# Prices and Markets: Microeconomics

# Prices and Markets: Microeconomics

### Charles W. Baird

California State University, Hayward

WEST PUBLISHING CO. | St. Paul • New York • Boston
Los Angeles • San Francisco

COPYRIGHT © 1975 BY WEST PUBLISHING CO.
ALL RIGHTS RESERVED

PRINTED IN THE UNITED STATES OF AMERICA

LIBRARY OF CONGRESS CATALOGING IN PUBLICATION DATA

BAIRD, CHARLES W.
    PRICES AND MARKETS.

    INCLUDES INDEX.
    1. MICROECONOMICS. I. TITLE.

HB171. 5.B194   330   75-7737
ISBN   0-8299-0060-8

*for Patti, Eric, and Elizabeth*

# Preface to Instructors

Economics, I feel, is an exciting subject because of the many real-world applications of economic theory. Yet many, if not most, students who sit through a course in microeconomic theory acquire the belief that the only use of economic theory is to provide employment to those who teach it. The main reason for this, I conjecture, is that teachers concentrate too much on the *tools* of the theory rather than on the theory itself and its many applications. In this text there is very little discussion of the mechanics of "curve bending" and even less of the mechanics of turning the mathematical crank. Curves are used, but I do not believe students should worry very much about why one curve looks exactly the way it does or why it intersects or is tangent to another curve at some precise point. Curves are useful only to the extent that they help the student keep track of the relationships among variables, and it is crucial that students see the usefulness of a diagram as soon as it is constructed. For example, in Chapter 4 I go through the usual discussion of the relationships among total, average, and marginal products. But after that is done I immediately show the importance of these relationships and how a diagram helps keep them in order, by illustrating how different specifications of property rights to a resource affect the intensity with which that resource will be used.

Students should also be made aware of the limitations of diagrams. In Chapter 8 I discuss how a legal ceiling price can induce a price searcher to increase the quantity of goods he makes available for sale, but that exposition is followed immediately by a discussion of the information problems involved in identifying and implementing the set of optimal ceiling prices.

At the intermediate level it is more important for students to see how economic theory explains real-world market phenomena than to be able to glibly discuss first- and second-order conditions for various optima. One who knows how to border a Hessian, but does not understand the competitive (rivalrous) uses of advertising, is more an applied mathematician than an economist. One who knows how to rewrite a Lagrangian function to take into account externalities, but does not understand that externalities emerge only when there are high costs of defining, enforcing, and exchanging private property rights, perhaps can pass an exam in economic theory but cannot make any intelligent policy recommendations regarding pollution. The intemperate use of mathematics in theory classes suppresses the importance of market processes and magnifies the importance of conditions that exist in equilibrium states. It leads students to the rather silly notion that if only we could get a sufficiently large computer we could do away with markets altogether. I agree with Hayek when he says that economic theory is more than just the "Pure Logic of Choice". The formal mathematics usually used in intermediate micro theory courses consists of the calculation of certain optima when known ends and known means are assumed to exist. An equally important question is: How do people acquire knowledge about available means and desired ends.

Apart from its deemphasis of tools and emphasis on the applicability of economic theory as a general methodological approach, there are other ways in which this text is different from most others. Following the lead of Gary Becker (in his graduate-level text, *Economic Theory*), I derive the demand curve holding measured *real* income, rather than *money* income, constant. All of the subsequent analysis is based on this definition of the demand curve. Constant measured real income rather than constant utility is used as the basis of the definition because, while econometric studies of demand functions can (and invariably do) use the ratio of money income to some price index as one of the independent variables determining the quantity demanded, there is no operational way to derive a constant utility demand curve empirically. Constant real income is used rather than constant money income because it is the purchasing power of a person's paycheck, rather than its nominal value, that effectively constrains his ability to participate in the market process. In this age of constant inflation it is crucial that students understand the difference between purchasing power and nominal income as well as the distinction between nominal (or money) prices and relative (or real) prices.

In a world where information is not free, the usual taxonomy of market structures—perfect competition, monopolistic competition, oligopoly, and monopoly—makes little sense and is of little practical significance. It suggests to students that all they need do to determine how well a market functions is to count up the number of firms that exist in the market. It flatly asserts that direct rivalry among sellers—the main driving force of all actual market processes—is a sign of "market imperfection." It uses as a standard a market scenario that only makes sense if all buyers and all sellers possess all relevant information. The only thing "perfect" about perfect competition is its set of perfect mathematical properties, not its ability to help us understand the real world. In this text I follow the lead of Alchian and Allen in dropping the standard taxonomy in favor of the more useful distinctions between price takers and price searchers and between open and closed markets. The superiority of this approach is attested to by the larger set of real-world problems that can be understood using this framework rather than the more conventional one. For example, is the behavior of airline companies more affected by the fact that there are relatively "few" carriers or by the fact that they operate in a closed market? In what sense is advertising anticompetitive when, in a world of positive information costs, any interloper firm must make known its existence and terms of trade? In what sense is product differentiation an anticompetitive device when, in a world of positive information costs, sellers (and buyers) must constantly search for more attractive packages of price and quality?

The level of understanding of economic phenomena among politicians is abysmally low. Nowhere is this more apparent than in the almost universal political condemnation of futures markets. During the "food crisis" of the summer of 1973 there was certainly no shortage of politicians who asserted that greedy speculators in the futures market were responsible for the food shortages and volatile prices. I suspect that most economics majors would have trouble explaining why those politicians were wrong. Most texts do not even mention futures markets. They explain all about ridge lines and cardinal utility, but they do not arm students against the folly of politicians. Students must see that economics enables them to talk meaningfully to people other than other students of economics, else they will come to the conclusion that economic theory can safely be ignored except in the classroom. To that end an entire chapter (Chapter 12) is devoted to futures markets. The mechanics of futures trading are outlined, but more importantly, the vital roles played by speculators and speculation are explained. Another chapter (Chapter 11) explains the notion of present value. Investment decisions in human and nonhuman capital, conservation, the used textbook market, planned obsolescence, and the alleged predatory pricing tactics of John D. Rockefeller are used as examples of the power of present-value analysis.

The last chapter (13) is unlike any chapter in other micro theory texts. The first part of the chapter deals with general equilibrium, but not in the usual fashion. Following Axel Leijonhufvud and Robert Clower I derive Say's Principle, which merely follows from the definition of transactors as neither thieves nor philanthropists, and applies only to planned excess demands, not to effective excess demands. General equilibrium is defined with reference to Say's Principle. Next Walras' auctioneer and *tatonnement* are introduced. Then Clower's important insight that without *tatonnement*, and in a money-using economy, the sum of the effective excess demands for all good including

money is *at most* zero is explained. (This is the bridge between microeconomics and the economics of Keynes.) It is shown that in a Walrasian *tatonnement* (zero information cost) system the good called money has no unique attributes. Indeed, in such a system there is no role for money to play at all. Next the distinction is made between Say's Principle (not Say's Law) and Walras' Law. The discussion of general equilibrium ends with an exposition of the geometry of a two-transactor, two-good Walrasian *tatonnement* and general equilibrium. A geometric proof of the existence of general equilibrium in such a system is given. The last section of the chapter follows Coase, Demsetz, *et al*, in the exposition of the modern property rights approach to the problem of externalities.

I want to express my appreciation to Professors W. P. Culbertson Jr., Ross D. Eckert, Eugene Silberberg, Courtenay C. Stone, and Wesley Yordan for their helpful comments on this manuscript. They will recognize many of their suggestions in the final version. Sandra Anderson's speedy and accurate typing, together with her patience and occasional help with spelling made my job much easier. Finally, to the extent that my past English teachers would be proud of the way this book is written, Frances Maurier's labors as copy editor must be given much of the credit.

# Preface to Students

You need not search too long in the daily newspapers, news magazines, and television news broadcasts to gain the impression that economics is an important subject, even to people other than economists. Its importance derives from the fact that most of the major political issues of the day are related to economics. This has always been the case—in fact, economics used to be called political economy. Economics is exciting and important precisely because, and only because, of the many real-world applications of economic theory. Too often, however, economic theory has been taught by almost exclusive reference to esoteric mathematical and geometric techniques. These techniques are only the tools that economists use; they are not, by themselves, the theory upon which the discipline of economics is built. Some economists have become enamored of the tools because the tools appear to put economics on the same intellectual footing as the physical sciences. Political economy has become economics, and the applications of economic theory have often become forgotten, or at least almost ignored.

In this text you will be exposed to some mathematics (mostly in Chapter 3, and all at the level of high school algebra) and quite a bit of geometry (charts and diagrams). It is, after all, necessary that those of you who are economics majors learn about the tools, but it is even more important for all of you—majors and non-majors—to learn what economic theory has to say about the real world. The emphasis in this text is always on the applications of economic theory. The tools are used to establish principles, and the principles are used to shed light on much of what you read in newspapers and magazines, hear in social science classrooms, and see on television. If you are patient and work your way through the text you will find yourself taking an increasingly critical view of what politicians and journalists say about economic matters. You may become depressed as you come to recognize the quality of existing public policy and public debate on economic issues. On the other hand, you may become determined to do what you can to improve the situation. I hope the latter proves to be the case.

# Table of Contents

**1** An Overview of Prices and Markets *1*

- relative prices and absolute prices *2*
- the consumer price index *2*
- relative prices as conveyors of information *4*
- relative prices and inflation *6*
- uses and misuses of diagrams in economics *7*
- the meaning of competition *13*
- questions for discussion *13*

**2** Indifference Curves and Exchange *15*

- the method of economic enquiry *15*
- the basic assumptions of indifference curve analysis *16*
- indifference curves *18*
- exchange without a middleman *19*
- exchange with a middleman *20*
- open and closed markets *21*
- the edgeworth exchange box *23*
- questions for discussion *25*

**3** Demand Theory *27*

- the budget constraint *27*
- depicting changes in real income and changes in relative price *29*
- the optimum consumption basket *31*
- the engel curve—superior and inferior goods *33*
- income elasticity of demand *34*
- aggregate engel curves *36*
- the demand curve and the first fundamental law of demand *37*
- alleged exceptions to the first fundamental law of demand *39*
- price elasticity of demand *41*
- the second fundamental law of demand *42*
- the combined demand curve and the slutsky equation *43*
- the demand curve: real income constant money income constant *45*
- the relative prices of related products *46*
- market demand curves *47*
- market demand curves and sellers total revenue *48*
- questions for discussion *49*

**4**

**Production Theory**

*51*

- the production function *51*
- processes and process rays *53*
- isoquant with two processes *54*
- adding a third process *56*
- convexity of isoquants *57*
- isoquants with many processes *58*
- the slope of an isoquant *59*
- the short run—one fixed input *60*
- property rights and fishing: application of the average-marginal relationship *63*
- the stages of production *66*
- the long run—returns to scale *69*
- questions for discussion *71*

**5**

**Cost Theory**

*73*

- the meaning of cost *73*
- short-run cost curves *74*
- two roads: the social function of private property *79*
- long-run cost curves *81*
  - isocost lines *82*
  - the optimal input combination *83*
  - the expansion path *84*
  - the long run average cost curve *85*
- the relationship between long run and short-run average costs *87*
- capacity *90*
- long-run and short-run marginal cost *91*
- effects of ceilings and floors *92*
- questions for discussion *93*

**6**

**The Firm**

*95*

- why firms exist *96*
- the objectives of private firms *98*
- market structure *99*
- questions for discussion *103*

**7**

**Price Takers**

*105*

- introduction *105*
- demand curves *107*
- marginal revenue *108*
- the firm's short-run supply curve *109*
- short-run market supply curves *110*
- short-run market, firm, and buyer equilibrium *111*
- market and individual adjustment to a shift of market demand curve *112*
- long-run equilibrium for a firm *113*
- the long-run market supply curve *116*
- a reminder *118*
- an exercise *118*
- price controls may result in higher prices *118*
- the demand for and supply of housing services *120*
- gifts of specific resources versus cash gifts *123*
- looking ahead *124*
- questions for discussion *124*

**8**

**Price
Searchers**

*125*

- price and marginal revenue *125*
- individual and market demand curves *127*
- the price searcher's optimum price *129*
- price searcher equilibrium—closed market *130*
- price searcher equilibrium—open market *131*
- comparison of price takers and
  price searchers *132*
- barriers to entry *133*
  - legal *133*
  - economies of scale *134*
  - ownership of vital or superior resources *135*
  - "imperfect" capital markets *135*
- price discrimination and multipart pricing *136*
  - price discrimination *136*
  - multipart pricing *139*
- patents and royalties *141*
- an exercise *142*
- questions for discussion *143*


**9**

**Cartels
and Mergers**

*145*

- the instability of cartels *145*
  - the free rider *147*
  - different marginal cost curves *147*
  - nonprice rivalry *148*
- the market concentration doctrine *149*
- horizontal mergers *151*
- vertical mergers *152*
- questions for discussion *155*


**10**

**Distribution
Theory**

*157*

- quantity of resources owned *157*
- the prices of services of resources *159*
  - short-run demand curve for productive services *159*
  - long-run demand curve for productive services *163*
  - determinants of the price elasticity of demand
    for inputs *165*
  - the supply curve of labor *166*
  - determination of the wage for a particular
    type of labor *168*
- monopsony *172*
- the role of unions *175*
- bilateral monopoly *176*
- the negative income tax *177*
- questions for discussion *180*


**11**

**Capital Values and
Investment Decisions**

*181*

- why there is a positive rate of interest *181*
- present values *182*
- the firm's investment decision *184*
- the internal rate of return *185*
- annuities *188*
- occupational choice *188*
- perpetuities *190*
- some further application of present
  value calculations *191*
  - conservation *191*
  - the used textbook market *192*
  - predatory pricing *195*
- questions for discussion *196*

**12**

**Futures Trading**

*199*

- the mechanics of futures trading *199*
- the transactors: speculators and hedgers *202*
- the time allocation of consumption *205*
- the volatility of prices *206*
- questions for discussion *207*

**13**

**General Equlibrium, Property Rights, and the Coase Theorem**

*209*

- say's principle and general equilibrium *210*
- effective demand, tatonnement, and walras' law *212*
- the geometry of walrasian general equilibrium *216*
- externalities and property rights *219*
- the coase theorem *220*
- the nfl player draft *222*
- pollution *223*
- conclusion *224*
- questions for discussion *224*

# 1
# An Overview of Prices and Markets

Since Adam ate the apple it has been impossible for human beings to obtain goods (things we want more of rather than less of) for nothing. We are confronted with the sad fact that in order to get more of one good we have to give up some of some other good(s). Imagine making up a list of the things you would want if you could obtain any good in any amount that you desired without incurring any cost (i.e., without having to give up anything else you want). The list would most likely be quite extensive and probably entertaining to read. Imagine now that each person makes up such a list and that we consolidate all lists into one grand shopping list of human wants. God's vengeance in the Garden was to see to it that mankind's time and ingenuity, together with the earth's natural resources, are incapable of generating enough goods to meet all those wants. In other words, mankind is confronted with *scarcity*. Since we cannot obtain all of what we want, we must pick and choose from our individual shopping lists those things and those quantities that we want more than others. We must decide what and how much we are willing to give up in order to obtain those other things that we want.

To get the most out of our scarce human and nonhuman resources we must transfer resources from uses where they are less valuable to uses where they are more valuable. The value of a given quantity of resources in any specific use is the amount people are willing to pay for the good that is produced by the resources in that use. Here the word "pay" does not refer to money. A person pays for good $A$ by giving up the opportunity to obtain some of another good $B$. Suppose people are willing to pay for one unit of good $A$ a greater amount than the amount of $B$ that must be sacrificed to make an additional unit of $A$ available. For example, suppose that people value one unit of $A$ at three units of $B$, but that one unit of $A$ can be produced with the same amount of resources used to produce only one $B$. People are made better off (they get more out of their scarce resources) by the production of additional units of $A$ (and fewer units of $B$), since they acquire the units of $A$ for much less than they would be willing to pay. People continue to consider themselves better off as more and more $A$ (and less and less $B$) is produced until the amount they are willing to pay no longer exceeds the amount that they must pay.

The major task of this text is to explain how decentralized decision making, guided by prices that emerge when many people voluntarily exchange resources and products, results in obtaining the most from the human and nonhuman resources with which we are endowed. The first step in this exposition is to make clear the distinction between relative prices and absolute prices.

## Relative Prices and Absolute Prices

Consider a world with only two goods, $X$ and $Y$, and a unit of account in which all absolute prices are expressed (for instance, dollars). The real (or relative) price of a unit of good $X$ is the amount of good $Y$ that must be given up to acquire an additional unit of $X$. That real price could be expressed as the ratio of the two absolute money prices, $P_x$ and $P_y$. Specifically, the real price of $X$ is the absolute price of $X$ divided by the absolute price of $Y$, where both absolute prices are in dollar units. Suppose the price of $X$ is $6, and the price of $Y$ is $2. To acquire one $X$, $6 must be surrendered. This $6 could have been used to purchase 3 $Y$'s. Thus, the $Y$ price of $X$ is three $Y$'s, or $P_x/P_y = 3$.

In a world with more than two nonmoney goods the real price of any one of these goods can be expressed in terms of any other of the goods. In the case of $n$ goods there are $n - 1$ real prices for each good. Each of the $n - 1$ real prices is in terms of one of the $n - 1$ other nonmoney goods. Rather than concern ourselves with $n - 1$ real prices for each nonmoney good, it is customary to express the relative (or real) price of any good $X$ as the ratio of the absolute price of $X$ to the *average* price of all nonmoney goods; e.g., the relative price of gasoline is the dollar price of gasoline divided by the average price level as measured by some price index such as the consumer price index.

In your principles class you learned that demand curves for any good—say, gasoline—are negatively sloped with respect to price. The diagram drawn to represent this relationship had price on the vertical axis and quantity purchased per unit of time on the horizontal axis. But which price belongs on the vertical axis? The correct answer is the relative, or real, price of gaso-

line. As we shall see in Chapter 3, all demand theory refers to *relative* price. The fact that the demand curve for gasoline is negatively sloped does not mean—even in the absence of changes in the purchasing power of buyers of gasoline, or anything that shifts the demand curve to the right—that a 5% increase in the absolute price of gasoline will necessarily be accompanied by a reduction in the quantity of gasoline purchased. If when the price of gasoline increases by 5% the average of all prices increases by 8%, the relative price of gasoline *decreases*. A 5% increase in the dollar price of gasoline, under these circumstances, would result in an increase in the quantity of gasoline demanded. The total dollars it takes to buy a tank of gasoline would have increased, but the purchasing power of these dollars over all other goods would have decreased. Of course, in 1973 and 1974 the money price of gasoline increased by much more than the average of all prices. This substantial increase in the relative price of gasoline reduced the quantity of gasoline demanded as people joined car pools, used buses, bought smaller cars, took fewer pleasure trips, etc.

## The Consumer Price Index

Since the consumer price index in its decimal form $(P)$ is used to express the generalized form of relative prices—$P_x/P$—it is of interest to see how the index is formed. In Chapter 3, when we discuss real income as well as real price, we will see that once we understand what the consumer price index is we can construct geometric representations of conceptual experiments such as changing real price while maintaining constant real income.

Periodically the Bureau of Labor Statistics (BLS) conducts expenditure surveys on randomly selected urban, wage-earning, families of two or more. There are approximately 4,000 families in the sample, chosen from various cities and regions. All of the data are obtained through the voluntary cooperation of the sampled families. Each family reports a complete account of its expenditures for a calendar year, and the data are collected by personal interview through the use of questionnaires. Each family reports the total number of dollars it spent on each of the various items it purchased (including services). From these data the BLS selects approximately 400 items to make up a "market basket." The market basket is selected to represent the way a typical urban, wage-earning family spends its money. (A complete list of the items in the market basket currently used to compute the consumer price index—CPI—for various dates can be found in the BLS *Handbook of Methods,* Bulletin 1711, pp. 84–87. A complete discussion of the formation of the CPI can be found in the same publication on pages 59–95.) From the expenditure survey the BLS knows the typical family's expenditure, in the survey year or "base period," on each of the items in the market basket, and it also knows the typical family's total expenditure on the market basket in the base period. The Bureau then collects information on the prices charged in the base period for each of the items in the market basket by sampling stores and service establishments in various cities across the country. To construct the CPI for any given period, say the first quarter of 1973, the BLS would sample stores and service establishments during that period to determine the then existing average price of each item in the market basket. The data collected in the survey for the base period, together with the new data on prices in the first quarter of 1973, are then used to compute the CPI for the first quarter of 1973 in the following way.

The amount of money spent by the average family for each item in the market basket in the base period is multiplied by the ratio of that good's 1973 price to its base period price. In symbols, for any specific good such as good $i$, we can write this multiplication as

$$P_i^0 \cdot q_i^0 \times \frac{P_i^t}{P_i^0}$$

where $P_i^0 \cdot q_i^0$ is the total expenditure on good $i$ in the base period, $P_i^t$ is the average price of the $i$th good at time $t$ (1973), and $P_i^0$ is the average price of the $i$th good in the base period. Note that this is algebraically equivalent to $P_i^t \cdot q_i^0$, which can be thought of as the expenditure necessary in time $t$ to buy the quantity of good $i$ that is in the market basket. (The quantities of the goods in the market basket are not calculated directly. They are implicit in the data on total expenditure on the various goods in the base period together with the data on base period prices and current period prices.) This multiplication is done for each good in the market basket, and the products are added together. The resulting total is the amount of money that is necessary to purchase the entire market basket in time $t$ (1973). This total is then divided by the total expenditure needed to buy the market basket in the base period, and the result is multiplied by 100 to get the CPI.

For example, suppose the base period is 1967 and the total cost of the market basket in 1967 was $2,456. Suppose that the same collection of goods in 1973 costs $3,125. (Notice that the market basket defined in 1967 is what is priced in 1973.) The consumer price index would then be $P$ = 3,125/2,456 = 1.27. It would be reported as 127, meaning that the cost of the basket defined in the 1967 survey in 1973 prices is 127% of what the basket cost was in 1967. Suppose the 1973 dollar price of a tape recorder is $152, and the consumer price index is (in its decimal form) 1.27. The real price of a tape recorder in 1973 would be $P_x/P$ = $152/1.27 = $119.68. That is, the number of real things that would have to be given up in 1973 to get a tape recorder is the number of real things that could have been bought in 1967 with $119.68.

Let us suppose that the price index for 1972, computed using 1967 as the base, is 1.20, and that the 1972 dollar price of a tape recorder was $150. Between 1972 and 1973 did the real price of a tape recorder go up? The absolute price did: from $150 to $152. However, the real price of a tape recorder fell from 1972 to 1973. The real price in 1972 was $150/1.20 = $125. We have already seen that the 1973 real price was $119.68. The number of real things that had to be given up in 1972 to get a tape recorder was the real things that could be purchased by $125 in 1967. The number of real things that had to be given up in 1973 to get a tape recorder was the real things that could be purchased with $119.68 in 1967.

The consumer price index is also used to compute real income. Suppose your monthly money income in 1972 was $1,000 and in 1973 it was $1,010. In terms of dollars of 1967 puchasing power your income fell from 1972 to 1973. In 1972 your real income ($I/P$) was $1,000/1.20 = $833.33. In 1973 it was $1,010/1.27 = $795.27. In 1972 your monthly income gave you claim to the real goods and services that $833.33 could have bought in 1967. In 1973 the number of real goods and services you could claim as monthly real income was the amount of goods and services that $795.27 could have bought in 1967.

In many microeconomics texts the consumer price index is not discussed in this context.[1] Demand curves are drawn with the absolute money price of the good on the vertical axis. The discussion in these texts is correct as long as there is no change in the average price level. In the absence of inflation or deflation, a 5% change in the absolute money price of a commodity is a 5% change in its relative (or real) price. Microeconomic theory is generally exposited with the assumption (often not explicit) that the average price level is constant. Changes in the average price level are regarded as appropriate subject matter for courses in macroeconomics. However, the most important skill you can acquire as students of economics is how to diagnose and understand real-world phenomena. Macrophenomena and microphenomena occur simultaneously in the real world. I believe that, to avoid confusion, it is sometimes necessary to drop the distinction between micro- and macroanalysis.

## Relative Prices as Conveyors of Information

As you proceed through this text you will come to see that relative prices and changes in relative prices have important functions to perform. Prices that buyers are willing to pay for a good indicate the value of resources when they are used to produce that good. The cost of making an additional unit of a good available indicates the value of the same resources when used to produce some other good. Costs, expressed as amounts of dollars of fixed purchasing power, are the payments that must be made to resource owners in order to induce them to devote their resources to a given use rather than to some other use. These payments depend on what the resource owners could receive if their resources were employed in the other use. (We will elaborate on this point in Chapter 5.) The payments that could be earned in the other use depend on the value buyers place on what is produced by the resources in that use. In short, prices (output prices and input prices) *convey information* which is needed if transactors (independent decision-making units such as households, firms, and individuals) are to make the decisions that permit the most to be gained from our scarce resources.

Increases in the relative price of a good convey to buyers and sellers the information that the good is now more scarce than it used to be (less of it is available relative to the amount that people want at the old price). No individual buyer or seller need know why the good is more scarce. It may be because a new use for the good has been found so that more of it is wanted than before, or it may be that one (or more) of the sources of the supply of the good has been eliminated. In either case the message of increased scarcity is transmitted, and buyers and sellers are induced to respond in ways that permit the most to be ob-

---

[1] The outstanding example of an exception to this statement is Gary Becker's *Economic Theory* (New York: Alfred A. Knopf, 1971).

tained from our scarce resources under the new circumstances. The higher relative price induces those buyers who place lower values on units of the good to stop purchasing them and it induces resource owners to divert some resources away from goods that people value less and toward the good that is now valued more highly.

Decreases in the relative price of a good also convey information. Specifically, they indicate that the good has become less scarce than it was before (more of the good is available relative to the amount that people want at the old price). Here again it is not necessary that any person know why the good has become less scarce. It may be because people's tastes have changed so that they place a lower value on the good and hence want less of it than they used to at the old price, or it may be because additional sources of supply of the good have been found. In either case the lower relative price will enable people who place lower values on the good than the previous relative price to now obtain some of the good, and it will induce resource owners to search for alternative uses of their resources to produce goods that people value more highly than they now value this good. Again, people are induced by the changed relative price to act in ways that enable the most to be obtained from our scarce resources under the new circumstances.

No one in such a voluntary exchange (sometimes called open market) setting has to decide on the grand design of the allocation of our scarce resources. Individual decisions in response to price incentives interact to establish coordination of the plans and desires of the millions of individual transactors. When buyers want more of something no petition must be made to a central authority to pass down orders to produce more of that thing. More of it will be produced because the increase in demand makes its relative price go up. The increase in relative price means that it is in the interest of producers to produce more. When buyers desire less of a thing sales rates of that thing will decline, inventories will start to accumulate, and prices will be lowered in order to move the inventories.

The lowered prices will mean decreased production. Again, in such a system no central authority must pass down orders to producers to curtail manufacture. In Chapters 7 and 8 we will elaborate on this theme.

The information conveyed by relative prices not only determines what goods will be made available and in what amounts, it also determines the particular mix of resources that will be used to produce the various goods. As long as producers can keep the net returns from their productive activity, they will strive to minimize the costs they incur when they make goods available. Thus if the price of using labor services is high relative to the price of using capital services, goods will tend to be produced with production techniques that employ a low ratio of labor to capital. A low price of labor services relative to the price of capital services will induce producers to use more labor-intensive production techniques. These ideas are fully examined in Chapters 4 and 5.

This relationship between relative input prices and the input combinations that will be used in production is the major reason why there cannot be a long-run problem of technological unemployment. If machines replace people in many jobs at the same time, an excess supply of labor will result—the quantity supplied will be greater than the quantity demanded. This will result in a decrease in the relative cost of using labor, which in turn will induce substitution to more labor-intensive processes.

Of course, if prices are not permitted to change when supply and demand conditions change, the market will not be able to make the requisite adjustments because relative prices will not convey accurate information. A minimum wage law would greatly hamper those who are displaced from their jobs by technical change in their attempts to find alternative employment. Such people must acquire a new set of skills and abilities. The most effective retraining technique is on-the-job training, but in order for employers to be willing to incur the training costs, workers will have to accept lower wages during the training period. (As we shall see in Chapter 10, wages paid to these workers will quite naturally rise as they acquire the new skills and abilities.) Those whose skills are so few that they cannot make a "living wage" are not protected by a minimum wage law. The actual minimum wage is zero—the wage earned when one is not employed. If someone can do something that is worth only $1.50 per hour, he will not be hired when the law makes it illegal to pay him any less than $2.20 per hour. Minimum wage laws outlaw the employment of relatively unproductive people.

Because of scarcity, more of something for one person necessarily means less of something for someone else. No one of us can obtain all that he wants of all goods because we all must compete for the limited amounts of all available things. Competition is the natural result of scarcity, and competition takes many forms. There are more applicants for admission to Harvard's freshman class than there are places available. The successful applicants win in a competition based on high school grades, performance on the Scholastic Aptitude Test, and letters of recommendation. In societies that are centrally directed and controlled by public officials, competition for many scarce goods, especially personal privileges, is based on an individual's skill at political manipulation. The major form of competition for scarce goods in a decentralized, voluntary exchange society is ability and willingness to pay.

We have already seen that with voluntary exchange it is people's willingness to pay that directs the allocation of scarce resources toward more highly valued uses. In Chapter 3 we shall examine in detail what determines the prices that individuals are willing to pay. One of the major determinants is the individual's real income—the purchasing power of the payments he receives when he sells the services of the human and nonhuman resources he owns. In Chapter 10 we will discuss the major determinants of an individual's real income or purchasing power. To anticipate that discussion, let us note here that the single most important determinant of an individ-

ual's real income is his ability to produce goods and render services that other individuals are willing to pay for, and nature has not distributed this ability equally. Thus we see that the prices that result from voluntary exchange not only determine what is produced, in what amounts, and by what techniques, but they also affect the size of the claim any individual can make to the available supply of scarce goods. It is here, many people feel, that a voluntary exchange economy breaks down. In such an economy resources are directed toward more highly valued uses, but what is "more highly valued" depends on what people are willing and *able* to pay. In turn, people's ability and willingness to pay depend on the amount of purchasing power they have. The valuation of goods in a voluntary exchange economy is not independent of the distribution of purchasing power. Most of the criticism of the "capitalist" system concerns the distribution of the claims to scarce goods that results from voluntary exchange. Even many friends of the system consider this such a serious problem that they are willing to intervene in the voluntary exchange process by fixing some prices. Minimum wage legislation is one example, and attempts to hold down the prices of the "more important" things that poor people buy is another. In Chapters 7 and 8 we shall see that this technique of helping those with little purchasing power inevitably has many undesirable side effects. If prices cannot move they cannot coordinate the plans of the millions of independent transactors. If prices cannot make all the pieces fit together, the economy must be centrally directed by authoritarian decisions. An alternative technique for attaining what many would consider a more equitable distribution of income, one that leaves prices free to carry out their normal functions, is the negative income tax plan. We will discuss that proposal in Chapter 10.

## Relative Prices and Inflation

The key variable in any voluntary exchange system is relative price. Changes in relative prices are what direct resources to their most highly valued uses. Politicians, journalists, and television commentators typically pay less attention to relative prices than to the average price level. In June 1973, concern over the rate of change of the consumer price index led to the implementation of a freeze on the absolute money price of practically every commodity produced and sold in the United States. Inflation, caused by a prolonged period of too rapid growth of the money stock, was about 9% per year. In order to stop the rate of growth of the average price level, politicians passed a law against it. (This is much like curing the common cold by making it illegal.) The effect of any such law is to freeze the pattern of relative prices. If relative prices cannot change the entire market mechanism breaks down. If buyers decide they want more of one thing and less of another, the appropriate price signals cannot be emitted. Shortages of the thing that is wanted more will develop. Shoppers will be greeted by empty shelves, although the price tags on the shelves will indicate low prices. Inventories of the thing that is wanted less will accumulate, but because there is no commodity which has become more profitable to produce there will be diminished incentive for resources to move out of their current employment.

One almost immediate result of the June price freeze was the drowning of thousands of chickens by their owners. At the frozen prices it was not possible for chicken ranchers to pay all of their costs. Tomato prices were frozen at 18 cents per pound—the price at which they were selling during the period that was used to determine legal prices. New Yorkers had been eating tomatoes from Florida at 18 cents a pound, but by the end of June the Florida crop was no longer available. New Yorkers then had to rely on California tomatoes, which cost 30 cents a pound when transportation costs were added in. But 30 cents a pound was an illegal price. The result was that New Yorkers went without tomatoes, comforted, no doubt, by the thought that the tomatoes they couldn't get cost 18 cents per pound.

To politicians, and to others who do not

understand economics, increases in individual prices are the cause of inflation. These people do not understand the difference between relative prices and the average money price level. Imagine that Congress passes a law that enables each person to add one zero (to the left of the decimal point) to his current balance in his checking account and to the face value of each Federal Reserve note (paper currency) he owns. Money bids for all goods would increase, causing all money prices to rise by a factor of ten. Relative prices (or real prices) would not be affected, but there would be an increase in the average money price level—i.e., there would be inflation. Now suppose that the aggregate amount of money held as currency and as checking account deposits is held fixed and many sources of supply of food and gasoline are suddenly eliminated. The resulting excess demand for gasoline and food would cause the relative prices of those things to rise substantially. Since the supply of money is fixed this change in relative prices would take the form of increases in the money prices of food and gasoline and *decreases in the money prices of some other goods*. The average money price level would not change. If people are using more of their money balances to purchase food and fuel they must be using less of them to purchase some other goods, as long as aggregate money balances are not increased. (Remember that when a buyer draws down his money balances the seller from whom he bought increases his money balances. The total amount of money balances stays the same.) Changes in individual prices do not cause inflation. The *definition* of inflation is increases of the average money price level. The *cause* of inflation is increases of the supply of money relative to the supply of the nonmoney goods that are purchased with money.

## Uses and Misuses
## of Diagrams in Economics

Each of you has had at least an introductory course in economics. You are, therefore, aware that economists (at least those who write textbooks and teach) are wont to use many diagrams in their exposition of the relationships amoung economic variables. This text is no exception. However, in this text the emphasis is not on why a given diagram looks the way it does, or why one curve either cuts or just touches another curve at a particular point. The emphasis is always on the *conclusions* that can be derived from the diagrams and the *applications* of the theory that the diagrams partially represent. It is easy to fall into the trap of concentrating too much on the "curve bending" mechanics of the diagrams, and to lose sight of the economic content of the theory. If economics is taught with exclusive reference to the construction of diagrams, students easily forget (or maybe never hear) that what goes on during adjustments to changes in economic variables is at least as important as the characteristics of the equilibrium values of those variables.

This point is perhaps best made by an example. You all remember that two of the most frequently used curves in economics are supply and demand curves. You probably think that the most significant part of supply and demand diagrams is the point at which the two curves intersect. This intersection point indicates the "equilibrium" or "market clearing" price and the quantity that goes with it. However, you must remember that the diagram is nothing more than a succinct summary of the behavior of many individual buyers and sellers. The behavior that lies behind the diagram is not explicitly stated by the diagram. The curves as drawn can be interpreted as succinct summaries of one or the other of two very distinct behavior patterns. Moreover, even though the supply and demand curves intersect, the equilibrium price may or may not be attainable. It depends on which behavior patterns are assumed to lie behind the picture. To see this let's consider the mechanism of market adjustment as an example of a homeostatic device.[2]

A homeostat is a control mechanism that compares the desired value of some variable (such as temperature) with the actual value of the variable, and on the basis of this comparison, emits orders (to a furnace for example) to correct any discrepancy between the actual and desired values. A common thermostat is the simplest of such devices. The desired temperature is selected depending on the tastes of the person in the room. The thermostat compares this target with the actual temperature reading and if the actual is too low it instructs the furnace to turn on. The furnace continues to operate until the "error"— the difference between the desired and actual values—is eliminated. If the actual is greater than the desired temperature, the thermostat instructs the air conditioner to operate until that error is corrected. Once the error is corrected the thermostat continues to monitor the actual temperature, ensuring that if any error emerges, forces will be set in motion to counteract it.

Markets can be thought of in this manner, although market mechanisms are much more complex than any temperature-monitoring device. To begin with, there are two variables of concern rather than one. Markets involve price and quantity adjustments, while the thermostat is concerned only with temperature. Market participants do not know what the correct values of price and quantity are, and no external force determines the desired values of price and quantity. The homeostat cannot, therefore, directly measure any discrepancy between desired and actual values of either price or quantity. Instead it operates on the basis of an indirect search for something called "equilibrium." Markets are pictured as operating with one or the other of two separate homeostatic devices—the Walrasian homeostat and the Marshallian homeostat.[3]

The Walrasian homeostat is designed to

[2]This discussion follows Axel Leijonhufvud, "Notes on the Theory of Markets," *Intermountain Economic Review* (Fall 1970).

[3]Cf. Leon Walras, *Elements of Pure Economics,* trans. William Jaffe (Homewood, Ill.: Richard D. Irwin, 1954); and Alfred Marshall, *Principles of Economics,* 8th ed. (London: Macmillan & Co., 1938).

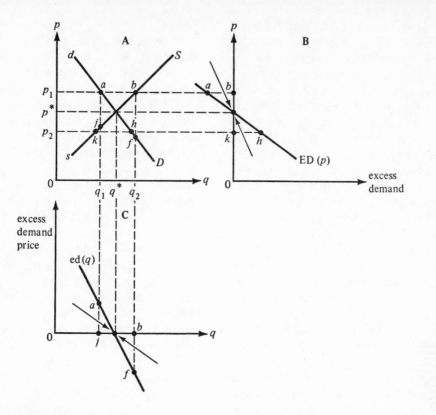

**Figure 1-1.**
Search for equilibrium with normally-shaped curves.

affect prices, but it does not know what the correct price is. The homeostat cannot read any divergence between desired and actual price; it operates on the basis of observations on quantity to determine when it has the correct price. It knows that with an incorrect price there will be a discrepancy between quantity supplied and quantity demanded. The homeostat can sense this discrepancy. When there is an excess supply—quantity supplied greater than quantity demanded—it tries a lower price; when there is an excess demand—quantity demanded greater than quantity supplied—it tries a higher price.[4] The Walrasian homeo-

stat searches for the correct price on the basis of input on actual quantities supplied and demanded. The behavioral assumption behind the mechanism is that individuals decide on the amount they want to buy and sell on the basis of price.

The Marshallian homeostat affects quantity on the basis of observations on price. Here again the homeostat does not know what the desired quantity is, but it knows when the actual quantity is the correct quantity. The correct quantity is that which carries with it no discrepancy between supply price and demand price. "Supply price" is the minimum price that sellers must get per unit if they are to continue supplying the quantity they are currently supplying. "Demand price" is the maximum price that can be charged per unit if buyers are to continue to purchase the quantity they are currently purchasing. The Marshallian homeostat works on the assumption that the price that actually exists is always equal to the demand price. If demand price is greater than supply

[4]In Chapter 13 we shall discuss the Walrasian system in detail. Walras constructed a fictional economic scenario he called *tatonnement* in order to provide a nonmathematical interpretation of the solution of his general equilibrium equations. The central figure in the *tatonnement* is an auctioneer. It is the auctioneer who "tries" the various prices as he gropes his way toward equilibrium.

price—i.e., if there is an excess demand price—the homeostat gives instructions to sellers to increase the quantity of the commodity on the market. If supply price is greater than demand price—excess supply price—the homeostat gives instructions to sellers to decrease the quantity of the commodity on the market. The behavioral assumption behind this mechanism is that individuals decide on the price they are willing to pay or accept on the basis of the quantity involved in the transaction.

With normally shaped curves—negatively sloped demand ($D$) and demand price ($d$) schedules, and positively sloped supply ($S$) and supply price ($s$) schedules—both homeostatic devices will be successful in their search for equilibrium. In Figure 1-1, panel A depicts such normally shaped curves. First we interpret the diagram as depicting the Walrasian homeostat. At relative price $p_1$ the quantity supplied is $ab$ units greater than the quantity demanded. There is an excess supply (negative excess demand) of $ab$ drawn in panel B at price $p_1$. At price $p_2$ the quantity demanded exceeds the quantity supplied by $kh$ units. There is an excess demand (ED) of $kh$ units drawn in panel B at price $p_2$. The Walrasian homeostat would observe the excess supply at price $p_1$, know that price $p_1$ was not the correct (or equilibrium) price, and thus would try a lower price. The lower price would induce transactors to increase the quantity demanded and decrease the quantity supplied. If the lower price was higher than $p^*$, there would still be some excess supply, and a still lower price would be tried. This process would continue until $p^*$ was reached. The homeostat would then sense that the price was correct because there would be zero excess demand (ED). Note that in panel B the indicated ED at price equal to $p^*$ is zero. The homeostat would know that $p_2$ was not the correct price because of the positive excess demand at that price, and would try a higher price. At a higher price transactors would decrease the quantity demanded and increase the quantity supplied. At price equal to $p^*$ there would again be zero ED—i.e., the market would be in "equi-

librium."

Panel A can also be understood to depict the Marshallian homeostat. In this case the negatively sloped line would be a demand price schedule, and the positively sloped line would be a supply price schedule. At quantity $q_1$ the demand price exceeds the supply price by $ja$ units. In panel C a positive excess demand price (ed) of $ja$ units is drawn for quantity $q_1$. The Marshallian homeostat would sense that $q_1$ was not the correct quantity because of the existence of the nonzero excess demand price. The homeostat would instruct sellers to increase the quantity supplied to the market. At larger quantities suppliers have higher supply prices (the minimum price per unit suppliers insist on receiving increases as they are asked to supply larger quantities), while buyers have lower demand prices (the maximum price buyers will pay per unit decreases as they are asked to buy more units). At quantity $q_2$ the excess demand price (ed) is negative—the supply price exceeds the demand price by $fb$ units. In panel C a negative ed of $fb$ is drawn for $q$ equal to $q_2$. The homeostat would recognize that $q_2$ was not the equilibrium $q$ because of the nonzero excess demand price. Instructions to decrease the quantity supplied would be emitted and this would again result in supply price and demand price becoming equal. Both the positive and the negative excess demand price cause quantity adjustments in the direction of $q^*$—the equilibrium quantity. The arrows drawn in panels B and C indicate that the feedback in the control system moves the market to the equilibrium price (Walras) or quantity (Marshall).

Figure 1-2 depicts circumstances where a successful search for equilibrium depends on the search rule (homeostat) used. If we interpret panel A to depict the Walrasian mechanism, one negatively sloped line is a demand curve ($D$) and the other negatively sloped line is a supply curve ($S$). At price $p_1$ there exists a positive excess demand, and that positive ED is depicted in panel B. The homeostat will sense an incorrect price, but will try a higher price. Remem-

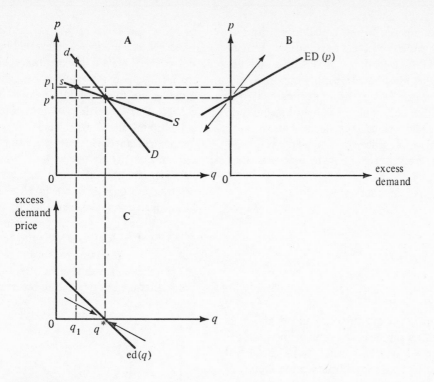

**Figure 1-2.**
Search for equilibrium with abnormally-shaped curves.

ber, the search rule is, with a positive excess demand try a higher price and with a negative excess demand try a lower price. A price higher than $p_1$ would create an even larger excess demand. The search for $p^*$ will not be successful.

If we interpret panel **A** to depict the Marshallian homeostat, however, a successful search for equilibrium can be carried out. In this case one negatively sloped line in panel **A** is a demand price schedule ($d$), and the other is a supply price schedule ($s$). At quantity $q_1$ there exists a positive excess demand price which is also shown in panel **C**. The homeostat will sense a disequilibrium quantity and will instruct sellers to increase the quantity available on the market. The increase in the quantity eliminates the positive excess demand price. The arrows in panels **B** and **C** indicate that the Walrasian search process will lead away from equilibrium, while the Marshallian search process leads toward equilibrium. If the $sS$ line in panel **A** were steeper than the $dD$ line, the Walrasian search would be successful while the Marshallian search would

not. (You should construct the relevant diagrams to satisfy yourself of this.)

Not only does this example illustrate the importance of the human action that lies behind the diagrams of economic theory, it also illustrates a danger in the use of mathematics in economics. A mathematician would say that the Walrasian and the Marshallian equations are simply the inverses of each other. That is, whereas Walras considers quantity demanded and quantity supplied to be the dependent variables and price to be the independent variable, Marshall considers demand price and supply price to be the dependent variables and quantity to be the independent variable.[5]

---

[5]An equation is typically written with one variable by itself on the left-hand side and a number of variables together with coefficients on the right-hand side. The variable on the left is called the dependent variable because its value can be determined only after the values of the other variables are known. The variables upon which the dependent variable depends are called independent variables.

Each imposes a third equation on the system which defines equilibrium. Walras' equilibrium condition is that quantity demanded must equal quantity supplied, and the search is for the one price that will establish this equality. Marshall's equilibrium condition is that demand price must equal supply price, and the search is for the one quantity that will establish that equality.

If Walras' equations are

$$q^d = f(p)$$

$$q^s = g(p)$$

$$q^d = q^s$$

where $q^d$ is quantity demanded and $q^s$ is quantity supplied, the equilibrium price ($\hat{p}$) can be found by solving $f(p) - g(p) = 0$ for $\hat{p}$. At this equilibrium price there will be a single quantity demanded and supplied. These same Walrasian equations could be put into Marshallian form by "inverting" them. Walras' demand function, which expresses $q$ in terms of $p$, could be rearranged to express $p$ in terms of $q$. The same could be done to Walras' supply function.

The equations in Marshallian form would be

$$p^d = f^{-1}(q)$$

$$p^s = g^{-1}(q)$$

$$p^d = p^s$$

where $p^d$ is demand price and $p^s$ is supply price. (Mathematicians denote a function that has been derived from another function simply by reversing the roles of the dependent and independent variables, by using the exponent $-1$.) Marshall's equilibrium quantity would be the value of $q$ that made $f^{-1}(q) - g^{-1}(q)$ equal zero. This equilibrium $q$ must be the same as the common quantity supplied and quantity demanded at Walras' equilibrium price. Likewise, the common demand price and supply price in the Marshallian equilibrium

must be the same as Walras' equilibrium price. When equations are inverted none of the coefficients in the original equations are changed, so the equilibrium values of variables in the equation system cannot change. Our discussion of the search for equilibrium shows that even though a mathematician could turn the mathematical crank and come out with the same values for equilibrium price and quantity whether the equations are in Walrasian or Marshallian form, the mathematics may or may not have any economic meaning. It is insufficient to look only for the intersection points in diagrams—or for the result of the simultaneous solution of a set of equations—that are constructed to represent human action.

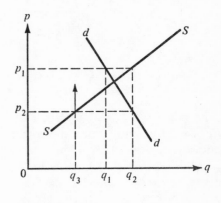

**Figure 1-3.**
Coupling the two search mechanisms.

If we put the Marshallian search mechanism together with the Walrasian search mechanism we could find situations where, although equilibrium is mathematically defined, and although either the Marshallian mechanism by itself or the Walrasian mechanism by itself would establish that equilibrium, the two together will lead us away from equilibrium. In Figure 1-3 the negatively sloped line (dd) is a demand price schedule. The positively sloped line (SS) is a supply schedule. As in the Marshallian mechanism we assume that the actual price that exists is the demand price. Hence, if the actual quantity is $q_1$, the actual price will be $p_1$. At $p_1$, following the Walrasian mechanism, the quantity supplied is $q_2$, which causes price to fall, a la Marshall, to $p_2$. This in turn will cause suppliers to reduce quantity supplied to $q_3$, etc. We can see in the diagram that if one set of transactors (sellers) behaves according to Walrasian rules and decides quantity supplied on the basis of actual price, while the other set of transactors (buyers) behaves according to Marshallian rules and bids price to the demand price for the quantity that actually exists, the interaction of the two sets can lead the market away from equilibrium price and quantity. If the absolute value of the slope of $dd$ is less than the slope of $SS$, the coupling of the two search mechanisms will lead the market to the equilibrium point. (Again, you should verify this by constructing the appropriate diagram.)

## The Meaning of Competition

Throughout this text we shall be concerned primarily with how market processes work, not with equilibrium states. We shall see that the major driving force of market processes is rivalry—rivalry among sellers and rivalry among buyers. Before you took your introductory economics class you probably used the word "competition" to mean rivalrous behavior. In that class, however, you learned that many economists reserve the word "competition" to describe an ideal market situation which they call "perfect competition." In a perfectly competitive market information is free, which is just a succinct way of saying that all transactors know all there is to know about the market behavior of other transactors. Buyers know what their own tastes and preferences are. Buyers know the terms of trade that the various sellers offer, and sellers know of the terms of trade that the various buyers offer. Buyers know not only the quantities and prices that are offered but they also know about the array of qualities available. Sellers know what various buyers and groups of buyers consider to be optimal combinations of quality and price. With all this information that is simply assumed to exist there is never any need for advertising,

product differentiation, or market research. Buyers never have to search for the most favorable terms of trade, never make purchases they later regret, and find brand names to be useless. In short, there is never any human action that we would classify as rivalry in a perfectly competitive market.

No actual market can be described in these terms, but it has become traditional to think of the ideal voluntary exchange system in this way, and students are encouraged to measure real-world markets against this ideal as a benchmark. This concentration on the characteristics of the ideal has led some to reject voluntary exchange systems, and the economic theory that is supposed to explain them, on the grounds that "too many assumptions are necessary to make it work." Others consider observations of rivalrous behavior such as advertising and product differentiation to be evidence of "imperfect" markets.

In this text the word "competition" means rivalry. While we shall frequently refer to equilibrium in various types of markets, our chief concern will be to understand real-world market processes. If we are to examine these processes, the assumption of zero information costs must be discarded right from the start. In Chapter 7 we shall discuss price taker markets, which are essentially perfectly competitive markets with positive costs of acquiring information. As we shall see, there are many examples of price taker markets in the real world, and advertising and other forms of rivalry have important functions to perform in these markets as well as others.

Before we can thoroughly discuss any kind of market, however, we must first consider the theories of exchange, demand, production, and cost. It is to these tasks that we now turn.

## Questions for Discussion

1. Even in relatively wealthy societies, such as the United States, scarcity has not been and never will be eliminated. Why? Does it have anything to do with

avarice or greed or the economic system? Why not? Why would scarcity not be eliminated even if enough could be produced to give each person all that he "needs?"

2. From the text's description of the computation of the CPI, show that a change in the price of a given good receives a weight equal to the percent of total expenditures spent on that good by the average family. Rising food prices receive a weight of approximately 22%. This overstates the resulting increase in the cost of living for some and understates it for others. Which is which?

3. On March 26, 1974, the *Wall Street Journal* reported that John Gibbons of the Federal Energy Office (the name has recently been changed to the Federal Energy Administration) said it was necessary to carry out a "propaganda blitz" to convince citizens to undertake such measures as reduced driving, better planning of shopping excursions, purchase of higher mileage cars, and increased use of storm windows and insulation in homes. Can you think of a more direct way to accomplish the desired end that does not also restrain individual freedom of choice?

4. Minimum wage legislation has always been vigorously supported by labor unions and established manufacturers, especially in the Northeast. Why?

5. President Ford and Henry Kissinger excoriated the Arabs in the United Nations for causing worldwide inflation. Why is that charge completely unfounded? Can labor unions or corporations cause inflation without the support of the Federal Reserve? Why not?

6. What kinds of competition are considered all right for obtaining public office but are not approved for attaining success in private business? Why?

7. In the text we saw how different and changing prices can be thought of in the context of a search for equilibrium. Explain how product differentiation—different qualities and styles of essentially the same good—can also be thought of as a similar search phenomenon.

# 2
## Indifference Curves and Exchange

### The Method of Economic Enquiry

In this chapter we make some basic assertions about human behavior. Upon these assertions we shall construct a theory. The assertions may or may not be "true" (although one doesn't have to stretch his imagination too far to agree with the ones we shall make). It is perfectly conceivable that a good (useful) theory could be constructed upon unrealistic assumptions or assertions. In an important book about the methodology of all scientific enquiry, Thomas S. Kuhn, a physicist, has pointed out that the theory based on the assumption that the earth was the center of the universe served man quite well for a long period of time.[1] This Ptolemaic model was capable of answering the questions that were asked of it. It was sufficient, for example, for navigation purposes. Indeed, even today when navigators use the heavens to plot their courses they pretend that the Ptolemaic model is an accurate description of reality. For navigation purposes the Ptolemaic model is superior to any other.

Only when more complex questions were asked, questions that the Ptolemaic model couldn't answer, did it become necessary to adopt the new frame of reference advanced by Copernicus. Copernicus was succeeded by Newton, who in turn was succeeded by Einstein. In each case, whenever a new framework was adopted it was because the existing theory proved to be inadequate to answer the questions that were being asked of it.

In economics we do the same thing. We consider a theory or a model to be a good one if it works—that is, if it helps us answer questions that we ask of it, and if those answers are empirically verified. We do not worry about the realism of the assumptions upon which our models are built. If we have two models, A and B, and both answer the questions we ask of them equally well, we prefer the one that is built upon the more realistic assumptions. If model A permits us to make better predictions than model B, if it can answer a larger set of questions than model B, we would prefer model A to model B even if the former were based on fanciful assumptions while the latter was based on assertions that no one would deny. We would stick to model A until a model that was even more useful came along. Our approach is very pragmatic. We wish to be able to predict, for

---

[1] Thomas S. Kuhn, *The Structure of Scientific Revolutions* (Chicago: University of Chicago Press, 1962).

instance, the consequences of an increase in minimum wages, a lowering of import quotas for oil, the implementation of a rent control program, the imposition of a tax on incomes, or the impact of a negative income tax plan. A good model is one that enables us to make accurate predictions of these effects. A better model is one that enables us to make even more accurate predictions. Ask not, "Are the assumptions realistic?"; instead, ask "How well does the model work?"[2]

### The Basic Assumptions of Indifference Curve Analysis[3]

**1. Every Person Wants More Than He Has of Many Goods.** This assumption merely states that no one is satiated with everything. All of us would like to have more than we do of at least some things. The reason that we don't have all we want is because of the cost of acquiring it. The word "good" merely means something that we *want* to have more of rather than less of (ignoring costs). Goods are of two types—free and economic. A free good is one that we can obtain additional amounts of without anyone having to give up anything in payment. Don't confuse free goods with goods that are distributed at a zero price. Some schools have "free" school lunches, but someone must pay for them even though the consumers of the lunches do not. Many nonfree goods are distributed at zero prices—lunches, books at public libraries, medical services in Britain, etc. But how many actually *free* goods can you think of? Are there *any* goods that can be obtained without someone paying something for them? Air is perhaps the only example, and clean air in metropolitan areas is no longer free. Urban dwellers must sacri-

fice something—some automobile travel, for example—in order to get additional clean air. In any case, if you can think of some truly free goods, don't worry about them. Economics is not concerned with free goods; its concern is with *scarce* or *economic* goods. A scarce (or economic) good is one that we can get additional amounts of only if we, or someone, is willing to give up some of some other goods in payment. As we saw above, this includes practically everything that we think of when we use the term "goods." Economics concerns making choices about more or less of one thing in exchange for less or more of something else. We cannot get all that we want of everything, so we have to figure out how to do the best we can with the opportunities we have. A better stereo may mean a shorter vacation, additional bourbon means less expensive theater seats, more resources devoted to the space program mean fewer resources available for education, more expensive cuts of meat mean a less extensive wardrobe, and more resources devoted to welfare programs mean less resources available for national defense.

**2. There Is Some Amount of Some Good Which Is Sufficient to Induce Each Person to Give up Some of Any Other Good.** In other words, people substitute more of one thing for less of another all the time. No one, we assume, steadfastly refuses to give up some of anything. Similarly, no one demands more of anything no matter what the price. A person is willing to sacrifice some bit of any good he has if he can obtain a sufficient amount of something else in exchange. A person can be dissuaded from acquiring more of anything by a sufficiently high price for the thing.

People substitute one thing for another even when it comes to such important goods as clean air and pure water. We have already seen that we willingly sacrifice some clean air so that we may have some transportation services. In Chapter 13 we shall see why this particular substitution has most likely gone too far, but the basic point remains—we are willing to give up at least some clean air to get something else

---

[2]For a thorough discussion of these points see Milton Friedman, "The Methodology of Positive Economics," in his *Essays in Positive Economics* (Chicago: University of Chicago Press, 1953).

[3]The discussion here is an adaptation of that by Alchian and Allen, *Exchange and Production* (Belmont, Calif.: Wadsworth, 1969), Chap. 2.

that we want. Consider the case of water. Water is not used only to drink. It is used to bathe, to keep lawns green, to keep cars clean, etc. Our substitution assumption says that there is a real price of water that is sufficiently high to induce an individual to take only three showers a week instead of seven, or to tolerate a brown lawn and a dirty car. Individuals are willing to give up some water if they can get in exchange something else that they want.

The minimum amount of some good $Y$ which an individual will insist on getting in order to induce him to give up one unit of some other good $X$ is called that person's marginal rate of substitution between $X$ and $Y$. It is also called that person's marginal evaluation of $X$ in terms of $Y$. These terms are similarly defined for exchange in the opposite direction—acquiring $X$ in exchange for $Y$. In this case their meaning is the maximum amount of $Y$ the individual would be willing to pay to get an additional unit of $X$. Consider an individual whose marginal rate of substitution between $X$ and $Y$ is 3. The individual has some amount of both $X$ and $Y$, and the value he places on one unit of $X$ in terms of $Y$ is three units of $Y$. This means that if someone paid our individual (let's call him Mr. A) three units of $Y$ for one $X$, Mr. A would be no better and no worse off than he was before he entered into that exchange. He would have been paid exactly what he thought the $X$ was worth to him. Similarly, if Mr. A were sold another unit of $X$ for three units of $Y$, he would also be no better and no worse off. Again the trade has merely replaced three $Y$'s with their equivalent (equivalent in the mind of the individual)—one $X$. If he got by with paying any amount of $Y$ less than this (even a tiny bit less) for the $X$, or if he could get more than three $Y$'s by giving up an $X$, he would consider himself to be better off and would happily trade.

Notice what the word "value" means in this analysis. It is entirely a subjective notion. The value of an economics text to me could be different from the value of the same text to you. "Value" is either the maximum amount that the individual

would pay to get one unit of $X$ or the minimum amount that the individual would insist on getting to induce him to give up a unit of $X$. *There is no such thing as intrinsic value.* Nothing is embodied in a good which gives it value. No matter what is necessary to produce a good, the good's value is merely what people are willing to pay for it. Clearly, if it costs more to produce a good than its value (what people are willing to pay for it), it won't be produced. If the value of a good exceeds its cost of production, more of that good is likely to be produced. *Value is not cost of production.*

Since we assume that individuals are willing to trade less of one thing for more of another, we hesitate to use the term "need" to mean a want that takes priority over other wants. To begin with, if a group of ten or more people were asked to make a list of things that people *need*, in decreasing order of importance, the group would find it impossible to come to a consensus on what should be on the list and in what order the items should appear. Food would probably be at the top of every list, followed by water, shelter, medical care, and clothing. Beyond this, agreement on whether something is a "need" would be difficult to obtain. Secondly, agreement on the *quantities* of each of the items that constitutes "need" would be even more difficult to obtain. What amount of food is a need? When does eating stop being a satisfaction of a need and begin becoming an indulgence in conspicuous consumption? Even though food is at the top of nearly everyone's list, no one would give up *all* of his clothing before he gave up *any* food. Suppose that to prevent 100 people from going to bed hungry we had to scrap the entire space program. Would you want to do it? Our assumption that people trade among desirable things says there is some price which you would consider too high to accomplish the admirable goal of feeding 100 persons more adequately.

Using the word "needs" or ranking wants from most important to least important is a matter of individual value judgment. There are no universally agreed-to objective standards that permit any person from passing on the value judgments of another. In economics, because of this difficulty, we talk only about *wants*, not needs. One want is the same as any other want; we do not set up a hierarchy of wants.

**3. A Person's Marginal Evaluation of a Good Declines as the Amount of the Good that the Person Has Increases.** This implies an individual's marginal evaluation of a good increases as the amount of the good the person has decreases. In other words, the maximum price you are willing to pay (by giving up some other good) for an additional unit of some good $X$ will be lower when you already have 10 $X$'s than when you start with two $X$'s. Notice that this is not an assumption regarding any nonobservable variable such as "utility" or "satisfaction." The amount a person is willing to pay for something and the amount he is willing to sell something for are observable in the real world. Note also that when we talk about paying for something, or the amount something is sold for, we are not talking about dollar amounts. The payment is made and received in units of some other nonmoney good. The assumption concerns the rate at which an individual is willing to trade one good for another.[4]

### Indifference Curves

These three assumptions enable us to construct a very useful geometric device called an indifference curve. Consider Figure 2-1. An individual has $0G$ units of $X$ and $0E$ units of $Y$. He is at point $A$. He contemplates losing $GD$ units of $X$. Our second assumption states that there is some amount of $Y$ that will be sufficient to compensate the individual for the loss of $GD$ of

---

[4]This assumption states that even if the amount of $Y$ that a person has is constant, his marginal evaluation of $X$ is higher when he has less $X$ than when he has more $X$. We shall have to consider this point again in the next chapter when we discuss "inferior goods."

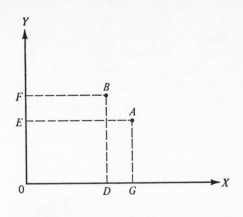

**Figure 2-1.**
Equally desirable combinations.

$X$. Let's suppose that amount is $EF$ units of $Y$. If the individual receives exactly $EF$ units of $Y$ in payment for the $DG$ units of $X$, he will have moved from point $A$ to point $B$. He has neither improved his well-being nor impaired it. He will be indifferent between point $A$ and point $B$. He would be willing to decide between $A$ and $B$ by tossing a coin. We say that $A$ and $B$ are on the same indifference curve.

An indifference curve through point $A$ connects all the points that the individual regards as neither better nor worse than point $A$. Since $X$ and $Y$ are both goods, the first assumption tells us that an indifference curve must be downward sloping. Less of $X$ must be compensated for by additional $Y$ if the individual's well-being is not to be impaired. $X$ and $Y$ are both things the individual wants more of rather than less of. Taking away some $X$ must be compensated for by giving the individual more $Y$ if the individual is to be no better and no worse off than he was originally.

The third assumption tells us that an indifference curve gets steeper as it gets closer to the $Y$ axis and gets more shallow as it gets closer to the $X$ axis. Consider Figure 2-2. Beginning with only $0C$ of $X$ and $0K$ of $Y$, the individual would be willing to pay up to $JK$ of $Y$ for an additional $CD$ units of $X$. If the individual began with $0E$ of $X$ he would be willing to pay a maximum of only $HG$ of $Y$ for $EF$ (which equals $CD$) of $X$. The $Y$ value of $X$ declines as more $X$ is acquired, in accordance with our third assumption.

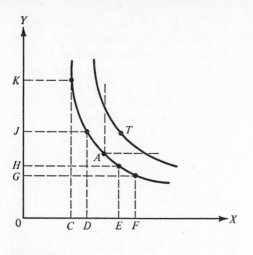

**Figure 2-2.**
Indifference map.

Point $T$ involves more of both goods than point $A$. Since goods are things the individual wants more of, we can say that point $T$ is preferred to point $A$. The first two assumptions assure us that there are many points which the individual considers to be just as good as (but no better than) point $T$. The line that connects all such points would be the indifference curve through $T$. All points on the indifference curve through $T$ are preferred to all points on the indifference curve through $A$. After all, all points on the line through $T$ are the same (in the person's mind), and all points on the line through $A$ are the same. $T$ is preferred to $A$; hence all points on the line through $T$ must be equally preferred to $A$, and all points on the line through $A$ must

be regarded as equally inferior to $T$. We say that $T$ is on a "higher" indifference curve than $A$.

Our assumptions assure us that there is an indifference curve through every point in Figure 2-2. A diagram that contains two or more indifference curves is called an indifference map. No two indifference curves in an indifference map can intersect, because that would mean that the combination of goods represented by the intersection point would be preferred to itself—a proposition that defies understanding.

## Exchange without a Middleman

Indifference curves enable us to analyze the process of exchange and to see that exchange involves gains to all parties. It is not unusual to hear the claim that trade (and all sorts of economic activity) involves gains for some at the expense of losses for others. This is utter nonsense, as our analysis will show.

Consider Figure 2-3. Two individuals, Mr. A and Mr. B, have some amounts of two goods $X$ and $Y$. The marginal evaluation of $X$ in terms of $Y$ is not the same for the two individuals. Mr. A values a unit of $X$ at three units of $Y$, and Mr. B thinks an $X$ is worth only one $Y$. That is, given that Mr. A starts with the combination of $Y$ and $X$ represented by point $E_A$ ($E_A$ is called A's endowment point), and Mr. B starts

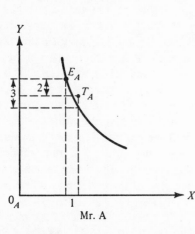

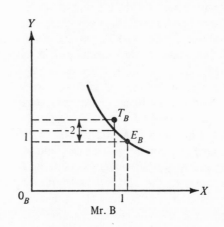

**Figure 2-3.**
Exchange without a middleman.

with the combination of $Y$ and $X$ represented by point $E_B$, and given Mr. A's and Mr. B's tastes, Mr. A places a higher value on $Y$ than Mr. B does. Mr. A thinks an $X$ is worth three $Y$'s, or that one $Y$ is worth one-third $X$. Mr. B thinks that an $X$ is worth one $Y$, or that one $Y$ is worth one $X$. Both can be made better off if each acquires more of the good he values more highly from the other.

For example, suppose Mr. B gives one $X$ to Mr. A in exchange for two $Y$'s. If he received only one $Y$ he would not have improved his situation. He would have remained on his initial indifference curve. But he receives two $Y$'s for the $X$, moving to point $T_B$, a point that is clearly on a higher indifference curve. Saying that he is on a higher indifference curve merely says that he prefers point $T_B$ to point $E_B$. Mr. B is clearly better off.

What about Mr. A? He would have been willing to pay up to three $Y$'s for the $X$, but he gets away with paying only two $Y$'s. If he paid three $Y$'s he would have remained on his initial indifference curve. Giving up only two $Y$'s puts him at point $T_A$, a point clearly on a higher indifference curve. Mr. A is unambiguously better off.

With only two individuals we cannot say what the exchange value of an $X$ in terms of $Y$ will be. Mr. B would like to get as many $Y$'s as he can for one $X$, but the most he can get is three $Y$'s (Mr. A's demand price). Mr. A would like to pay as little as he can for the $X$, but the least he can get away with is one $Y$ (Mr. B's supply price). The actual price will be somewhere between three $Y$'s and one $Y$. Exactly where depends on the relative bargaining skills of the two individuals. When many individuals are involved in buying and selling $X$'s and $Y$'s, the actual exchange prices are determinate, as we shall see.

Note that as Mr. A and Mr. B move from their endowment points to $T_A$ and to $T_B$, respectively, their marginal evaluations come closer to each other. Assumption 3 assures us that this is true. Mr. A has acquired an $X$ and has got rid of some $Y$'s. His $Y$ value of $X$ must decline. Mr. B has got rid of an $X$ and has acquired some additional $Y$'s. His $Y$ value of $X$ must increase. The possibility of mutual gains from trade will continue to exist as long as the two individuals have unequal marginal evaluations. The trading itself will eventually result in equal marginal evaluations, and at this point trading will stop.

Marginal evaluation of $X$ in terms of $Y$ is merely the number of additional $Y$'s that a given individual thinks is exact compensation for the loss of one $X$. It is the negative of the *slope* of the individual's indifference curve at the point which represents the combination of $Y$ and $X$ that the individual actually has. The slope of an indifference curve is negative (downward sloping). Marginal rates of substitution (or marginal evaluations) are expressed as positive numbers, hence the marginal rate of substitution is the absolute value of the slope of an indifference curve. Mutually beneficial trade can take place, therefore, whenever the slopes of two individuals' indifference curves at the points which represent the combinations of $X$ and $Y$ they actually have are different. The two individuals could start with the same combination of $X$ and $Y$ and still engage in mutually beneficial trade as long as the slopes of their indifference curves at the starting point are different.

### Exchange with a Middleman

An implicit assumption in the preceding section was that Mr. A and Mr. B knew about each other, could communicate with each other at zero cost, and could transport $X$'s and $Y$'s at zero cost. In other words, we implicitly assumed that the costs of engaging in exchange (sometimes called transactions costs) were zero. This is obviously unrealistic, and by dropping this assumption our model becomes more useful in understanding the world we see around us. Since transactors generally do not know about each other, and thus cannot communicate directly, a middleman is needed. The role of the middleman is to reduce the costs of engaging in exchange.

To analyze the role of the middleman, let's go back to the example of the previous section. Suppose Mr. A and Mr. B did not know each other. They would have to search for opportunities for mutually beneficial trade. These search costs would be diminished if there was a third person who would arrange the trade for them, for a fee. This third person would be a specialist in collecting information about bids and offers from the various transactors who wish to trade. Such specialists permit these transactors to effect their trades with less expenditure of time and effort than would otherwise be necessary. Mr. A and Mr. B would be happy to pay a fee that was less than the costs of search they would have to bear in the absence of the middleman. The middleman could offer Mr. B 1.5 $Y$'s for an $X$. Mr. B would be better off if he accepted the offer, since he would receive more than his supply price (the minimum price he will accept—1 $Y$). We say that the middleman's "bid" price is 1.5 $Y$'s. The middleman could then take the $X$ and offer it to Mr. A for 2.5 $Y$'s. If Mr. A agreed to that price he would be better off because that price is less than his demand price (the maximum price he is willing to pay—3 $Y$'s). We say that the middleman's "ask" price is 2.5 $Y$'s. The middleman ends up with 1 $Y$, the difference between his "bid" and his "ask" prices.

The middleman's fee is collected from both transactors, since each transactor ends up with less $Y$'s than he did when the trade was carried on without the middleman. This does not mean that the middleman was a parasite. To the contrary, once we recognize the costs of engaging in exchange we must conclude that both Mr. A and Mr. B are better off than they would be without the middleman. Without the middleman trade would not have taken place, or if it did, resources worth more than one $Y$ would have been used up in search, bargaining, and transportation costs. The middleman minimizes these costs.

The middleman is forced to perform his functions efficiently—i.e., in the least-cost manner—because if the spread between bid and ask prices is larger than the costs he incurs from performing his services (including income he could earn doing something else), other middlemen will offer their ser-

vices to Mr. A and Mr. B for a smaller fee. It is the competition among middlemen that keeps them honest. Middlemen do not compete with consumers; they compete with other actual or potential middlemen.

We often hear that we can save money if we skip the middleman. But buying directly from the factory or bakery, say, at lower prices, is frequently a false economy. Retail stores are generally more conveniently located than manufacturers. They devote space to showrooms, provide delivery service, provide clerks with specialized information about the product, carry inventories so that customers will not have to order ahead, and provide return privileges to customers who are dissatisfied with their purchases. If we never used retail stores the dollar price of what we purchased might be lower, but the total paid for the commodity plus the costs of transportation, information collection, and time would exceed the prices we pay using middlemen. If this were not true, how would you explain the fact that middlemen exist and flourish?

## Open and Closed Markets

We said earlier that middlemen compete with each other rather than with consumers. If the revenue collected by a middleman exceeds his costs plus enough to represent a rate of return on his investment at least equal to the rate of return he could earn by purchasing bonds, other middlemen will want to start providing similar services so that they, too, can make this "economic profit." Economic profit (a profit rate larger than the rate that can on average be made on alternative types of investments) attracts competitors like honey attracts bees. If there are no legal impediments to keep new competitors from setting up shop, economic profit will be eliminated as new middlemen enter and drive down the ask (retail) prices and drive up the bid (wholesale) prices.

Unfortunately not all markets are open to new competitors. Frequently we hear of sellers of some commodity or service appealing to state legislatures to keep potential competitors out. They claim that these interlopers are unqualified sellers who would engage in practices that would be detrimental to the public interest. To protect the unsuspecting, gullible public from these charlatans it is necessary, the existing sellers claim, to institute licensure laws. Existing sellers may form a state board of examiners who will determine who the qualified sellers are. This board will see to it that the number of new sellers each year does not exceed the number that ensures an "orderly market." "Cutthroat competition" will not be permitted. Does this sound farfetched? Why do barbers, drycleaners, and morticians have to be licensed? Why, in the state of Massachusetts, is it illegal for prepaid medical groups such as Kaiser to practice medicine? For that matter, why do physicians have to be licensed at all?

The answer to this last question seems obvious. There are high information costs in the medical market. That is, it is difficult for buyers in the medical market to obtain information about the qualifications of sellers. We clearly don't want sick people to be tricked into spending money on unqualified quacks who may permanently incapacitate or even kill them. A license at least ensures that each seller of medical services has *some* expertise in medicine.

It is true that the licensure laws reduce the risk involved in picking a seller of medical services. The license *does* provide important information to patients. However, the license is also used to restrict entry into the medical profession. A person cannot even sign up to take the licensure exam unless he has graduated from an approved medical school. The list of approved schools is determined by the American Medical Association and the American Association of Medical Colleges. As a result of this regulation, the number of medical students in American medical schools in 1958 was only 5,200 more than the number of medical students in 1910.[5]

There is an alternative way of coping with high information costs in the medical market that would not permit the restriction of entry the existing regulation carries with it.[6] Let anyone who wants to, practice medicine. Require only that all practitioners take an extensive examination which could be administered five days a week for a month and would examine knowledge of pharmacology, clinical laboratory procedures, ability to diagnose and prescribe, etc., and require that each seller post his grade on this exam on all his stationery, his prescription slips, on his door, and on the walls of his office. The exam could be retaken as often as any practitioner wished, but would have to be retaken at least every five years. Under this system patients could identify the qualifications of physicians. For some ailments (such as broken bone, lacerated finger, upper respiratory infection, the flu), a grade C physician would be adequate. For other, more complicated problems, a grade A physician, who would charge a higher price, would be called. Grade C physicians, afraid of malpractice suits, would refer cases they couldn't handle. Anyone who wished to buy from a grade F physician would not affect anyone but himself. If he knowingly purchased grade F services, that would be up to him. It is difficult to see any legitimate public interest involved.

Another device that is often used to restrict competition and protect economic profit is the obtaining of an exclusive franchise from some government body to sell in that government's jurisdiction. The Los Angeles Yellow Cab Company has such an exclusive franchise in downtown Los Angeles and at the Los Angeles International Airport. It is impossible to determine how this government action is in the public interest.

In California there is a milk marketing board that sets *minimum* retail prices on milk. The Sherman Antitrust Act makes it illegal for General Electric and Westing-

[5]Reuben A. Kessel, "Price Discrimination in Medicine," *Journal of Law and Economics* (October 1958).

[6]See Charles W. Baird, "A Market Solution to Medical Inflation," *Journal of Human Resources* (Winter 1971).

house to collude on prices, but dairy companies can collude and set price through their representatives on the milk marketing board. The Civil Aeronautics Board enforces *minimum* as well as maximum fares on airline travel. Price competition among airlines is illegal, so the airlines compete with more leg room, zero price champagne, and attractive stewardesses.

There are all sorts of ways to prevent open market competition, and there are all sorts of arguments that these impediments are in the public interest. Most of the time the regulations act in the interest of a legal cartel of sellers who have been successful in convincing government officials that what is in the interest of sellers is in the public interest.

## The Edgeworth Exchange Box

In Figure 2-3 we constructed separate indifference curve diagrams for two transactors, $A$ and $B$. $A$'s marginal rate of substitution between $X$ and $Y$ was 3, meaning that $A$ would pay a maximum of three $Y$'s to get an additional $X$. $B$'s marginal rate of substitution between $X$ and $Y$ was 1, meaning that the minimum number of $Y$'s that $B$ would insist on getting in exchange for one $X$ was 1. We imagined that trade actually took place at the rate of two $Y$'s for an $X$ and demonstrated that such a trade would put both transactors into preferred positions. The Edgeworth exchange box is an alternative geometric device for depicting such an exchange.[7]

In Figure 2-4 the indifference curve diagram for $A$ is presented just as it was in Figure 2-3. $A$ begins with $Y_A$ of $Y$ and $X_A$ of $X$ and has a marginal rate of substitution equal to three $Y$'s for an $X$. The indifference curve diagram for $B$ in Figure 2-3 has been rotated 180° and $B$'s endowment point ($X_B$ of $X$ and $Y_B$ of $Y$) has been placed on top of $A$'s endowment point. The origin of $B$'s diagram is in the upper

right-hand corner of the Edgeworth box. $B$'s indifference curve is negatively sloped and convex toward $B$'s origin, even though it is concave toward $A$'s origin. $B$'s marginal rate of substitution is one for one, just as it was in Figure 2-3.

Note that the width of the exchange box is equal to the sum of the amount of $X$ with which $A$ starts and the amount of $X$ with which $B$ starts. Its height is equal to the sum of $A$'s endowment of $Y$ and $B$'s endowment of $Y$. Since the box was constructed by superimposing the two endowment points, one point (point $E$ in Figure 2-4) represents the individual endowments. At point $E$, since the marginal rates of substitution (the absolute values of the slopes of the indifference curves) are different, the indifference curves intersect. The two starting indifference curves form a football-shaped area. Points in this area are points on higher indifference curves for both transactors.

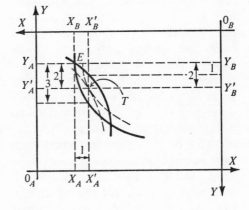

**Figure 2-4.**
Edgeworth exchange box.

Let us examine the geometry of the same trade that we discussed in Figure 2-3 within the context of the Edgeworth box. Both transactors begin at point $E$. $A$ acquires one additional $X$ (goes from $X_A$ to $X_A'$) in exchange for two $Y$'s (from $Y_A$ to $Y_A'$). $B$ gives up the unit of $X$ (from $X_B$ to $X_B'$) and acquires the two units of $Y$ (from $Y_B$ to $Y_B'$). Notice that when $B$ decreases his holdings of $X$ he moves from left to right along the top of the box, and when

[7]Named for Francis Ysidro Edgeworth, who first constructed and used it in his *Mathematical Psychics*, 1881.

he increases his holdings of $Y$ he moves down along the right side of the box. These moves exactly correspond to the left-to-right move along the bottom of the box as $A$ increases his holdings of $X$ and the downward move along the left side of the box as $A$ gives up $Y$'s. What one transactor gives up the other transactor acquires.

If $A$ were to stay on his original indifference curve he would have to give up three $Y$'s for his additional $X$. If $B$ were to stay on his original indifference curve he would acquire only one $Y$ for the $X$ that he gives to $A$. The actual exchange rate is two $Y$'s for the $X$, hence both transactors are on higher indifference curves. They move to the two dashed indifference curves in Figure 2-4, and are at the common point in the box labeled $T$. If at $T$ the two indifference curves intersected, further gains from trade would be possible, because if indifference curves intersect at a point they have different slopes at that point, and if they have different slopes the two transactors have unequal marginal rates of substitution. The potential for gains from trade comes from unequal marginal rates of substitution. If the two indifference curves are tangent to each other at point $T$ (as they are in Figure 2-4), the transactors will have equal marginal rates of substitution and no further gains from trade are possible.

Figure 2-5 is an Edgeworth box diagram with many indifference curves drawn in for both $A$ and $B$. If the common endowment point were $E_1$, $A$ would be on indifference curve $A_1$ and $B$ would be on indifference curve $B_3$. Exchange would occur until the transactors arrived at some point on the line segment $CD$. The line that connects points $C$, $D$, $F$, and $G$ is called a *contract curve*. It is the set of all points of tangency between indifference curves of the two transactors. It is, in other words, the set of all points of equal marginal rates of substitution. Thus if the starting point is $E_1$, trade will stop only when equal marginal rates of substitution are obtained, and the trading cannot result in either $A$ or $B$ becoming worse off (on lower indifference curves) than when they started. Point $C$ is

the point on the contract curve that is on $A$'s original indifference curve. $A$ will not voluntarily move southwest of point $C$ because that would mean that he was moving to lower (less preferred) indifference curves. Point $D$ is the point on the contract curve that is on $B$'s original indifference curve. $B$ will not voluntarily move northeast of point $D$ because that would mean he was moving to lower indifference curves. (Remember that $B$'s indifference curves are drawn with the upper right-hand corner of the Edgeworth box as their origin.) Thus voluntary exchange between $A$ and $B$ starting from point $E_1$ will culminate at some point on the line segment labeled $CD$.

If the total amount of $X$ and $Y$ available were the same as before, but the initial distribution of the commodities were such that $E_2$ was the starting point, voluntary exchange would culminate at some point on the line segment labeled $FG$. Voluntary exchange will lead (in the absence of transactions cost) to some point on the contract curve, for only points on the contract curve are points of tangency of indifference curves. All other points in the Edgeworth box are points of intersection of two indifference curves.

If the process of exchange itself takes resources it may not pay the transactors to trade to the point of equal marginal rates of substitution. For example, if the difference between the marginal rates of substi-

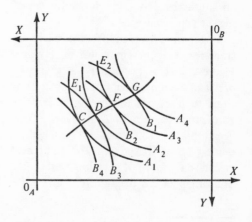

**Figure 2-5.**
Contract curve.

tution is 0.5 $Y$'s, and if the cost of getting together and actually engaging in trade is the equivalent of one $Y$, it will not be worthwhile to carry out the exchange that would equate the marginal rates of substitution.

In the next chapter we will see how indifference curves are used to develop important notions in the theory of demand. In Chapter 13 we will see how the Edgeworth exchange box is used to illustrate some notions that are important in general equilibrium analysis.

## Questions for Discussion

1. Does assumption 3 in the text imply that a loss of $10 of income means less to a rich man than to a poor man? Why not?

2. Use the basic assumptions discussed in the text to construct an indifference curve that represents an individual's attitude toward different combinations of a bad (something he wants less of rather than more of) and a good. Make a list of some common bads about which we all must make tradeoff decisions.

3. Does trade emerge only when the traders have produced surpluses above what they need themselves? Why not? Can you construct an operational definition of "surplus?"

4. In *The American Way of Death*, Jessica Mitford attacked the mortician profession for its abuses of bereaved family members. Morticians were then and still are licensed sellers of their services. Explain the connection between the licenses and the abuses.

5. Fair trade laws make it illegal for retailers to sell certain goods (e.g., *Sony* TV's and *Timex* watches) for less than a minimum price set by manufacturers. To whom are the fair trade laws fair? Why do manufacturers want these laws? Why do specialty shops want them and large department stores not want them?

6. The contract curve of the Edgeworth box diagram is sometimes called the "conflict curve." Why?

7. Use an Edgeworth box diagram to show why rationing by fixed allotments without the possibility of exchange leaves people worse off than they would be if exchange were permitted.

# 3
# Demand Theory

In the previous chapter we derived indifference curves from some basic assumptions about human behavior. In this chapter[1] we shall put indifference curves together with another geometric device called the budget constraint to derive two other relationships: the Engel curve and the demand curve. An Engel curve[2] depicts the relationship between the quantity demanded of some good $X$ and the real income of the buyers of $X$ when the real (or relative) price of $X$ is held constant. A demand curve depicts the relationship between the quantity demanded of some good $X$ and the relative price of $X$ when the real income of the buyers of $X$ is held constant. In each case we shall derive the curves first for an individual and then for the market as a whole. In addition, we shall analyze the impact on the quantity demanded of some good $X$ of changes in the relative prices of substitutes for and complements with $X$, when both the relative price of $X$ and the purchasing power of the buyers of $X$ are held constant.

## The Budget Constraint

Here, as before, we shall assume that a buyer buys only two goods, $X$ and $Y$. There are actually many goods upon which we spend our incomes, but if we restrict the mathematics of our exposition to geometry we can discuss at most three goods. Since two-dimensional diagrams are easier to construct and to understand than three-dimensional diagrams, we shall limit our discussion to a two-good world. Fortunately, the two-dimensional analysis can be generalized to the multigood case. In a multigood world, one of the "goods" that we could spend some income on is saving. We spend money on saving by not spending it on other goods. Since our two-dimensional analysis stands for the multigood case, we will adopt the convention that each transactor spends all of his income on the two goods $X$ and $Y$. That is, no transactor will have any money income left over after he has purchased his desired quantities of $X$ and $Y$. (One possible thing that either $X$ and $Y$ could stand for is saving.)

Consider a transactor who earns $1,000 income each month. He spends his income on two goods: $X$, which has a unit price of $50, and $Y$, which has a unit price of $25. If each month he spent all of his income on $X$ he could purchase $1,000/$50 = 20 units

[1]The discussion in this chapter follows Gary Becker, *Economic Theory* (New York: Alfred A. Knopf, 1971), pp. 14–45.

[2]Named for Ernst Engel, a 19th Century German statistician.

of $X$. If he spent all of his income on $Y$ he could purchase $1,000/$25 = 40$ units of $Y$. For every unit less of $X$ he purchases, $50 is freed for the purchase of $Y$'s. With $50, two $Y$'s can be purchased. With a dollar price of $X = $50$ and a dollar price of $Y = $25$, the transactor can purchase two $Y$'s for every $X$ that he doesn't purchase. Thus the real price of an additional $X$ is two $Y$'s. The real price of $X$ is the dollar price of $X$ $(P_x)$ divided by the dollar price of $Y$ $(P_y)$, or $P_x/P_y = 2$ $Y$'s.

These simple observations can be put into a picture. Consider Figure 3-1. On the vertical axis physical units of good $Y$ are plotted. The horizontal axis indicates physical units of good $X$. If no $X$ were purchased the individual's $1,000 income could purchase the amount of $Y$ indicated by the point where the line in the diagram cuts the vertical axis. That amount of $Y$ is, as we indicated above, $1,000/$25 = 40$ $Y$'s. If no $Y$ were purchased, the $1,000 income could purchase the amount of $X$ indicated by the point where the line in the diagram cuts the horizontal axis: $1,000/$50 = 20$ $X$'s. The absolute value of the slope of the line in the diagram is

the number of $Y$'s that can be acquired for each unit less of $X$ bought. For example, if instead of purchasing 20 $X$'s the individual purchased only 10 $X$'s, he would thus save enough money to purchase 20 $Y$'s. The absolute value of the slope of the line is 20/10, which equals 2—the number of $Y$'s that can be acquired *per unit less* of $X$ bought.

The combination of 20 $Y$'s and 10 $X$'s costs $25(20) + $50(10) = $1,000$. Any point on the line in the diagram costs $1,000, because when less of one good is purchased the money so saved is used to purchase more of the other good. Thus we can write that $1,000 = $25y + $50x$, where $y$ and $x$ are the amounts of good $Y$ and good $X$, respectively, that will cost a total of $1,000, given that the price of $Y$ is $25 and the price of $X$ is $50. As you can see in the diagram, there are many combinations of $X$ and $Y$ that cost a total of $1,000. In fact, for any amount of $X$ you wish to consider, there is a specific amount of $Y$ which, if purchased together with $X$, would cost a total of $1,000. We can derive the formula that will permit us to find the $y$ that goes with any $x$ we pick in the following manner. We know that $1,000 = $25y + $50x$. Therefore $25y = 1,000 − 50x$. Dividing both sides of this equation by 25, we get

$$y = 1,000/25 − (50/25)x \qquad (3\text{-}1)$$

Equation 3-1 is called the *budget constraint* equation. Its intercept on the vertical axis (the value that $y$ takes when $x$ equals zero) is $1,000/25 = 40$ units of $Y$. Its slope is $−50/25 = −2$. The absolute value of the slope is 2—the number of $Y$'s that can be purchased per unit decrease in the amount of $X$ purchased. The general form of the budget equation is

$$y = I/P_y − (P_x/P_y)\,x \qquad (3\text{-}2)$$

where $I$ is the amount of money income the transactor has to spend, and $P_x$ and $P_y$ are the dollar price of $X$ and the dollar price of $Y$, respectively. The intercept on the vertical axis of any budget line is $I/P_y$ and the slope of any budget line is $−P_x/P_y$.

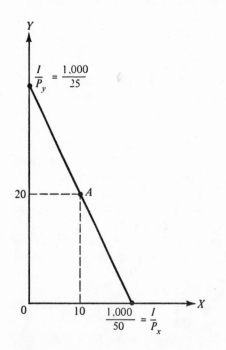

**Figure 3-1.**
Budget constraint.

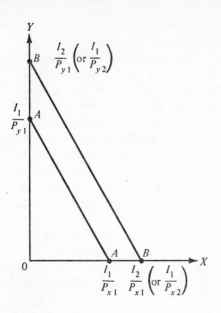

**Figure 3-2.**
Changed real income with
constant relative prices.

## Depicting Changes in Real Income
## and Changes in Relative Price

In our exposition of the theory of demand we shall use a geometric representation of changes in the purchasing power (real income) of transactors with relative price constant, as well as changes in relative price with real income constant. In this section we shall discover how to show these changes in our budget constraint diagram.

In the first chapter we defined real income to be the ratio of money income ($I$) to an average price level, specifically the consumer price index ($P$). One way to increase real income is to increase money income while holding both the price of $X$ and the price of $Y$ constant. If each price is constant, the average of the two prices (and their ratio) is constant. Another way to increase real income would be to lower the average of the two prices while holding money income constant. We wish, however, to depict changes in real income with unchanged relative prices; thus if we are to increase real income through a decrease in the average price level, we must do it while keeping the ratio of the two prices constant.

Consider Figure 3-2. Initially, the budget line faced by the individual transactor depicted is line $AA$. The transactor has money income equal to $I_1$, and the price of $Y$ and the price of $X$ are $P_{y1}$ and $P_{x1}$, respectively. The absolute value of the slope of line $AA$ is $P_{x1}/P_{y1}$. Now imagine that this transactor receives an increase of money income to $I_2$, while $P_y$ and $P_x$ are not changed. The individual's budget line becomes line $BB$. Its slope is the same as the slope of line $AA$ because the ratio of the two money prices has not changed. The increase in real income with unchanged relative prices shows up as a parallel shift to the right of the budget line. The same shift to the right could have been accomplished by lowering both $P_x$ and $P_y$ while keeping their ratio and the transactor's money income constant. Clearly there is some pair of prices, $P_{x2}$ and $P_{y2}$, such that

$$I_1/P_{x2} = I_2/P_{x1}$$

and

$$I_1/P_{y2} = I_2/P_{y1}.$$

A decrease in real income with fixed relative prices would show up as a parallel shift to the left of the budget line.

The question of how to depict a changed relative price with a fixed real income is more difficult to answer. In Figure 3-3, let the initial budget constraint be line $AA'$, and let the relative price of $X-P_x/P_y$—increase. One way to increase the relative price of $X$ would be to increase $P_x$ and leave $P_y$ unchanged. If money income did not change this would cause the budget line to become line $AC$. The vertical intercept is unchanged because neither $I$ nor $P_y$ has changed. The absolute price of $Y$ has not changed, but the relative price of $Y$ has fallen. The relative price of $Y$ is the number of $X$'s that must be given up if one is to purchase an additional $Y$. The relative price of $Y$ is $P_y/P_x$—the reciprocal of the relative price of $X$. Clearly, with only two goods, if the relative price of $X$ is increased the relative price of $Y$ declines.

When only the absolute price of $X$ is increased and the absolute price of $Y$ and

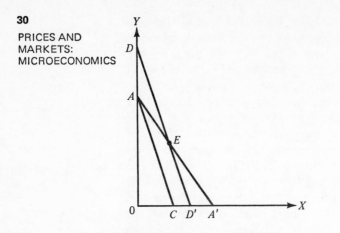

**Figure 3-3.**
Representing constant real income.

money income are held constant, real income declines. There are two ways of seeing this. First, if the price of one thing increases while the price of the other doesn't change, the average of the two prices increases. With a fixed money income the ratio $I/P$—real income—declines. Second, in the diagram it is clear that the area $A0C$ is less than area $A0A'$. When the budget line is $AC$ the transactor has a smaller number of opportunities to pick from. He can be anywhere on line $AC$ or, if he doesn't necessarily spend all of his income, anywhere in area $A0C$. If the budget line is $AA'$ the set of opportunities that he can pick from is represented by area $A0A'$. Clearly the transactor has a larger command over $X$'s and $Y$'s in the latter case—in other words, in this case his purchasing power (or real income) is larger than when the budget constraint is line $AC$.

How shall we represent the new higher relative price of $X$ with an unchanged real income? Real income means purchasing power. We could represent unchanged real income with the higher relative price of $X$ by a budget line that is parallel to $AC$ but one that bounds roughly the same opportunity area that the transactor had when the budget line was $AA'$. Budget line $DD'$ is such a line. With the higher relative price of $X$, opportunities represented by points in area $ED'A'$ are no longer available; but this is compensated for by the opportunities represented by points in area $DAE$ that

were not available previously.

We have not, however, defined real income as the area of opportunities available to the transactor. Rather, we have defined real income as the ratio of money income to the consumer price index. This means that the new budget line must be parallel to line $AC$ (reflecting the higher relative price of $X$), and it must pass through the point on the original budget line (the one before the change in relative prices) that the transactor chose before the change. That is, with the original relative prices and real income the transactor purchased $X$'s and $Y$'s in some combination. Let us say that the combination picked was the combination represented by point $E$ in Figure 3-3. The relative price of $X$ increases and we want the transactor to have the same purchasing power as before. Well, if one of the points that he *could* choose under the new circumstances is the point that he in fact *did* choose under the old circumstances, it could be said that he has unchanged purchasing power. His income is *capable* of claiming the same combination of goods that it used to claim.

In Chapter 1 we saw that the consumer price index is the ratio of the cost of purchasing a given basket of goods in two different time periods. Let the base year be the period when the budget line was line $AA'$. Let the other period be when the relative price of $X$ increased. Let us see what real income is in the two time periods. Real income initially is $I_0/P_0$, where $I_0$ is money income in the initial period and $P_0$ is the consumer price index in the initial period. The initial period is the base period, therefore $P_0 = 1$. Money income in the initial period is the amount spent when combination $E$ was purchased. Thus

$$I_0 = P_{x0}x_E + P_{y0}y_E$$

where $P_{x0}$ and $P_{y0}$ are the money prices of $X$ and $Y$, respectively, in the initial period, and $x_E$ and $y_E$ are the amounts of $X$ and $Y$, respectively, in the combination represented by point $E$. Real income in the other period is $I_1/P_1$, where $I_1$ is money income in the later period and $P_1$ is the consumer price index for that period. $I_1$ is the amount of money it would take to purchase combination $E$ in the second period. All points on line $DD'$ involve the same expenditure of money that point $E$ does with the new prices.

$$I_1 = P_{y1} y_E + P_{x1} x_E$$

where $P_{y1}$ and $P_{x1}$ are the money prices of $Y$ and $X$, respectively, in the second period. (We are no longer necessarily holding the absolute price of $Y$ constant. We have changed the *ratio* of the two prices and we want to maintain constant real income.)

$$P_1 = \frac{P_{x1} x_E + P_{y1} y_E}{P_{x0} x_E + P_{y0} y_E}$$

This is the ratio of the cost of basket $E$ in the two time periods. Real income, then, is

$$I_1/P_1 = \frac{P_{x1}\, x_E + P_{y1}\, y_E}{\dfrac{P_{x1}\, x_E + P_{y1}\, y_E}{P_{x0}\, x_E + P_{y0}\, y_E}}$$

This equals

$$\frac{1}{\dfrac{1}{P_{x0}\, x_E + P_{y0}\, y_E}}$$

which equals $P_{x0}\, x_E + P_{y0}\, y_E$. This, you will recall, was real income in the original period. Money income and real income in the original period were equal because the consumer price index for the original period was equal to 1. Thus we see that the geometric counterpart to an increase in the relative price of $X$ with real income held constant is a steeper budget line ($DD'$) that passes through the original consumption basket (point $E$).

## The Optimum Consumption Basket

In the previous section we said that the transactor chooses a consumption basket from among those baskets that his purchasing power makes attainable. How does a transactor decide which combination of

goods to purchase? To answer this question we must put our indifference curve diagram together with our budget constraint diagram. The transactor would like to get as much of both $X$ and $Y$ as possible. (Both $X$ and $Y$ are goods—something he wants more of rather than less of.) Unfortunately, the purchasing power of his income is limited. His task, then, is to purchase the combination of goods that he is most satisfied with from among all the combinations he could buy. To any outside observer the basket chosen by the transactor must be regarded as the most preferred one, else why did he pick it? We represent this choice process in Figure 3-4.

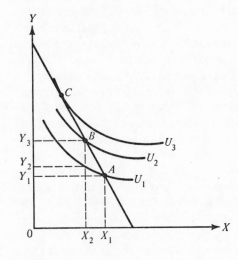

**Figure 3-4.**
Attaining the optimum
consumption basket.

Suppose the transactor purchases combination $A$ on his budget constraint. Point $A$ is attainable, as are all the points on the budget constraint. From the last chapter we know that an indifference curve passes through each point in the $X$-$Y$ plane. The indifference curve through point $A$ is labeled $U_1$. The indifference curve gives us useful information. With it we can deduce that combination $A$ is not the most preferred point on this transactor's budget constraint. If the transactor decreased his purchase of $X$ by $X_1 - X_2$ units, he would save enough money to purchase $Y_3 - Y_1$ units of $Y$. (The budget constraint tells us that.) Only $Y_2 - Y_1$ units of $Y$ are sufficient to exactly compensate the transactor for the loss of $X_1 - X_2$ of $X$. (The indifference curve tells us that.) The transactor can get on to a higher indifference curve (purchase a combination of $X$ and $Y$ that he prefers to combination $A$) by using the money that he saves on the $X_1 - X_2$ units of $X$ to purchase $Y_3 - Y_1$ of $Y$. This would mean that he moves from point $A$ to point $B$ on his budget constraint.

At point $B$ the transactor is on indifference curve $U_2$. The (absolute value of the) slope of indifference curve $U_2$ at point $B$—the marginal rate of substitution between $X$ and $Y$—is the amount of $Y$ that the transactor considers to be exact compensation for the loss of an $X$. The (absolute value of the) slope of the budget constraint is the amount of $Y$ that can be purchased in the market with the money that is saved when one unit less of $X$ is purchased. As long as the indifference curve is flatter than the budget line the individual can attain higher indifference curves (purchase preferred consumption baskets). The transactor moves along the stationary budget line until he reaches a point on an indifference curve that has the same slope as the budget line. Such a point is labeled point $C$ in Figure 3-4. Point $C$ is said to be the transactor's optimum consumption basket given that his choices are limited by the depicted budget constraint. At point $C$ the budget constraint is tangent to indifference curve $U_3$.

The (absolute value of the) slope of an indifference curve is the marginal rate of substitution between $X$ and $Y$. The symbol that is customarily used for this is $\text{MRS}_{xy}$. The (absolute value of the) slope of the budget line is, as we saw earlier in this chaper, $P_x/P_y$. Thus at the optimum consumption basket, the basket that the transactor would choose to purchase from among all those he could choose, $\text{MRS}_{xy} = P_x/P_y$. This is merely a formal way of saying that the transactor will continue to change the combination of goods he buys until he can no longer get more of one good per unit of some other good given up than the amount that leaves him just as well off (as he sees it) as he is with the basket he has.

This, we must admit, is no great insight. All we have done is develop a way of making a picture of this process. The picture is valuable only because it helps us make deductions about how a transactor will respond to *changes* in real income and *changes* in relative prices. The diagram can also be used to depict how a transactor responds to a *change* in his tastes. Of course, no one needs such an elaborate apparatus to predict that, if the transactor acquires more of a liking for $X$ relative to $Y$ than he had before, he will buy more $X$ and less $Y$. Nevertheless it may serve to reinforce your understanding of the diagram if we illustrate how to show such a change in tastes using it.

Suppose that a transactor is at point $A$ in Figure 3-5. Point $A$ is this transactor's optimum consumption basket when his tastes are reflected by indifference curve $U_1$. Indifference curve $U_1$ and the budget constraint are tangent at point $A$. Now let the transactor's tastes change so that he prefers $X$ relative to $Y$ more than he did before. In Chapter 2 we saw that the (absolute value of the) slope of an indifference curve is the value placed on a unit of $X$ in terms of the number of $Y$'s that the transactor considers to be equivalent to an $X$. If we wish to show a higher relative value for $X$ in our picture, we must show that at each point in the $X$-$Y$ plane the indifference curve through that point is steeper

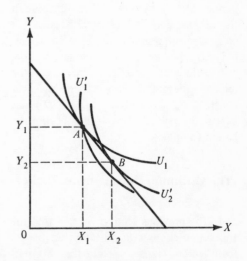

**Figure 3-5.**
Representing changed tastes.

than it used to be. For example, the indifference curve through $A$ becomes $U_1'$ rather than $U_1$. The whole indifference map becomes generally steeper. The point on the budget constraint that is now tangent to an indifference curve is point $B$—a point involving more $X$ and less $Y$ than point $A$. The transactor responds to the taste change by moving from point $A$ on the budget constraint to point $B$ on the same budget constraint. Since the transactor's tastes have changed, his entire indifference map changes. We cannot compare any indifference curve from the original indifference map with any indifference curve from the new indifference map. Specifically, points on $U_2'$ are not necessarily preferred to points on $U_1$ in the figure.

## The Engel Curve—Superior and Inferior Goods

Consider the transactor depicted in Figure 3-6 who has money income equal to $I_1$ and faces a money price of $X$ equal to $P_x$ and a money price of $Y$ equal to $P_y$. His budget constraint intersects the vertical axis at $I_1/P_y$ units of $Y$ and intersects the horizontal axis at $I_1/P_x$ units of $X$. His optimum consumption basket is represented by point $A$. Suppose this transactor's money income increases to $I_2$ and the prices of $X$ and $Y$ remain unchanged. His real income has increased and relative prices are unchanged; hence, his budget constraint shifts to the right but remains parallel to his original budget constraint. How will the transactor respond to such a "pure" change of real income? (A "pure" change of real income is one that occurs while *relative* prices are unchanged.) All we can say is that he will move from point $A$ to some point on the new budget constraint between points $D$ and $E$. We can say this because only points between $D$ and $E$ are on higher indifference curves than $U_1$.

If the transactor chooses a basket between points $B$ and $C$, the new basket will contain more of both $X$ and $Y$. In that case, both $X$ and $Y$ are said to be *superior* (sometimes called "normal") goods. A superior good is one that a person buys more

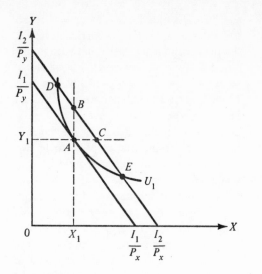
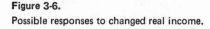

**Figure 3-6.**
Possible responses to changed real income.

of as his real income increases and less of as his real income decreases. If the person chooses a consumption basket between points $B$ and $D$, he will buy less $X$ and more $Y$ than he did before his real income increased. In that case, we would say that $X$ is an *inferior* good and $Y$ is a superior good.[3] An inferior good is one that a per-

[3]If the person chooses a consumption basket between points $B$ and $D$, one of the indifference curves from his indifference map will be tangent to the new budget line at the point that represents that consumption basket. The slope of this indifference curve at that point will be the same as the slope of $U_1$ at point $A$ (because the two budget lines have the same slope). Since indifference curves are convex, the new indifference curve must be *flatter* directly above point $A$ than $U_1$ is at point $A$. A point directly above point $A$ represents more $Y$ and the same amount of $X$ as point $A$. The third assumption of the last chapter states that with more $Y$ and the same amount of $X$ the individual would value an additional unit of $Y$ less than he does at $A$. The value of $Y$ in terms of $X$ is the reciprocal of the slope of an indifference curve; hence the new indifference curve should be *steeper* directly above point $A$ than $U_1$ is at point $A$. The third assumption seems to rule out inferior goods. Actually the assumption only rules out inferior goods in the two-good case. With three or more goods the existence of inferior goods is perfectly consistent with our third assumption. Since we are using the two-good case as a proxy for the more general multigood case, we shall include inferior goods in our discussion.

son buys less of as his real income increases and more of as his real income decreases. If the person chooses a basket between points $C$ and $E$, $X$ would be a superior good and $Y$ would be an inferior good. Notice that while it is possible that both goods could be superior goods, it is not possible that both goods could be inferior goods. It is impossible for the transactor to be at two separate points on his new budget constraint at the same time.

A curve that depicts the quantity bought by a transactor of some good $X$ as a function of that transactor's real income (holding the relative price of the good constant) is called an Engel curve. Such a curve is drawn in Figure 3-7. From low levels of real income up to real income $i_2$, the quantity purchased of $X$ increases as real income increases. For this range of income, $X$ is a superior good. As real income increases beyond $i_2$, the quantity purchased of $X$ by the depicted transactor declines. Good $X$ has become an inferior good for this transactor. Consider ground beef as an example. If you were a married student living on $200 a month from a fellowship in 1973, you would probably eat ground beef once or twice a month. If your fellowship check increased to $300 per month, you might eat ground beef as much as once a week. In fact, ground beef would be on your plate with increasing frequency as your monthly check increased up to (say) $500. Ground beef would be a superior

good to you for that income range. Now consider what you would do if your monthly income increased beyond $500. You might decrease your purchase of ground beef in favor of ground round and an occasional steak. In this higher range of purchasing power, ground beef would be an inferior good to you.

### Income Elasticity of Demand

A commonly used measure of the responsiveness of the quantity demanded of some good $X$ to changes in real income when the relative price of $X$ is constant is the coefficient of income elasticity. The symbol we shall use for this coefficient is the Greek letter eta—$\eta$. Starting with a given level of real income, say $i_1$ in Figure 3-7, let real income change by some amount, say +5%. This increase of real income will cause a transactor to change the quantity he demands of $X$, say by +10%. The coefficient of income elasticity in this case would be +2. It is calculated by dividing the percentage change in real income into the resulting change in the quantity demanded of $X$. In this case, a positive change in real income caused the quantity demanded to increase; hence, the coefficient of income elasticity is positive. That is to say, good $X$ is a superior good for the income change that took place. In general, the formula for income elasticity is:

$$\eta = \frac{\% \ \Delta \ \text{in quantity demanded}}{\% \ \Delta \ \text{in real income}}$$

where the Greek letter delta—$\Delta$—means "change." In words, this formula reads: income elasticity is equal to the percentage change in quantity demanded divided by the associated percentage change in real income.

Let $\Delta q/q$ stand for the percentage change in quantity demanded and $\Delta i/i$ stand for the percentage change in real income. Then:

$$\eta = \frac{\Delta q/q}{\Delta i/i} = \frac{\Delta q}{q} \cdot \frac{i}{\Delta i}$$

$$\eta = \frac{\Delta q}{\Delta i} \cdot \frac{i}{q} \qquad (3\text{-}3)$$

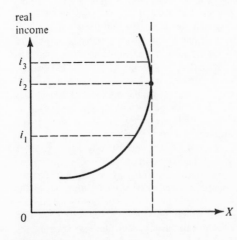

real
income

$i_3$

$i_2$

$i_1$

0

$X$

**Figure 3-7.**
Engel curve.

Equation 3-3 is the most frequently used form of the formula for income elasticity.

We can see that the coefficient of income elasticity changes as real income changes. For example, in Figure 3-7, the coefficient of income elasticity would be positive for all income levels from zero up to $i_2$ and negative for all higher income levels. This implies that it is usually incorrect to say that an Engel curve displays some specific elasticity. Income elasticity of demand is different at each different point on a given Engel curve.

An exception to this rule occurs when the Engel curve is a straight line that comes out of origin. In this case, the income elasticity is +1 at each point on the Engel curve. In other words, a percentage change in income will result in that same percentage change in consumption of the good. To see this, consider Figure 3-8.

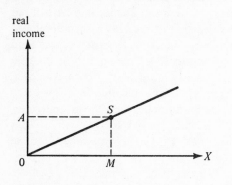

**Figure 3-8.**
Unitary income elasticity.

Arbitrarily pick any point along the straight-line Engel curve coming from the origin, such as point $S$. Refer back to Equation 3-3. That equation tells us that to find the income elasticity at a given point on an Engel curve, we must multiply the reciprocal of the slope of the Engel curve at the point by the ratio of the real income at that point to the quantity demanded at that point. In Figure 3-8 the slope of the Engel curve is the same at every point, since the Engel curve is a straight line. The reciprocal of the slope is $0M/0A$. Real income at point $S$ is $0A$ and the quantity demanded at point $S$ is $0M$. Hence,

$\eta = 0M/0A$ multiplied by $0A/0M$, and that is clearly +1. The same technique would yield the same result no matter which point on the Engel curve was used.

This does not hold for straight-line Engel curves that do not come out of the origin. To see this, consider Figure 3-9. The Engel curve in this diagram cuts the vertical axis at point $R$ and cuts the horizontal axis at point $T$. The reciprocal of the slope of the line is $0M/AR$. (Distance $0M$ equals distance $AS$.) Real income at point $S$ is $0A$, and the associated quantity demanded is $0M$. Hence, $\eta = 0M/AR$ multiplied by $0A/0M$. This equals $0A/AR$, which is clearly greater than one and which changes value as point $S$ moves along the Engel curve.

We can plot the relationship between a person's real income and the amount he demands of each good he buys when the relative prices of the goods he buys are constant. For each good, we would draw a separate Engel curve. However, these separate Engel curves are not independent of each other. We have already seen (Figure 3-6) that not all Engel curves can have a negative slope at the same income level, because not all goods can be inferior goods at once. But we can say more than this. Specifically, we can say that the average income elasticity (average of the income elasticities for the various goods at a specified income level) must be +1. The proof of this proposition is fairly easy. Initially, the individual purchases goods $X$ and $Y$ (and as many others as you care to include) by spending all his money income ($I$). Thus $I = P_x x + P_y y$, where $x$ is the amount of good

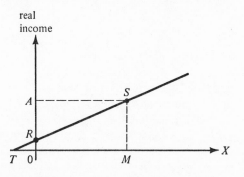

**Figure 3-9.**
Nonconstant income elasticity.

$X$ bought, $y$ is the amount of good $Y$ bought, $P_x$ is the price of $X$, and $P_y$ is the price of $Y$. Let this individual receive an increment of income equal to $\Delta I$, and hold both prices fixed. All of the $\Delta I$ will be spent either on $X$ or $Y$ or both, or even by decreasing the amount bought of one while increasing the amount bought of the other. Let $\Delta x$ be the change (either positive or negative) in the amount of $X$ bought and $\Delta y$ be the change (positive or negative) in the amount of $Y$ bought. Then

$$\Delta I = P_x \Delta x + P_y \Delta y \qquad (3\text{-}4)$$

Divide both sides of Equation 3-4 by $\Delta I$.

$$\frac{\Delta I}{\Delta I} = P_x \cdot \frac{\Delta x}{\Delta I} + P_y \cdot \frac{\Delta y}{\Delta I} \qquad (3\text{-}5)$$

Next, multiply the first term on the right-hand side of Equation 3-5 by $x/x$ and $I/I$, and multiply the second term by $y/y$ and $I/I$.

$$1 = P_x \cdot \frac{\Delta x}{\Delta y} \cdot \frac{x}{x} \cdot \frac{I}{I} +$$

$$P_y \cdot \frac{\Delta y}{\Delta I} \cdot \frac{y}{y} \cdot \frac{I}{I} \qquad (3\text{-}6)$$

Now, look back at Equation 3-3. Since prices are constant, given percentage changes in money income indicate the same percentage changes in real income. Equation 3-6 can be rewritten as

$$1 = \frac{P_x x}{I} \cdot \frac{\Delta x}{\Delta I} \cdot \frac{I}{x} +$$

$$\frac{P_y y}{I} \cdot \frac{\Delta y}{\Delta I} \cdot \frac{I}{y} \qquad (3\text{-}7)$$

Let $P_x x/I$, the percent of income spent on $X$, be represented by $k_x$ and $P_y y/I$, the percent of income spent on $Y$, be represented by $k_y$. Equation 3-7 then becomes

$$1 = \eta_x k_x + \eta_y k_y \qquad (3\text{-}8)$$

where $\eta_x$ is the income elasticity of the demand for $X$ and $\eta_y$ is the income elasticity of the demand for $Y$. Equation 3-8 states that the weighted average of the income elasticities of the demand for all goods purchased by an individual at a given level of income must be +1, where the respective weights are the percent of income spent on each good.

One implication of this theorem is that if there is a good that is strongly inferior, i.e., one whose income elasticity is a large negative number, there must be either one that is even more strongly superior or many fairly strongly superior goods to offset it, because the average must be +1. Very strongly superior goods, those with income elasticities significantly greater than one, must be offset by others with income elasticities significantly smaller than one. Another implication of the theorem is that if a good takes a large percent of an individual's budget, its income elasticity is likely to be small. The income elasticity of the demand for food in an underdeveloped country is most likely small because food represents such a large portion of total expenditures in underdeveloped countries. Suppose, for example, that food takes 80% of the average budget. If the income elasticity of the demand for food were larger than +1¼ (= 10/8), the average income elasticity of demand for all other goods must be negative (0.8 times 10/8 equals 1). This situation is highly unlikely since most goods are superior goods.[4]

### Aggregate Engel Curves

Up to now we have discussed the relationship between an individual's real income and the quantity he demands of various goods. What about a total or market Engel curve for some good? Such a curve would indicate the total amount demanded as a function of aggregate real income. We must proceed very carefully when going from *individual* Engel curves for some good

---

[4]See Becker, *op. cit.*, p. 18.

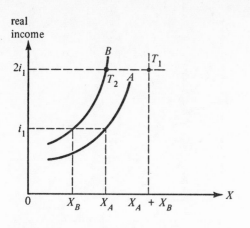

**Figure 3-10.**
A point on an aggregate Engel curve.

*X* to *market* Engel curves for good *X*. Consider Figure 3-10. Mr. A's Engel curve is labeled *A*, and Mr. B's Engel curve is labeled *B*. Suppose that both individuals had real income equal to $i_1$. The quantity demanded by Mr. A is $X_A$, and the quantity demanded by Mr. B is $X_B$. Total income is $2i_1$, and total quantity demanded is $X_A$ plus $X_B$. Point $T_1$ is a point on the aggregate Engel curve *if both individuals have the same income.* Suppose total income is $2i_1$ and that Mr. B has all of it. Point $T_2$ would be a point on the total Engel curve. The message should be clear—we cannot add together individual Engel curves in any meaningful way unless we specify the distribution of total income among the individuals. Furthermore, suppose we want to derive, from the individual Engel curves, the total amount demanded when total income increases beyond $2i_1$. We cannot do this unless we specify how the additional total income is distributed between Mr. A and Mr. B. The weight that any individual receives in determining the total quantity bought is proportional to the percent of the total income that person has claim to. In practice, aggregate Engel curves are not formed by adding together individual Engel curves. Rather, they are derived by studying aggregate data on income and quantity bought. The most widely used aggregate Engel curve relates aggregate national income to aggregate expenditures by house-

holds on everything except new houses. This is the famous "consumption function" of Keynesian economics.

## The Demand Curve and the First Fundamental Law of Demand

An individual's demand curve depicts the quantity demanded of some good *X* as a function of the relative price of the good under the assumption that the indiviual's real income and the relative prices of related products are held constant. We shall discuss the role of the relative prices of related goods later in this chapter. In this section we shall consider the implications for the quantity demanded of a good of a "pure" change in relative price. A "pure" change in relative price is one that occurs when real income doesn't change. Earlier in this chapter we saw that the way we depict a change in the relative price of *X* with real income held constant is to change the slope of the budget line but to pass the new budget line through the point that represents the consumption basket that the individual chose before the change in relative price (Figure 3-3). We wish now to see how a given transactor will respond to such a pure change in relative price. Remember that the only reason for setting up the indifference curve—budget constraint diagram in the first place was that the diagram permitted us to predict responses to changes in real income and relative price. We have seen that the response to changes in real income with fixed relative price is ambiguous, depending on whether the good in question is a superior or an inferior good. On the other hand, our apparatus permits us to say *unambiguously* that a transactor will respond to a pure change in the relative price of good *X* by changing the quantity demanded of the good in the opposite direction. This is the basis of the so-called *first fundamental law of demand*: demand curves are downward sloping with respect to the relative price of the good in question.

Some authors define a demand curve in a slightly different fashion. They say that a

demand curve depicts the relationship between the quantity demanded of a good
and that good's relative price when *money*
income doesn't change. Later we shall discuss the relationship between these two
definitions and state why the present
author, and others, prefer the definition
that holds *real* income constant.[5]

Consider Figure 3-11. The initial budget
constraint is line *AA*. The initial optimum
consumption basket is represented by
point *E*. Let there be a fall in the relative
price of *X* (which is the same thing as an
increase in the relative price of *Y*), but imagine that the transactor's real income remains the same. After all, in the real world
we constantly confront changes in the rate
of exchange between goods at the same
time that the general purchasing power of
our income is constant. The result of the
pure decline in the relative price of *X* in
our two-good diagram is that the budget
constraint becomes flatter but passes
through point *E*. Since line *AA* was tangent
to indifference curve $U_1$ at point *E*, a flatter line that passes through point *E* must
intersect indifference curve $U_1$ at that
point. A glance at Figure 3-11 reveals that
only points on line *BB* (the new budget
constraint) that lie southeast of point *E* are
on higher indifference curves. The transactor will always try to attain the highest
indifference curve possible subject to whatever budget constraint he faces; hence the
transactor will move to some point southeast of point *E*. All points southeast of *E*
involve more *X* and less *Y*. The relative
price of *X* has decreased and the relative
price of *Y* has increased. This has unambiguously caused an increase in the quantity
of *X* demanded and a decrease in the
quantity of *Y* demanded. Notice that our
conclusion was derived from changing the
*slope* of the budget line. The (absolute
value of the) slope of the budget line is the

[5]See, for example, Milton Friedman, "The
Marshallian Demand Curve," *Journal of Political
Economy* (December 1949); Martin J. Bailey,
"The Marshallian Demand Curve," *Journal of
Political Economy* (June 1954); and Gary
Becker, *op. cit., passim.*

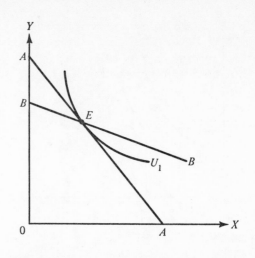

**Figure 3-11.**
First fundamental law of demand.

relative price of $X-P_x/P_y$. It is the *relative*
price of a good to which the quantity demanded of something is related, *not* its *absolute* price.

The discussion above was simple and
straightforward enough, but do you think
that you understand it? To test your understanding, begin with some initial optimum
consumption basket and investigate the individual's response to a pure increase in the
relative price of *X* or decrease in the relative price of *Y*. The conclusion is again
unambiguous: there will be a decrease in
the quantity of *X* demanded and an increase of the quantity of *Y* demanded.

Figure 3-12 is an individual transactor's
demand curve for good *X*. On the vertical
axis we plot different quantities of *X* demanded. Instead of writing the relative
price of *X* as $P_x/P_y$, we write it in its more
general form, $P_x/P$. We do not actually live
in a two-good world. We use a two-good
diagram to get results that we can gen-
eralize to the multigood case. When we
wish to refer to a specific relative price of
*X*, we shall use the symbol $p_x$. The lower
case *p* means that the absolute money price
has been divided by the consumer price
index.

Our indifference curve–budget constraint analysis reveals that demand curves
must be downward sloping. We cannot say
whether they are concave, convex, both, or
a straight line. All we can say for sure is
that they are downward sloping. At relative

price $p_1$, the quantity demanded will be $X_1$. At a lower relative price, say $p_2$, the first fundamental law of demand states that the quantity demanded will be larger than $X_1$, say $X_2$. Each point on the demand curve refers to a different relative price of $X$, but real income and the relative prices of related goods are the same at all points on the demand curve. If the transactor's real income increases, and if $X$ is a superior good, the demand curve for $X$ will shift to the right. At each relative price of $X$ a larger quantity of $X$ will be demanded by this transactor than before the increase of his real income. If $X$ is an inferior good, an increase in the transactor's real income will cause his demand curve to shift to the left, indicating that at each relative price of $X$ he will demand less $X$ than before.

## Alleged Exceptions to the First Fundamental Law of Demand

The first fundamental law of demand is the single most important proposition in economic theory. It has many implications that may not immediately occur to you. For example, it implies that an increase in the legal minimum wage, if it increases the *real* wage (the money wage rate divided by the consumer price index), will *cause* additional unemployment. As Milton Friedman has said, a bill before Congress to increase the minimum wage should really be called "a bill to increase unemployment."[6] We shall examine this implication of the first fundamental law of demand in detail in Chapter 10. Another implication of the law is that when university budgets are cut, so that professors must either pay graduate students out of their own pockets or else do their own reading of exams and term papers, fewer and shorter term papers will be assigned and essay exams will tend to be replaced by multiple choice exams or by short-answer exams. Professors consider making students work to be a good, but as with all goods and all consumers, professors will decrease their consumption of this good when its real cost *to them* increases.

A less obvious implication of the first fundamental law of demand is that privately owned profit-making firms will tend to be run more efficiently than government-owned firms (such as the Los Angeles Department of Water and Power and the U. S. Post Office). The private owner of a firm has his personal wealth at stake in the operation of that firm. His wealth increases if costs are kept low and profit is made, and his wealth decreases if losses are incurred. The decision maker in a government firm does not have his personal wealth at stake. He works for a salary which is most likely independent of performance, and his job is protected by Civil Service rules. It is very difficult to monitor a firm effectively to make certain that costs are as low as possible. It is much easier to relax and let happen what will. Taking it easy is considered a good. But the cost of the good to the private owner of a firm is much higher than its cost to a governmentally employed manager. For that reason the private owner will be more diligent to promote efficiency than will his counterpart in a government firm.[7]

Since the first fundamental law of de-

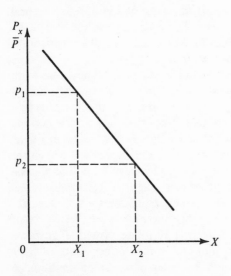

**Figure 3-12.**
Demand curve.

---

[6]Milton Friedman, "Legislating Unemployment," *Newsweek* (July 3, 1972). •

[7]Cf. Alchian and Allen, *Exchange and Production* (Belmont, Calif.: Wadsworth, 1969), pp. 161–164.

mand is so important, we had better consider some commonly alleged exceptions to it.[8] On July 20, 1973, the existing price freeze was lifted on all food items except beef. (This was Phase 4 of President Nixon's anti-inflation policies.) The frozen prices that preceded this Phase 4 freeing of prices were far below market clearing levels and had disastrous effects on the supply of poultry, pork, and eggs. On Saturday, July 21, 1973, many supermarkets raised their prices on eggs, chicken, bacon, etc. Shoppers responded by purchasing unusually large amounts of these products—much larger than their usual weekly purchases during the price freeze. Their real income hadn't increased in so short a period of time. Prices of products that are substitutes for pork and poultry and eggs did not increase relative to the prices for these products. This seems to be a case of a pure increase in relative price causing an *increase* in the quantity demanded. The demand curves for these products seem to be *positively* sloped.

The reason shoppers increased their purchases of these products was that they expected the prices of these products would go even higher in the future. "Stocking up" immediately was seen as a way of being more able to decrease the quantity purchased when prices increased further. Instead of a refutation of the first fundamental law of demand, this episode was an affirmation of it. Relative to expected future prices, current prices fell; and, consistent with the first fundamental law of demand, shoppers bought more.

You have probably heard that an increase in the price of a product sometimes makes buyers think of that product as a "prestige" or a "snob" good, and they therefore purchase more. An imitation fur wrap may sell better at a price of $100 than it would at $35. A $35 wrap, after all, can be purchased by anyone. Those who purchase fur wraps want to distinguish themselves from the ordinary person and

so would be attracted by a higher rather than a lower price tag. This, too, seems to be an exception to the first fundamental law of demand, but it really isn't. That law states that the quantity demanded of a given good, *with well defined and unchanging characteristics in the minds of buyers*, will decrease as the relative price of that good increases. If, when the price increases, buyers' perceptions of what the good is and what the good will do for them change, we are really dealing with two different goods. Given the new perception of what the good is, a further increase in its relative price will decrease the quantity demanded. A good is defined in the mind of the buyer. It is not, in economic theory, merely defined by its physical characteristics. The first fundamental law of demand states how *people* react to pure changes in the relative prices of goods as those goods are perceived by those people.

Another alleged exception to the first fundamental law of demand is similar to the one we just discussed. This involves the effect of a change of price on buyers' perceptions of the *quality* of a good. I would buy fewer Sears tires if their price were $5 apiece than I would if their price were $25 apiece. That is because I know that the tire market is competitive and therefore that a tire of given quality could not for long sell at two different prices. It is, nevertheless, also true that if I knew that the $5 tire was exactly the same as the $25 tire, I would replace the tires on my car more frequently than I now do, and the replacements would be the $5 tires.

No buyer has perfect knowledge about products available on the market. Collecting information is a costly enterprise. It is generally true that when one product yields above-average profit rates to a seller, new sellers of similar products will emerge to get in on the gravy train. The presence of these new sellers will reduce prices until only average profit rates are earned. This means that prices are at least fair indicators of quality. It makes sense for buyers to economize on their information collection costs by using price as an indicator of quality. They will sometimes be fooled, but the rivalrous behavior of actual and

---

[8]These alleged exceptions are discussed in Alchian and Allen, *op. cit.*, pp. 76–77.

potential other sellers of the product will most often rescue them from their folly.

## Price Elasticity of Demand

Just as the coefficient of income elasticity of demand is a measure of the responsiveness of quantity demanded to pure changes in real income, the coefficient of price elasticity of demand is a measure of the responsiveness of the quantity demanded to pure changes in relative price. The symbol we shall use for this coefficient is $\epsilon$—the Greek letter "epsilon." The formula for the coefficient of price elasticity of demand is

$$\epsilon = \frac{\% \text{ change of quantity demanded}}{\% \text{ change of relative price}}$$

For example, if the relative price of eggs increased by 2% and this caused a 5% reduction in the quantity demanded of eggs, we would say that the price elasticity of demand for eggs, for this price change, would be −2.5. The algebraic sign of $\epsilon$ will always be negative because of the first fundamental law of demand. If we let $\Delta p/p$ be the percentage change of relative price and $\Delta q/q$ be the associated percentage change of the quantity demanded, the formula for $\epsilon$ may be written as

$$\epsilon = \frac{\Delta q/q}{\Delta p/p}$$

$$= \frac{\Delta q}{q} \cdot \frac{p}{\Delta p}$$

$$= \frac{\Delta q}{\Delta p} \cdot \frac{p}{q} \qquad (3\text{-}9)$$

Equation 3-9 is the most frequently used formula for the price elasticity of demand. The convention is to say that if the absolute value of $\epsilon$ is greater than one, the demand relationship is "elastic" and if the absolute value of $\epsilon$ is less than one, the demand relationship is "inelastic." When the absolute value of $\epsilon$ equals one, the de-

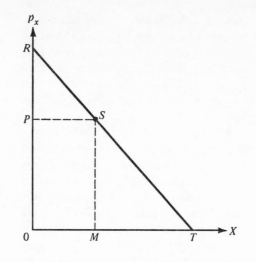

**Figure 3-13.**
Measuring price elasticity.

mand relationship is said to be "unit elastic."

The value of $\epsilon$ will be different at each different point on a given demand curve; hence it is generally incorrect to talk about the elasticity of a demand curve. Rather, we must refer to the price elasticity of demand at a given price or a given quantity. To see this, consider Figure 3-13. Pick any point on the straight-line demand curve $RT$, such as point $S$. Let the quantity that goes with point $S$ be $0M$ and the price that goes with point $S$ be $0P$. Look back at Equation 3-9. That formula says that $\epsilon$ equals the reciprocal of the slope of the demand curve at the point we have picked, multiplied by the ratio of the price that goes with the point to the quantity that goes with the point. Thus

$$\epsilon = \frac{MT}{0P} \cdot \frac{0P}{0M} = \frac{MT}{0M} \qquad (3\text{-}10)$$

The slope of the demand curve is always negative, hence $\epsilon$ will always be negative. Equation 3-10, however, doesn't take note of the negative sign; it will always give us the absolute value of $\epsilon$. It is clear from Figure 3-13 and Equation 3-10 that $\epsilon$ will have different values at each point on the demand curve. If the quantity that goes with the point of concern is half-way between the origin and point $T$, the (absolute) value of $\epsilon$ will be one. For larger quantities, the (absolute) value of $\epsilon$ will be less than one; and for smaller quantities the (absolute) value of $\epsilon$ will be greater than one. We shall call Equation 3-10 the "horizontal axis formula" for $\epsilon$ because it uses only the ratio of two distances on the horizontal axis.

We can derive a similar formula for $\epsilon$ that involves the ratio of two distances on the vertical axis. Again consider Figure 3-13 and Equation 3-9. Another way to write the reciprocal of the slope of the demand curve in Figure 3-13 is $0M/PR$. If we multiply this ratio by the ratio of the price to the quantity—$0P/0M$—we get $(0M/PR) \cdot (0P/0M)$. Hence

$$\epsilon = \frac{0P}{PR} \qquad (3\text{-}11)$$

Equation 3-11 is the "vertical axis formula" for the (absolute) value of $\epsilon$.

Consider the two demand curves in Figure 3-14. Which one exhibits the greater price elasticity of demand at price $0P$? That is, is the elasticity at point $A$ on $R_1 T_1$ greater than, less than, or equal to the elasticity at point $B$ on $R_2 T_2$? Using the vertical axis formula we see that the elasticity at point $A$ is $0P/PR_1$, and the elasticity at point $B$ is $0P/PR_2$. Clearly the former is greater than the latter. If you tried to answer the question by looking only at the slope of the two demand curves you would have given the wrong answer. When comparing the price elasticity of demand on two demand curves at a given price, the larger elasticity will be found on the demand curve that intersects the vertical axis closer to the origin. If two demand curves intersect each other at some positive price and quantity, the larger elasticity will be found at the point on the flatter of the two lines. But that is not because the line is flatter; it is because, in this case, the flatter line will have the smaller vertical intercept. *Do not confuse elasticity and slope.* Two parallel demand curves will have different elasticities at each price, with the greater elasticities on the demand curve that is closer to the origin. Two demand curves that intersect the vertical axis at the same price, but have different slopes,

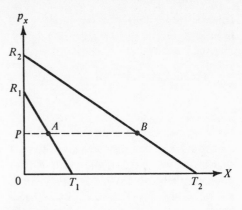

**Figure 3-14.**
Comparing price elasticities.

will have equal elasticities at each price.

We can apply our horizontal and vertical axis formulae to demand curves that are not straight lines. Equation 3-9 says, to find $\epsilon$ at any point on any demand curve, merely multiply the reciprocal of the slope of the demand curve at that point by the ratio of the price at the point to the quantity at the point. On a nonstraight-line demand curve we construct a tangent to the point of concern, label the place where that tangent cuts the vertical axis point $R$, and label where it cuts the horizontal axis point $T$. Label the quantity that goes with the point we have picked $0M$, and label the price that goes with the point we have picked $0P$. Our two formulae can then be used.

## The Second Fundamental
## Law of Demand

The second fundamental law of demand states that for a given change in price the resulting change in quantity demanded will be larger in the long run than in the short run. In other words, the price elasticity of demand is greater for a long-run demand curve than for a short-run demand curve. Consider a 10% increase in the real price of gasoline. The first fundamental law of demand states that this will immediately result in some decrease in the quantity of gas demanded as people take fewer trips, drive more slowly, and check their tire compression more often. The second fundamental law of demand states that if the new price persists there will be a further reduction in the quantity of gasoline demanded as individuals begin to get more frequent tune-ups and replace worn-out cars with smaller, more economical models.

In general, there are two reasons why long-run quantity adjustments will exceed short-run quantity adjustments to a given price change. First, it takes time for people to adjust their buying patterns. In the example of the car, it takes time for people to switch from large, low-mileage cars to smaller, more economical cars. Second, it takes time for word of the price increase to get around. Gasoline prices are well advertised, so the cost of acquiring information about price changes is fairly small. But for other commodities, say cotton fabric, this is not the case. An individual may not buy any of some particular kind of shirt because at some time in the past he discovered that its relative price was too high. If the price falls, this individual may not know about it so he continues to buy none. The initial quantity adjustments are made by people who customarily purchase the good; longer term adjustments include individuals who previously weren't in the market for that good at all.

## The Combined Demand Curve and the Slutsky Equation

In many textbooks demand curves are derived in the following way. Imagine a transactor with a given money income ($I$) facing a price of $Y$ equal to $P_y$ and a price of $X$ equal to $P_{x1}$. That person's budget constraint would intersect the vertical axis in Figure 3-15 at $I/P_y$ and intersect the horizontal axis at $I/P_{x1}$. The optimum consumption basket would be represented by point $A$, and quantity $X_1$ of $X$ would be purchased. Now imagine a decline in the absolute price of $X$ to $P_{x2}$ when the price of $Y$ and the individual's *money* income are held constant. The budget constraint will intersect the vertical axis in the same place it did before (neither $P_y$ nor $I$ is changed), but it will intersect the horizontal axis at point $I/P_{x2}$. The optimum consumption basket becomes that represented

by point $B$, and quantity $X_2$ of $X$ would be purchased. The decline of the absolute price of $X$ means that the relative price of $X$ falls. Thus we have two relative prices of $X$—one before and one after the change in the absolute price of $X$. For each of the two relative prices of $X$, we have a specific quantity of $X$ purchased—$X_1$ before the change in the price of $X$, and $X_2$ after the change in the price of $X$. We could therefore draw a demand curve that would picture these two combinations of relative price and quantity. Such a curve would not be the same as the demand curve we derived earlier in this chapter. Here we are not holding real income constant, but we are holding money income constant and lowering one of two absolute prices; hence we are unambiguously *increasing* real income.

The increase from $X_1$ to $X_2$ in the quantity demanded has, therefore, two parts. First there is the increase that would be observed if the relative price of $X$ fell and *real* income were held constant. This is sometimes called the "substitution effect." It is really nothing more than the change in quantity demanded caused by a pure change in relative price—a movement along what we have called the demand curve. You could say that our earlier definition of demand curves includes only substitution effects, since no change in real income is permitted. The second part of the increase from $X_1$ to $X_2$ in Figure 3-15 is the change

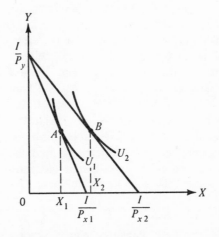

**Figure 3-15.**
Money income constant demand.

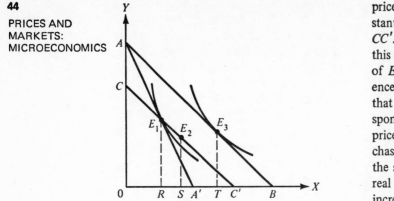

**Figure 3-16.**
Income and substitution effects.

in the quantity purchased which is caused by the fact that real income has increased. If $X$ is a superior good, it must mean that the substitution effect increased the quantity demanded from $X_1$ to some quantity less than $X_2$. Due to the increase in real income, quantity $X_2$ is then attained. This is sometimes called the "income effect." It really is nothing more than a move along an Engel curve. Thus we see that the money income constant demand curve is really a combination of a real income constant demand curve and an Engel curve relationship.

An important equation called the Slutsky equation[9] specifies how the real income constant demand relationship and the Engel curve relationship are combined into the money income constant demand curve. Consider Figure 3-16. Initially the transactor faces budget constraint $AA'$, and his optimum consumption basket is $E_1$, which includes $0R$ of good $X$. The price of $X$ falls, the price of $Y$ remains the same, and money income is constant. The budget constraint becomes line $AB$, and the new consumption basket becomes $E_3$, which includes $0T$ of $X$. The total increase in the purchase of $X$ is $RT$. We can divide this total into its two parts—the substitution effect and the income effect. To find the substitution effect, note that if the transactor faced the same change in the relative

price of $X$ but his real income were constant, his budget constraint would be line $CC'$. The optimum consumption basket in this case would be a point on $CC'$ southeast of $E_1$, say point $E_2$. (There is an indifference curve that is not shown in the diagram that is tangent to $CC'$ at point $E_2$). In response to such a pure change in the relative price, the individual would increase his purchases of $X$ by $RS$. $RS$ is, in other words, the substitution effect. But the individual's real income is *not* constant; it has, in fact, increased due to the fall in the absolute price of $X$ while money income and the price of $Y$ are fixed. His budget line is not $CC'$; it is $AB$. Thus his optimum consumption basket after the change in the relative price of $X$ is not $E_2$; it is $E_3$. The change in real income increases the purchases of $X$ by $ST$. $ST$ is, in other words, the income effect.

Now it is clear that $RT = RS + ST$. Let $RT$ be represented by $\Delta X_T$, the total change in $X$. Let $RS$ be represented by $\Delta X_s$, the change in $X$ due to the substitution effect; and let $ST$ be represented by $\Delta X_i$, the change in $X$ due to the change in real income. Note that the change in real income equals the change in the absolute price of $X$ times the amount of $X$ originally bought. If the original amount of $X$ bought was 10 units, for example, and if the change in the price of X was −50 cents, the individual would have to spend $5 less on basket $E_1$ after the price change than he did before the price change. This $5 is thereby freed to buy other things, and the purchasing power of the individual's money income has increased. In other words, his real income has increased by $5. In symbols,

$$\Delta i = -\Delta P_x X = -(-\$0.5)(10) = \$5$$

We have

$$\Delta X_T = \Delta X_S + \Delta X_i \qquad (3\text{-}12)$$

Dividing both sides of Equation 3-12 by $\Delta P_x$ and multiplying the last term by

$$\frac{\Delta i}{\Delta i} \cdot \frac{i}{i}, \text{ we get}$$

---

[9]Named for E. E. Slutsky, who developed a version of the equation in a famous journal article in 1915.

$$\frac{\Delta X_T}{\Delta P_x} = \frac{\Delta X_S}{\Delta P_x} + \frac{\Delta X_i}{\Delta P_x} \cdot \frac{\Delta i}{\Delta i} \cdot \frac{i}{i} \qquad (3\text{-}13)$$

Multiplying both sides of Equation 3-13 by $P_x/X$, we have

$$\frac{\Delta X_T}{\Delta P_x} \cdot \frac{P_x}{X} = \frac{\Delta X_S}{\Delta P_x} \cdot \frac{P_x}{X} +$$

$$\frac{\Delta X_i}{\Delta P_x} \cdot \frac{\Delta i}{\Delta i} \cdot \frac{i}{i} \cdot \frac{P_x}{X} \qquad (3\text{-}14)$$

Substituting $-\Delta P_x X$ for the top $\Delta i$ in the last term of Equation 3-14, cancelling out the $\Delta P_x$'s in the last term, and rearranging the last term, we get

$$\frac{\Delta X_T}{\Delta P_x} \cdot \frac{P_x}{X} = \frac{\Delta X_S}{\Delta P_x} \cdot \frac{P_x}{X} -$$

$$\frac{\Delta X_i}{\Delta i} \cdot \frac{i}{X} \cdot \frac{P_x X}{i} \qquad (3\text{-}15)$$

Let $E_x$ be the total price elasticity of demand (for constant money income but changed real income), $\epsilon_x$ and $\eta_x$ stand for the price elasticity of demand with constant real income and income elasticity of demand, respectively, and $k_x$ be the percent of real and (since we are using the initial situation as our base period) money income originally spent on $X$. Equation 3-15 becomes

$$E_x = \epsilon_x - \eta_x k_x \qquad (3\text{-}16)$$

Equation 3-16 is the Slutsky equation in its elasticity form. It says that the price elasticity of demand for a money income constant relative price change is a combination of the price elasticity of demand for a pure relative price change and the income elasticity of demand for the product times the percent of income that is spent on the specific product in question. The $\epsilon_x$ indicates the substitution effect and the $-\eta_x k_x$ indicates the income effect.

Suppose that good $X$ is a superior good. This means that $\eta_x$ will be positive. The $\epsilon_x$ is always negative (the first fundamental law of demand), and the $k_x$ is always posi-

tive (it is merely the percent of income spent on $X$). In this case, $E_x$ will be a larger negative number than $\epsilon_x$. The income effect will reinforce the substitution effect. If price should fall, the substitution effect will say "buy more." The price fall will mean a higher real income and this will also mean more will be bought. The negative $\epsilon_x$ will combine with the negative $-\eta_x k_x$ to make $E_x$ more negative than $\epsilon_x$.

If good $X$ is an inferior good, the income effect will work counter to the substitution effect. A fall in the price of $X$ will cause more of $X$ to be bought, due to the substitution effect. The fall in the price of $X$ will also increase real income which, in the case of an inferior good, will tell the transactor to buy less $X$ than he would if only the substitution effect were to be considered. This time the expression $-\eta_x k_x$ becomes positive because $\eta_x$ is itself negative. The negative $\epsilon_x$ combines with the positive $-\eta_x k_x$ to make $E_x$ less negative than $\epsilon_x$.[10]

In sum, at any given price the price elasticity of demand on a real income constant demand curve is smaller than the price elasticity of demand on a money income constant demand curve in the case of a *superior* good. The reverse is true in the case of an inferior good.

### The Demand Curve: Real Income Constant versus Money Income Constant

The ultimate purpose of all theoretical models is to enable us to understand and to make predictions about real-world phenomena. Our demand theory is exposited within the context of a two-good model merely because that is the most convenient expository device to use when we choose to limit our use of pure mathematics. The two-good model, however, is merely a proxy for the multigood economic environ-

---

[10]It is even possible (although it is never observed) that $E_x$ could be made positive. This is a special case of an inferior good called a Giffen good.

ment within which we all transact. In this environment we are often faced with changes in the relative prices of various things that we purchase, and the purchasing power of our paychecks is not appreciably changed by these price changes. We are in either the situation where some absolute prices are increasing and others are decreasing or the situation where most absolute prices are increasing but at different rates. This latter situation is called inflation, and during inflation it is also true, for most people, that money income keeps up with the inflation. In other words, real income does not change very much, except that it increases gradually over time.

Our demand apparatus exists to help us analyze buyers' reactions to changes in the real price of some commodity when "other things are the same." This expression "other things the same" is ambiguous. If only one dollar price changes and money income is constant, real income changes. If real income is constant in the face of a change in the dollar price of a good, then either the price of some other good or money income must change. There is no such thing as a change in the dollar price of one good with all other relevant economic variables unchanged. In a two-good world, when the absolute price of one good changes and money income is held constant the result is a substantial change in real income. In the actual multigood world, when the absolute price of one good changes, the effect on the purchasing power of an individual's paycheck is very small. This means that in the multigood world even the change in the absolute price of only one good is (approximately) what we have called a *pure* change in relative price. In addition, in the real world it is never the case that only one absolute price changes at a time. The prices of many things change at the same time. Money income is constant, but so, too, is real income, since the general price index need not change if some absolute prices are going up while others are going down. Relative prices change, but, most of the time, real income is constant when these changes in relative price take place.

Another reason the present author pre-

fers to use the real income constant definition of the demand curve is that in most econometric studies that attempt to estimate actual demand relationships, the independent variables used in the regression equations are typically the absolute price of the specific good in question divided by the consumer price index (i.e., the relative or real price of the good), the absolute prices of related goods divided by the consumer price index (i.e., the relative prices of related goods), and per capita real income.[11] It seems silly to define demand relationships one way in theory and an entirely different way in econometric tests of the theory. Econometricians work with the theory exposited in this chapter, not with a hybrid theory that combines demand and Engel curve relationships.

## The Relative Prices of Related Products

A product can be related to a given product $X$ either as a substitute for $X$ or as a complement to $X$. If $X$ is butter, a substitute would be margarine. An increase in the relative price of margarine would increase the quantity demanded of butter at each relative price of butter. In other words, the demand curve for butter would shift to the right. A decrease in the relative price of margarine would shift the demand curve for butter to the left. The cross price elasticity of demand between butter and margarine would be positive. The coefficient of cross price elasticity is defined as the ratio of the percentage change in the quantity demanded of a good divided by the percentage change in the relative price of the substitute (or complementary) good. An *increase* in the price of margarine would *increase* the quantity of butter sold in the absence of a change in the price of butter; hence the cross elasticity would be positive.

---

[11]See, for example, Lawrence R. Klein, *An Introduction to Econometrics* (Englewood Cliffs, N. J.: Prentice-Hall, 1962), Chap. 2, especially pp. 19–24.

A complement to $X$ is a product that is used in conjunction with $X$. If $X$ is tennis balls, then a complement to $X$ would be tennis racquets. If the price of tennis racquets increased, then playing tennis would become more expensive. The first fundamental law of demand says that less tennis will be played—this will decrease the amount of tennis balls purchased although there has been no change in the price of tennis balls *per se*. The demand curve for tennis balls will shift to the left in response to an increase in the price of tennis racquets. The coefficient of cross price elasticity for complements is negative.

## Market Demand Curves

Up to this point we have discussed demand curves of individuals for specific goods. We must get from individual demand curves for a good to aggregate, or market, demand curves for that good. Markets, not individual buyers (or sellers), are our chief concern. We saw that it was practically impossible to derive aggregate Engel curves from individual Engel curves because not all individuals have the same real income nor do all individuals face the same changes in real income. Fortunately that is not a problem in the case of aggregate or market demand curves. It is most often true that the different buyers of a given good are each confronted with the same relative price of the good. Similarly, when the relative price changes for one buyer, all buyers face the same change in relative price.

In Figure 3-17 the demand curves of two individuals are drawn. $A$'s demand curve is $RA$ and $B$'s demand curve is $RB$. At each relative price of $X$ ($p_x$) we wish to find the total quantity demanded. At $p_1$, for example, the quantity demanded by $A$ is $q_A$ and the quantity demanded by $B$ is $q_B$. The total quantity demanded at $p_1$ is $q_T = q_A + q_B$. To get the total demand curve from individual demand curves we pick some price, determine the quantity demanded by each individual at that price, and add the quantities demanded together. The total quantity demanded will be the

horizontal coordinate and the given price will be the vertical coordinate of a point on the total demand curve. We do the same for each price. In other words, the individual demand curves are added together horizontally to get the market demand curve for a given product.

Notice that the market demand curve will always be flatter than any of the individual demand curves for the product. This is so because we add together the individual values of the variable on the horizontal axis but do not combine values of the variable on the vertical axis in any way. Even though the market demand curve must be flatter than any of the individual demand curves, it does not necessarily exhibit a greater price elasticity of demand at any price than any of the individual demand curves. In fact, in Figure 3-17 the elasticity of demand at each price on the total demand curve is the same as the elasticity of demand on each of the individual demand curves. We know this because all three demand curves are straight lines, and they intersect the vertical axis at the same point.

In general, the price elasticity of demand at each price on the market demand curve is a weighted average of the individual price elasticities of demand, where the weights are the percents of the total quantity demanded that are demanded by each individual. The proof of this proposition is as follows. Let the price elasticity of demand at a specific price such as $p_1$ in Figure 3-17 on the total curve be $\epsilon_T$, and

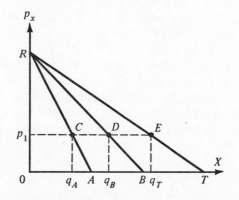

**Figure 3-17.**
Market demand curve.

the price elasticity of demand on $A$'s and $B$'s demand curves at the same price be $\epsilon_A$ and $\epsilon_B$, respectively.

The formula for $\epsilon_T$ is $\dfrac{\Delta q_T}{\Delta p} \cdot \dfrac{p}{q_T}$.

This equals

$$\frac{\Delta(q_A + q_B)}{\Delta p} \cdot \frac{p}{q_T}$$

which can be written as

$$\frac{\Delta q_A}{\Delta p} \cdot \frac{p}{q_A} \cdot \frac{q_A}{q_T} + \frac{\Delta q_B}{\Delta p} \cdot \frac{p}{q_B} \cdot \frac{q_B}{q_T}$$

This in turn is merely

$$\epsilon_A \cdot \frac{q_A}{q_T} + \epsilon_B \cdot \frac{q_B}{q_T}$$

and that is what we set out to prove.

### Market Demand Curves and Sellers' Total Revenue

A seller of a product is concerned with the total or market demand curve he faces. In Figure 3-18, the top panel is the market demand curve for good $X$. Suppose there is only one seller of $X$, so that the demand curve faced by that seller is identical to the market demand curve. Demand curve $RT$ is a straight line, and as we saw earlier for quantities less than $0M$ (point $M$ is halfway from origin to point $T$ on the horizontal axis), the (absolute) value of the price elasticity of demand is greater than one. This means that a reduction of price of 1% will result in an increase of more than 1% in the quantity demanded of $X$, and hence total revenue (price times quantity) will increase. Imagine our seller charging price $0R$. He would sell none, so his total revenue would be zero. We see the zero total revenue corresponding to zero quantity demanded in the lower panel of the figure. If the seller reduced his price from $0R$, he would sell some of $X$, so total revenue would begin to increase. Further reduc-

tions in the price he charges will cause total revenue to increase until he reaches price $0A$. At this price the (absolute) value of $\epsilon$ is equal to one. For lower prices the (absolute) value of $\epsilon$ is less than one. This means that if he continues to lower the price beyond $0A$, the percentage increase in quantity demanded will be less than the corresponding percentage decrease in price, and thus total revenue will decline. Total revenue will again be zero when $0T$ is sold, because the price that the seller must charge to sell $0T$ is zero. Maximum total revenue is attained when the seller charges price $0A$, which permits him to sell quantity $0M$. At this price and quantity the (absolute) value of $\epsilon$ equals one.

Do not jump to the conclusion that sellers will always search for the price that makes their demand elasticity equal to one. Firms are not in business to maximize *revenue;* they attempt to maximize *profit.* To see the price that must be searched for to maximize profit we must introduce costs as well as revenue. But before we can discuss costs we must discuss production theory, a task to which we turn in the next chapter.

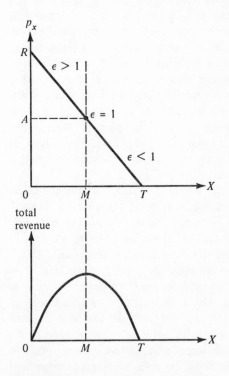

**Figure 3-18.**
Price elasticity and total revenue.

1. Show that even if consumers decided which combination of two goods to purchase merely by randomly choosing among all attainable combinations, the first fundamental law of demand would still hold. (*Hint:* examine what happens to the attainable combinations as relative prices change.)

2. The CPI is said to measure changes in the "cost of living." If a given standard of living is represented by different points on a given indifference curve, show that the CPI will overstate any increase in the cost of attaining a given standard of living whenever inflation occurs but relative prices change.

3. An individual gets a 10% increase in his monthly money income. He plans to increase his monthly purchases of fifths of bourbon by 12%. He is accustomed to spending 1% of his income on bourbon. He then discovers that the CPI has risen by 10% and that the price of bourbon has increased by 4%. He thus revises his plans and decides to decrease his purchases of bourbon. Is economic theory consistent with this individual's behavior? Why not?

4. Consider an inferior good that is not a Giffen good. In one diagram draw both a real income constant demand curve and the corresponding money income constant demand curve. Explain your diagram.

5. Suppose we know that with a fixed real income a decrease of 10% of the relative price of $X$ will cause Mr. A to increase his purchases of $X$ by 2%, that the income elasticity of the only other good Mr. A buys is 2.0, and that Mr. A customarily spends 80% of his income on $X$. By what percentage would Mr. A's purchases of $X$ change in response to a 2% decrease of the relative price of $X$ if his money income were constant?

6. What effect would the advent of no fault automobile insurance have on the number of wills drawn up by attorneys? Why?

7. An entrepreneur gets satisfaction out of profits and such emoluments as pretty secretaries, a fancy office, and a staff of suitably obsequious assistants. Using indifference curve—budget constraint analysis, show that an "excess" profits tax will increase the extent to which emoluments will be consumed and thus raise the costs of produced goods.

8. The notion of an upward sloping supply curve can be derived from the first fundamental law of demand. How?

9. Even if individual demand curves have vertical sections in them, market demand curves will be negatively sloped throughout. Why?

10. It is quite common for commercial airplanes to have to queue up for landing clearance at many major airports during peak travel hours. Landing fees that airlines must pay are based on aircraft weight. Can you see a way to eliminate the landing queues (and thus also eliminate the "need" for more and bigger airports)?

11. Freeways are typically congested during peak commuter hours. Can you see a way to eliminate the congestion (and also eliminate the "need" for fixed track rapid transit systems)?

# 4
# Production Theory

When an economist discusses production theory he is concerned with general laws of production that apply to all productive activity. He does not profess to know how to produce any particular commodity (other than economic insight) or service; nevertheless, he is willing to apply his theory to the production of any particular good or service. For example, an economist doesn't know how to manufacture steel, but he does know some general principles of interaction among inputs that help him identify the more profitable input combinations to use in the manufacturing process. Even if the chemical composition of steel is fixed, the production process that brings the chemical components together is not. For example, a finished ton of steel can be produced using as much as 65,000 gallons or as little as 1,400 gallons of water in the process. The typical amount used is 40,000 gallons.[1] The steel manufacturer can choose a process that is relatively "capital intensive" (one that involves a high ratio of capital to labor) or one that is relatively "labor intensive" (one that involves a low ratio of capital to labor). The economist's theory tells him such

things as what happens to the productivity of one input as the utilization of some other input is varied and what happens to the rate at which one input can be substituted for another input to produce a given quantity of output as that substitution proceeds. The purpose of this chapter is to exposit general principles of production of this sort.

## The Production Function

The basis of production theory is the idea of a systematic relationship between the rate of utilization of two or more inputs and the resulting output. It is asserted that, for any specified combination of (for example) capital and labor used for a specified period of time, there is one maximum quantity of output that can be produced in that specified period of time, given the existing technology. Technology is the total know-how or knowledge concerning production that exists in an economy at a point in time. For a given state of know-how (or state of the art, as it is sometimes called) there is a maximum amount of output per period that will be the result of using a given combination of inputs for that same period. The mathematical expression of this technical relationship between various

---

[1]Alchian & Allen, *Exchange & Production, op. cit., p. 74.*

combinations of inputs and the resulting output is called a production function. It is written as $q = F(A_1, A_2, A_3, . .)$, where $q$ is the quantity of output per time unit and $A_i$ refers to the amount of the $i$th input that is used per time unit.

Just as we used two goods, $X$ and $Y$, to stand for the multigood world of buyers in our demand theory, we shall use two inputs to stand for the multi-input world of producers. It is customary to call these two representative inputs "capital" and "labor," but it is clear that there are many different kinds of labor that a producer of a given product would use. Some are executives and others are engineers. Some have lots of formal training; others have little. Draftsmen would be one of the $A_i$'s in the production function; typists would be another. Similarly, there are many different kinds of capital that a given producer would use. Lathes, typewriters, conveyors, buildings, and computers each are different types of capital. Each different type would be one of the $A_i$'s in the production function. We want to use only two inputs for our discussion. We could use two different types of labor or two different types of capital, or we could pretend that there was only one type of each. In all cases, we would be concerned with the interaction among inputs that are used together to produce some output.

We shall base our discussion on an abbreviated production function that is written as $q = F(K, L)$, where $q$ is output per time period, $K$ is number of machine hours of capital services, and $L$ is number of man-hours of labor services used per unit of time. For example, suppose that $q = 20$ per month, $K = 5$ per month, and $L = 10$ per month. That would mean that if we used 5 machine hours of capital services together with 10 man-hours of labor services over the period of a month, we would produce 20 units of output during that month. When $L = 10$ that could mean that 10 people each work for one hour during the month, or five people each work for two hours in the month, or two people each work for five hours in the month, etc. It is the *services* of labor that constitute the input, not the labor itself. To use labor

the producer contracts with people to perform specified services for specified periods of time. The contract calls for the worker to be remunerated for his work time at the rate we call a "wage."

Similarly, it is the *services* of capital that is the input, not the capital itself. If the producer rents capital equipment, he contracts for its use for a specified period of time at a rate of remuneration we call the "rental fee." If the producer buys the capital equipment, it is still the capital services that we are interested in. The wage rate is the cost of using labor. The corresponding price for the capital input is the cost of *using* capital, not the cost of its purchase. When a piece of capital equipment is purchased, the firm merely exchanges one asset (cash) for another of equal value (the machine). On the other hand, when the firm hires an additional unit of labor services it draws down on an asset (cash) and acquires in exchange a flow of services that do not appear directly as another asset. Labor services are an expense item, not an asset. The firm incurs expenses analogous to labor expenses through the *use* of capital.

The cost of using capital includes depreciation of the capital good, maintenance expenditures, and the interest foregone by the firm because it has its wealth in the form of the machine instead of in bonds. The sum of these depreciation, maintenance, and interest costs is called the *user cost of capital*. For any production period we can calculate the sum of these costs and divide by the number of machine hours of use the firm has received during the production period to get the *user cost of capital per machine hour*. (Machine hours equal the number of machines used times the number of hours each machine was used.) If the firm rented its capital equipment it would have to pay the owner of the equipment at least enough to cover the owner's depreciation, maintenance, and interest costs. If the rental fee were larger than these costs, additional equipment owners would be induced to rent out their machines, and the rental rate would decrease. Thus a firm would have to pay roughly the same cost to acquire capital services whether it rented machines or bought them. For this reason, the user cost of capital is sometimes called the "implicit rental rate."

## Processes and Process Rays[2]

A production process is a technique or method used to produce some specific output. The process is specified by the proportions of the inputs that are needed to yield a specific quantity of output. Inputs include the ingredients embodied in the finished good as well as the use of capital and labor services to put the ingredients together during the actual act of production. The easiest way to understand what we mean by a "process" is to think of a cake recipe in a cookbook. The recipe specifies the types and proportions of ingredients as well as the specific way that these ingredients are put together. The cook performs the labor services, and the oven and mixing tools provide the capital services. The recipe plus the capital and labor services make up the production process for a cake.

Suppose we set up a given production process and it yields 10 units of output per time unit. If we *exactly* duplicate the process, that is, if we set up the same combination of ingredients, capital, and labor services in another corner of the room, the expectation would be that the same output would again result. A doubling of *all* inputs will usually lead to a doubling of output. The word "all" in the previous sentence is crucial. It is generally impossible to increase all inputs proportionately. For example, management is an input. While it is possible to acquire additional raw materials, labor services, and capital services, it is not usually possible to expand the management team proportionately. The larger a firm becomes, the more difficult it is for management to do a good job of monitoring the production processes. For this reason, it is generally thought that most firms

[2]The discussion in this and the next three sections is derived from Kelvin Lancaster, *Introduction to Modern Microeconomics* (Chicago: Rand McNally, 1969), pp. 62–70.

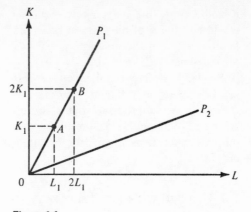

**Figure 4-1.**
Process rays.

will eventually encounter less than proportional increases in output when inputs other than management are increased.

If we assume that there are only two inputs involved in any production process, we can represent such a process as a ray (a straight line emanating from the origin) in a diagram such as Figure 4-1, which measures units of capital services on the vertical axis and units of labor services on the horizontal axis. The slope of such a ray measures the ratio of capital services to labor services that are used in the production process represented by the ray. Each different process will be represented by a different ray. The process represented by ray $0P_1$ requires a larger number of capital services per unit of labor services than does the process represented by ray $0P_2$.

If the first process ($P_1$) were used to the extent represented by point $A$ (that is, used to the extent that $K_1$ units of capital services per time unit and $L_1$ units of labor services per time unit were utilized), some specific quantity of *output* per time unit would be the result. Suppose that quantity were 10. If capital and labor were the *only* two inputs required for process $P_1$, doubling the use rate of both of them would result in a doubling of the resulting output rate. Starting from point $A$, if we doubled both the amount of capital services used and the amount of labor services used, we would be at point $B$ on process ray $0P_1$, and the resulting output would be 20. If instead of doubling the use rates of the inputs we tripled them, the result (as long as

$K$ and $L$ were the *only* inputs required) would be tripling of output, and we would be at a point on the process ray that had the coordinates $3K_1$ and $3L_1$.

Similarly, different points on process ray $0P_2$ represent different intensities of use of the second process. Proportional increases of both inputs would result in equiproportionate increases of the resulting output.

## Isoquant with Two Processes

A process is said to be "technically efficient" if it is not possible to show, without any information on the prices of the inputs, that the process would be more costly to use than some other process. Process Two is not "technically efficient" if it requires more of both inputs to produce a given output than Process One does. Similarly, Process Two is not technically efficient if it requires more of one input and the same amount of the other input to produce a given output than Process One does. In either of these cases, Process Two is more expensive to use to produce a given amount of output than Process One, no matter what the prices of the inputs are (as long as both prices are positive).

Consider Figure 4-2. Suppose that the use of Process One ($P_1$) at the intensity represented by point $A$ resulted in 100 units of output per time unit and that an employee of the firm invents a new way (process) to produce the product. Should management give this employee a raise, or should he be fired? Let the new process be represented by process ray $0P_2$. (The employee has invented a more labor intensive way of doing things.) If, in order to produce 100 units of output per time unit using the new process, it was necessary to operate the new process at an intensity represented by point $D$, the new process would be technically inefficient and the employee would not get his raise. Point $D$ uses the same amount of capital services as point $A$, but it uses more labor services. No matter what the user cost of capital and the wage rate are, point $D$ is a more expensive way to produce 100 units of output

than is point $A$. If the point that yields 100 units of output using the new process were northeast of point $D$, more of *both* inputs would be required to produce 100 units of output and the employee would stand a good chance of getting fired. On the other hand, suppose that the point on $0P_2$ that yields 100 units of output is point $C$. Point $C$ involves the same amount of labor services as point $A$ but fewer capital services. The first process would be technically inefficient relative to the new process. The employee would get his raise. If the point that yields 100 units of output on $0P_2$ were southwest of point $C$, less of *both* inputs would be required to produce the 100 units of output, and the employee would probably be promoted.

If both of the processes are technically efficient, the point that yields 100 units of output on $0P_2$ is between points $C$ and $D$. In this case, it is impossible to tell which process is the cheapest way to produce the 100 units of output without knowing the input prices.

In Figure 4-3 we have two technically efficient production processes. That means that a straight line connecting the input combination point on $0P_1$ that yields 100 (or any given number) units of output with the input combination point on $0P_2$ that yields the same output must have a negative slope. The second process ($P_2$) uses less of one input but more of the other input to produce the given amount of output than does the first process ($P_1$); hence

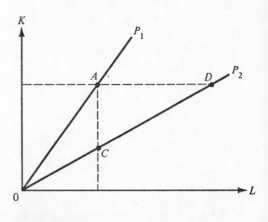

**Figure 4-2.**
Technical efficiency.

we don't know which process is less expensive until we know the input prices. Let the input combination needed using $P_1$ to produce $q^*$ of output be point $A$ and the input combination needed using $P_2$ to produce $q^*$ of output be point $B$. Pick any point on line segment $AB$ and label it point $C$. Draw a line from point $C$ parallel to $0P_2$ and label the point where this line cuts $0P_1$ point $D$. Consider the triangle $0AB$. Line $DC$ is in the interior of the triangle and is parallel to one of the triangle's sides. From plane geometry, you will recall that a line in the interior of a triangle that is parallel to one of its sides cuts the other two sides into proportionate parts. That is, the ratio $CB/AB$ equals the ratio $0D/0A$. If point $C$ is 20% of the distance from $B$ to $A$, point $D$ is 20% of the distance from $0$ to $A$.

From analytic geometry we know that the way to add two points in a Cartesian plane together is to draw a line from each point to the origin. These two lines will form two sides of a parallelogram. If we complete the parallelogram, the two sides that we must draw will intersect at a point that is the sum of the two starting points. In Figure 4-3 point $C$ is the sum of points $D$ and $E$ (where point $E$ is the point where a line parallel to $0P_1$ through point $C$ cuts $0P_2$).

We know that point $A$ and point $B$ each yields $q^*$ units of output. Point $C$ also yields $q^*$ units of output. If point $C$ is 20% of the distance from $B$ to $A$, $P_1$ is operated at point $D$, which means that 20% of $q^*$ is produced by $P_1$ and the remaining 80% is produced using $P_2$. (If point $C$ is 80% of the distance from $A$ to $B$, point $E$ is 80% of the distance from $0$ to $B$.) Point $C$ does *not* represent a new process—it represents producing a given output rate, $q^*$, using a *combination* of the first and second process. $P_1$ is operated at 20% of the intensity at which it would have to be operated if all of $q^*$ were to be produced by $P_1$, while $P_2$ is operated at 80% of the intensity at which it would have to be operated if all of $q^*$ were produced by $P_2$. Point $C$ represents a different ratio of capital services to labor services from that for either of the two production processes. For example, suppose $P_1$ combines capital services and

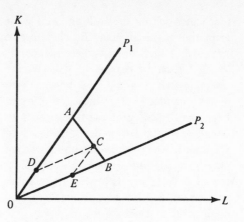

**Figure 4-3.**
Isoquant with two processes.

labor services in the ratio 2/1, while $P_2$'s $K/L$ ratio is 1/2. Using $P_1$ with 2 units of $K$ and 1 unit of $L$ yields (let's say) one unit of output. Using $P_2$ with 1 unit of $K$ and 2 units of $L$ also yields one unit of output. Suppose $q^* = 10$. Point $A$ in Figure 4-3 would involve using 20 units of $K$ and 10 units of $L$, while point $B$ would involve 10 units of $K$ and 20 units of $L$. If point $C$ were 20% of the distance from $B$ to $A$, that would mean that 2 units of output would be produced with $P_1$ using 4 units of $K$ and 2 units of $L$ (20% of 20 and 10 respectively), and 8 units of output would be produced with $P_2$ using 8 units of $K$ and 16 units of $L$. Together, $4 + 8$ units of $K$ and $2 + 16$ units of $L$ would be used. The $K/L$ ratio would be $12/18 = 2/3$.

*Any* point on the line segment $AB$ has an interpretation similar to our interpretation of point $C$. The closer the point in question is to point $A$, the larger the portion of $q^*$ that is produced using $P_1$, and the smaller the portion of $q^*$ that is produced using $P_2$. The line segment $AB$ is called an *isoquant*. The isoquant for quantity $q^*$ is made up of all the points (remember that each point is an input combination) that yield $q^*$ units of output. There is a different isoquant for each output rate. The isoquant for a quantity larger than $q^*$ would be a line parallel to $AB$ but farther away from the origin. If point $A$ yields $q^*$ units of output, the point that yields $2q^*$ on $0P_1$ will be twice as far from the origin as point $A$. Similarly, the point that yields $2q^*$ on $0P_2$ will be twice as far from the origin as point $B$. Therefore, a straight line that connects these two points for $2q^*$ must be parallel to $AB$. (We are assuming that $K$ and $L$ are the *only* two inputs required to produce our output. Using any given process, if we wish to double the output we must double each of the inputs. When we double inputs, we are merely exactly *duplicating* a given productive activity. There is no reason to think the output will be any different for the duplicate than it was for the original.)

With only two technically efficient production processes, the isoquant for any given output rate is a *negatively* sloped straight line. The end points on each isoquant represent producing the given quantity using only one of the processes. Points other than the end points represent using both of the processes to different extents.

## Adding a Third Process

Suppose we have two technically efficient production processes and we wish to consider whether a third process is also technically efficient. The first thing we must notice is that it is possible that this third process could be so good that it uses less of both inputs than either of the original two processes. In that case, the original two processes will no longer be technically efficient. A technically efficient process is one that is not clearly inferior to any other known process. "Clearly inferior" means that we know it is more expensive than some other process even without any information on input prices. It either uses more of both inputs or the same amount of one and more of the other input than does some other known process. We must, therefore, as we check to see whether the third process is technically efficient, also check to see whether it makes either of the other two processes technically inefficient.

Consider Figure 4-4. Initially there are two technically efficient production processes: $P_1$ and $P_2$. Line segment $AB$ is the isoquant for output rate $q^*$. A third process, $P_3$, is to be considered for use. The main question of importance is: Where is

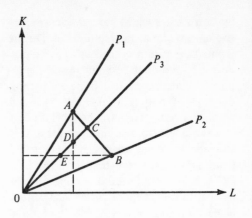

**Figure 4-4.**
Addition of third process.

the point on $0P_3$ that yields $q^*$ units of output? Point $C$ is already attainable by using $P_1$ and $P_2$ in combination (i.e., point $C$ is a point on line segment $AB$). Clearly, if the input combination needed to produce $q^*$ using $P_3$ is represented by a point (let's call it point $Z$) northeast of point $C$, $P_3$ is technically inefficient. The combination of $P_1$ and $P_2$ represented by point $C$ uses less of both inputs than any point northeast of point $C$. If point $Z$ coincides with point $C$ there would be no reason to go through the trouble of setting up the new process, since point $C$ is already attainable by a combination of $P_1$ and $P_2$. If point $Z$ is between point $C$ and point $D$, all three processes would be technically efficient. A straight line drawn from such a point $Z$ to $A$ would be negatively sloped and would represent various ways of producing $q^*$ using combinations of $P_1$ and $P_3$. A straight line drawn from the same point $Z$ to point $B$ would also be negatively sloped and would represent various ways of producing $q^*$ by combinations of $P_3$ and $P_2$. The isoquant for output $q^*$ would be made up of the two line segments, $AZ$ and $ZB$, and $ZB$ would be flatter than $AZ$. If point $Z$ coincided with point $D$, $P_1$ would no longer be technically efficient because it uses more $K$ and no less $L$ than $P_3$ does to produce $q^*$. The isoquant in this case would be the line drawn to connect points $D$ and $B$. If point $Z$ were between points $D$ and $E$, $P_1$ would be even more technically inefficient, and the isoquant for $q^*$ would be the line drawn to connect points $Z$ and $B$. Such a line would have a negative slope, while a line drawn to connect points $Z$ and $A$ would have a positive slope, indicating that $P_1$ would use more of both inputs to produce $q^*$ than would $P_3$. If point $Z$ coincided with point $E$ or were southwest of point $E$, $P_2$ would not be technically efficient. In this case, the isoquant would simply be point $Z$. Both $P_1$ and $P_2$ would be revealed to be inferior to $P_3$. *Note that isoquants are composed of points on, and lines connecting points on, technically efficient process rays only.*

We noted in the previous paragraph that if all three processes are technically efficient, point $Z$ must be between points $D$ and $C$ in Figure 4-4. In that case, the isoquant would be composed of two line segments, with the second one flatter than the first. Look at Figure 4-5. With only two technically efficient production processes, $P_1$ and $P_2$, the isoquant for $q^*$ is $AB$. With the addition of a third technically efficient production process, the isoquant for $q^*$ becomes $AZB$. $AB$ is no longer the isoquant (or any part of it) because for any point on $AB$ there is a point on either $ZA$ or $ZB$ that uses less of both inputs than that point on $AB$. With the addition of technically efficient process $P_3$, combinations of $P_1$ and $P_2$ will never be used, because combinations of either $P_1$ and $P_3$ or $P_3$ and $P_2$ use less of both inputs.

## Convexity of Isoquants

Suppose we begin with three technically efficient production processes, $P_1$, $P_2$, and

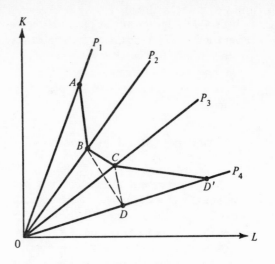

**Figure 4-6.**
Convexity of isoquants.

$P_3$ (see Figure 4-6). The isoquant for output $q^*$ is $ABC$. A fourth process, $P_4$, comes up for consideration. If $P_4$ is technically efficient, and if the three original processes continue to be technically efficient, the line that connects point $C$ on $0P_3$ with the point on $0P_4$ that also yields $q^*$ (let's call it point $D$) must be flatter than line segment $BC$. To see why this is so, consider the implications if it were not so. Line segment $CD$ in Figure 4-6 is negatively sloped, but it is steeper than line segment $BC$. Because it is steeper, a line drawn between points $B$ and $D$ would be closer to the origin than line segments $BC$ and $CD$. This means that for any point on $BC$ or $CD$ (an input combination that yields $q^*$ by a combination of $P_2$ and $P_3$ or $P_3$ and $P_4$, respectively) there is a point on $BD$ (an input combination that yields $q^*$ by a combination of $P_2$ and $P_4$) that uses less of both inputs. $P_3$ would no longer be technically efficient. The isoquant for $q^*$ would be $ABD$. On the other hand, suppose the point on $0P_4$ that yields $q^*$ is $D'$. Line segment $CD'$ is flatter than line segment $BC$. Combinations of $P_2$ and $P_4$ would not be superior to combinations of $P_2$ and $P_3$ and of $P_3$ and $P_4$. All four processes would be technically efficient, and the isoquant for $q^*$ would be $ABCD'$.

Line segments that make up isoquants must get successively flatter as they are drawn from process rays that represent

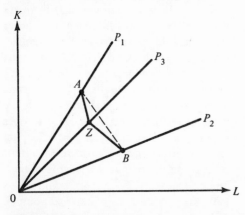

**Figure 4-5.**
Isoquant with three processes.

high $K/L$ ratios to process rays that represent lower $K/L$ ratios. Isoquants must, in other words, be "bent" toward the origin. We say that isoquants must be *convex* toward the origin, as well as negatively sloped.

## Isoquants with Many Processes

We have seen that if there are only two technically efficient processes the isoquant for any specific output will merely be a negatively sloped straight line. With three technically efficient processes isoquants are made up of two negatively sloped straight line segments with the one farther down and to the right flatter than the other one. With four technically efficient production processes, isoquants are made up of three negatively sloped line segments that become successively flatter as we move down and to the right. With $n$ technically efficient production processes, isoquants would be made up of $n - 1$ negatively sloped straight line segments that become successively flatter. If $n$ is a large number such as 15 or 20, each of the straight line segments would be very small. If there were as many as 25 technically efficient production processes one would need a magnifying glass to see the individual straight line segments. With 35 technically efficient production processes, isoquants would be practically indistinguishable from the smooth, negatively sloped, convex-to-the-origin isoquants drawn in Figure 4-7.

Each isoquant in Figure 4-7 is made up of points that indicate input combinations that yield the quantity associated with the particular isoquant in question. Production of quantity $q_1$ of output is attainable at point $A$ (using $K_A$ of $K$ and $L_A$ of $L$) and equally attainable at point $B$ (using $K_B$ of $K$ and $L_B$ of $L$). All other points on isoquant $q_1$ could just as easily be used and would result in precisely the same output, namely $q_1$. A producer who desires to maximize his profits when he produces $q_1$ will choose that one point (input combination) on isoquant $q_1$ that is the least expensive. To determine which point that is,

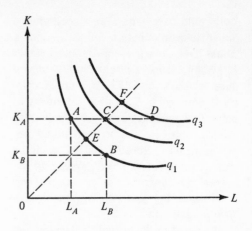

**Figure 4-7.**
Isoquants with many processes.

he would have to know the prices of $K$ and $L$. We shall discuss this search for the least-cost production process in the next chapter, which is devoted to the theory of cost.

As Figure 4-7 indicates, there are many input combinations that could be used to produce output $q_2$ and also many input combinations that will result in output $q_3$. Isoquants merely indicate that "there are many ways to skin a cat." No producer is limited to only one way to produce a given product, nor is he limited to just one way to produce a given quantity of that product. Like indifference curves, isoquants cannot intersect. If two isoquants intersected this would mean that two different maximum quantities of output would be attainable from one given input combination—a proposition that, again, defies understanding.

Figure 4-7 also indicates that there are many different ways in which a producer can change his output rate. For example, working with a fixed amount of $K-K_A$—the producer could increase his output from $q_1$ to $q_2$ to $q_3$ by moving from point $A$ to point $C$ to point $D$, i.e., by using increasing amounts of labor services together with the fixed amount of capital services. Another way to increase output from $q_1$ to $q_2$ to $q_3$ is to use more of both inputs. One way to do this would be to move from point $E$ to point $C$ to point $F$. This would mean that the ratio of $K$ to $L$ was constant, but increasing amounts of both would be used. Another alternative would be to move from point $B$ to point $C$ to point $D$. Output would increase, but the ratio of capital to labor would be different at each output rate. Which way will actually be chosen by a profit maximizer depends on which way is the least cost way.

## The Slope of an Isoquant

As we move from one point on an isoquant to another point on the same isoquant we are increasing the usage of one input and decreasing the usage of the other, while we maintain a constant output rate. Mathematicians define the term "slope" to be a change in the value of the variable plotted on the vertical axis divided by the associated change in the value of the variable plotted on the horizontal axis. In the case of an isoquant the slope is $\Delta K/\Delta L$—the number of units change in the amount of capital used per unit change in the amount of labor used, as output is held fixed. We have already seen that an isoquant must have a negative slope. For each unit change in $L$ let's say there is a two-unit change in $K$. The negative slope tells us that the direction of change of $K$ will be opposite the direction of change of $L$, but we still report the number of units change in $K$ as two—a positive number. In other words, the number of units change in $K$ per unit change in $L$ is the *absolute value* of the slope of the isoquant at the point from which we make the change. Since an isoquant is convex to the origin its slope is different at each point.

The *marginal product of labor* ($MP_L$) is defined as the change in output that results when there is a one-unit change in the amount of labor used and the amount of capital used is fixed. The *marginal product of capital* ($MP_K$) is the change in output that results when there is a one-unit change in the amount of capital used together with a fixed amount of labor. Suppose $MP_L =$ 10 and $MP_K = 5$. Starting at point $A$ in Figure 4-8, consider a one-unit increase in the amount of labor used while the amount of capital used is fixed (a move from point $A$ to point $B$.) Since the marginal product

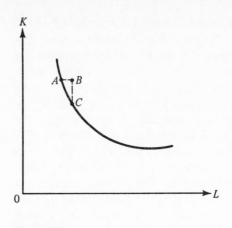

**Figure 4-8.**
Slope of isoquant.

of labor is 10, at point $B$ output would be 10 units greater than it is at point $A$. We wish to know by how many units to decrease our use of capital so that we return to the same output rate as before. In other words, how far straight down from point $B$ must we move to get back on the original isoquant? As we move from point $B$ straight down we are decreasing the amount of capital we are using, but we are holding fixed the amount of labor we are using. The marginal product of capital is 5, so for each unit decrease in the amount of capital used, output will decrease by 5 units. The unit increase in the amount of labor used increased output by 10, so we have to lower the use rate of capital by 2 units to get output back to where it was before. Distance $BC$ is 2 units of $K$. The absolute value of the slope of the isoquant is, therefore, 2, and this equals $MP_L/MP_K$ ($= 10/5$). The amount of change in the use rate of capital that compensates for a unit change in the use rate of labor, $\Delta K/\Delta L$, is two units.[3]

Since the slope of an isoquant tells us the amount of $K$ that compensates for a unit change in $L$ so that output is held fixed, the slope is called the *marginal rate*

---

[3]Actually $(-)$ 2 is the average slope of the isoquant over the range $A$ to $C$ in Figure 4-8. The slope exactly at any specific point is determined by imagining tiny (in the limit zero) changes of $L$ ($dL$) and finding the associated change of $K$ ($dK$). The ratio $dK/dL$ is still read as the change in $K$ per unit change in $L$.

*of technical substitution* between $K$ and $L$. As we move from point $A$ to point $C$ in Figure 4-8 we are substituting labor for capital while we produce the same output. If we were to move from point $C$ to point $A$ we would be substituting capital for labor, again producing the same output. The slope indicates either the reduction of $K$ when $L$ is increased by one unit or the increase of $K$ when $L$ is reduced by one unit. The convexity of an isoquant indicates that the marginal rate of technical substitution between labor and capital declines as labor is substituted for capital and increases as capital is substituted for labor.

## The Short Run—One Fixed Input

Under the rubric "capital" we include such things as plant and equipment. At any point in time a business firm has a given size building and a given number of machines and other equipment that it can use. It is possible to get additional plant and equipment fairly rapidly, but the more quickly a firm adjusts its plant and equipment, the more costly it is to do so. A new building could be constructed and outfitted in one week, but that would require work around the clock, offering high bids for the resources needed, and not spending any time investigating alternative ways of accomplishing the task. Therefore the decision maker in a firm will construct a plant of the scale that is the most efficient for the rate of output he plans to produce. If after a plant of given scale is constructed it turns out that the decision maker made a bad guess about the rate of output he desires to produce, he will want to alter his scale of plant. But he will not do this immediately. He will, at least for a while, use the scale he has to produce the quantity he desires to produce. Any plans to alter the scale of plant will be carefully put together and only eventually carried out.

The *short run* is defined as the period of time during which a firm operates with an unchanged scale of plant. Notice that the short run is *not* defined as the period of time over which the scale of plant *cannot* be altered. The scale of plant can *always* be

altered, but the more quickly it is altered the more costly the alteration will be.

Look back at Figure 4-7. Suppose a firm had built a scale of plant that is represented by quantity of capital services $K_A$. In the next chapter we shall see why the firm did this, but for now let's just suppose that $K_A$ is the scale of plant (amount of capital services) that the firm restricts itself to using. The firm could alter its output rate by altering the amount of labor services that it uses together with $K_A$. As output increased the firm would be moving from left to right along the dashed horizontal line emanating from $K_A$. For each rate of use of labor services there would be a different rate of output. The isoquant diagram of Figure 4-7 is not very good at depicting this relationship between output and labor input because neither of the axes in that diagram measures output. In contrast, the vertical axis of Figure 4-9 does measure output, and its horizontal axis measures the amount of labor services used. Since the amount of capital services used is always the same, there is no need to have a separate axis that measures $K$.

The output curve in Figure 4-9 is drawn with an "S" shape. With no labor used, no output will be produced even though capital services are available. At first, as additional workers are hired output increases at an increasing rate. This is shown by the lower part of the "S" shape. The slope of the output curve is $\Delta q/\Delta L$, which is the

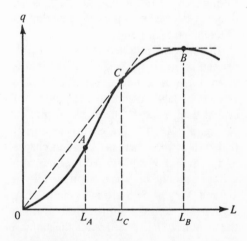

**Figure 4-9.**
Total product curve.

amount of additional output produced per unit increase in the amount of labor used. Since capital is held fixed, $\Delta q/\Delta L$ is nothing other than the marginal product of labor. Why do we expect the amount of additional output produced when one more worker is hired to *increase* as we hire additional workers over the initial range of $L$ (from 0 to $L_A$ in the figure)? The additional output produced when one more worker is hired is made up of two parts: the amount that the additional worker himself produces and the amount by which his presence affects the productivity of workers who are already there. At first there is likely to be a strong positive effect of an additional worker on the productivity of others. Two men working together can lift more than the total of the amount lifted by each working separately. However, the strength of this positive effect of an additional worker on the productivity of others is likely to diminish (and eventually even become negative) as more and more workers are hired. It seems unlikely that a fifth man added to a team of men who are lifting objects augments the productivity of the first four as much as the second man on the team augmented the productivity of the original worker. Thus at first we expect to observe output increase at an increasing rate, but eventually output will increase at a diminished rate. The point of maximum rate of increase is labeled point $A$ in Figure 4-9. It is the point where the output curve has its maximum slope. (Mathematicians call this point the point of inflection.) Beyond point $A$ output continues to increase, but the output curve gets flatter and flatter. At point $B$ the output curve reaches its maximum. The marginal product of labor is zero. This means that when an additional worker is hired the amount of output that he produces is exactly offset by the reduction in the amount of output that is produced by the workers that were already there.

It is generally impossible to identify the amount of output that is produced by any particular person. (We will examine this more closely in Chapter 6.) When we say "the amount produced by an additional

worker" (or by any worker) we generally refer to the *average product of labor* ($AP_L$). $AP_L$ is simply calculated by observing the total amount produced and dividing this amount by the number of units of $L$ used to produce it. This gives us output per unit of $L$. *Note that the marginal product of labor is not the amount produced by an additional unit of labor.* The amount produced by an additional unit of labor is the *average* product of labor. The marginal product equals the average product corrected for the positive or negative effect of an additional worker on the productivity of workers already working.

$$MP_L = AP_L + \Delta AP_L \cdot L$$

where $\Delta AP_L$ (change of average product) is positive if an additional worker augments the productivity of the others and negative if an additional worker impairs the productivity of the others. The $\Delta AP_L$ must be multiplied by the original number of workers ($L$) to calculate the change in output due to this interrelationship of productivities. For example, suppose that initially five workers are working and the initial output per worker is 10 units. A sixth worker is hired and his presence lowers the amount that each worker produces to 9 units (i.e., the *new* average product is 9 units). The new worker produces 9 units, just as every worker does when he is there. The amount by which output has increased when the sixth man is hired (i.e., the marginal product of labor when the sixth man is hired) is 4.

$$MP_L = AP_L + \Delta AP_L \cdot L$$

$$= 9 + (-1)5 = 4.$$

From 0 to $A$ in Figure 4-9 the $\Delta AP_L$ is increasingly positive. We know this is so because $MP_L$ is increasing. At point $C$ the *average* product of labor is at its maximum. The slope of a straight line from origin to a point on the output curve is the ratio of $q$ to $L$ at that point. There is no line steeper than line $0C$ that connects the origin to any point on the ouput curve; therefore point $C$ is the point of maximum $AP_L$. For values of $L$ greater than $L_C$ the average product declines. The average product declines only when $\Delta AP_L$ is negative; therefore, for values of $L$ between $L_A$ and $L_C$, $\Delta AP_L$ is positive but getting smaller and smaller. Beyond $L_C$, $\Delta AP_L$ is negative, and at $L_B$ the strength of the negative feedback on the productivity of others is exactly sufficient to offset the amount that is produced by an additional worker, so $MP_L = 0$.

The output curve in Figure 4-9 (sometimes called the total product of labor curve) can be used to derive two other curves—the marginal product of labor curve and the average product of labor curve. We have already seen that the marginal product of labor is merely the slope of the total product of labor curve. From 0 to $L_A$ in Figure 4-9 the marginal product of labor is increasing. At $L_A$ it is at its maximum, and between $L_A$ and $L_B$ it declines, reaching zero at $L_B$. The top panel of Figure 4-10 is a reproduction of Figure 4-9, while the bottom panel depicts the marginal and average products. The marginal product of labor curve in the lower panel is labeled $MP_L$. It is drawn so that its maximum is at $L_A$, and it reaches zero at $L_B$. The average product of labor curve in the same diagram is labeled $AP_L$. Notice that it reaches its maximum at $L_C$. As we noted above, the average product of labor is merely $q/L$; its value at any point is the slope of the straight line drawn from the origin to that point on the total product curve (the top panel). Line $0C$ is steeper than any other line connecting the origin with a point on the total product curve; hence $L_C$ is the value of $L$ at which $q/L$ is at its maximum. Notice that all of the lines drawn from the origin to the points on the total product curve that correspond to values of $L$ between 0 and $L_C$ (line $0D$ for example) have smaller slopes than the slope of the total product curve itself at those points. The slopes of all the lines drawn from the origin to points on the total product curve that correspond to values of $L$ greater than $L_C$ are bigger than the slope of the total product curve itself at those points. In other words, when the average product is increasing (between 0 and $L_C$) the marginal

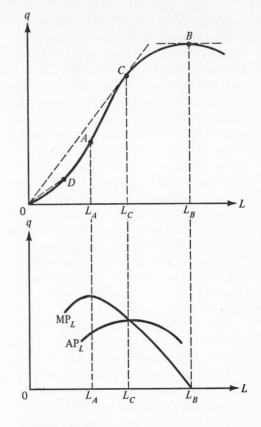

**Figure 4-10.**
Total, average, and marginal products.

product is above the average product, and when the average product is declining (beyond $L_C$) the marginal product is below the average product. The bottom panel of Figure 4-10 depicts these relationships.

For any total product curve we can derive the corresponding average and marginal product curves. All that we must do is note the location of the *three critical points* on the total product curve—the point of maximum slope (point $A$), the point of maximum average product (point $C$), and the point where the total product is maximum (point $B$). While this does not tell us the values of the average and marginal products, it does tell us when each is rising and falling and what the relationship between the average and marginal products is at each value of $L$. This is all the information we will need for our purposes.

The relationship between the average product and the marginal product is always the same—*when the average product is rising the marginal product is greater than* the average product, and when the average product is falling the marginal product is below the average product. This average-marginal relationship is universal. In the next chapter we will discuss average and marginal costs. There we will see that when average cost increases, marginal cost is greater than average cost, and when average cost decreases marginal cost is less than average cost. The word "marginal" refers to what happens when you do one more or one less of something (hire one more or one less worker or produce one more or one less unit of output). The word "average" simply means the total (total output or total cost) divided by the number of individual contributors to the total (number of workers or number of units of output).

Consider one particular average-marginal relationship that is very important to every student—average and marginal grades. The grade you get in this class will change your grade point average if it is different from your existing grade point average. The grade you get in this class is the "marginal," or additional, or new, grade. If it is higher than your existing grade point average it will pull your grade point average up; if it is below your existing average it will pull the average down. If the grade you get in this class is the same as your grade point average, the average will not change. This is the universal average-marginal relationship. *When the marginal is above the average the average rises, when the marginal is below the average the average falls, and when the marginal is the same as the average the average neither rises nor falls.*

## Property Rights and Fishing: Application of the Average-Marginal Relationship

You have often heard that the buffalo was almost made extinct during the late 19th century because hunters overkilled the herds. No one has ever claimed that a similar threat existed in the case of cattle. The reason that there was no overkilling of cattle herds was that private property rights in cattle were well defined and enforced.

Owners of cattle had every reason to ensure that each year a sufficient number of new cows would be available to replace those that were sold for slaughter. Those who slaughtered the cows, since they had to pay for the right to slaughter them, had every reason to ensure that they didn't slaughter any more cows than consumers of meat were willing to pay for. On the other hand, nobody had private property rights in buffalo, thus no one was motivated to conserve them. Each hunter had the incentive to kill as many as he could since the right to slaughter buffalo was available at a zero price. Although his decisions affected others, he was not forced to take others into consideration because he did not have to pay anyone for their consent to slaughter the buffalo. The nonexistence of defined and enforced private property rights always results in the overutilization of a resource. In Chapter 13 we shall see that pollution is the direct result of the absence of private property rights in clean air. Pollution is one example of a class of phenomena economists call "externalities"—when the action of one person affects another person and there is no price that is paid, or reward that is received, that forces the individuals to take the interdependence into consideration when they make their decisions. All externalities arise because of the absence of private property rights.

We can use our diagram of marginal and average products to see how three different specifications of the rights to use a resource (a lake full of edible fish) will result in three different intensities of use of that resource. In Figure 4-11 the curve labeled $AP_F$ (average product of fishermen) depicts the amount of fish caught per fisherman as a function of the number of fishermen on the lake. The number of fishermen on the lake is plotted on the horizontal axis, and the amount of fish caught by each fisherman is measured on the vertical axis. For example, if $F_2$ fishermen were fishing, the catch per person would be $F_2B$ fish. The $AP_F$ curve first rises and then falls as additional fishermen come on the lake. (At first when an additional fisherman comes on the lake his line may attract more fish to the vicinity of the other fishermen, but after a while the lake becomes so congested that each fisherman catches fewer fish.) The curve labeled $MP_F$ (marginal product of fishermen) tells us what happens to the *total* amount of fish caught when an additional fisherman comes on the lake. For example, if $F_2-1$ fishermen were on the lake and an additional fisherman arrived, the total amount caught (adding the catch of each fisherman together) would increase by $F_2A$ fish. Each fisherman, including the new one, would catch $F_2B$ fish, but the size of each individual's catch would be smaller with the new fisherman there than it was before he arrived. When an additional fisherman comes on the lake the change in the total catch (i.e., the *marginal* catch) equals the catch of the new person plus the change in the amount caught by the people who were already on the lake. The catch of the new person is $F_2B$ fish, but before he came on the scene the other fishermen each caught more than $F_2B$ fish. (i.e., the $AP_F$ curve is falling in the region of $F_2$ fishermen). Thus the change in the total amount of fish caught will be less than the amount caught by the new fisherman—it will be $F_2A$ fish. In general we can say that

$$MP_F = AP_F + \Delta AP_F \cdot F,$$

where $AP_F$ is the new amount caught by each fisherman, $\Delta AP_F$ is the change (negative in the region of $F_2$) in the amount caught by each fisherman, and $F$ is the number of fishermen on the lake before

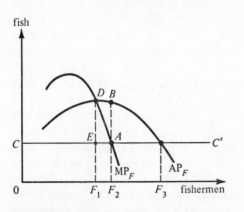

**Figure 4-11.**
Marginal and average catch.

the new person arrives. This is the usual formula for the marginal product in terms of the average product.

Now suppose that if a given person decided not to fish he could do something else (make shoes for example) that is worth $0C$ fish. $0C$ fish is the *opportunity cost* of fishing. It tells us what a person gives up if he makes the decision to fish. Line $CC'$ tells us that this opportunity cost is the same no matter how many fishermen are on the lake.

Consider three specifications of the right to fish on the lake:

1. The first person on the lake can decide how many fishermen will be allowed to fish, but he cannot charge anyone for his permission to fish.
2. The lake is the private property of someone who allows individuals to fish on his lake if they pay him a fee. Each fisherman must be charged the same fee for the fishing rights.
3. The lake is public property—anyone who wants to can fish on the lake.

How many fishermen will be observed fishing on the lake in each of these three cases? The answers to the first and the third cases are the easiest to see, so let's consider them first.

*Case 1*: The first person on the lake will be interested in maximizing the amount of fish that he catches. He will, therefore, allow $F_1$ fishermen on the lake. At $F_1$ fishermen the $AP_F$ curve is at its maximum. The amount caught by each fisherman will be $F_1D$ fish.

*Case 3*: Each person, in deciding whether or not to fish, will consider the amount of fish that he can catch compared to the value (in units of fish) of what he could do if he did not fish. A person will elect to fish if, and only if, the catch he makes is larger than his opportunity cost (i.e., if, and only if, $AP_F$ is larger than $0C$). If $F_2$ fishermen were on the lake the amount caught by each would be $F_2B$ fish, which is clearly larger than $0C$. A person who chose to fish under these circumstances would make a gain of $AB$ fish over the value of what he could do if he did not fish. Such a gain is possible until $F_3$ fishermen are on the lake. At this point there is no longer any difference between the amount of fish caught by each fisherman and the opportunity cost of the fisherman's time, hence $F_3$ fishermen would elect to fish if the lake were public property.

*Case 2 (The Private Property Case)*: The owner of the lake must decide what fee to charge for the right to fish. The most he could charge is the difference between the amount caught by each fisherman and the opportunity cost of the fisherman's time. For example, if $F_1$ fishermen were on the lake the highest fee the owner could possibly charge would be $ED$ fish. If exactly $ED$ fish were set as the fee, each fisherman would end up with $EF_1$ fish for himself—exactly the same as what he would have if he used his time in an alternative pursuit ($EF_1 = 0C$). If the owner were to lower his fee he could induce additional fishermen to fish. For example, if he set the fee at $AB$ fish and only $F_1$ fishermen were on the lake, others would join them, since the sum of $AB$ and the opportunity cost would be less than their catch. This would continue to be true until $F_2$ fishermen were on the lake. Charging a lower fee will attract additional fishermen to pay the fee, but it means that less of a of a fee will be collected from those who already fished at the higher fee. (Everybody must be charged the same fee.) The owner of the lake, when deciding whether or not to lower his fee enough to attract one more fisherman onto the lake, will compare the benefit of so doing with its cost. The benefit is the fee collected from the new person. This equals the difference between $AP_F$ and $0C$ when the additional person is there. The cost is the fact that less revenue will be collected from those who chose to fish when the fee was higher. This equals the reduction in the fee ($\Delta AP_F$) times the number of fishermen who were previously fishing ($F$). $\Delta AP_F$ is negative, so the cost (a positive number) is $-\Delta AP_F \cdot F$. The owner will continue to lower his fee until the benefit is no longer greater than the cost of so doing, or until, in other words,

$$AP_F - 0C = -\Delta AP_F \cdot F$$

This condition may be rewritten as

$$AP_F + \Delta AP_F \cdot F = 0C,$$

and we know that

$$AP_F + \Delta AP_F \cdot F = MP_F$$

Hence, the owner will lower his fee until he attracts $F_2$ fishermen onto the lake. The marginal product of fishermen equals the opportunity cost of fishing only when $F_2$ fishermen are on the lake. The fee that the owner will settle on is $AB$ fish.

In sum, the specification of the rights to use a resource will affect the way that resource is used. A resource will always be used less intensively if it is privately owned than if it is publicly owned and made available at a zero price. In the previous section we saw that total product (in this case the total amount of fish caught) is at its maximum when marginal product is zero. It follows that the total catch *net of the total opportunity cost* ($0C$ times the number of fishermen) is at its maximum when $MP_F$ *net of the unit opportunity cost* ($0C$) is zero—i.e., when $MP_F = 0C$. Thus, the private property specification of rights results in the optimal use of the resource—the use that yields the largest net gain after costs have been taken into consideration. With reference to Figure 4-11, $0C$ is the lost output in the nonfishing sector when an additional person fishes, and it is also the gain in output in the nonfishing sector when one less person fishes. (Output in the nonfishing sector is measured in units of fish.) $MP_F$ is both the gain in the output of the fishing sector when one more person fishes and the loss of output in the fishing sector when one less fishes. If less than $F_2$ are fishing, the gain in output in the fishing sector is larger than the loss of output in the nonfishing sector when one more fishes. If more than $F_2$ are fishing, the gain in output in the nonfishing sector is larger than the loss of output in the fishing sector when one less fishes. Thus $F_2$ represents the ideal allocation of effort between the two sectors. The maximum possible output (fishing plus nonfishing) is obtained from scarce resources by the institution of private property.

## The Stages of Production

Our discussion of total, average, and marginal products of labor was constructed within the context of the following conceptual experiment: maintain a constant amount of capital for labor to work with, vary the amount of labor utilized, and observe what happens to total output. From observations on total output, calculate average and marginal products of labor. Once we have carried out this conceptual experiment it may seem quite natural to carry out a second. Hold constant the amount of labor capital has to work with, vary the amount of capital utilized, and observe what happens to total output. From the observation on total output, calculate the average and marginal products of capital. Fortunately, it is not necessary to carry out the second experiment once we have carried out the first. *The results of the first experiment contain within themselves the results of the second.*

Suppose that the first experiment was carried out holding $K$ fixed at 2 units and that observations were made on total output when $L$ had the values 1, 2, 3, and 4. The results for total and average products of labor are given in Table 4-1.

### Table 4-1

| $K$ | $L$ | $q$ | $q/L$ |
|-----|-----|-----|-------|
| 2 | 1 | 5 | 5 |
| 2 | 2 | 12 | 6 |
| 2 | 3 | 21 | 7 |
| 2 | 4 | 24 | 6 |

We could construct a second experiment holding labor fixed and varying capital, but if we agree that labor is to be held fixed at *one unit* and the different amounts of capital used are to be the amounts which equal $K/L$ from the first experiment, we do not have to bother with a second experiment. Look at the first row in Table 4-1. Labor already has the value 1, and the corresponding amount of $K$ equals $K/L = 2/1$. If two units of capital and one unit of labor previously produced 5 units of output, they will again. Now consider the second row of the table. $L$ equals 2 and we want it to equal 1, hence we reduce $L$ by one-half. We also reduce $K$ by one-half since $K/L = 2/2 = 1$. Both inputs have been reduced by one-half, hence the resulting output will be one-half of what it was before.[4] It was 12 before, so it becomes 6 now. Note that the total output when $L = 1$ and $K = 1$ equals the average product of labor when $L = 2$ and $K = 2$. Next consider the third row of Table 4-1. $L = 3$ and we want it to equal 1, so we multiply the existing $L$ by 1/3. We also multiply the existing $K$ by 1/3, since $K/L = 2/3$. Since we have multiplied both inputs by 1/3, we know that the total output will be one-third of what it was before. It was 21 before, so it is 7 now. Again note that the total output when $L = 1$ and $K = 2/3$ equals the average product of labor when $L = 3$ and $K = 2$. Finally, consider the fourth row of Table 4-1. $L = 4$; we want it to equal 1, so we multiply $L$ by 1/4. We also multiply $K$ by 1/4 since $K/L = 2/4$. The resulting total output will be 6, an amount equal to the average product of labor for row 4 of Table 4-1.

We are not *actually* changing the amount of capital at all. The amount of capital is fixed, and we are varying the amount of labor. As we increase the amount of labor working with the fixed amount of capital the ratio of $K$ to $L$ decreases. In other words, the amount of capital used per one unit of labor decreases. We treat this as if labor were held fixed at one unit and capital were actually decreased. Similarly, when the amount of labor that works together with the fixed cap-

---

[4]Here again we are assuming that $K$ and $L$ are the *only* two inputs, so that when the inputs used are changed by some proportion we would normally expect that output will change by the same proportion. This notion is discussed more fully in the last section of this chapter.

ital decreases, the ratio of $K$ to $L$ increases. In other word, the amount of capital used per one unit of labor increases. We treat this as if there were an actual increase in the amount of capital and the amount of labor were held fixed at one unit.

Table 4-2 summarizes the results of our numerical example. The first column shows decreasing amounts of capital as we read it from top to bottom. The second column shows a fixed amount of labor—one unit—and the third column depicts the total output that results from the different amounts of capital working with the one unit of labor. This third column is called the total product of capital, just as the output that results when labor is varied and capital is held fixed is called the total product of labor.

### Table 4-2

| $K$ | $L$ | $q$ |
| --- | --- | --- |
| 2/1 | 1 | 5 |
| 2/2 | 1 | 6 |
| 2/3 | 1 | 7 |
| 2/4 | 1 | 6 |

Comparing Table 4-1 and Table 4-2 we see that the average product of labor in Table 4-1 equals the total product of capi-

tal in Table 4-2. In Table 4-2 the amount of capital used with the fixed amount of labor increases as we read from the bottom to the top. In Table 4-1 the amount of labor used together with the fixed amount of capital increases as we read from the top to the bottom.

Figure 4-12 depicts the data of our two tables. The curve in the figure may be interpreted as either the average product of labor (from Table 4-1) or the total product of capital (from Table 4-2). With the former interpretation the horizontal axis is Scale A, which measures increasing amounts of $L$ (with $K$ held fixed at two units) as we read from left to right. With the latter interpretation the horizontal axis measures increasing amounts of $K$ (with $L$ held fixed at one unit) as we read from right to left. The vertical axis measures the average product of labor with the former interpretation, and the total product of capital with the latter interpretation. One curve does double duty.

If the amount of $K$ that is used with varying amounts of $L$ were one unit instead of two units, the total product of labor would be the same as the average product of capital. The average product of capital is, after all, output per one unit of capital. When two units of capital are used, the total product of labor equals output per two units of capital and the average product of capital is one-half of that. The average product of capital curve exactly lines up with

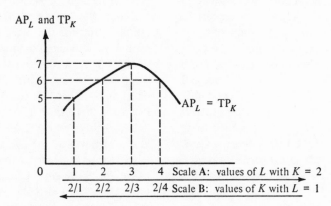

**Figure 4-12.**

Identity of average product of labor and total product of capital with alternative interpretations of horizontal scale.

the total product of labor curve. That is, the three critical values of $L$—point of maximum slope, point of maximum average, and point of zero slope—are the same for the total product of labor curve as they are for the average product of capital. For our purposes, then, we can regard the total product of labor curve as the average product of capital curve, with the understanding that we read increasing values of $K$ from right to left and increasing values of $L$ from left to right.

Consider Figure 4-13. In the top panel the total product of labor is plotted in the usual fashion. In the bottom panel the marginal and average product of labor curves are derived from the total product of labor curve. We have seen that we can regard the average product of labor as the total product of capital, and we can regard the total product of labor as the average product of capital. Since the total product of capital curve (bottom panel) reaches its maximum at $0A$ units of labor, the marginal product of capital curve must reach zero at $0A$ units of labor. Since the average product of capital curve (top panel) reaches its maximum at $0B$ units of labor, the marginal product of capital curve must cut it at $0B$ units of labor. The marginal product of capital curve is labeled $MP_K$ in the top panel of the figure.

At this juncture it is wise to pause and remind ourselves what we are doing. There is some fixed amount of capital and varying amounts of labor are used with it to produce output. We know that over certain values of $L$ the average product of labor rises, and over other values of $L$ it falls. We also know that over some values of $L$ the marginal product of labor is positive, and over other values of $L$ it is negative. *Implicit in all of the things that we know about the average and marginal product of labor is similar information about the average and marginal products of capital.* For any given value of $L$ working together with the fixed amount of $K$, there is a definite ratio of $K$ to $L$. This ratio can be thought of as an amount of capital working together with one unit of labor. Thus each change of $L$ working with the fixed $K$ can be regarded as a change in $K$ working with a

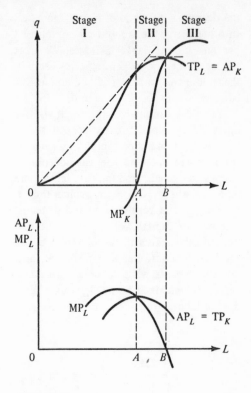

**Figure 4-13.**
Stage symmetry.

fixed amount (one unit) of $L$. $K$ really doesn't change, but when $L$ does change it is exactly the same thing as a change in $K$, since the ratio $K/L$ (capital per one unit of labor) changes. For each different value of $L$ working with the fixed $K$ there is a unique value of the marginal product of labor and a unique value for the average product of labor. For this same value of $L$ working with the fixed $K$ there is also a unique value for the marginal product of capital as well as a unique value for the average product of capital. If we know what is happening to the average product of labor (whether it is rising or falling), we know whether the marginal product of capital is positive or negative. The reason we know this is that the average product of labor can be regarded as the total product of capital. Since what happens to the total product of labor also happens to the average product of capital, we can make further deductions about the marginal product of capital simply by looking at the total product of labor.

Look at Figure 4-13. There we can see

that when the average product of labor is rising (from 0 to $A$ on the horizontal scale) the marginal product of capital is negative. Similarly, when the average product of capital is rising (moving from right to left toward point $B$ on the horizontal scale) the marginal product of labor is negative. When both marginal products are positive (from $A$ to $B$ on the horizontal scale) both average products are falling ($AP_L$ falls as we read from left to right, and $AP_K$ falls as we read from right to left). These three ranges on the horizontal axis are called *stages of production*. From 0 to $A$ is Stage I, from $A$ to $B$ is Stage II, and beyond $B$ is Stage III.

The first useful insight that can be gained from all of this is that a producer who has his personal wealth at stake will always operate somewhere in Stage II. If he used so little labor that he was in Stage I the marginal product of capital would be negative. Using a small amount of labor together with the fixed amount of capital implies a high ratio of $K$ to $L$—a high amount of capital working with one unit of $L$. It is so high that if he reduced the amount of capital working together with one unit of labor, output would increase. But the amount of capital the producer has is fixed; therefore the only way he can decrease the amount of $K$ working with one unit of $L$ is to *increase the amount of L he uses*. He will continue to do so until he is somewhere in Stage II. If he used so much labor with his fixed capital that he was in Stage III, the marginal product of labor would be negative. This would mean that if he reduced the amount of $L$ used, his output would increase. Again he will continue to do so until he is in Stage II. Since a producer will always operate in Stage II, he will always hire more labor than the amount that maximizes output per unit of labor; that is, he will go beyond the point of maximum average product of labor into the region of declining average product of labor.

We can also see from Figure 4-13 that in Stage II—the only relevant stage—when the amount of labor increases with a fixed amount of capital, the marginal product of labor declines and the marginal product of

capital increases. Similarly, when additional capital is used with a fixed amount of labor (reading from right to left), the marginal product of capital declines and the marginal product of labor increases. This interdependency of the marginal products will be crucial when we come to discuss distribution theory in Chapter 10.

## The Long Run—Returns to Scale

In the previous three sections one input (capital or a lake full of fish) was held constant and the amount of another input (labor or fishermen) was varied. The resulting output was observed, and from these observations average and marginal products were derived. All of this was the "short run," which merely means that at least one input was held fixed. The "short run" can be a very long period of time. It lasts for as long as there is a constant amount of one input, no matter why the input is constant. The long run is defined as that period of time over which all inputs are changing. A firm may have a given scale of plant and be quite content with it over a long period of time. Our short-run production theory would apply in this case. When a firm becomes unhappy with the scale of plant it has, it begins to make plans to change the scale. Those plans will be based on the relationship between output and different amounts of all inputs; hence they will be based on our long-run production theory.

The basic question we ask in long-run production theory is what happens to output when we change the *scale* of a firm's operations. The phrase "changes of scale" has two different meanings. It is sometimes used to refer to equiproportionate changes in literally *all* inputs used in a given production activity, and it is sometimes used to refer simply to equiproportionate changes in the amount of capital, labor, and materials used. The normal expectation is that when literally *all* inputs are changed by the same percentage amount, the resulting output will change by the same percentage amount. The only time when we would not expect this result is when not only is the amount of some

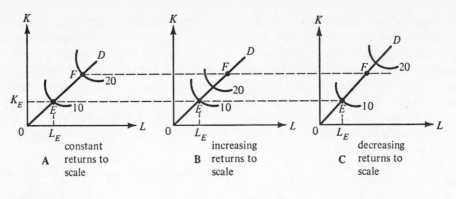

**Figure 4-14.**
Returns to scale.

input changed, but its *characteristics* change as well. Sometimes when a firm grows it may be able to use techniques that it could not use before. An automobile firm may use a custom workshop technique if it produces only a few cars, but an assembly line would be set up if it produced thousands of cars. It may use 10 times as much capital, labor, and materials as before, but it may get 100 times as many cars. However, additional entrepreneurial services (the services of those who coordinate the enterprise and make it go) cannot generally be obtained as readily as can additional capital, labor, and materials. While an automobile firm may initially be able, due to changes in input characteristics, to get a larger *percentage* change in the quantity of cars produced than in the quantity of capital, labor, and materials used, eventually the additional difficulty of coordinating the enterprise will offset (or even more than offset) the gains from assembly line production.

In our two-input model we will define "changes of scale" to refer to equiproportionate changes in both of the inputs. Figure 4-14 depicts the three possible cases of *returns to scale*. If we change the amounts of $K$ and $L$ used by the same percentage we will maintain a constant ratio of $K$ to $L$. We will be moving from point to point along a ray from the origin such as that labeled $0D$ in the diagrams. In each of the panels we begin at point $E$, producing 10 units of output and utilizing $K_E$ of $K$ and $L_E$ of $L$. We now wish to double our output. In panel **A** we depict the case where, in order to increase output to 20 units and

maintain a constant ratio of $K$ to $L$, both inputs must be doubled. We must move from $E$ to $F$ on $0D$. This is called *constant returns to scale*—a doubling of both inputs results in a doubling of output. In panel **B** we see that in order to double the output while maintaining a constant ratio of $K$ to $L$, we must less than double both inputs. This is called *increasing returns to scale*—if we should double both inputs we would more than double the output. Panel **C** depicts the case where, in order to increase output from 10 to 20 while maintaining a constant ratio of $K$ to $L$, we would have to more than double the amounts of $K$ and $L$ used. *This is called decreasing returns to scale.*[5]

The underlying source of increasing returns to scale is changes in production techniques made possible by increases in the desired output rate. The underlying source of decreasing returns to scale is the fact that one input—entrepreneurial and management services—is held fixed as $K$ and $L$ are increased.

---

[5]In mathematical economics the three cases of returns to scale are represented by production functions which are homogeneous of various degrees. A production function is homogeneous of degree $k$ if its algebraic structure is such that when all the independent variables (the inputs) are multiplied by an arbitrary number $t$ the dependent variable (output) is multiplied by $t^k$. Thus if $k = 2$ and all inputs are tripled ($t = 3$), output would be multiplied by $9 = 3^2$. This is a case of increasing returns to scale. When $k = 1$ the production function exhibits constant returns to scale, and when $k$ is less than 1 the production function exhibits decreasing returns to scale.

As we shall see in the next chapter, whether we have constant, increasing, or decreasing returns to scale determines whether we will encounter constant, decreasing, or increasing unit production costs as we alter our scale of operations.

## Questions for Discussion

1. Suppose we collect data on inputs and output for two firms, one privately owned and operated for a profit and the other government-owned. In both cases we use statistical regression techniques to derive a production function. Which production function would most closely follow the definition of a production function given in the text? Why?

2. Evaluate the following:

   Since production is really a technical relationship between inputs and outputs, economists can add nothing to what engineers have to say about production. Leave production to the engineers and leave marketing to economists.

3. Try to construct an indifference curve for two goods using the same approach we used to construct an isoquant in this chapter. Why is this impossible?

4. In a community with 100 people and 10 firms, consider two property rights structures:

   All of the firms are government-owned—that is each person is 1/100 owner of each of the 10 firms, but ownership shares cannot be exchanged.

   All firms are privately owned corporations—initially each person owns 1/100 of each of the 10 firms, but ownership shares can be exchanged.

   Suppose that, for each person, 1/10 of his time devoted to any of the firms would result in $1000 worth of value. Under the second rights structure, ownership shares could be exchanged so that each person becomes a 1/10 owner of only one firm and concentrates his efforts on that one firm. What advantages could be gained from this exchange? Note that with both rights structures there is an egalitarian distribution of ownership claims, yet the rights structures do make a difference.

5. In the private property case of the fishing example used in this chapter, each fisherman is forced by the fee he is charged to internalize (to make decisions on the basis of) the effect he has on other fishermen. Why?

6. Explain the following:

   If the marginal product of labor, when added to a fixed amount of land, always increased, the whole of the world's food supply could be grown in a flower pot.

7. Does the law of diminishing returns have anything to do with returns to scale? What does it refer to?

# 5
## Cost Theory

### The Meaning of Cost

Resources can be used to produce many different things, but when a given set of resources is used to produce commodity $A$ it cannot at the same time be used to produce anything else. If the resources used to produce commodity $A$ had only one alternative use—the production of commodity $B$—the cost of producing a specific amount of $A$ would be the value of the amount of $B$ that could not be produced because the resources are used to produce the $A$. However, if the resources required to produce the $A$ could be used to produce many different things, the cost of the amount of $A$ produced is the most highly valued of those things that cannot be produced because the resources are used for $A$. To an economist *the cost of anything is the value of the best alternative given up in order to get that thing.* To emphasize the idea of a sacrificed alternative, economists sometimes refer to this concept of cost as "opportunity cost." The term "opportunity cost" is really redundant because the word "cost" is defined as a foregone oportunity.

In popular discussion the cost of producing commodity $A$ is defined as the sum of money payments made to acquire resources for the production of $A$. Since resource owners (and this includes entrepreneurs) sell their services to the highest bidders, the sum of money payments made to acquire resources for the production of $A$ must at least equal the value of the same resources in their best alternative use. Thus the economist's concept of cost does not necessarily contradict the popular concept of cost.

The rate of return that an entrepreneur can earn by setting up shop to produce commodity $B$ is part of the cost of producing commodity $A$. After all, an entrepreneur must make at least as much from the production of $A$ as he could make from the production of $B$, or he wouldn't produce $A$. If an entrepreneur made more from the production of $A$ than other entrepreneurs made from the production of other things, these other entrepreneurs would attempt to get into the production of $A$ and out of the production of these other things until there was no longer any differential return made from the production of $A$. However, the entrepreneur producing $A$ may be the sole owner of one of the resources necessary to do the job he is doing. For example, he may possess unique entrepreneurial skills required in the production of $A$. In this case he would continue to earn more by producing $A$ than he could if he did something else, and other entrepreneurs would continue to earn less than he does even if they produced *A*. The differential obtained by the superior entrepreneur is called *rent*. Rent is a payment received by a resource owner which is greater than the minimum payment necessary to get him to do what he is doing. The minimum payment necessary to get him to do what he is doing equals the best payment he could obtain by doing something else. Rent is not part of cost. Cost consists only of sacrificed alternatives, and thus cost is limited to payments made to resource owners that are equal to what they could receive if their resources were used elsewhere.

Although the popular concept of cost as the sum of money payments made to acquire resources for some purpose is consistent with the economist's definition of cost, the concept is frequently misused in popular discussion. Suppose that I purchase an apartment house for $100,000 in 1973, and I continue to own and operate it for 11 years. In 1984 I entertain the idea of selling the apartment house, collect information on the market for apartment houses, and discover that the highest bid I would receive is $50,000. (Things are bad all over in 1984.) How should the $100,000 that I initially paid for the apartment house affect my decision as to whether to sell? *Not at all.* The fact that I paid $100,000 in 1973 in no way affects the alternatives I now face.[1] The money was paid in the past and is history. It is a *sunk cost.* Sunk costs are not costs at all, in the economist's sense, because they do not represent a currently available alternative that is sacrificed. The cost of selling the apartment house is the annual flow of net income (rent receipts less property taxes, maintenance, and depreciation expenses) that I would receive if I did not sell it. Let's suppose that annual flow is $4,000. The cost of not selling the apartment house is the annual stream of payments I could earn by using the $50,000 I receive from the sale to purchase the asset that yields

the largest annual net revenue. Suppose that asset is $50,000 worth of triple A bonds that pay 10%; the cost of not selling the apartment house would be $5,000 annually. Since the cost of not selling is larger than the cost of selling, I would sell. *Cost is a currently sacrificed alternative.*

Do you ever allow historical costs to affect current decisions? Many of us do, even though it makes no sense. While driving through Massachusetts on a summer day you stop at a restaurant that sells fried clams. You have been driving for a while and are hungry, so you order a quart of clams for $3.50 instead of a pint for $2.00. After you have eaten half the quart you realize that you are full, but you stuff the other half down because you don't want to waste $1.50. But that $1.50 was already "wasted," and you are making matters worse by incurring indigestion. The cost of discarding half the quart of clams depends on what you could do with them if you did not discard them. If your best alternative is to eat them and get indigestion that cost is actually *negative.*

## Short-Run Cost Curves

The "short run" is the period of time over which a firm operates with a fixed amount of plant and equipment. The plant and equipment are obtained, of course, through either purchase or rental. In the purchase case the owner incurs certain costs which are independent of the firm's output rate as long as he *continues possession* of the plant and equipment. The plant and equipment will, at least to some extent, depreciate whether it is used or not. This cost is relatively minor. More importantly, if the money to purchase the plant and equipment was borrowed, interest must be paid to the lenders whether or not the firm produces anything. Even if the money was not borrowed the owner still incurs an interest cost—the return he could make if he sold the plant and equipment and used the proceeds to buy bonds. If the plant and equipment are rented, the rental contracts specify periodic payments which must be made as long as the entrepreneur

---

[1] I am ignoring the effects of the transaction on current tax liability.

*continues possession* of the plant and equipment, and these payments are independent of the firm's output rate. These costs which are independent of the firm's output rate are called "fixed costs" or sometimes "continued possession costs." Since they are the same whether the firm produces zero units or 500 units per week, they are, in the short-run, not production costs at all. The cost of the production of some quantity of output is the outlay that *could be avoided* if that output were not produced. Only *that* outlay represents a currently available alternative that is sacrificed when the output is produced. Outlays that can be avoided by not producing (while continuing possession of the plant and equipment) rather than producing, or by producing less rather than more, are called "variable production costs," "variable costs," or "operating costs". Depreciation related to the intensity of use of the plant and equipment and rental payments tied to production rates would fall into this "variable cost" category.

Fixed production costs are, of course, unavoidable only so long as the entrepreneur continues possession of the plant and equipment. In the rental case, the rent payments can be avoided by simply turning over the plant and equipment to its owners. If the rental contracts have not matured and they stipulate an early termination fee, that fee, *and only that fee,* is unavoidable. If the entrepreneur owns the

plant and equipment he has the option of selling it. After he has sold it he avoids the depreciation and interest costs of continued possession.

In the previous chapter we saw in our two-input model that when one input, $K$, is held fixed and the other input, $L$, is varied we will obtain varying amount of output. The curve that depicts the relationship between the varying amounts of $L$ and the resulting output, $q$, is "S" shaped; this curve is reproduced in panel **A** of Figure 5-1. From this total product of labor curve we can derive another curve which depicts what happens to the amount of money that is spent on labor as different rates of output are produced. The total product of labor curve tells us how much output will be produced when the firm uses any specified amount of labor services together with its fixed plant and equipment. Each amount of output is associated with a specific amount of labor services used. If we know the price of each unit of labor services—the wage rate, $W$—we can calculate the amount of money that must be spent on $L$ (the variable input) in order to obtain any specified quantity of output. We simply use the $\text{TP}_L$ curve to find the amount of $L$ required for the $q$ that we are interested in, and multiply this $L$ by $W$. Panel **B** measures the product of $W$ and $L$ on the vertical axis and the different $q$'s on the horizontal axis, while panel **A** measures the different $q$'s on the vertical axis and the

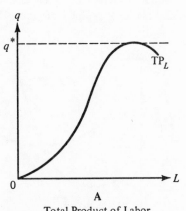

**A**
Total Product of Labor

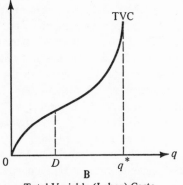

**B**
Total Variable (Labor) Costs

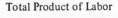

**Figure 5-1.**
Derivation of total variable cost curve.

various amounts of $L$ on the horizontal axis. To get the curve that depicts the total amount of money spent on $L$ when the various $q$'s are produced—the total variable cost curve (TVC)—we merely reverse the axes of the $TP_L$ diagram and multiply $L$ by the wage rate. The wage rate is the same no matter how much $L$ is used. Since the axes are reversed, if the $TP_L$ curve is "S" shaped the TVC curve is shaped as an inverse "S" as in panel **B** of Figure 5-1.

Inspection of the TVC curve reveals that, at first, variable costs increase at a decreasing rate (over the output range from 0 to $D$). This follows from the fact that initially as increasing amounts of $L$ are used, output increases at an increasing rate. It doesn't take much additional $L$ to get additional $q$ at first, so costs don't increase proportionately with $q$ at first. Eventually as additional $L$ is used the rate of increase of $q$ decreases; thus to get additional $q$ we must use larger and larger increments of $L$—i.e., labor costs eventually begin to increase at an increasing rate. In panel **A** the maximum $q$ obtainable is $q^*$; hence beyond $q^*$ in panel **B** total variable costs become infinite.

Just as we derived the total variable cost curve from the total product of labor curve, we can derive curves that represent average variable cost and marginal cost from the average product of labor curve and the marginal product of labor curve, respectively. Average variable cost (AVC) is defined as total variable cost divided by output. That is, for each $q$ we know the total amount that must be spent on the variable input. If we divide this amount by the $q$, we get variable cost per unit of output. AVC = TVC/$q$, but TVC = $WL$; hence AVC = $WL/q$. This can be rewritten as $W/(q/L)$, which is merely the wage rate divided by the average product of labor ($AP_L$). To derive the AVC curve from the $AP_L$ curve we merely turn the $AP_L$ curve upside down (from $q/L$ to $L/q$) and multiply by the wage rate. The curve labeled AVC in Figure 5-2 depicts average variable cost (vertical axis) as it relates to the quantity of output (horizontal axis). Since the $AP_L$ curve (not shown) is shaped as an inverse "U," the AVC curve must be "U" shaped.

The $AP_L$ curve tells us the amount of output per unit of $L$ for the various amounts of $L$. Suppose that $AP_L$ = 5. Since each unit of $L$ produces 5 units of output, only 1/5 units of $L$ are necessary to produce one unit of output ($L/q$ = 1/5). That one unit of output would then cost W times 1/5 man-hour to produce; that is, variable costs per unit of output would be W/5.

Marginal cost (MC) is defined as the change in total cost when there is a one-unit change in the quantity of output produced; i.e., it is the change in total cost per unit change in output ($\Delta C/\Delta q$). With only one variable input there is only one source of a change in total costs—a change in labor costs or variable costs.

$$MC = \frac{\Delta C}{\Delta q},$$

but

$$\Delta C = W(\Delta L);$$

hence

$$MC = \frac{W(\Delta L)}{\Delta q}$$

This can be rewritten as

$$\frac{W}{\Delta q/\Delta L}$$

which is merely the wage rate divided by the marginal product of labor. Here, as be-

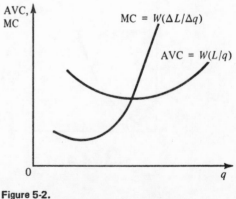

**Figure 5-2.**
Average variable and marginal costs.

fore, to get from the product curve to the cost curve (in this case to get from the marginal product curve to the marginal cost curve) we simply invert the product curve and multiply by the wage rate. We invert $\Delta q/\Delta L$ to get $\Delta L/\Delta q$, and we multiply by $W$. Since the marginal product of labor curve is shaped as an inverse "J," the marginal cost curve is "J.. shaped. The marginal cost curve is labeled MC in Figure 5-2.

Note that the usual average-marginal relationship holds: when the average is falling the marginal is below the average, and when the average is rising the marginal is above the average. When the average is neither rising nor falling (when it reaches its minimum in Figure 5-2) the marginal equals the average.

Accountants are often concerned with "total costs" of production, by which they mean the sum of variable costs and fixed costs. We have seen that, given the decision to continue possession of a given amount of plant and equipment, fixed costs (costs of continued possession which are independent of production rates) are not rightfully attributable to output since they cannot be avoided by the decision to alter output. They are not really production costs because cost is currently available sacrificed alternative, and outlays that *must* be made are not currently available for *any* alternative. Since they are not production costs they should not affect the entrepreneur's decision on how much to produce, or even, given the decision to continue possession, whether to produce or not.

Consider a firm that has $2,000 per month worth of fixed outlay related to its plant and equipment. Let's say the firm is producing 1,000 units of output per month, its total variable costs (the outlays that could be avoided if there were zero production but if the entrepreneur continued possession of the plant and equipment) amount to $3,000 per month, and the 1,000 units sell for $4.00 apiece. "Total cost" equals $5,000 per month, but monthly revenue amounts to only $4,000. An accountant would say that this firm is experiencing a loss of $1,000 per month. A bad accountant would advise the entrepreneur to shut down—to cut production to

zero. It is easy to see why this is bad advice. At a zero output rate the entrepreneur still must pay out $2,000 per month. If output were to continue at 1,000 (we assume that 1,000 is the output that results in the least possible loss) the entrepreneur would receive $4,000 of revenue. Only $3,000 would be used to cover variable costs, so $1,000 would be left over to pay half of the monthly fixed costs. The monthly loss would be only $1,000 instead of the $2,000 loss that would be experienced if zero output were produced and zero revenue were collected.

Now this clearly cannot go on forever. If the entrepreneur anticipates that his revenue will not increase he will reevaluate his decision to continue possession of the plant and equipment. He may decide to leave this market altogether. In this case he would sell the plant and equipment to the highest bidder, and use the proceeds of the sale to acquire other assets which yield a positive rate of return. Perhaps he would decide to reduce the size of his operation by selling only a portion of his plant and equipment. In either case the amount of plant and equipment used by the firm would change. Since the "short run" is the period of time over which a firm operates with a fixed amount of plant and equipment, this decision takes us into the realm of the "long run." The main point now is that if an entrepreneur expects soon to be able to cover his continued possession costs as well as operating costs he should operate in the short run even if only his operating costs are covered.

Panel **A** of Figure 5-3 depicts a total variable cost curve labeled TVC. It has the usual shape. The horizontal line in the same diagram represents an outlay of $0E$ dollars which is independent of the amount of output ($q$) produced; that is to say, it is fixed. If, at each $q$, we add together the variable costs and the $0E$ dollars of fixed outlay we will have the total outlay made for each $q$. We call this total outlay "total costs" (TC). The TC curve is $0E$ dollars above the TVC curve at each $q$. The TC curve must have the same shape as the TVC curve since variable costs are the only source of change in total costs.

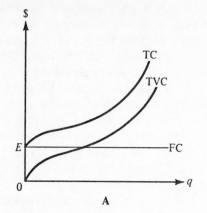

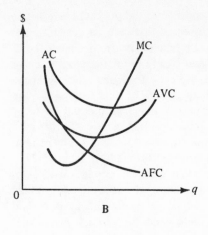

**Figure 5-3.**
Short-run cost curves.

Panel **B** of Figure 5-3 depicts an average variable cost curve (AVC) and a marginal cost curve (MC), each of which has its usual shape. If we divide the $0E$ dollars of fixed outlay (from panel **A**) by each of the various $q$'s and plot that ratio against $q$ in panel **B**, we will trace out a declining curve such as that labeled AFC (average fixed cost). If $0E$ equals $70 and the rate of output is 35 units, average fixed cost equals $2. This is usually interpreted to mean that $2 of fixed cost is attributed to each unit of output. If the rate of output were 70 units, $1 of fixed cost would be attributed to each unit of output. An accountant would say that the "overhead" is being "spread out" over more units so each unit has to bear a smaller portion of the total. If at each $q$ we add average variable cost to average fixed cost, we will get average cost. The average cost curve is labeled AC in panel **B**. Notice that the AC curve gets closer and closer to the AVC curve as $q$ gets bigger. This is because the difference between AVC and AC is AFC, and AFC gets smaller and smaller as $q$ gets bigger. Notice also that the marginal cost curve stands in the usual average-marginal relationship with respect to the AC curve as well as with respect to the AVC curve. This is because marginal cost is simply the rate at which total cost changes as $q$ changes. The only source of change in total cost is change in variable cost; hence a curve that depicts the rate of such change in variable cost will also depict the rate of such change

in total cost. The minimum point on the AC curve occurs at a larger $q$ than does the minimum point on the AVC curve. Since AC = AVC + AFC, the slope of the AC curve (AC') equals the slope of the AVC curve (AVC') plus the slope of the AFC line (AFC'). AC' = AVC' + AFC'. AFC' is always negative (AFC declines as $q$ gets bigger). When the AVC curve is at its minimum, AVC' equals zero, hence AC' = AFC'. Since AC' is negative where AVC' is zero, AC is falling at that point, and therefore it cannot yet be at its minimum.

Marginal cost is the change in total cost that is brought about when there is a unit change of quantity (for example, quantity of output). When one more unit of output is produced, total cost increases. This increase has two parts: the amount it costs to produce the new unit, and the effect that production of the new unit has on the costs of producing the amount that used to be produced. Suppose that when 20 units are produced per period the average cost—the amount each unit costs—is $5 and that when the rate of production is increased to 21 per period each unit (including the 21st unit) costs $6. What does marginal cost equal? In other words, by how much does total cost go up when the production rate is increased from 20 per period to 21 per period? Total costs before were $5 times 20 units, which equals $100. Total costs now will be $6 times 21 units, or $126. The increase in cost is $126 − $100 = $26. This figure could also be calculated in the following way. When the output rate is increased to 21 an additional unit is produced which itself costs $6. In addition, each of the first 20 units per period now costs $1 more than before, so there is a further $1 times 20 units increase in cost. The total increase in cost—the marginal cost— will be $6 + $20 = $26. The formula for marginal cost in terms of average cost is

$$MC = \quad MC = AC + \Delta AC \cdot q,$$

where $\Delta AC$ is the change of average cost when one more is produced, $q$ is the original amount produced, and AC is the new average cost when the additional unit is produced. This formula corresponds to the one we used in the previous chapter for the marginal product of labor in terms of the average product of labor.

## Two Roads: The Social Function of Private Property[2]

In the original edition of *The Economics of Welfare* (1918), A. C. Pigou claimed he could show that if transactors are left free to choose the extent to which they invest in particular industries there will always be an overinvestment (from "society's" point of view) in those industries that exhibit increasing average costs. To illustrate his proposition he constructed an example of two roads that connected two localities. One road was paved but narrow. As long as there were not too many cars on this road the time each traveler would have to spend driving between the two localities—the average cost in units of time— would be less than the time required on the second road. This second road was unpaved but extremely broad—so broad, in fact, that no matter how many cars were on it, it would not become congested. The time

each traveler would have to spend in transit between the two localities on this second road was greater than the amount required on the first road as long as there were not too many travelers on the first road. The first road, because it was narrow, could become congested, so that if too many travelers elected to travel on it the time spent by each traveler would exceed the amount of time he would have to spend if he elected to travel on the unpaved broad road.

In Figure 5-4 the vertical axis in each diagram represents time spent in transit between the two localities while the horizontal axis measures the number of travelers ($T$) on the road. The time spent by each individual on Road A would be $OJ$ hours as long as no more that $OL$ travelers are on the road at one time. The curve labeled $AC_A$ shows what happens to the time that each traveler must spend in transit on Road A as the number of travelers increases. If more than $OL$ travelers are on the road the time spent by each traveler increases. For example, if $OF$ travelers are on the road the time spent by each one will be $FH$ hours, and if $OC$ travelers are on the road the time each will spend in transit will be $CD$ hours. The curve labeled $MC_A$ depicts what happens to the total time spent in travel (adding all individuals' travel times together) as increasing numbers of travelers use the road. As long as there are no more than $OL$ travelers on the road, when an additional person uses the road the total time spent in travel on the road goes up only by the amount that that person spends in transit. If $OF - 1$ people are already using the road and an additional person uses it, the time each will spend in travel will become $FH$ hours. However, total time spent on the road (adding all individual times together) will increase by $FG$ hours. This is because, as the additional person comes on the road, he increases the transit time spent by each person. Each person had a transit time of less than $FH$ hours per trip before the new person used the road; now each has a transit time of $FH$ hours. The increase in the total transit time equals the time spent by the additional person plus the extra time spent by all the other travelers:

[2]This section is based on F. H. Knight, "Some Fallacies in the Interpretation of Social Cost," reprinted in Stigler and Boulding, *Readings in Price Theory* (Homewood, Ill.: Richard D. Irwin, 1952).

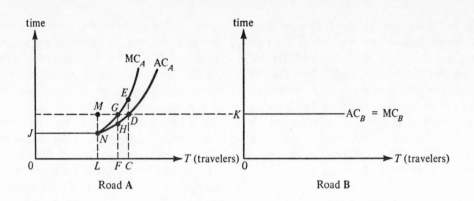

**Figure 5-4.**
Marginal and average time costs.

$$MC_A = AC_A + \Delta AC_A \cdot T,$$

where $\Delta AC_A$ is the increase in transit time for each traveler, $T$ is the original number of travelers, and $AC_A$ is the new transit time for each traveler when the new traveler uses the road. Over the range 0 to $L$ average transit time neither increases nor decreases, so marginal transit time equals average transit time. Beyond $0L$, travelers' average transit time on Road **A** increases, so marginal transit time is above average transit time. On Road **B** average transit time is constant, hence marginal transit time always equals average transit time. No matter how many travelers use Road **B**, when an additional one uses the road the increase in the total time spent on the road merely equals the time spent by the additional traveler.

Now suppose that travelers were free to choose which road to use. Individual travelers would elect to travel on Road **A** until $0C$ travelers were on the road. If fewer travelers than that were on Road **A**, the transit time per trip on Road **A** would be less than the transit time per trip on Road **B**. Each new traveler would choose Road **A** until this difference in transit times no longer existed. However, if a dictator could tell people which road to use, he could reduce the total time spent in travel between the two localities. (The total time spent in travel between the two localities is the sum of the individual times spent on Road **A** plus the sum of the individual times spent on Road **B**.) When $0C$ travelers use Road **A**, the marginal transit time is $CE$ hours.

That means that if one less person used Road **A**, the total time spent in transit on Road **A** would decline by $CE$ hours. That person could use Road **B** instead, and the total time spent in transit on Road **B** would increase by only $0K$ ($= CD$) hours. If a dictator ordered one person from **A** to **B**, the total time spent in transit between the two localities would decrease by $DE$ hours. From "society's" point of view (looking at the *total* time spent in travel), too many travelers will elect to use Road **A**. Free choice leads to a suboptimal use of the roads.

The suboptimal use of the roads results because when an additional person chooses to use Road **A** (beyond $0L$ travelers), he increases the transit time of everybody else on the road, *and he is not forced to take this effect into consideration when he makes his choice of the road to use.* As Professor Frank Knight pointed out in the article referred to in the last footnote, this misallocation of travelers on the two roads would be remedied if Road **A** were a privately owned toll road. (It must be privately owned because only a private owner would have sufficient incentive to search for the optimal toll to charge.)

The maximum toll the owner could charge would be an amount of money equal in value to the difference between the transit times on the two roads. This difference in the transit times ($AC_B -$ $AC_A$) depends on how many travelers use Road **A**. If $0L$ travelers use Road **A**, the maximum toll is the dollar equivalent of $MN$ hours; if $0F$ travelers use the road the maximum toll is *GH*, and if *0C* use the road the maximum toll is zero. The owner will choose the toll that maximizes the revenue he collects. (We are ignoring any costs of collecting the toll.) If he picks toll *MN*, only *0L* travelers will use the road because, if any additional travelers used it, the sum of $AC_A$ (transit time on **A**) and the toll would exceed $AC_B$ (transit time on **B**). If he charged toll *GH* and only *0L* travelers were on the road, additional travelers would be attracted to the road because the sum of the transit time on **A** and the toll would be less than the transit time on **B**. Individual travelers would pick Road **A** until the sum of the transit time on Road **A** and the toll was no longer less than the transit time on Road **B**.

When the owner lowers the toll sufficiently to attract one more traveler to the road he collects that toll (which equals $AC_B - AC_A$) from the new person. But, if *0L* or more travelers are already on the road, he will collect less revenue from the travelers who elected to use the road at the higher price. The owner will lower the toll until the amount collected from the new person ($AC_B - AC_A$) no longer exceeds the lost revenue from the other travelers. The lost revenue from the other travelers equals $\Delta AC_A \cdot T$. Thus the optimum toll occurs where $AC_B - AC_A = \Delta AC_A \cdot T$ or where $AC_A + \Delta AC_A \cdot T = AC_B$. The optimum toll is *GH* because only when *0F* travelers use Road **A** does $MC_A$ (which equals $AC_A + \Delta AC_A \cdot T$) equal $AC_B$.

If Road **A** were privately owned and a toll of *GH* were charged the allocation of travelers between the two roads would be optimal—even from "society's" point of view. If one traveler left Road **A** and used Road **B** instead, the amount by which total transit time on **A** would decrease ($MC_A = GF$) would equal the amount by which total transit time on Road **B** would increase ($MC_B = 0K$). No reallocation of travelers between the two roads would result in a reduction of total time spent in transit between the two locatlities; thus the allocation of travelers between the two roads is optimal from "society's" point of view. Since the sum of transit time on **A** and the toll equals the transit time on **B**, no indi-

vidual could make himself better off by switching roads; hence the allocation of travelers between the two roads is optimal from the individual's point of view. The imposition of the toll forces an additional traveler on Road **A** to recognize the effect he has on the transit time of his fellow travelers. *The charging of a price forces individual transactors to recognize and act on whatever "spillover" effects they have on others.* Pigou's criticism of free choice is not valid; it is instead a valid criticism of the absence of private property rights in a scarce (congestible) resource.

California freeways are congested at peak use (commute) hours precisely because the right to use them is distributed at a zero price. While no public administrator of freeway fees would have the incentive to search out the optimal fee to charge, the freeway congestion problem could be greatly ameliorated by the imposition of tolls at peak use hours. Such tolls would encourage businesses to stagger their working hours, encourage users who could just as well travel at nonpeak hours to do so, encourage greater use of car pools and buses, and eliminate the "need" for multibillion-dollar investments in fixed-track rapid transit systems which always must be subsidized out of general tax revenues.

## Long-Run Cost Curves

The expression "the long run" refers, as we said before, to a situation where the amounts of all inputs used by a given firm are variable. Long-run cost curves are relevant to a decision maker in a firm at the planning stage of the firm's operations, before any contractual obligations related to plant and equipment are incurred. The decision maker at the planning stage chooses the amount of plant and equipment to set up by identifying the combination of inputs that minimizes the cost of producing the quantity of output he wants to produce. There are no restrictions on the *availability* of any of the inputs, but each input that is used must, of course, be paid for. Long-run cost curves are also relevant to a firm's decision maker when he is dissatisfied with the amount of plant and equipment that he has. It often happens that the initial estimate of the best rate of output to produce turns out to be a bad estimate. Perhaps demand conditions change, or perhaps actual demand conditions were initially perceived incorrectly. In either case, the least-cost way to produce the new desired rate of output calls for a different amount of plant and equipment. Our derivation of long-run cost curves is based upon the identification of least-cost input combinations.

## Isocost Lines

We base our formal exposition of the theory on only two inputs, $K$ and $L$, as defined previously. Consider Figure 5-5. Suppose the firm uses the input combination represented by point $A$. That is, it uses $K_A$ of $K$ and $L_A$ of $L$. If we know the unit cost of $L$ (the wage rate, $W$) and the unit cost of $K$ (the user cost of capital, $\phi$) we can calculate the total outlay the firm must make to use that input combination. That total outlay (or total cost) will equal $WL_A + \phi K_A$. If $L_A = 20$ man-hours $K_A = 60$ machine hours, $W = \$5$, and $\phi = \$2.50$, the total cost, $C_1$, would be $\$5(20) + \$2.50(60) = \$250$. With $\$250$ the firm could secure the use of $C_1/W = \$250/\$5 = 50$ man-hours of labor services, but if it did so it would not have any money left over to acquire any capital services, so it would be at point $E$ in the figure. The firm could also use $\$250$ to purchase $C_1/\phi = \$250/\$2.50 = 100$ units of capital services and zero labor services (point $F$). These three options—points $F$, $A$, and $E$—are not the only input combinations that cost $\$250$ (or $C_1$). Each time an additional unit of $L$ is used, five additional dollars must be spent on $L$. That $\$5$ is no longer available to spend on $K$. Since each unit of $K$ cost $\$2.50$, the use of an additional $L$ means that two units less of $K$ must be used if the total outlay is to remain at $C_1$. The firm's decision maker could acquire the use of $AB$ additional units of $L$, but if he wanted to continue to spend only $C_1$ on inputs he would have to decrease his use of $K$ by $BD$

($= 2AB$). Each point on line $FE$ represents a different input combination, but all of these input combinations cost $C_1$. Line $FE$ is called an *isocost line*. (The prefix "iso" means "the same.")

Isocost lines are negatively sloped because when *larger* amounts of one input are used, *smaller* amounts of the other have to be used to keep total cost the same. Since units of $K$ are plotted on the vertical axis and units of $L$ on the horizontal axis, the slope of an isocost line is $\Delta K/\Delta L$. This is read as the number of units change in $K$ made necessary by a one-unit change in $L$—a positive number. The number of units change in $K$ per unit change in $L$ depends on the wage rate relative to the user cost of capital. In our numerical example $W$ was $\$5$ and $\phi$ was $\$2.50$; hence for every unit change in $L$ there had to be a two-unit change in $K$. The absolute value of the slope of an isocost line equals $W/\phi$.

The equation for an isocost line is easy to derive. A given isocost line refers to a specific total outlay, say $C_1$. If the wage rate equals $W_1$ and the user cost of capital equals $\phi_1$, then $C_1 = W_1L + \phi_1K$. Solving for $K$ as a function of $L$ (since $K$ is on the vertical axis in our diagrams), we get $K = C_1/\phi_1 - (W_1/\phi_1)L$. This is the equation of a straight line (since $K$ and $L$ are both to the first power) that cuts the vertical axis at $C_1/\phi_1$ (the amount of $K$ that could be acquired if zero $L$ were used) and that has a

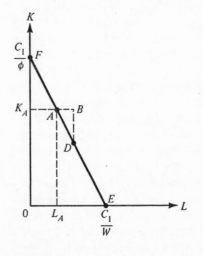

**Figure 5-5.**
Isocost line.

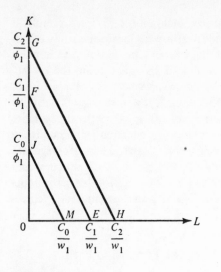

Figure 5-6.
Family of isocost lines.

increases—the entire family of isocost lines becomes steeper. The amount of $K$ that can be acquired (or must be given up) when one unit less (or more) of $L$ is paid for increases. Similarly, if the $W/\phi$ ratio declines (such as from an increase in $\phi$ or a decrease in $W$) the entire family of isocost lines becomes flatter. The amount of $K$ that can be acquired (must be given up) when one unit less (more) of $L$ is paid for decreases.

### The Optimal Input Combination

In Chapter 3 we put indifference curves together with the budget constraint to determine the optimum consumption basket. We now shall put an isoquant together with a series of isocost lines to identify the least-cost way to produce the quantity of output represented by the isoquant. The least-cost way to produce a given output rate is called the *optimal input combination* for that output rate. Consider Figure 5-7. The wage rate and the user cost of capital are specified and generate a family of isocost lines that have the slope depicted. Suppose the quantity of output produced is $q^*$ and that it is produced using the input combination represented by point $A$. Point $A$ is not the optimal input combination for $q^*$. The amount of $L$

slope equal to $-W_1/\phi_1$ (the negative of the ratio of the given wage rate to the given user cost of capital). The equation of a specific isocost line permits us to find all the combinations of $K$ and $L$ that could be acquired for the specified total outlay and the specified input prices.

Once the input prices are given (and therefore the slope of any isocost line determined) we can generate a "family" of isocost lines such as those in Figures 5-6. All the isocost lines in a given family are parallel (since the input prices are fixed), while each isocost line corresponds to a different total outlay. For input prices specified as $W_1$ and $\phi_1$ the general equation for the family of isocost lines is

$$K = \frac{C}{\phi_1} - \frac{W_1}{\phi_1}L$$

Each individual isocost line corresponds to a different value of $C$. For example, line $GH$ in the figure corresponds to $C = C_2$, while line $FE$ corresponds to $C = C_1$, a smaller total outlay. Line $JM$ corresponds to an even smaller expenditure, $C_0$. Points on a given isocost line represent input combinations that are each attainable for the same total cost—specifically the value of $C$ that corresponds to the line in question.

If the wage rate increases relative to the user cost of capital—i.e., if the ratio $W/\phi$

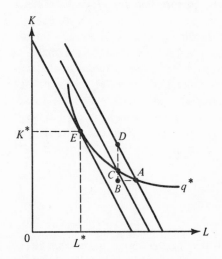

Figure 5-7.
Optimal input combination.

used could be reduced by (for example) *AB*, and the money thus saved could be used to purchase *BD* additional units of *K*. (The isocost line through point *A* tells us that.) The isoquant tells us that if we reduce the amount of *L* used by *AB* we only need *BC* additional units of *K* to continue to produce *q\**. The correct thing to do, if we wish to produce *q\** in a less expensive manner, is to cut back on the use of *L* by *AB* units, acquire *BC* units of *K*, and save the money that could be used to purchase the *CD* units of *K* we don't need. If we did so we would be at point *C* on the *q\** isoquant and on a lower isocost line. The isocost line through point *C* involves less total cost than the one through point *A*. But we shouldn't stop there, for it continues to be the case that the amount of *K* we *could* buy with the money that we save per unit decrease in our use of *L* (the slope of the isocost lines) is greater than the amount of *K* we *must* buy in order to continue to produce *q\** (the slope of the isoquant). We should continue to move up along the *q\** isoquant, getting onto lower and lower isocost lines, for as long as we can. We will have exhausted all oportunities to do so when we have reached point *E* on the *q\** isoquant. The optimal input combination for *q\**, given the specified input prices, is *K\** of *K* and *L\** of *L*. At point *E* the slope of the isoquant equals the slope of the family of isocost lines and we are on the lowest isocost line that touches the isoquant (i.e., that permits *q\** to be produced). Since the slope of an isoquant at a given point is the ratio of the marginal product of labor at that point to the marginal product of capital at the point (see Chapter 4), and since the slope of an isocost line is the ratio of the given wage rate to the given user cost of capital, at the optimal input combination

$$\frac{W}{\phi} = \frac{MP_L}{MP_K} \, .$$

If the specified input prices were different the family of isocost lines in Figure 5-7 would have a different slope, and thus point *E* would no longer be the optimum

input combination for *q\**. For example, if the *W/ϕ* ratio were lower the family of isocost lines would be flatter and a point down and to the right along the *q\** isoquant would become the optimum input combination. A lower wage rate relative to the user cost of capital means that a more labor-intensive production technique is the optimal technique, while a higher wage rate relative to the user cost of capital would mean that a more capital-intensive production technique would be employed to produce *q\**.

## The Expansion Path

Once input prices (and therefore the slope of the family of isocost lines) are specified we can identify the optimum combination for each output rate. In Figure 5-8 we suppose that the input prices are such that the isocost lines have the slope of line *AB*. Each output rate is represented by an isoquant (only three output rates are indicated in the diagram) and there is one point on each isoquant to which an isocost line is tangent. To find these tangency points, imagine pushing line *AB* in a northeasterly direction while maintaining its slope. As it moves it will hit isoquants that represent successively higher output rates. It hits (is tangent to) isoquant $q_0$ at point $E_0$, isoquant $q_1$ at point $E_1$, and isoquant $q_2$ at point $E_2$. Points $E_0$, $E_1$, and $E_2$ are therefore the optimum in-

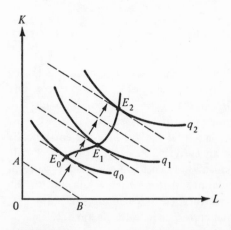

**Figure 5-8.**
Expansion path.

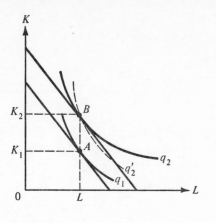

$K$

$K_2$ — — — $B$

$K_1$ — — — $A$

$q_2'$   $q_2$

$q_1$

$0$        $L$        $L$

**Figure 5-9.**
Positive slope of expansion path.

put combinations for output rates $q_0$, $q_1$, and $q_2$, respectively. A line which connects all of these optimum input combinations is called an *expansion path*. We can see from inspection of Figure 5-8 that such a line need not be a straight line, but it must have a positive slope as long as an increase of one input causes the marginal product of the other one to increase.

Consider Figure 5-9. If the optimum input combination for output $q_2$ (point $B$) were directly above the optimum input combination for $q_1$ (point $A$), the same amount of $L$ would be indicated for each output rate. The slope of an isoquant at a specific point is the ratio of the marginal product of labor at that point to the marginal product of capital at the point. For both point $A$ and point $B$ to be on the expansion path, isoquant $q_2$ at point $B$ must have the same slope as isoquant $q_1$ at point $A$. (The isocost lines are parallel, and curves tangent to parallel lines must themselves be parallel at the points of tangency.) But it is logically impossible for isoquant $q_2$ at point $B$ to be parallel to isoquant $q_1$ at point $A$. The slope of isoquant $q_2$ at point $B$ equals $MP_L$ at point $B$ divided by $MP_K$ at point $B$. (Notice that point $B$ involves the same amount of $L$ as point $A$ but more $K$ than point $A$.) The slope of isoquant $q_1$ at point $A$ equals $MP_L$ at point $A$ divided by $MP_K$ at point $A$. In the previous chapter we saw that as the amount of $K$ is increased while the amount of $L$ is held constant, $MP_L$ increases and $MP_K$ decreases. Thus $MP_L$ at point $B$ is larger than

$MP_L$ at point $A$, and $MP_K$ at point $B$ is smaller than $MP_K$ at point $A$. It follows that the slope of isoquant $q_2$ at point $B$ must be bigger (in absolute value) than the slope of isoquant $q_1$ at point $A$. The isoquant for $q_2$ must look something like the dashed isoquant labeled $q_2'$, and a tangency between an isoquant and the isocost line through point $B$ must be northeast of point $A$. Thus an expansion path cannot be vertical. A similar set of considerations reveals that an expansion path cannot be horizontal. (You can test your understanding of this argument by seeing if you can construct a similar argument for the horizontal case.) The proposition that an expansion path must have a positive slope means that if there is an increase in the desired rate of output, more of both inputs will be used (in the long run) to produce the additional output.

## The Long-Run Average Cost Curve

Suppose the expansion path that exists with specified input prices $W_1$ and $\phi_1$ is $0E$ in panel **A** of Figure 5-10. The optimal input combination for $q_1$ would be $K_1$ and $L_1$. This means that the least total cost that the firm could get by with if it produced $q_1$ would be $W_1 L_1 + \phi_1 K_1$. The average cost would be this total divided by $q_1$. Let's use $c_1$ to stand for the average cost when output is $q_1$ and the optimal input combination is being used to produce $q_1$. Panel **B** of the figure measures this long-run average cost (LAC) on the vertical axis and the output rate on the horizontal axis. Now suppose we have the case of constant returns to scale, so that if we double both inputs (move from $E_1$ to $E_2$ along the expansion path) we will double the output rate. In this case $q_2$ will equal $2q_1$. The least total cost of producing $q_2$ will be $W_1(2L_1) + \phi_1(2K_1)$, which is exactly double the least total cost of producing $q_1$. Since $q_2 = 2q_1$ the least average cost (i.e., long-run average cost) possible when producing $q_2$ is the same as the long-run average cost when producing $q_1$. The long-run average cost curve would be horizontal over the range $q_1$ to $q_2$ (which in this case

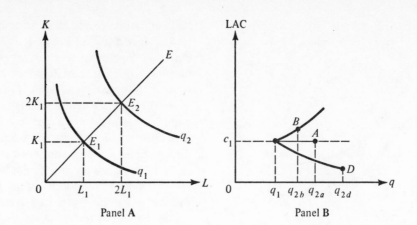

**Figure 5-10.**
Expansion path and long-run average cost.

appears as $q_{2a}$ in panel **B**).

However, suppose that instead of constant returns to scale we have decreasing returns to scale.[3] That means that when we double our inputs we less than double the output. In this case $q_2$ is an amount less than $2q_1$ (it appears as $q_{2b}$ in panel **B**). We have doubled our inputs and the input prices haven't changed; therefore we have doubled our total cost. But we have less than doubled the output, so the long-run average cost of producing $q_2$ is higher than the long-run average cost of producing $q_1$. The long-run average cost curve rises over the range $q_1$ to $q_2$ (which appears as $q_{2b}$ in panel **B**).

The third possibility is that we have increasing returns to scale, so that when we double our inputs we will more than double the output. In this case $q_2$ will be larger than $2q_1$ (it appears as $q_{2d}$ in panel **B**). Again we have incurred a total cost that is double the total cost of producing $q_1$, but now the result is a more than doubled output. Long-run average costs decline over the range $q_1$ to $q_2$ for this case.

Take special note of the fact that when we talk about long-run average cost at a specified output we mean the *least possible*

average cost of producing that output. Each point on a long-run average cost curve refers to a point on the expansion path. All points on an expansion path are points of optimum (i.e., *least-cost*) input combinations. As we move along an expansion path we change *both* inputs; hence we refer to this least average cost as the long-run average cost.

In the previous chapter we said it is likely that over the initial ranges of output we would encounter increasing returns to scale (declining long-run average costs) because of the possibility of changing the characteristics of some of the inputs we use as well as their amounts. The example we used was the automobile plant that used a custom workshop technique for small output rates but, for larger output rates, an assembly line that uses different types of machinery and permits specialization and division of labor. We also said that as the firm gets bigger and bigger (produces increasing quantities of output with optimal input combinations), it probably will become increasingly difficult to manage and it will be increasingly difficult to ensure that all operations are executed in the least-cost way. Thus we expect to eventually encounter decreasing returns to scale (rising long-run average costs). The elongated "U" shaped long-run average cost curve in panel **A** of Figure 5-11 depicts all of these considerations. Over the range of output from 0 to $q_1$ average costs fall, depicting the gains made possible by using large-scale pro-

---

[3]It can be shown that all homogeneous production functions (see footnote 4 in the previous chapter), no matter what the degree, generate straight line expansion paths. Thus the linear expansion path in panel A of Figure 5-10 can be used to discuss all three cases of returns to scale.

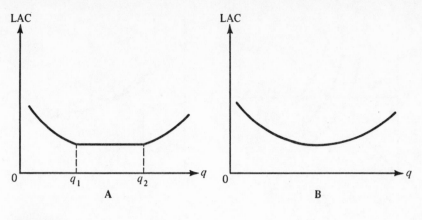

**Figure 5-11.**
Long-run average cost curves.

duction techniques which involve specialization and division of labor. From $q_1$ to $q_2$ average cost is constant, indicating that any advantages of large-scale production are offset by decreasing returns due to the difficulties of managing a large-scale enterprise. Beyond $q_2$ the difficulties of management become so great that they offset any further advantages from using large-scale equipment and further specialization and division of labor. A number of empirical studies have been done which indicate that long-run average cost curves actually look like the one drawn in panel **A**, and that most firms operate in the horizontal portion of the long-run average cost curve, so that *experienced* long-run average cost curves apear to be "L" shaped.[4] The smooth, "U" shaped, long-run average cost curve drawn in panel **B** of Figure 5-11 is the one that has traditionally been used in textbook expositions of economic theory. We shall use both types of long-run average cost curves in this text.

## The Relationship between Long-Run and Short-Run Average Costs

At a given point in time a firm will have a specific plant and a specific amount of equipment it may use. The average cost it experiences with that plant and equipment

is what we have called short-run average cost, for the term "short run" refers to a fixed amount of capital services. The firm's decision maker may or may not be happy with the amount of $K$ that he has. He will be happy with it if, and only if, it is the amount that is indicated by the optimal input combination for his desired rate of output. If that is the case, the experienced average cost will be a point on the long-run average cost curve as well as on the short-run average cost curve. All points on the long-run average cost curve correspond to optimal input combinations for each output rate. The short-run average cost curve depicts what happens to actual average cost, given the amount of $K$ actually available. Experienced (or actual) average cost is always read off the short-run average cost curve, but if the amount of $K$ the firm has is just right for the output rate it is producing, actual average cost will also be a point on the long-run average cost curve.

Consider Figure 5-12. Panel **A** is an isoquant expansion path diagram, and panel **B** depicts both short-run and long-run average cost as a function of the quantity of output produced. Suppose that over the output range $q_0$ to $q_2$ there are increasing returns to scale. That means that as the firm moves along its expansion path, $OE$, from point $F$, to point $A$, to point $C$ in panel **A**, long-run average cost declines from point $F$, to point $A$, to point $C$ in panel **B**. Each point along the expansion path and each point along the long-run average cost curve (LAC) refers to a different

[4]See A. A. Walters, "Production and Cost Functions," *Econometrica* (January 1963).

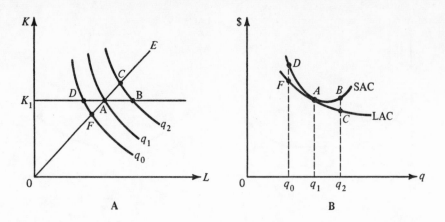

**Figure 5-12.**
Long-run and short-run average costs—increasing returns to scale.

amount of $K$. Suppose the amount of $K$ that the firm actually has is $K_1$ in panel **A**. That amount of $K$ is *just right* for output $q_1$. That is, if the firm desired to produce at the rate $q_1$ for a prolonged period of time it would seek to employ the optimal input combination for $q_1$. The optimal input combination for $q_1$ is represented by point $A$ in panel **A**, and it involves $K_1$ units of $K$.

If the firm produced $q_2$ while it had only $K_1$ units of $K$, it would use the input combination represented by point $B$ in panel **A**. The least-cost way to produce $q_2$ is with the input combination represented by point $C$ in panel **A**, but that calls for more $K$ than the firm now has. If point $C$ in panel **A** were attainable, the average cost when $q_2$ is produced would be that indicated by point $C$ in panel **B**. This is the least average cost possible when $q_2$ units are produced. Since the firm must be at point $B$ in panel **A** to produce $q_2$, it will incur an actual average cost higher than this least average cost. The average cost actually incurred will be that indicated by point $B$ on the short-run average cost curve (SAC) in panel **B**. This SAC curve corresponds to the AC curve of Figure 5-3.

Suppose the firm produced quantity $q_0$ with a scale of plant represented by $K_1$. We can see in panel **A** that the least-cost way to produce quantity $q_0$ is with the input combination represented by point $F$ (point $F$ is on the expansion path). This calls for less $K$ than $K_1$, and thus it seems that the

firm would use this input combination. (After all, the firm doesn't have to use all of the available plant and equipment. It cannot use more, but it can use less.) However, the firm must pay for all $K_1$ units of $K$ whether it uses them or not. Point $F$ in panel **A** is the least-cost way to produce $q_0$ only if the firm has no prior commitment to pay for a larger amount of $K$ than that indicated by point $F$. Since $K_1$ units must be paid for whether they are used or not, the firm will produce $q_0$ using the input combination represented by point $D$ in panel **A**. This involves less $L$ than point $F$ and the same *expenditure* on $K$ as would be necessary at point $F$. If the firm had no prior commitments to pay for any specific amount of $K$, it would choose input combination $F$ in panel **A** and incur average costs indicated by point $F$ in panel **B**. All points on the long-run average cost curve correspond to points on the expansion path. Since $q_0$ is actually produced using input combination $D$ in panel **A**, the average cost actually incurred will be that indicated by point $D$ in panel **B**. The short-run average cost curve depicts *actual* average cost given that no more than $K_1$ of $K$ can be obtained and at least $K_1$ of $K$ must be paid for.

The amount of $K$ the firm has at a given point in time is just right for some specific output rate—$q_1$ in the example we have been discussing. For that output rate, short-run average cost and long-run average cost are equal. For any other output rate, short-run average cost must be greater than long-run average cost, since long-run average cost is defined as the *least possible* average cost for each output rate. The SAC and LAC curves are tangent at the $q$ for which the $K$ the firm has is just right.

The least possible average cost is attainable only if there are no constraints on the availability of either of the inputs and if there are no prior commitments to pay for a specific amount of either input. For this reason the long-run average cost curve is sometimes called the *planning* curve. It represents the average cost attainable at the planning stage of the firm's decision making, before any commitments have been made in regard to any inputs. Plant and equipment represented by $K_1$ of $K$ in Figure 5-12 would be set up only if at the planning stage the firm's decision maker thought that $q_1$ would be his desired rate of output for a prolonged period of time. If after this plant and equipment are set up it turns out that the decision maker misjudged the market and his desired output is changed to $q_2$ (for example), he will begin to alter his scale of plant to the one that is just right for $q_2$. He will, in this case, enlarge his scale of plant to the amount of $K$ indicated by point $C$ in panel **A**. When he has accomplished this, the short-run average cost curve he actually faces will be one that has the usual "U" shape but is tangent to the long-run average cost curve at point $C$ in panel **B**.

Panel **A** in Figure 5-12 could just as easily represent constant or decreasing returns to scale as increasing returns to scale. Let's suppose that it represents constant returns to scale. In that case, the long-run average cost curve would be a horizontal line over the relevant output range. Since the firm has $K_1$ units of $K$, it will experience actual average costs equal to the long-run average cost only at output rate $q_1$. Panel **A** of Figure 5-13 depicts this case. The short-run average cost curve has its usual "U" shape, and it is tangent to the long-run average cost curve at $q_1$—the output for which the capital that the firm has is just right. If $q_2$ were produced with $K_1$ of $K$, the actual average cost would be that indicated by point $B$, and if $q_0$ were produced with $K_1$ of $K$ the actual average cost would be that indicated by point $D$. Points $F$ and $C$ are attainable only if the optimal input combination is used (and paid for) to produce $q_0$ and $q_2$ respectively.

Panel **B** of Figure 5-13 depicts the case of decreasing returns to scale. Here again all of the points of the LAC curve are attainable if, and only if, the respective optimal input combinations are used to produce each output rate. Since the amount of $K$ the firm has (and must pay for) is just right for output $q_1$ only, the SAC and the LAC curves are tangent at output rate $q_1$. The actual average cost of producing any output other than $q_1$ is read off the SAC curve—the SAC curve that exists when plant and equipment are held fixed at $K_1$ units of $K$.

Figure 5-14 depicts a "U" shaped long-run average cost curve. First there are

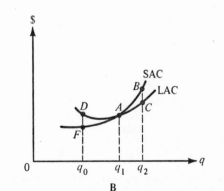

**Figure 5-13.**
Constant and decreasing returns to scale.

increasing, then constant, then decreasing, returns to scale. There is a least-cost way to produce each output rate. The LAC curve depicts what average cost would be for each output rate if the optimal input combination were used for each output rate. If the firm has the amount of $K$ that is just right for output rate $q_1$, experienced average cost will be $q_1A$, and the existing short-run average cost curve will be $SAC_1$. With a scale of plant that is just right for $q_1$, if $q_2$ were produced, actual average cost would be $q_2B$. This is less than $q_1A$, but it is more than $q_2C$. $q_2C$ is the least average cost of producing $q_2$, and it is not attainable because the firm does not have the amount of $K$ that is just right for $q_2$. Notice that from $q_1$ to $q_2$ actual or short-run average cost declines. Since $LAC$ declines at the point where $SAC_1$ is tangent to it, $SAC_1$ must also decline at the same point. Even though the LAC curve depicts the least average cost for each $q$, it is *not* made up of the minimum points of SAC curves. The short-run average cost for $q_2$ is lower that the short-run average cost for $q_1$, but it is not the least average cost possible for $q_2$. If the decision maker in the firm thought his desired output rate would be $q_2$ for a prolonged period of time he would alter his scale of plant to that that is just right for output rate $q_2$. He would then confront a different short-run average cost curve—the one (not shown) that is tangent to LAC at point $C$.

If the firm had the amount of $K$ that is just right for output rate $q_3$, the short-run average cost curve that would exist would be $SAC_3$. This SAC curve is tangent to the LAC curve at its own minimum point, but this is only because $q_3$ is the output rate for which LAC is minimum. This is not true for any other output rate.

If the firm had just the right amount of $K$ for output rate $q_5$, the existing SAC curve would be $SAC_5$. The least possible average cost when $q_5$ is produced is $q_5G$. If $q_4$ were produced with the scale of plant that was just right for $q_5$ the actual average cost would be $q_4E$. If the decision maker thought he would want to produce $q_4$ for a prolonged period of time, he would construct the scale of plant that is just right for $q_4$, and thus he would incur an average cost equal to $q_4F$. There would be a new short-run average cost curve (not shown) that would be tangent to LAC at point $F$.

By now you are aware of the ambiguity of the phrase "minimum average cost." Average cost has its absolute minimum value at output rate $q_3$ (Figure 5-14), but there is nothing to guarantee that a firm will always want to produce the quantity for which its long-run average costs are minimum. $q_1A$ is the minimum average cost of producing quantity $q_1$, and $q_2B$ is the minimum average cost possible for producing quantity $q_2$ when the scale of plant is just right for output rate $q_1$. When the expression "minimum average cost" is used you must be careful to sort out which "minimum" is meant.

## Capacity

The term "capacity" is frequently used in reference to a firm, though it is not so easy to define. We usually think of some upper limit on the amount of output a firm can produce. In the long run, however, since the scale of plant can be altered, there is no such upper limit. Capacity must logically be a short-run notion. The term is used with reference to a given amount of plant and equipment, but there is really no firm upper limit to the amount of output that can be produced with a given scale of plant. A firm could use increasing amounts

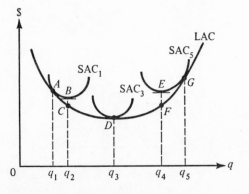

**Figure 5-14.**
Least average cost.

of variable inputs with a given scale of plant and continue to produce increasing amounts of output. Of course, if the firm did this it would encounter rapidly rising costs. The "U" shaped short-run average cost curve indicates that more and more output can be produced even though the firm operates on the upward-sloping portion of the curve.

Perhaps we should reserve the word "capacity" for that output at which a given scale of plant can be operated at minimum average cost. Look back at Figure 5-14. With this definition of capacity, and with an amount of plant and equipment that gives us the short-run average cost curve labeled $SAC_5$, capacity would be $q_4$. Presumably an entrepreneur who was operating his plant at above capacity would eventually want to increase the scale of plant. However, we know that $q_5$ (which exceeds $q_4$) is the amount of output that would make the entrepreneur happy with the scale of plant that gives him $SAC_5$ as his short-run cost curve. At $q_5$, average cost would be $q_5G$, and this is the least possible average cost of producing $q_5$. If the entrepreneur were producing at the rate $q_5$ he would have no desire to change the scale of plant at all. If he were producing at the rate $q_4$ he would want to reduce the scale of plant, thereby reducing his average cost from $q_4E$ to $q_4F$.

It seems rather silly to define capacity as the output rate that minimizes the average cost of producing with the given scale of plant when most of the time an entrepreneur will not desire to operate at the minimum point of his short-run cost curve. The definition of capacity of a given scale of plant that is used by most economists is the output rate that provides the entrepreneur with no incentive to change the scale of plant. In other words, the capacity of a given scale of plant is the output at which short-run and long-run average costs are equal. Again with reference to Figure 5-14, the capacity of the scale of plant that generates $SAC_5$ as the short-run cost curve is $q_5$. With that scale of plant, if any other output were produced for long, the entrepreneur would desire to change the scale of plant.

Earlier in this chapter we saw that there is a marginal cost curve that is related to the short-run average cost curve in the usual fashion: when the average rises the marginal is above the average, when the average declines the marginal is below the average, and when the average neither rises nor falls (e.g., at its minimum point) the marginal equals the average (see Figure 5-3). As you might expect, there is another marginal cost curve—the long-run marginal cost curve—that is related to the long-run average cost curve in the usual fashion. But it is also related to the short-run marginal cost curve in a specific manner.

Consider Figure 5-15. Suppose the scale of plant that exists is the one that is just right for output rate $q_1$. The short-run average cost curve that exists is $SAC_1$, and it is tangent to the long-run average cost curve at point $A$. The short-run marginal cost curve is labeled $SMC_1$, and it stands in the usual relationship to $SAC_1$. The long-run marginal cost curve is labeled LMC, and it too stands in the usual relationship to its average curve—LAC. At point $A$, short-run and long-run average costs are equal; therefore short-run and long-run total costs are equal. For output rates from 0 to $q_1$, SAC is bigger than LAC, and LAC is getting closer and closer to SAC. Therefore, over this same range, short-run total cost (which is increasing) must be larger than long-run total cost

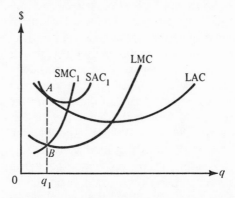

**Figure 5-15.**
Long-run and short-run marginal costs.

(which is also increasing), and long-run total cost must be getting closer and closer to short-run total cost. The rate of increase of short-run total cost (which is merely short-run marginal cost) must be less than the rate of increase of long-run total cost (which is merely long-run marginal cost) over the range from 0 to $q_1$. (How else could long-run total cost, which starts below short-run total cost, catch up to short-run total cost at $q_1$?) As output is increased beyond $q_1$, SAC is again larger than LAC, and this time they are getting farther apart. Thus short-run total cost is equal to long-run total cost at $q_1$ but gets larger and larger relative to long-run total cost for $q$'s bigger than $q_1$. Short-run marginal cost (the rate of change of short-run total cost) must exceed long-run marginal cost (the rate of change of long-run total cost) for $q$'s bigger than $q_1$. If SMC is smaller than LMC for $q$'s smaller than $q_1$ and larger than LMC for $q$'s bigger than $q_1$, it must equal LMC at $q_1$. In Figure 5-15 we show this relationship between LMC and SMC. The marginal cost curves intersect at point $B$, at the same quantity ($q_1$) for which the average cost curves are tangent. (The student should test his understanding of this line of reasoning by constructing a SAC curve that is tangent to the LAC curve in the rising portion of the LAC curve, and then constructing the relevant marginal cost curves.)

## Effects of Ceilings and Floors

Up to now we have considered two situations: no restriction on the amount of either of the inputs that can be used (the long run) and an absolutely fixed amount of one of the inputs (the short run). Suppose now that there is some minimum amount of capital services that we must use because we have contracted to pay for that amount. We will call this a "floor" on the amount of capital that must be used. Suppose also that we can obtain additional capital services, if we want them, up to some limit. We will call this upper limit on the available capital services a "ceiling." If the input prices are specified and constant,

and if the underlying production function exhibits constant returns to scale, the existence of such a ceiling and a floor will mean that the average cost curve (a kind of hybrid between a long-run curve and a short-run curve) will be shaped as an elongated "U" like the average cost curve in panel B of Figure 5-16.

Line $0E$ in panel A of Figure 5-16 is the expansion path. Since we are assuming constant returns to scale we know that if we could be on the expansion path (i.e., use the optimal input combination) for each output rate the result would be a horizontal average cost curve. Let's say that the average cost would be $0C^*$ in panel B. However, since we must pay for $K_F$ units of capital services whether we use them or not, we know that any output less than $q_2$ (the output rate for which $K_F$ is just right in panel A) will be produced using $K_F$ units of capital services and the corresponding amount of labor services. For instance, if we produced $q_1$ we would do so with input combination $D$ in panel A. Since $D$ is off the expansion path, we know that the average cost we will incur will be greater than $0C^*$. It will (for example) be $q_1D$ in panel B. Since $K_F$ is just the right amount of $K$ for $q_2$, since any amount of $K$ between $K_F$ and $K_C$ may be used, and since $K_C$ is just the right amount of $K$ for $q_4$, we know that average cost will equal $0C^*$ for output between $q_2$ and $q_4$ in panel B. Output $q_3$, for example, is represented by an isoquant that cuts the expansion path at a value of $K$ between $K_F$ and $K_C$; hence average cost when output is $q_3$ must be $0C^*$. For all outputs larger than $q_4$ we must again be off the expansion path. $K_C$ is the ceiling amount of $K$ available; hence $q_5$ (for example) must be produced using input combination $G$ rather than the optimal input combination for $q_5$. Since point $G$ in panel A is off the expansion path, average cost when $q_5$ is produced must be greater than $0C^*$. It is shown as $q_5G$ in panel B.

The effect of having both a ceiling and a floor on the amount of capital services that can be used is to make average cost first decline (for outputs between 0 and $q_2$), then remain constant (for outputs between

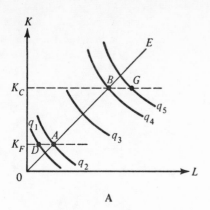

A

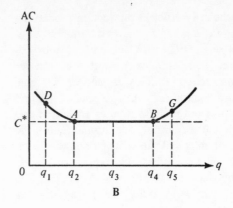

B

**Figure 5-16.**
Ceiling and floor.

$q_2$ and $q_4$), and finally rise (for outputs greater than $q_4$). From the shape of the average cost curve we can deduce the shape of the corresponding marginal cost curve. Since average cost is falling from 0 to $q_2$, marginal cost must be below average cost for this range. Since average cost is constant from $q_2$ to $q_4$, the marginal cost curve must coincide with the average cost curve for this range. Since average cost rises after $q_4$, marginal cost must be above average cost beyond $q_4$. As an exercise, draw the marginal cost curve that goes with the average cost curve in panel **B**.

We have now completed our discussion of cost theory. In the coming chapters we shall put the cost theory together with our demand theory of Chapter 3 to form the theory of the firm. But before we discuss the formal theory of the firm, we must consider the nature of the firm. The next chapter is devoted to this topic.

## Questions for Discussion

1. In September, 1974, Governor Ronald Reagan of California signed a bill extending a half-cent sales tax to subsidize the Bay Area Rapid Transit (BART) system. BART had not been able to generate enough passenger revenue to cover even its operating expenses. The reason Governor Reagan gave for his action was that if he didn't do this, BART would have to shut down and all of the money that had already been spent to construct BART would have been wasted. Did the governor use sound economic reasoning? Why not?

2. Explain why the following statement is wrong:

   Since the incremental cost of an airline flight includes only such things as fuel, crew salaries, and landing fees and excludes such things as executive salaries, insurance fees, and interest, airlines cannot be allowed to compete by offering lower fares. The fares would cover only the incremental costs; thus companies would eventually go bankrupt and leave the industry until only one or two airlines were left. (This argument is frequently used to get the government to eliminate price competition.)

3. Evaluate the following statement:

   The two-roads exercise in this chapter is inapplicable to the case of freeway congestion because there is almost never a road with the characteristics of Road **B** to serve as an alternative to a freeway.

4. Show that at any point on a long-run average cost curve, marginal cost is the wage rate divided by the marginal product of labor and is also the user cost of capital divided by the marginal product of capital.

5. Suppose that the wage rate is $3 and the user cost of capital is $4. There are four

technically efficient production processes— $P_1, P_2, P_3$, and $P_4$. $P_1$ uses 5 units of capital services ($K$) and one unit of labor services ($L$) to produce one unit of output per time period. $P_2$ uses $3K$ and $2L$ for one unit of output, $P_3$ uses $2K$ and $3L$ for one unit of output, and $P_4$ uses $1K$ and $5L$ for one unit of output. The floor amount of $K$ is 30 units and the ceiling amount of $K$ is 90 units. Construct an isoquant map with isoquants for output rates 6, 10, 15, 30, and 90. Derive and plot average costs and marginal costs.

# 6

# The Firm

We have now derived individual and market demand curves that depict the behavior of buyers in a given market. We have also derived curves that depict costs of producing a given product. These costs, of course, are incurred by the sellers of the product. But who are the sellers, and what are their objectives? Sellers are typically organizations that we call "firms," but why is most selling done by firms and not by individual transactors? What *is* a "firm" in the first place? What do decision makers in firms try to accomplish? Our demand theory says that buyers strive to "get on the highest possible indifference curve subject to their budget constraints" (i.e., to identify and purchase the basket of goods that they are most pleased with out of those their real income permits them to buy). What do decision makers in firms strive to do? In this chapter we shall address these (and other) questions.

## Why Firms Exist

Consider the assembly line at some Ford plant. Imagine that each person on that assembly line was an independent businessman who rented space under a common roof with other independent businessmen. As each piece of a car was made it would

be sold to the next person down the line so that he could "do his thing" with it. Your first reaction to such a scenario is, doubtless, that it would be chaotic. In order to manufacture a car there must be some central direction, some overall plan, or else there will be too many of some parts and not enough of others, or the parts may not fit together. But stop and think a moment. In the world as it is, there are many independent *firms* who manufacture pieces of automobiles and sell them to Ford Motor Co. These independent economic agents are directed by market prices as they make their decisions about how much to supply and whom to supply. The size and shape of the parts are specified by the buyer of the parts, who in turn has the specifications of those to whom he sells in mind when he places his own orders. Independent economic agents pay attention to those to whom they sell and from whom they buy because they must do so to carry on a profitable enterprise. Since this is true for independent firms, why couldn't we carry the logic one step farther and say that there is no need for firms to exist? Individuals could simply specialize in what they do best, buy their supplies from other individuals, and sell the finished product to still other individuals who would in turn do something to it and pass it farther along the way toward becoming the final consumer good. The number of individuals performing any given function would be determined by the demand for the product or service relative to the cost to the individual of such performance. The multitude of individual transactors would be coordinated by the price—market mechanism.

Yet in the real world we see firms; that is, we see coordination carried on without using the price mechanism. Within a firm individuals are directed by specific rules and orders, not by prices. One definition of a firm is that it is an organization within which market exchanges are eliminated and replaced with an entrepreneur who monitors and directs production.[1] Why is the price—market coordination device used for some transactions (e.g., between firms) but not for others (within firms)? In other words, why do firms exist?[2]

Much productive activity is best carried on in a *team* manner. Team production is indicated whenever total output by cooperative effort is larger than the simple sum of outputs produced by the team members each acting independently. Examples of such situations abound. More fish will be caught by a team made up of one oarsman and one netter than will be caught by each of the two working separately. More lumber will be cut by two men working a two-man saw than by each working a one-man saw. More cargo will be loaded by two workers lifting pieces together than by each lifting pieces independently. This interdependence of the productivity of individuals is a necessary, but not a sufficient, condition for the use of team production. Team production will be used if the amount by which the resulting total output exceeds the sum of independent production is larger than the cost of organizing and disciplining the team members.

In general it is not possible in team production to identify which part of the total output is attributable to any particular team member. Five men make up a basketball team, play a game, and score a total of 100 points. Can the coach say that Player *A* produced 40 points while Player *B* produced only 10 points? Not really, because Player *A* may not have sunk as many baskets as he did had it not been for the activity of Player *B* and the other three team members. The 100 points were the result of a collective, or team, effort. It is not possible to look at the total or changes in the total and see who is responsible. This is true for both positive and negative changes. Perhaps, for instance, the team could have scored more than 100 points had it not been for the almost imperceptible shirking of one or two team members. Interdependence of individual productivities means that the total is not separable into individual parts.

It is simple to measure the production of a producer who works independently. All that is produced is attributable directly to him, and his reward for that production is tied directly to the production itself. An independent producer can acquire more of what he wants only by producing more of what he produces to exchange with others. If the independent producer shirks in his effort he bears the full consequences of such shirking. Shirking means that he will produce less, and thus he will be able to claim less of other things. When it comes to production by teams of individuals, metering is no longer so easy. Since the total is not separable into parts contributed by individuals it is difficult to detect whether a given team member is shirking, or how much he is shirking. If one individual shirks, the effect is spread out over all team members. The total costs are not borne by the individual shirker alone. He bears only a fraction of the decrease in total output that results from his shirking. Each team member recognizes that everyone is better off if no one shirks, but each team member also recognizes that if he alone shirks the costs to him will be small. He can shirk and get a "free ride" on the efforts of the other team members. Since the cost to the indi-

---

[1]R.H. Coase, "The Nature of the Firm," *Economica* (1937); reprinted in Stigler and Boulding, *Readings in Price Theory* (Homewood, Ill.: Richard D. Irwin, 1952), pp. 332-335.

[2]The answer given here is that given by Armen A. Alchian and Harold Demsetz in "Production, Information Costs, and Economic Organization," *American Economic Review* (December 1972).

vidual of shirking in team production is less than the costs of shirking in independent production, the first fundamental law of demand indicates that more shirking will be done in team production.

One way that team members can cope with this problem is to hire another team member to act as a monitor of the productive activity of all team members. If he is to be effective, this monitor must have the authority to discipline other team members. He must have the authority to deal with individual shirkers without having to terminate the entire productive enterprise. He must, in other words, have the authority to tell a shirker that the team withdraws its future business from him—that he is fired. This is precisely the same thing as if I "fired" my dry cleaner because he did not give me satisfactory service. For one transactor or a group of transactors to "fire" another simply means that future business is withheld from him.

The monitor watches and directs the other team members by their common consent. We can say either that the team members "hire" the monitor or that the monitor "hires" the team members. In either case each team member has a contract with the monitor that specifies what is expected of both. The monitor is the only team member with whom each of the other team members has a contract. Team members enter into these contracts because they know that someone must meter the performance of each member if the team as a whole is going to produce the maximum possible amount net of costs. They all seek to increase their reward from their productive activity and hence they confer on the monitor the right to control and alter individual membership and performance.

*But who monitors the monitor?* After all, the monitor is just as subject to the temptation to shirk as anyone else. How can the team members be certain that the monitor is diligent in his search for ways of improving the performance of the team? One way is to make the monitor the *residual claimant* on the output of the firm. That is, each team member contracts to do a specific job for a specified salary. Whatever is left over after other costs are deducted

goes to the monitor. If the monitor gets to keep the residual of net output above what all the other team members get by contract, he will be very diligent to see that there is as much left over as possible. Since the payments to the other team members are specified by contract this means that the monitor will strive to maximize the net output that results from the team effort. Other team members are interested in achieving the maximum possible net output because they know that the larger the total net output the larger the amount that each team member can contract for in the future. It is in everybody's interest to cut down on shirking. The monitor policies the other team members to cut down on their shirking, and his desire for a larger residual claim policies his behavior against his own shirking.

The essence of the organization we call a "firm" is that there are numerous people (team members), each with a contract with the same central figure (the entrepreneur or residual claimant) whose job it is to monitor and direct activities of all inputs. It is in the interest of all people—team members as well as the monitor—to maximize the difference between total output and costs. To ensure that this is done, all team members agree to submit to the supervision and discipline of a monitor. The monitor is supervised and disciplined by making him the residual claimant—the one who keeps what is left over of the difference between total product and costs after the contractual obligations to the other team members have been met. To have a residual claim on the output of an organization is to have private property rights to that residual. Thus we see that entrepreneurs "own" firms and run them for a "profit." To "own" a productive enterprise is to control the productive activity of the inputs involved in the enterprise.

There is nothing essentially authoritarian, dictatorial, or exploitive in the relationship between "employees" and "employers." Employees "order" employers to pay them the amounts specified in the hiring contract every bit as much as employers "order" employees to abide by the provisions of the hiring contract. The employee-employer relationship is merely a contractual agreement negotiated for the mutual benefit of both. It is another example of mutually beneficial exchange.

To sum up: firms exist whenever team or cooperative effort results in a larger total output than the sum of output from individual effort, and when this difference is at least as large as the costs of organizing and disciplining team members. In any team effort it is impossible to attribute any part of total output to individual team members; hence, if a team member shirks he may not be detected. Since the probability of detection is lowered, and the consequences of the shirking are visited on all team members rather than concentrated on the shirker, more shirking will be done than would be the case if the individual worked independently to produce something. Each team member recognizes that everyone would be better off if no shirking were done, but each also recognizes that if he alone shirks the cost will be spread out over the whole team and he will not suffer too much. Each team member is tempted, therefore, to get a "free ride" on the effort of the other team members. Since all team members recognize this danger they agree to have one team member specialize in seeing to it that no team member becomes such a "free rider." In order to ensure that the monitor himself is diligent, the other team members agree to work for a specified reward and allow the monitor to keep whatever is left over. They each, in other words, contract to sell their services for a *wage* to a person whose reward we call a *profit*.[3]

As W. H. Hutt has pointed out in an analysis that somewhat anticipates that of Alchian and Demsetz (*The Strike-Threat*

[3]In Chapter 7 we shall see that economists reserve the word "profit" for a residual claim that represents a rate of return to the owner of a firm in excess of what, on average, he could earn from other investments. Since in order to induce an owner to set up and operate a particular firm he must earn at least this average rate of return, the average residual claim is actually a *cost* of operation of the firm—without at least an average residual claim the owner would not for long continue to operate the firm.

*System*, Arlington House, 1973, Chapter 6), the standard employer-employee taxonomy is very misleading. It inculcates an image of "workers" and "managers" as antagonists rather than as complementary team members. *Consumers* are the actual employers of both "workers" and "managers." And consumers are ruthless, authoritarian employers. They lay off or fire whole teams with abandon as they decide whether or not to purchase the output of given firms. Since the "owners" of firms are the residual claimants they are much more vulnerable to the whims of the consumer—employer than the "workers" who are the *contractual claimants*. The contractual claimants are shielded from the exigencies of demand in the short run because contractual payments must be made no matter what happens to the size of the residual claims. In the long run, as long as there are no barriers to mobility (such as closed shops), workers can seek out alternative hiring contracts which will again provide them with the protection of contractual claims. Residual claims, on the other hand, fluctuate up and down immediately as consumers pass judgment on the prices and qualities of products. Residual claimants do not have the buffer provided by contractual claims. In Hutt's analysis, unlike the Alchian-Demsetz analysis, it is the high degree of risk faced by the residual claimants that accounts for the fact that they are the central figures that "control" their respective firms. In order to get a residual claimant to bear the risk it is necessary for the other team members to allow him to monitor their performance against shirking.

## The Objectives of Private Firms

Our discussion of the nature of a firm indicates that what the owner-entrepreneur-monitor-decision maker in a firm tries to maximize is the size of the residual claim—i.e., profit. Profit maximization is the keystone of the theory of the firm just as satisfaction maximization is the keystone of demand theory. In the next three chapters we shall consider a number of topics that have to do with how firms respond to various changes in cost and demand. Our basic procedure will be to discover what kind of response will maximize the firm's profit, and to predict that that response will be the one chosen by the firm's decision makers.

It is frequently asserted that profit maximization, while an accurate description of the goal of a small owner-managed firm, is not an accurate description of the goals of the managers of large corporations. The managers of large corporations are not the owners of the firms. They often work for salaries (and sometimes bonuses and stock options) rather than a residual claim. Salaries are, it is asserted, related to the size of a firm's operations (its total sales) or to the share of a given market that is held by the firm. Therefore, managements will attempt to maximize sales subject to the constraint that they make enough profit to keep the stockholders happy.[4]

To this two responses can be made. First, there exists a competitive (rivalrous) market in managers. The existing management of any firm constantly faces the possibility that some other management team may convince the stockholders that they can make more profit for the firm and hence larger dividends for the stockholders. If the existing management personnel spend too many resources on fancily decorated offices, thick carpets, pretty secretaries, and other emoluments at the expense of profit for the stockholders, they can expect to have to search for alternative employment. They can get away with some such behavior because of the costs that stockholders must incur to detect and correct it. But if the sacrifice of profit exceeds these costs, management is in trouble. Similarly the sacrifice of profit for the sake of sales cannot be carried on with abandon. A loss of profit smaller than the costs of detecting the behavior is all that management can get away with.

Secondly, not only must existing stockholders be kept happy, but *potential* stockholders must also be considered. In Chapter 11 we shall see that the price of a firm's common stock is tied to the stream of returns (dividends) that a stockholder can expect to receive from ownership of the stock. The price of a firm's common stock depends on the "present value" of that stream of payments. If current management is not maximizing long-run profits, the current price of the firm's common stock will be less than it otherwise would be. The stock would be "undervalued" relative to what it could be if the existing management were tossed out and replaced with a management team that *would* maximize long-run profit. In common usage, the corporation would be "ripe for a takeover bid." Other corporations or a group of individual investors would see a chance to purchase the common stock at its depressed price, install a new management team that will maximize profits, and later sell the stock at its full-valued price. This opportunity for capital gains serves as an effective policeman against shirking by nonowner managers.

It is frequently asserted that because the 200 largest corporations own an increasing share of total manufacturing assets, the American economy is becoming less and less competitive. Actually such data do not mean any such thing. Contrast two situations. There are 1,000 independent firms, each one being the single seller in one of 1,000 separate markets, and there are 200 independent firms, each one selling in *each* of 1,000 separate markets. Clearly the second scenario indicates more rivalrous behavior in pursuit of satisfied customers than does the first. Many of the 200 largest corporations are conglomerates—firms that sell in many unrelated markets at the same time. These conglomerates are formed by perceptive individuals who are constantly on the lookout for undervalued stock to purchase. The threat of being taken over by a conglomerate serves as an effective brake on nonprofit-maximizing behavior of managers.

## Market Structure

Our discussion of the theory of the firm in subsequent chapters will be constructed

---

[4]See William J. Baumol, *Economic Theory and Operations Analysis*, 2nd ed. (Englewood Cliffs, N. J.: Prentice Hall, 1965), Chap. 13.

on the distinction between two kinds of firms: *price takers* and *price searchers*. A firm is a *price taker* if the existing market price for the kind of product it produces does not appreciably change when the firm supplies either more or less of the product. A price-taker market is one in which no firm acting by itself can change the going price for a product by a significant amount. Whether the firm produces zero of the product or produces as much as its "capacity"[5] will allow, the going rate for the product will not change appreciably. A firm is a *price searcher* if it makes up a large enough portion of the total supply of a product type to affect the market clearing price of that product type by its decision to produce more or less.

This is not the usual classification of market structures. Most texts discuss four market types: perfect competition, monopolistic competition, oligopoly, and monopoly. A perfectly competitive market is said to exist when:

1. There are many buyers and sellers of each product (or service), so many that, in equilibrium, each buyer can buy all he wants at the going price, and each seller can sell all he wants at the going price.

2. All buyers and all sellers are fully informed about each other's prices and about market conditions in general, and become instantly aware of any changes in prices and market conditions.

3. All sellers in a given market produce a homogeneous product. That is, each seller produces a product that is indistinguishable (to buyers) from the product produced by every other seller in the same market.

4. Resources are free to enter or to leave any market with no impediments at all (i.e., at zero cost).

Monopoly is the polar extreme of perfect competition. There is only one seller

of the product instead of a multitude of sellers of a given (homogeneous) product. A monopolist may maintain his monopoly position because the profit rate that he makes is no higher than the profit rate that could on average be made in other markets. In this case there is nothing to attract rival entrepreneurs onto the scene. If the monopolist makes a profit rate that is above what on average can be earned in alternative pursuits, rival entrepreneurs will be induced to set up shop and sell the same, or almost the same, product. There are three exceptions to this rule. If the monopolist's average cost curve lies below the *market* demand curve over almost the entire range of output that would be bought, even at very low product prices, the monopolist is said to be a "natural monopolist." Public utilities are an example of this case, and we shall discuss them in Chapter 8. Another way that rival entrepreneurs can be prevented from setting up competing enterprises in the face of above-average profit rates being earned by an existing monopolist is if the existing monopolist can somehow get Congress or some state legislature to create legal barriers to market entry. The third way that rival entrepreneurs can be kept out is if the existing monopolist owns the only source of a vital raw material or other resource used in the production process. This barrier to entry is usually temporary, because alternative sources of raw materials are eventually discovered and advances in technology make the use of substitute resources possible. In any event, in Chapter 8 we shall discuss these actual barriers to competition as well as some commonly alleged, but not actual, barriers.

Notice that in the case of perfect competition and in the case of monopoly there is no difficulty in defining the "product." Each firm in perfect competition produces the same product as all other firms in a given market, and there is only one firm and one product in the case of monopoly. If a monopolist makes an above average rate of return, most of the time rival entrepreneurs will set up shop ("enter the market") and produce a product that buyers consider to be a good substitute for the

---

[5]As defined in the previous chapter.

monopolist's product. We would like to be able to say that the rival entrepreneur would produce the same product, but in the real world firms use brand names and other devices to differentiate their products in the minds of buyers. We cannot say that Camel cigarettes are the same product as Lucky Strikes as long as buyers do not consider them to be the same.

Monopolistic competition is characterized by many sellers producing similar, but differentiated, products; oligopoly refers to the situation in which there are only "a few" sellers of similar, but differentiated, products. But since the products are different, we can say that both monopolistic competition and oligopoly are merely cases of monopoly where the demand curve faced by the monopolist seller is more price-elastic than if there were no rival entrepreneurs selling similar products. Nothing much is added to the theory of the firm by the discussion of monopolistic competition and oligopoly.

Some have claimed that monopolistic competition, like perfect competition and unlike monopoly, is characterized by many firms that in equilibrium do not make an above average rate of return. But this could just as well be said in many cases where there are only "a few" firms, because there are few effective barriers to rival entrepreneurs whose competition eliminates above-average rates of return. It does not matter whether a market is called monopolistically competitive, oligopolistic, or monopolistic; the important distinction is between open and closed markets—i.e., between markets where interlopers can and cannot enter.

The term "monopoly" is itself ambiguous. If we define the product narrowly enough, every seller could be said to be a monopolist. Farmer Jones is the only producer of Farmer Jones' wheat, even though Farmer Brown's wheat is a good substitute for it. A loaf of bread at the corner mom-and-pop grocery store is a different product from a loaf of bread at the supermarket located a mile away, especially if your car won't start. On the other hand, if the product being produced is defined broadly enough, no seller is a monopolist.

For a few years Alcoa was the only seller of aluminum in the United States. But Alcoa was not a monopolist in "building materials" or "structural metals."

Consider "perfect competition." Standard discussion of this model begins by assuming that all transactors have all the information they must have to establish a competitive equilibrium. But it is the process of market rivalry that creates and disseminates this information. Buyers find out about sellers and their terms of trade from friends and associates and, most importantly, through advertising. Advertising and attempts to build good reputations are common forms of rivalry among sellers. Sellers find out about buyers through market research and trial-and-error product differentiation, which are also common forms of rivalry among sellers. If we began our analysis with the assumption of full information there would remain no market rivalry, no market process, to analyze.[6]

Perfect competition assumes a homogeneous product. This is another example of an assumption that eliminates analysis. Some say that if a product is not homogeneous the competition in the market for that product must be "imperfect." If there are diverse types of tires, competition in the tire market must be "imperfect." Actually, if there is any imperfection it is one of *knowledge*, not of competition. Sellers acquire information about buyers' demand prices for various qualities and variations of products by constant trial-and-error experimentation with diverse qualities and variations of products—i.e., by product differentiation. Only in full equilibrium is it even remotely conceivable that only one version of a product would be found to satisfy its many independent buyers.

Buyers do not have immutable tastes and preferences which sellers must discover. Buyers acquire tastes and preferences as a result of their search for ways

---

[6]The discussion in this and the next three paragraphs follows F. A. Hayek, "The Meaning of Competition," in *Individualism and Economic Order* (Chicago: University of Chicago Press, 1948).

to improve their subjectively evaluated satisfaction or "utility"—i.e., as a result of their participation in market and non-market *processes*. Buyers' tastes and preferences are shaped by such things as education (who is *born* with an innate desire to read Shakespeare?) and advertising (who *innately knew* that a machine with the characteristics of a Volkswagon could provide so much satisfaction?).

Many take "perfect competition" to be the ideal market type—the way a decentralized, private property, voluntary exchange economy should look. No actual market looks at all like this, and because no market looks like this some conclude that a decentralized, private property, voluntary exchange economy cannot work. This is nonsense. It is the perfectly competitive model that doesn't work, not the voluntary exchange economy. Actual markets and actual market processes should be compared to the situation that would exist if there were no market rivalry rather than to a fanciful construct called "perfect competition."

In the real world all markets are characterized by *rivalrous behavior*. Indeed, according to one student of the development of economic theory (George Stigler) the meaning of the word "competition" to Adam Smith, the father of modern economics, was rivalrous behavior.[7] The currently fashionable use of "competition" to refer to a state of nonrivalrous harmony was the result of the search by many economists for the mathematical properties of a perfectly coordinated state—an economy in general equilibrium. What is "perfect" about perfect competition are its perfect mathematical properties, not its ability to help us understand real-world markets.

For these reasons we shall consider firms to be either price takers or price searchers. We shall be concerned with whether a given firm sells in an open or a closed market. The word "competition" will mean rivalrous behavior. Competition exists in all *open* markets, whether they are price-taker or price-searcher markets. A firm will be said to be a price taker when there are so many sellers of good substitutes for the product of the firm that the decision maker in the firm has practically no discretion over the price he can charge. There is a "going price" for the type of product he sells, and if he sets his price above this going price he will sell practically none of the product. A firm will be said to be a price searcher if its decision maker has a range of prices that he can charge and still sell significant amounts of his product. The higher the price he charges, the less he will sell, but he does have discretion over the price he can charge. He must, therefore, *search* for the best price to charge among the prices that he could charge. A price searcher faces a negatively sloped demand curve, and a price taker faces an almost horizontal demand curve.[8]

In the next chapter we discuss price-taker output markets (later on we shall consider input markets). Most of what we say would ordinarily be found in a chapter entitled "Perfect Competition," however, some of what we say would not be found there. For example, we shall discuss some implications of positive information costs in price-taker markets. One such implication is that advertising has a role to play in such markets; another is that market research also will be observed in such markets. Examples of price-taker markets include the housing market (both rental and owner-occupied), the market for beef and most other kinds of food, the car mechanics' market, and the restaurant market. To decide whether a given market is a price-taker market, ask yourself if the typical seller in the market is big enough to significantly affect the market price of the product or service in question by his own, and only his own, decisions and actions. If he is not, you have found a price-taker market.

---

[7]George Stigler, "Perfect Competition, Historically Contemplated," *Journal of Political Economy* (1957).

[8]In the next two chapters we shall see how to represent price takers and price searchers diagrammatically.

After the chapter on price-taker output markets we shall consider two chapters on price-searcher output markets. In most texts the material in these chapters can be found under the rubrics "Pure Monopoly," "Oligopoly," and "Monopolistic Competition." Here again, however, there will be some differences. We shall again investigate the implications of postitive information costs. Advertising will be considered a competitive, rather than a monopolistic, device. Rather than concentrating on the number of sellers in a given market, we shall emphasize the importance of the difference between open and closed markets. Examples of products sold in price-searcher markets include automobiles, steel, computers, news magazines, gasoline, and laundry detergents. To decide whether a seller is a price searcher, ask yourself if he is large enough relative to the total demand for his product type to affect its going price by his decision to supply more or less of the good. If the answer is yes, you have identified a price searcher.

## Questions for Discussion

1. Can coordination of millions of independent transactors be brought about by movements in relative prices? Each day the people in Los Angeles eat a wide variety and a large quantity of food. Who is in charge of seeing to it that the right amounts and kinds of food get to Los Angeles every day? Can you see why economists consider coordination achieved by orders and authority, as it is in firms, as a phenomenon to be explained rather than taken for granted?

2. Why can you not say that employees exploit employers by making employers bear the risk of unanticipated changes in demand? Why can you not say that employers exploit employees by making employees settle for contractual claims while employers get to keep what is left over? What does "exploit" mean?

3. Why is the employer-employee distinction useless and even misleading for purposes of economic analysis?

4. Evaluate the following statement:

    When there is a separation of management and ownership of a firm, profit maximization does not guide decision making within that firm.

5. Evaluate the following statement:

    The growth of conglomerates in the United States reduces the extent of competition within United States' markets.

6. Explain this sentence:

    The conditions that are assumed to exist in perfect competition could only be the result of market processes based on rivalry.

7. Explain the following statement:

    With positive information costs there cannot be any logical basis for a distinction between selling costs and production costs. All costs are undertaken for the purpose of selling the product.

# 7
## Price Takers

### Introduction

In Chapter 1 we defined "competition" as rivalrous behavior among transactors. In Chapter 6 we saw that it is customary to use the term "perfect competition" to refer to an ideal market type characterized by perfect information, costless resource transfers, a homogeneous product, an atomistic structure, and no rivalry. We also discussed some of the reasons why this book forsakes the usual taxonomy of market structures in favor of the price taker versus price searcher distinction. This chapter elaborates on the deficiencies of the model of perfect competition and exposits the theory of price-taker firms.

One of the most articulate critics of the model of perfect competition is F. A. Hayek. He writes:

The modern theory of competition deals almost exclusively with a state of what is called "competitive equilibrium" in which it is assumed that the data for the different individuals are fully adjusted to each other, while the problem which requires explanation is the nature of the process by which the data are thus adjusted .... Competition is by its nature a dynamic process whose essential characteristics are assumed away by the assumptions underlying static analysis ...

Nothing is solved when we assume everybody to know everything .... The real problem is rather how it can be brought about that as much of the available knowledge as possible is used. [1]

Unfortunately, although Hayek wrote this in 1946, practically no attention has yet been paid to this point. Established theory of the firm is still merely an equilibrium theory. It begins with known demand curves and known cost curves and consists of the computation of optimal (profit-maximizing) price and quantity combinations. Much of what we do in this and subsequent chapters will consist of this "Pure Logic of Choice." [2] This is necessary precisely because economists have spent so little time taking up Hayek's challenge. However, we shall drop the assumption of zero information costs, and we shall to some extent examine rivalrous behavior as the mechanism that propels the market process.

The main distinguishing characteristic of a seller who is a price taker is his small size relative to the market demand curve for

---

[1] F. A. Hayek, "The Meaning of Competition," *Individualism and Economic Order* (Chicago: University of Chicago Press, 1948), pp. 94-95.

[2] *Ibid.*, p. 93.

the product he sells. The term "atomistic" is sometimes used to describe price takers, to emphasize that they are small (relative to the market, not absolutely) and numerous. A large firm that sells many different products (a conglomerate) may be a price taker in one of the products that it sells and a price searcher in another. If a firm is a price taker in a given product, it is only one of many firms that sell the same (in the minds of buyers) product. For example, ITT is only one of many firms in the food vending machine market. When ITT acquired the Canteen vending machine operation it did not diminish the number of rival sellers of vending machine services. There were no economic reasons to force ITT to divest itself of Canteen. Since there are many sellers in a price-taker market, if any one firm raises its price above that charged by its rivals, if the prevailing price is no less than the equilibrium price (the price at which quantity supplied and quantity demanded are equal), and if buyers become aware of the price difference, that firm will lose most of its customers. Buyers simply have many alternative sellers from whom they may buy, so any one seller is constrained to charge the prevailing price. Of course, if all the separate sellers decided to raise price at the same time, each would suffer some decrease in quantity sold (market demand curves are downward sloping) but no single firm would lose most of its sales. An agreement among sellers to act in concert to restrict supply and thereby increase price is a collusive agreement. The large number of sellers in a price-taker market precludes successful collusion. With an atomistic market structure there are simply too many rivals who could undercut the price rise, and thereby capture the customers of those who increase price, to make collusion practicable.[3]

Rivalry is the discipline that one firm exercises over another, and rivalry exists in price-taker markets. When one firm doesn't go along with another firm's increase in price, the first firm is engaging in rivalrous behavior. This rivalrous behavior is effective only if buyers are aware of the price difference. One way that buyers acquire information about price differences is through advertising. Advertising is the device most commonly used to make a price taker "take" the prevailing price. Because there are so many sellers of many different goods and services it is difficult for any one advertiser to attract the attention of the public to his message. As a result advertisers resort to flamboyant tactics which appear to most of us to be totally specious. However, without advertising, buyers would find it much more costly to become aware of the alternative sellers and the alternative terms of trade that are available.

Firms that advertise hope that their efforts will create some degree of brand loyalty among buyers. If buyers believe that Brand $X$ is significantly different from Brand $Y$, the seller of Brand $X$ can more easily raise his price without losing most of his customers to Brand $Y$. In this sense advertising can be used partially to insulate a seller against his rivals. For this reason advertising is sometimes regarded as an anticompetitive device that is inconsistent with price-taker markets. Yet only if all transactors always possessed all relevant information about alternative terms of trade would advertising have no role to play in price-taker markets. For example, in any community there are many sellers of housing services. Different dwelling units (apartments and houses) provide different size packages of the homogeneous good called housing services. The larger the dwelling unit, for a given quality, the larger the package of housing services provided therein. Similarly, the better equipped the dwelling unit, for a given size, the larger the package of housing services yielded by the unit.[4] Landlords must take the prevailing price per unit of housing services that is

---

[3]However, a very large group of sellers can form an effective collusive group (cartel) if it is successful in getting government to enforce the group's rules against cheating on the collusion. We shall consider this in more detail in Chapter 9.

[4]See Edgar O. Olsen, "A Perfectly Competitive Theory of the Housing Market," *American Economic Review* (September 1969).

determined by the interaction of the many buyers and sellers of housing services.[5] Moreover, landlords must constantly advertise their existence and the particular size packages of housing services that they offer, if they are to be successful. Tenants don't know about the alternatives they face. They must search for that information, and advertising reduces the cost of that search.

It is sometimes said that in price-taker markets, because any individual seller is so small relative to the market demand for the product, any seller can sell all he wants at the prevailing price and thus there is no role for advertising to play. But a price-taker seller can sell all he wants to sell at the existing price only if that price is not higher than the equilibrium price. If the aggregate supply forthcoming at the existing price exceeds the aggregate quantity demanded at that price there must be some sellers who will not be selling all they wish to sell.[6] Equilibrium is attained only by the rivalrous behavior of transactors, and in this case advertising more favorable terms of trade is the most likely form the rivalry will take.

If at the existing price the aggregate quantity demanded exceeds the aggregate quantity supplied, the individual firms are temporarily no longer price takers. Any seller can raise his price even if his rivals do not raise theirs because his rivals are already satisfying all the demand they can handle.[7] Since price is lower than the equilibrium price, there are some buyers who have not been able to execute all their desired purchases and thus would be willing to buy some (less than before) of the good at a higher price. Sellers who become aware of this raise their prices. Other sellers will observe the success of their rivals and imitate them. This process will go on until the

equilibrium price is reached. The usual assertion that a price taker cannot charge a price higher than the existing price without losing most of his customers is only true if the existing price is not lower than the equilibrium price.

Of course if the price that exists is always the equilibrium price, there won't be any need for any sort of rivalrous behavior in price-taker markets. At the equilibrium price each seller can sell all he wants to, since aggregate quantity demanded is not less than aggregate quantity supplied. At the equilibrium price each seller knows that if he raises his price he will lose most of his customers, since there are no unsatisfied buyers who would pay a higher price rather than go without the product. The model of perfect competition assumes that all transactors possess all the information needed to establish an equilibrium, so there is no rivalry in perfect competition.

## Demand Curves

If the existing price is the equilibrium price, the demand curve faced by an individual price-taker firm is almost horizontal. Consider Figure 7-1. The top panel depicts the market demand curve (the horizontal sum of individual buyers' demand curves) for the product being produced by many price-taker firms. Suppose that initially the equilibrium price is $p_1$, the total quantity supplied and demanded is $0A$, and another price-taker firm enters the market. Any one firm (such as the new one) makes up (say) only $AB$ of the total quantity supplied to the market. Thus when the new firm enters there will be, at most, an increase of $AB$ in the quantity supplied. This increase will reduce the equilibrium price to $p_2$. ($p_2$ is the only price at which a total of $0B$ units will be demanded.) Now $AB$ is a very small distance on the horizontal scale of the top panel. We want to depict the demand curve faced by any single price taker, and if we confined ourselves to the top panel we would need a magnifying glass to see the relevant portion of the market demand curve. The bottom diagram is designed to remedy this situation. The hor-

[5]We shall elaborate on the housing market later in this chapter.

[6]Kenneth J. Arrow, "Toward a Theory of Price Adjustment," in Abramovitz, et al., *The Allocation of Economic Resources* (Stanford, Calif.: Stanford University Press, 1959), p. 46.

[7]*Ibid.*

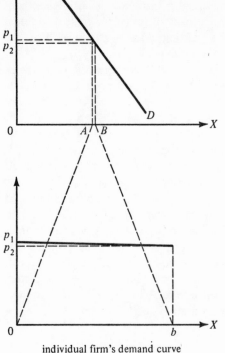

**Figure 7-1.**
Derivation of price taker's demand curve.

izontal axis of the bottom panel is distance $AB$ from the top panel stretched out like an elastic band. If any one firm decided to produce zero of the product, the equilibrium price would be $p_1$. If the same firm decided to produce as much as it is practicable for it to produce ($AB$ in the top panel and $0b$ in the bottom panel), the equilibrium price would decline to $p_2$. Thus, over the range of output that the single firm can control, its demand curve appears nearly horizontal as in the bottom panel. For all practical purposes the price taker must take a price not significantly different from $p_1$.

Actually the slope of the demand curve faced by the individual price taker is the same as the slope of the market demand curve over the relevant price range. The single seller's demand looks horizontal merely because we have stretched out the horizontal axis but have not changed the scale of the vertical (price) axis. The effect on the market clearing price of a given in-

crease in quantity is the same whether that increase in quantity comes from one firm alone or from many firms each increasing output by a few units. The slope of both the market demand curve and the individual firm's demand curve is $\Delta p/\Delta X$. The $\Delta p$ is the same in both cases, and so too is the $\Delta X$. The only difference is that the $\Delta X$ is measured on two different scales.

Although the slopes of the two demand curves are equal, the price elasticities of demand are not. In Chapter 3 we saw that the formula for the price elasticity of demand is

$$\frac{\Delta X}{\Delta p} \cdot \frac{p}{X}$$

Each of the terms in this formula would be the same for the individual seller and the market demand, except for $X$—the initial quantity. For the market the initial quantity is $0A$; for the individual seller it is zero. The price elasticity of demand for the individual seller is infinite, while the market price elasticity is finite. Another way to see this point is to recall that the definition of price elasticity is the ratio of the percentage change in quantity to the percentage change in price. The percentage change in price is the same for both the individual seller and the market. A given absolute change in quantity represents a small percentage change for the whole market, but it represents a large percentage change for the individual seller (an infinite percentage change if the individual seller originally produced zero).

## Marginal Revenue

Marginal revenue is defined as the change in total revenue collected from sales of the product when price is changed enough to cause a one-unit change in the quantity demanded. For any given market demand curve the change in price that is necessary to cause only a one-unit change in the quantity demanded will be very small. In Chapter 4 and again in Chapter 5 we saw that the marginal of any variable can be expressed in terms of the average of that variable. Here we can do the same thing again. Average revenue is total revenue $(pq)$ divided by the quantity sold $(q)$; thus average revenue is merely $p$—the price for which each unit of the commodity is sold. Each unit is sold for the same price. When an additional unit is sold the additional revenue coming in from sales will equal the price that the additional unit sells for minus any change in the total amount collected on the number of units that used to be sold. $MR = p - \Delta p \cdot q$, where MR is marginal revenue, $p$ is the price that must exist if an additional unit is to be sold per time period, $\Delta p$ is the difference between the price that existed at the old sales rate and the price that must exist if the sales rate is to be increased by one unit, and $q$ is the original sales rate. It is sometimes convenient to write this formula as

$$ p - \frac{\Delta p}{\Delta q} \cdot q. $$

This is the same as the formula above because the $\Delta q$ is one unit. The relevant change in price is always the change in price per one unit change in quantity.

The change in price per unit change in quantity $(\Delta p/\Delta q)$ is the slope of the demand curve. We have already seen that the slope of the price taker's demand curve is the same as the slope of the market demand curve. However, the individual price taker is small relative to the total demand for the product; therefore the original amount sold by an individual price taker will be tiny when compared with the original amount sold in the market as a whole. It follows that the $\Delta p/\Delta q \cdot q$ term in the formula for marginal revenue will be much larger for the market as a whole than it is for the individual price taker. In fact it is sufficiently small for an individual price taker that it is traditional to ignore it. For an individual price taker, when an additional unit is sold the addition to revenue (the marginal revenue) will almost equal the price for which the additional unit (as well as all other units) is sold. We cannot, however, ignore the difference between price and marginal revenue for the market

as a whole. For an individual price taker the tiny drop in price that is necessary to cause a one-unit increase in the quantity demanded is applied to the small quantity the price taker originally sold. The same price change must be applied to the much larger original quantity supplied by the market as a whole; thus the marginal revenue for the market as a whole is significantly lower than the new selling price. In other words, when the price is lowered sufficiently to cause a one-unit increase in the quantity sold, the resulting addition to the total revenue collected by all the price takers as a group is less than the addition to revenue of the one price taker who sells the additional unit. All the other price takers will be selling at the old rate, but at a lower price. This fact will be very important when we come to discuss cartels in Chapter 9.

## The Firm's Short-Run Supply Curve

In Chapter 5 we discussed the various short-run cost curves—those that pertain to a situation where a firm has a fixed scale of plant but uses varying amounts of labor. Two of those curves are relevant to our derivation of the firm's short-run supply curve—the marginal cost curve and the average variable cost curve. Consider Figure 7-2. Suppose the existing price for the product is $p_1$, and the decision maker in

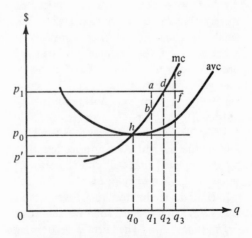

**Figure 7-2.**
Optimum quantity decision.

the firm knows that his marginal cost and average variable cost curves are in the positions indicated in the diagram. If the decision maker desires to maximize profit, he will decide to produce quantity $q_2$. The horizontal line from $p_1$ depicts the addition to revenue each time an additional unit is sold (marginal revenue). Since we are discussing price takers this is (almost) the same as the product price. The marginal cost curve indicates the addition to cost when an additional unit is produced and sold. An additional unit will be sold if the addition to revenue ($p_1$) is greater than the addition to cost (mc), because that means that profit will increase. For example, the firm's decision maker would not be content to produce and sell at the rate $q_1$ because an additional unit sold would add to revenue by $q_1 a$ (equals $p_1$) while it would increase total cost by only $q_1 b$. The addition to profit would be $ab$. If output were increased to $q_2$ from $q_1$, area $abd$ would be added to total profit. The firm's decision maker would not be content to produce and sell at the rate $q_3$ either. At $q_3$, if one *less* were produced and sold, the reduction in total cost would be $q_3 e$ while the reduction of total revenue would be only $q_3 f$. Profit would increase by $fe$ if one less were produced and sold. If production were cut to $q_2$ from $q_3$ the addition to profit would be area $def$. Profit is maximum at the quantity at which marginal cost equals the price the price taker takes.

To find the quantity supplied by an individual price-taker firm at any price, we merely find the quantity that makes marginal cost equal to that price. However, at some prices, $p'$ for example, the firm will produce zero of the product. $p'$ is below average variable cost (i.e., operating costs per unit). A firm will not produce any output if it cannot cover its variable (avoidable) costs with the revenue from the sale of the output. At any price less than $p_0$ the depicted firm will produce zero. At price $p_0$ the firm may or may not produce $q_0$. If it does, the resulting revenue ($p_0$ times $q_0$) will just equal total variable costs ($q_0 h$ times $q_0$). The firm's accounting losses will equal its fixed costs, but the firm must pay these fixed costs whether it

operates or not. Its losses are the same whether it operates or not when the price is $p_0$. For any price greater than $p_0$ the revenue collected will more than cover the variable costs; hence at least some revenue will be available to defray fixed costs. *The supply curve for an individual price-taker firm is the portion of its marginal cost curve that lies above its average variable cost curve.*

In Chapter 5 we saw that short-run marginal cost equals the wage rate divided by the marginal product of labor. Thus if the wage rate increased (and the marginal product of labor did not increase), the marginal cost curve (and therefore the firm's supply curve) would shift up, and if the wage rate decreased the marginal cost curve (and the supply curve) would shift down. The slope of the firm's supply curve depends on the relationship between the amount of labor used and the marginal product of labor. Shifts of the firm's short-run supply curve are caused by changes of the wage rate unaccompanied by compensating changes in the marginal product of labor.

## Short-Run Market Supply Curves

We have already seen that the market demand curve for a given product is derived by horizontally summing all the demand curves of individual buyers for that product. The same procedure is used to derive the market supply curve for a given product. Consider Figure 7-3. For simplicity suppose there are only two price taker firms that produce the product in question. The portion of the first firm's marginal cost curve that lies above its average variable cost curve is labeled $mc_1$. The same curve for the second firm is labeled $mc_2$. At price $p_A$ the profit-maximizing quantity for the first firm is $q_1$, and the profit-maximizing quantity for the second firm is $q_2$. Therefore at price $p_A$ the total quantity supplied is $q_T$ (equals $q_1 + q_2$). At any price below $p_B$ the first firm will produce zero because it would not be able to cover its variable costs. Therefore, the market supply curve would coincide with the

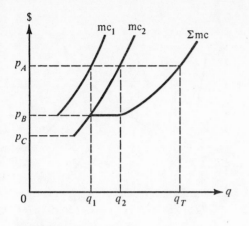

**Figure 7-3.**
Short-run market supply curve.

second firm's marginal cost curve for prices between $p_B$ and $p_C$. Below $p_C$ the second firm would produce zero; hence the market supply would be zero. If we added the quantity supplied by the first firm to the quantity supplied by the second firm at each price we would trace out the curve labeled $\Sigma$mc. (The Greek capital "sigma" means "sum.") This summed marginal cost curve is the short-run market supply curve for the product in question. Notice that although we call it the summed marginal cost curve we are *not* adding the marginal costs of the two firms together. Rather, we are adding together the quantities supplied at each price.

## Short-Run Market, Firm, and Buyer Equilibrium

For the market to be in short-run equilibrium the price must have the value at which total quantity demanded equals the total quantity supplied. For each firm to be in short-run equilibrium it must produce the quantity that makes its marginal cost equal the existing price. Figure 7-4 depicts such a situation. The summed marginal cost curve is labeled $S$. (It is the short-run market supply curve.) The market demand curve is labeled $D$. The only price at which the quantity supplied and the quantity demanded are equal is $p^*$. Each individual firm faces a nearly horizontal demand curve at price $p^*$. Given that the market-determined price is $p^*$, each firm maxi-

mizes its profit by producing the quantity that makes its marginal cost equal $p^*$. For the first firm that quantity is $q_1$, for the second firm it is $q_2$. The total quantity supplied and demanded is $q_1 + q_2$, which equals $q^*$.

For individual buyers to be in equilibrium they must be buying the quantity they want to buy at the existing price. The market demand curve in Figure 7-4 is the horizontal sum of individual buyers' demand curves. Figure 7-5 duplicates Figure 7-4 but adds the individual demand curves. (Again for simplicity we assume that there are only two buyers.) The market demand curve ($D$) is the horizontal sum of the two individual demand curves ($d^A$ and $d^B$). At the equilibrium price ($p^*$) the total quantity demanded equals the total supplied. Individual A desires to purchase $q_A$, and Individual B desires to purchase $q_B$.

$$q_A + q_B = q^*.$$

Each buyer and each seller can execute his desired transactions because the equilibrium price coordinates their individual plans.

If the price were higher than $p^*$ the quantity supplied would exceed the quantity demanded, and thus the individual firms would not be able to sell all they wanted to sell. This would induce each firm to advertise more favorable terms of trade to buyers. If the price were lower

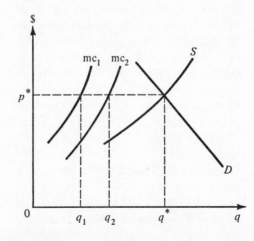

**Figure 7-4.**
Market and individual firm equilibrium.

than $p^*$ the quantity demanded would exceed the quantity supplied. This would mean that each firm could raise its price without losing its customers, since there are many buyers who cannot execute their desired purchases and would be willing to pay a higher price rather than go without the product.

## Market and Individual Adjustment to a Shift of Market Demand Curve

We have just seen that a market-determined equilibrium price coordinates the plans of many independent trans-actors—both buyers and sellers. Now we shall see how, when there is a change in market conditions, a new price can reestablish this coordination of plans. Suppose, for example, a new buyer becomes aware of the product we have been discussing and decides to purchase some of it. Figure 7-6 is like Figure 7-5 in that there are still only two firms producing the product and Mr. A and Mr. B are still buyers. When a third buyer enters the market the aggregate demand curve shifts from $D$ to $D'$. Mr. C's individual demand curve is labeled $d_C$. When we horizontally add $d_C$ to $D$ we get $D'$. The market supply curve does not shift because the same two firms are still the only sellers, and their marginal cost curves have not shifted. This increase in demand creates an excess demand (quantity demanded in excess of quantity supplied) of $RT$ at the initial equilibrium price $p^*$. How will Mr. C get any of the product? How can Messrs. A and B be induced to share with the newcomer? How can the suppliers be induced to supply more? The answer to all of these questions is the same—by an increase in price. Mr. C would rather have some of the product at a price higher than $p^*$ than go without, so he offers such a bid. Messrs. A and B also prefer to have some of the product (although less than before) at a higher price rather than go without, so they match Mr. C's bid. The higher bids induce each of the two sellers to increase the quantity they make available for sale. The plans and desires of each of the five transactors mesh when the price rises to

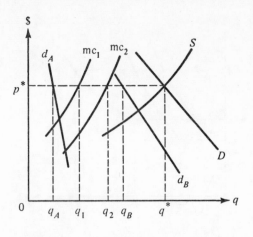

**Figure 7-5.**
Firm, buyer, and market equilibrium.

$p^{**}$. Such a price increase reduces A's quantity demanded from $q_A$ to $q_A'$, reduces B's quantity demanded from $q_B$ to $q_B'$, increases the quantity supplied by Firm 1 from $q_1$ to $q_1'$, increases the quantity supplied by Firm 2 from $q_2$ to $q_2'$, and limits the amount that C wants to $q_C$. The aggregate quantity supplied equals the aggregate quantity demanded, as we can see by the intersection of $S$ and $D'$.

The price that fully coordinates the plans of the many diverse transactors is not just any old price. Only the equilibrium price does the job. You should remember this the next time some politician says that some market-determined price is too high or is "unjust." Market prices are not randomly determined variables that can be

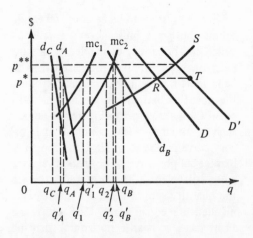

**Figure 7-6**
Consequences of market demand shift.

tinkered with with impunity. If a price is not left free to assume its market-determined value there will be a breakdown in the coordination of the plans of the buyers and sellers in that market. A "shortage" is one such breakdown. If the price for a product is held below its equilibrium value, more of that product will be wanted than is available. *Any* shortage (including a shortage of oil) can be made to disappear simply by allowing the market price to increase until the quantity that buyers want meshes with the quantity that sellers make available. The increased price decreases the quantity wanted, and *it also increases the quantity made available.* Some politicians advocate coping with the oil shortage by increasing the tax on gasoline. This will decrease the quantity demanded, but because sellers won't get the higher price it will not increase the quantity supplied.

If prices are not allowed to make the quantity wanted equal the quantity available, some other device must be used. The long lines at gasoline stations during the first two months of 1974 provide an excellent example of such nonprice rationing devices and their consequences. The limited gasoline was obtained by those most willing and able to pay the time costs involved in waiting in long lines. Politicians would not let price rise sufficiently to eliminate the need for the lines because they were concerned about the effect of the high price on the poor. (At least that was the reason they gave.) But the poor did not escape paying a high price for their gasoline. Rich and poor alike incurred extremely high costs for gasoline, while the sellers of the gasoline did not receive any benefit from the high costs paid by buyers. As a result sellers closed on weekends, stopped washing windshields and checking oil levels in engines, sold gasoline for only one or two hours per day, and were forced to sacrifice much of their customers' good will. The frustration felt by buyers and sellers, the uncertainty created by the situation, and the great waste of time all combined to make the true cost of gasoline much higher than it would have been if price had been permitted to do the rationing.

In 1967 there was an Arab-Israeli war.

As a result the Suez Canal was shut down and oil tankers had to travel around Africa on their way to Europe. This greatly reduced the supply of crude oil relative to the demand in Europe. The United States assisted its European friends by sending them large amounts of crude from its own sources. This created a "shortage" of crude oil in the United States, but the shortage was eliminated by increases in the relative price of oil products. There was no "gasoline crisis" in 1967 because markets were left alone to do their work.[8] Moreover, the 1974 crisis was made a lot worse because of the adverse supply effects of the price controls that had been in effect since 1971. What the Arab oil boycott couldn't do to us we did to ourselves by allowing our politicians to set prices.

## Long-Run Equilibrium for a Firm

We have seen that a firm seeks to maximize profit by producing the quantity that sets its marginal cost equal to the market-determined equilibrium price, providing the market-determined price is at least as large as average variable cost. In the long run, however, other considerations come into play. First, if the market-determined price is below average total cost (the sum of average variable cost and average fixed cost) not all of the costs of continued possession will be met. If the firm's decision maker thinks this situation will persist, he will decide not to continue possession of at least some of the plant and equipment now in use. Thus, in the long run, not only must marginal cost equal the market-determined price, but price must be at least as large as average total cost.

Second, the firm's decision maker must be content with the scale of plant that he has. This idea is best expressed with the aid of Figure 7-7. Suppose price is $0P$ and the firm has the scale of plant that is just right for output rate $q_0$. From Chapter

---

[8] Roger Leroy Miller, *The Economics of Energy* (Glen Ridge, N.J.: Horton, 1974), pp. 76-77.

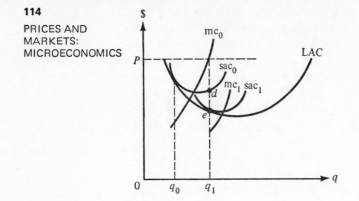

**Figure 7-7.**
Output and desired scale of plant.

5 we know that this means the marginal cost and the average total cost curves the firm now faces are $mc_0$ and $sac_0$ respectively. If the firm sets its marginal cost equal to the existing price it will produce at rate $q_1$. However, if the decision maker thought that in fact his optimal output rate would continue to be $q_1$ he would build a different scale of plant. With the plant scale he now has his costs per unit are $q_1 d$. If he built the scale of plant that was just right for output rate $q_1$ he would be on his long-run average cost curve, experiencing unit costs of $q_1 e$. A new scale of plant means a whole new average total cost curve (short-run average cost curve) and a whole new marginal cost curve. These new curves are labeled $sac_1$ and $mc_1$ respectively. Now we have a problem. Even if the price remained at $0P$ the firm would not want to continue to produce $q_1$, because $mc_1$ and the horizontal line from $0P$ do not intersect at $q_1$. The new scale of plant means that another output rate is optimal.

So far we know that price must equal marginal cost and must be at least as large as average total cost, and the decision maker in the firm must be content with the scale of plant he has. We can identify the output rate that meets all of these conditions with the aid of the long-run marginal cost curve developed in Chapter 5. Consider Figure 7-8. We know from Chapter 5 that short-run marginal cost (smc) equals long-run marginal cost (LMC) at the quantity of output for which the scale of plant the firm has is just right. If price is $0P$, and

if the decision maker knows the shape and position of his long-run average cost and long-run marginal cost curves, he can identify his optimal output rate as $q^*$ and build the scale of plant that is just right for $q^*$. He identifies $q^*$ as the quantity that makes LMC equal the market price and then builds the scale of plant that is just right for $q^*$. With this scale of plant, short-run marginal cost will equal long-run marginal cost when $q^*$ is produced. Thus the firm is in short-run equilibrium (price equals short-run marginal cost) as well as long-run equilibrium (price equals long-run marginal cost), and is content with its scale of plant.

However, we have not yet described a *full* equilibrium. In Figure 7-8 we see that when price is $0P$ it exceeds average total costs by $bd$. We saw in Chapter 4 that the user cost of capital includes the rate of return that can on average be made on alternative investments (the proxy often used for this is the rate of return on triple A corporate bonds), hence the average total cost curve includes this rate of return or "normal profit." The firm depicted in Figure 7-8 is collecting enough revenue from its sales to more than cover its necessary payments to its hired factors of production plus a normal profit; it makes more than a normal profit on each unit. Profits above normal are called "economic profits." The depicted firm is earning economic profits of $bd$ per unit of output. Of course the entrepreneur who operates this firm would be perfectly content to continue to earn

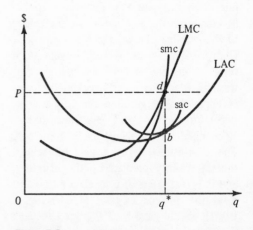

**Figure 7-8.**
Use of long-run marginal cost curve.

this above-average profit rate, but other entrepreneurs also enjoy making economic profit. If we interpret Figure 7-8 to depict the "representative firm" in this market there will be many entrepreneurs who are earning economic profit. Other entrepreneurs who are not in this market will, if they become aware of the high rate of return, desire to imitate these successful firms. If these potential interlopers are not prevented from entering the market by legal restrictions such as a licensure requirement or the requirement of a permit from some regulatory agency, or if they are not excluded because the existing firms control all the available quantity of one or more resources vital for the production of the product, they will become actual interlopers. When they enter the market they increase the supply of the product and thereby reduce its market price. With a new market price the firm depicted in Figure 7-8 will no longer want to produce $q^*$, and thus will no longer be content with its scale of plant. For a firm to be in full long-run equilibrium, not only must (1) price equal both short- and long-run marginal cost and (2) the firm's decision maker be happy with the existing scale of plant, but also the firm cannot be making any economic profit. This last condition means that price must equal average total cost. Look again at Figure 7-8. If price equals average total cost the price line must just touch the existing sac curve at its minimum point. This is so because the firm always equates price and short-run marginal cost, and short-run marginal cost equals average total cost only at the minimum point of the latter. If the firm's decision maker is to be happy with the existing scale of plant, his sac curve must touch the LAC curve at the quantity that is being produced. There is only one sac curve that has its minimum point on the LAC curve—the one that is tangent to the LAC curve at the minimum point of the LAC curve.

We conclude that full long-run equilibrium for a price-taker firm is depicted by a diagram such as Figure 7-9. Price, which equals $0P$, equals short-run marginal cost (smc) and long-run marginal cost (LMC). This is the profit-maximizing condition. In

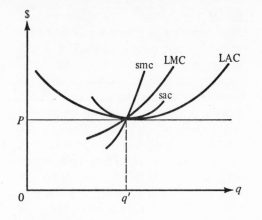

**Figure 7-9.**
Full competitive equilibrium.

addition, price equals average total cost, so that the firm earns only a normal profit. (Economic profit is zero.) This is necessary so that there is no incentive for additional firms to enter the market, and hence no pressure for the price to change. Finally, the firm's decision maker is content with his scale of plant, since short-run average cost (sac) equals long-run average cost (LAC) at the quantity produced ($q'$).

Since there can be only one equilibrium price at a time for a given product, it is of interest to consider whether *all* firms in full equilibrium make a zero economic profit. Not all entrepreneurs are equally efficient in monitoring their enterprises, so we would expect some long-run average cost curves to be lower than others. If Firm A's long-run average cost curve is lower than Firm B's, and Firm B is making just a normal rate of profit, Firm A must be making some economic profit. Perhaps we should say that full long-run equilibrium requires zero economic profit only for the least efficient entrepreneur in the market. More efficient entrepreneurs will enjoy some economic profit that cannot be competed away by interlopers. After all, if the least efficient entrepreneur is making just a normal profit no potential interloper could be more efficient than he is. If there is such an entrepreneur, why isn't he already in the market? The economic profit earned by superior entrepreneurs is a *rent*—a payment to a resource owner in excess of the minimum payment necessary to secure the use of the resource. The minimum payment necessary to induce a resource owner to use the resource in a particular way is the payment the resource owner could secure in the next most valuable use of the resource. Here the resource in question is superior entrepreneurial skills, which are a scarce resource. Owners of firms who do not have such superior skills will want to secure the services of the superior entrepreneur. Competitive bidding for these services will mean that the superior entrepreneur will have to count his own services at a higher cost than before. If he remains in his own business he sacrifices the high salaries he could earn working for others. The cost to the firm of its entrepreneur's skills will rise until the firm earns just a normal profit. The entrepreneur, an an entrepreneur, continues to receive his rent, but the entrepreneur as the owner of the firm just earns a normal profit.

The cost of securing any resource for use in a given firm depends on the highest bid for that resource in alternative uses. This is true whether or not the owner of the resource is also the owner of the firm that uses the resource. For this reason economists say that in full long-run equilibrium in any open market—one where there are no barriers (especially legal barriers) to entry—each firm in the market will make a zero economic profit. This is true for firms that are price searchers as well as those that are price takers, as we shall see in the next chapter.

## The Long-Run Market Supply Curve

We have seen that the short-run market supply curve is the horizontal sum of the marginal cost curves of the firms selling the product in question. However, the long-run market supply curve is not the horizontal sum of the individual firms' long-run marginal cost curves. The long-run market supply curve depicts the relationship between market price and the aggregate quantity supplied when each firm is in full long-run equilibrium at that price. Here again, a diagram is helpful. Figure 7-10 depicts a representative firm in panel A and market supply and demand curves in panel B. The initial market demand curve is labeled $D$ and the initial short-run market supply curve is labeled $S_1$. $S_1$ is, as we have seen, the horizontal sum of the individual short-run marginal cost curves. The initial short-run marginal cost curve for the representative firm is labeled mc. Since $S_1$ intersects $D$ at point $E_1$, the initial equilibrium price is $p_1$. At $p_1$ the representative firm is in full long-run equilibrium, since its initial long- and short-run average cost curves are LAC and sac, respectively. The representative firm produces $q_1$ and the aggregate quantity supplied (and demanded) is $Q_1$. (Note that the horizontal axes in the two diagrams have different scales: a given distance on the $Q$ axis measures much more output than it does on the $q$ axis.)

Now suppose this equilibrium is disturbed by an increase in the demand for the product. Additional buyers become aware of the product, and existing buyers want to buy more at every price. The product has perhaps become fashionable or perhaps some law has been passed that mandates increased use of the product (e.g., safety belts, smog control devices, or red tape). We show the increased demand by shifting the market demand curve to $D'$. The first effect of the increase in demand will be a higher price. In particular, the price will increase to $p_2$ (the intersection of $S_1$ and $D'$). Each firm will move along its short-run marginal cost curve and increase the quantity it supplies to $q_2$. In the market diagram this appears as a movement along the initial supply curve from $E_1$ to $b$, which indicates an increase in aggregate quantity supplied to $Q_2$. The rise in price from $p_1$ to $p_2$ also gets buyers to decrease the quantity demanded, and this is shown as a movement along the new demand curve from $a$ to $b$. If the price did not or could not change there would be an excess demand of $E_1 a$. The increase in price eliminates this excess demand by inducing an increase in the quantity supplied and a reduction in the quantity demanded. At $p_2$ there is zero excess demand, but full equilibrium has not been restored, for now the representative firm makes an economic profit of $hk$ per unit. This economic profit

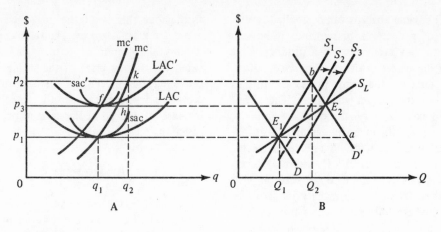

**Figure 7-10.**
Derivation of long-run market supply curve.

will attract interloper entrepreneurs. As new firms enter the market the short-run market supply curve shifts to the right. In addition, the new firms will be bidding for the resources used in the production of the product, and this will likely cause an increase in the prices of those resources. As resource prices rise the representative firm's cost curves—all of them—shift up. The economic profit is reduced in two ways: the increase in the number of firms makes the product price fall, and the increase in resource prices makes costs go up. The former is represented by rightward shifts of the short-run market supply curve, and the latter is represented by upward shifts of the cost curves. This process continues until the economic profit is eliminated. If there is zero economic profit there is no further entry and therefore no further downward pressure on price and upward pressure on cost. For example, full equilibrium would be restored if, when the short-run supply curve reaches $S_3$, the representative firm's cost curves are in the positions labeled LAC', sac', and mc'. Since $S_3$ intersects the new demand curve at point $E_2$, the price will be $p_3$. At $p_3$ the representative firm is back in full long-run equilibrium (point $f$). The long-run market supply curve ($S_L$ in the diagram) is derived by connecting the initial point of full equilibrium in the market diagram to the new point of full equilibrium in the same diagram, i.e., by connecting $E_1$ and $E_2$.

Let us review this market process. There

is an increase in the amount that people want of some product. At the existing price there is less available than is wanted. This leads to frustrated buyers bidding up the price. The higher price decreases the quantity wanted, and it also increases the quantity available; thus the "shortage" is eliminated. The higher price now means that firms producing the product will be making above-average profits. This will induce additional entrepreneurs to enter the market, thus increasing the amount of the product that is available even more. The additional supply reduces price, but the price does not fall back to its initial level because as entrepreneurs enter the market they bid up resource prices. The falling product price and the increasing resource costs reduce economic profit. The process continues until economic profit is again zero. The increase in demand sets in motion a chain of events that gets additional resources devoted to the product that is wanted more. No central authority must hand down a revised production plan. The process is quite automatic, and it is propelled by the pursuit of profit.

The market initially responds to an increase in demand with an increase in price and a small increase in quantity supplied, but as time goes on and new firms enter the market there are further increases in the quantity supplied and consequent reductions in price. The long-run market supply curve is more elastic than the short-run market supply curve.

This same analysis can be applied to the case of a decrease of demand. If buyers decide they want less of a product than they did before at the existing price, sellers will discover their inventories of unsold goods getting larger and larger. There will be an excess supply—the quantity supplied in excess of the quantity demanded—at the initial price. Sellers will reduce prices to reduce their inventories, and the lower price will induce them to cut back on production. If for any firm the price falls below average variable cost, that firm will shut down and the entrepreneur will presumably look for a more auspicious way to invest his wealth. The lower price eliminates the excess supply but it does not restore full equilibrium. The representative firm that was previously earning a normal profit is now making a less than normal profit—an economic loss. This will induce entrepreneurs to leave this market and devote their resources to alternative pursuits. Not all entrepreneurs leave, for as exit proceeds two things happen: the price of the product increases (the short-run supply curve shifts to the left) and, since there is less bidding for resources, the cost curves shift down. Exit proceeds only until these forces restore a normal profit to the representative firm. This will occur at a lower price than the initial equilibrium price because the cost curves shift down. The end result of this market process is a lower product price and fewer resources devoted to the production of the product. Here again it is not necessary for a central planner to give orders to devote fewer resources to a product that buyers no longer favor. We can count on individual self-interest to get producers to behave in the desired manner.

## A Reminder

Since the end of World War II people in the United States have become accustomed to seeing the money price of most goods increase most of the time. For this reason students are usually skeptical of any economic analysis that concludes that the price of a product will fall. Remember that throughout this book the prices we talk about are *relative* prices. The relative price of anything—input or output—falls even when the money price of that thing rises, providing the percentage increase of the average price level exceeds the percentage increase of the particular money price in question.

## An Exercise

We said that when there is an increase (decrease) of demand the resulting economic profit (loss) will induce entry (exit), and that this entry (exit) will mean higher (lower) resource prices and thus the cost curves of the representative firm will shift up (down). We saw that this means that the long-run market supply curve is positively sloped. (An increase of demand will ultimately result in a higher price and larger quantity, while a decrease of demand will result in a lower price and a smaller quantity.) Suppose that:

1. Entry and exit do not affect resource prices and therefore the cost curves do not shift, and

2. Entry reduces resource prices while exit increases them, so that cost curves shift down with entry and up with exit,

What will the slope of the long-run market supply curve be in these cases? The correct answers are: a horizontal curve in the first case, and a negatively sloped curve in the second case. The student should actually go through the graphical analysis with pencil and paper to make certain that these answers are understood.

## Price Controls May Result in Higher Prices

The foregoing discussion outlined the so-called law of supply and demand. The interaction of many buyers and many sellers determines the market price that coordinates the multitude of individual plans. Movements of prices cause fewer resources to be used to produce the things that buyers want less and more resources to be used to produce the things that buyers want more. Often we hear politicians lament the results of the interaction of supply and demand, and sometimes they go beyond lamentation and actually intervene in the market process in order to establish a "just price." Sometimes the just price is higher than the market-determined price. In this case the politician is courting the favor of the sellers of some product, such as milk. (If the government had no power to set milk prices there never would have been any illegal campaign contribution from the dairy industry in 1972.) Sometimes the just price is lower than the market clearing price. In this case the politician is trying to make points with the buyers of some product, such as gasoline. As buyers we generally prefer lower prices to higher prices. In Eden everything had a zero price, but we were dismissed from there. Now the amount that is wanted at a zero price always exceeds the amount that is available; hence price must be greater than zero. In particular, if everyone is to be successful in carrying out his purchasing and selling plans the price must be the market clearing price, and no amount of tinkering with a market can change that simple truth. If price is held below its market clearing level there will be a persistent excess demand. Many buyers will not be able to purchase as much as they want at the legal price, and producers will have no incentive to increase the amount that is available. The product will be acquired by those who arrive at the selling point first, or by those who are willing to make "under-the-counter" payments to sellers.

The extent to which under-the-counter payments will be used depends on the severity of the penalties that the politicians decide to visit on those who do not agree with them on what constitutes a just price. We can use supply and demand analysis to show that weakly enforced price controls, or price controls that do not carry severe penalties for violators, will result in higher prices than no price controls at all.[9] The

market supply and demand curves for a product are labeled $S$ and $D$, respectively, in Figure 7-11. The market-determined price is $p_m$. Suppose now that the price for this product is controlled, and the legal price is $p_c$. Sellers will supply a total quantity of $q_c$ at price $p_c$, while buyers desire a total quantity of $q_B$. There is an excess demand at $p_c$, which means that not all buyers will be able to purchase as much as they want to purchase at $p_c$. These disappointed buyers would be willing to pay a price higher than $p_c$ rather than go without the product. They offer a higher price to sellers, but the politicians require the sellers to turn down such offers—trade at a price in excess of $p_c$ is not in the "public interest." Sellers tell buyers that if they want more than $q_c$ to be made available they must offer the sellers an amount that would equal the normal price (the prices indicated on the $S$ line), and they must also offer enough to compensate the sellers for the risk of being penalized by the price controllers. Suppose, for example, that the penalty for selling at a price higher than $p_c$ makes sellers add $T_1$ onto the usual price they would charge for the various quantities. The supply curve that the buyers face is then the regular market supply curve up to quantity $q_c$, but for any quantity greater than $q_c$ it is $S + T_1$. The effective supply curve is discontinuous at $q_c$. This curve intersects the market demand curve at price $p_1$. Buyers pay $p_1$ per unit

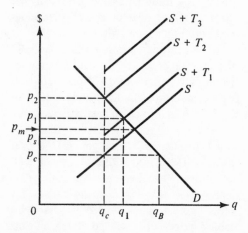

**Figure 7-11.**
Price controls and illegal payments.

[9]See Gary Becker, *Economic Theory, op. cit.*, pp. 106–109.

to sellers and the aggregate quantity supplied and demanded is $q_1$. The $p_1$ per unit that the sellers receive has two parts: the normal competitive price that would be charged for that quantity in the absence of controls ($p_s$), plus the additional $T_1$ per unit that is payment for incurring the risk of legal sanctions.

If the penalties for disobeying the politicians' orders were more severe the effective supply curve would be higher for quantities in excess of $q_c$. If the penalties were so severe that sellers would add on $T_2$ to their regular prices for the various quantities, the market clearing price would be $p_2$. If the penalties were still more severe, the market supply curve would be above $S + T_2$ for quantities greater than $q_c$. Since such a supply curve (e.g., $S + T_3$) does not intersect the market demand curve, the actual price would be the legal price, and the excess demand would persist. The product would then be rationed by queues, ration coupons, or the personal prejudices of the sellers. (The prettiest ladies get the best cuts of meat.)

Sometimes the politicians say that charging a price above the legal minimum is "price gouging" and they urge buyers to report such prices to the authorities. But who is being "gouged?" Buyers would clearly prefer a lower price if they could get the amount they wanted, but at that lower price not all buyers will be able to carry out their planned purchases. Buyers are really "gouged" by the controlled price: they cannot (legally) offer a higher price to sellers even though they consider that better than going without.

Price controls on one product can raise the average of prices on other products. During the summer of 1973 price controls were removed on food products except for beef. The legal price on beef was decidedly lower than the market clearing price. As a result people could not get all the beef they wanted. Faced with shortages of beef, consumers switched to chicken, pork, lamb, fish, etc. The demand curves for other protein foods shifted to the right, raising prices of those goods to all-time highs. Here the control of one price and not others raised the prices of these other

things higher than they otherwise would have been.

## The Demand for and Supply of Housing Services

To illustrate the long-run and short-run adjustments that a price-taker market goes through in response to a change in demand, consider the response of the housing market to the introduction of rent vouchers made available to sum dwellers.[10] We used to think that the best way to rid ourselves of slums was simply to bulldoze them down. Unfortunately both economic theory and actual experience indicate that this "slum clearance" merely results in relocation of the slum.

Each dwelling unit, whether it is an apartment or a house or a tenement, yields a specific amount of housing services. The larger the dwelling unit for a given quality, or the higher the quality of a dwelling unit for a given size, the larger the bundle of housing services that is yielded thereby. For example, if there are two apartments, alike in every respect except that one has a more effective heating system, that one yields more housing services and can be said to be a larger package, or bundle, of housing services. In long-run competitive equilibrium the price per unit of housing services must be the same no matter what size bundle they come in, and this price must equal the long-run average cost of producing a unit of housing services.

The amount of housing services yielded by a given dwelling unit can be changed by maintenance (or lack of it), repair, alteration, or addition. The jargon of the housing market is that dwelling units "filter" up or down. A unit "filters down" if the amount of housing services it yields declines, and it "filters up" if the amount of housing services it yields increases.

In Chapter 3 we saw that an individual's demand for something is constrained by

[10]This discussion follows Edgar O. Olsen, "A Perfectly Competitive Theory of the Housing Market," *op. cit.*

the real purchasing power the individual has. For each good, including housing services, we decide how much of our purchasing power to use on it by considering our preferences (or tastes) in conjunction with the price of that thing relative to the price of other things we also wish to buy. If there are two individuals with the same tastes who confront the same relative prices, the person who is more wealthy (has more real purchasing power) will demand more of any good than the other person. Our wants, or at least our effective wants, are tempered by our ability and willingness to pay.

Since there is a wide diversity of tastes and a wide diversity of real incomes there is a demand for many different sizes of housing services packages. There is a demand for packages that most of us consider to be slum housing, because there are many people who have such limited real purchasing power that they opt for small packages of housing services so they can have some of their purchasing power left over for other things they consider important. Slum clearance does nothing to alter the purchasing power of these people, nor does it alter the set of relative prices that these people face. Slum clearance does not, therefore, alter the demand for slum-sized packages of housing services. Individuals who are displaced by slum clearance will move to other areas. If the housing market in these areas is initially in long-run equilibrium, only a normal rate of return is being made on each size package of housing services. The influx of people with a demand for slum-sized packages will mean that the price of housing services in slum-sized packages will rise above long-run average cost. Since it becomes relatively more profitable to offer slum-sized packages, owners of packages of other sizes will allow their units to filter down, thereby increasing the supply of slum-sized packages and decreasing the supply of larger packages. If the long-run average cost of housing services does not change, the price per unit of housing services will be the same in the new equilibrium as it was previously. This means that the decrease in the supply of larger packages must be offset by the filter-

ing down of still larger units, or by new construction. The process continues until the supply adjustments reduce the price of services in all sizes of packages back to the long-run average cost of housing services. It is estimated that 90% of the adjustment is completed in seven years.

If the desired goal is to get people permanently out of slum dwellings, a much more effective policy, and one that avoids any necessity for public housing, is to increase the purchasing power of the poor in the housing market. Once we have defined the people that we wish to subsidize (e.g., by income class weighted by family size), the government could sell rent vouchers to them. These rent vouchers could be used by the poor to buy housing services. The poor would pay their rent with the vouchers, and the sellers of housing services would turn the vouchers in to the government in exchange for an amount of money specified on the face of the voucher. The poor would buy the vouchers from the government for a price less than the face value. The exact price any individual would have to pay would depend on his income and family size. The face value of the vouchers would equal the amount necessary to purchase the package of housing services that is thought (by the taxpayers) to be the minimum acceptable size package for people to dwell in. Let's say that this is a package of $Z$ units of housing services.

Now it may seem that such a proposal would merely increase the price that landlords get for their units since the proposal does nothing to increase the supply of $Z$-sized packages. Economic analysis suggests otherwise. The initial effect of the rent vouchers would be to shift the demand curve for $Z$-sized packages of housing services to the right. The short-run supply curve for $Z$-sized packages (and any size package) would be fairly steep, indicating that in the short run hardly any additional $Z$-sized packages would be made available. The only increase in the short run would be through reduced vacancy rates in existing $Z$-sized packages. This would mean a fairly large increase in the price of housing services in $Z$-sized packages. If the housing market was initially in equilibrium, the sellers of Z-sized packages would now earn some economic profit. Some of the recipients of the rent vouchers would temporarily have to remain in slum dwellings, but the promise of economic profit would ensure that additional Z-sized packages would eventually be made available. The higher price and the resulting economic profit from the provision of Z-sized packages would induce sellers of larger sized packages of housing services to allow their units to filter down. Therefore there would be a decrease in the supply of these larger packages, and the price of housing services in the larger packages would increase, making it profitable to construct more of them. Newly constructed dwelling units are usually larger packages of housing services than what most of us would consider to be the minimally acceptable standard; hence additions to the supply of Z-sized packages would probably come about through the filtering down of larger packages and some filtering up of what were slum dwellings originally. Slum landlords know that even if many of their tenants are forced to stay with them at first, these tenants will eventually leave as more Z-sized packages become available. The only way the existing landlords can keep these tenants is to alter their dwellings to yield Z units of housing services.

The increase in the supply of Z-sized packages through filtering and the increase in the supply of larger packages through new construction would continue until the price per unit of housing services was again the same in all size packages and equal to the long-run average cost of housing services. If this long-run average cost increased because of the additional construction, the final equilibrium price would be higher than the initial price but lower than the price of housing services in Z-sized packages immediately after the increase in demand brought about by the rent vouchers. If the long-run average cost of housing services did not increase during this process, the new equilibrium price of housing services would be the same as the initial price.

The process we have just described can be represented in a standard supply and demand diagram. Consider Figure 7-12. The

horizontal axis measures the quantity of Z-sized packages of housing services, and the vertical axis measures the price per unit of housing services in Z-sized packages. Initially this submarket is in equilibrium with the price per unit of housing services in this size of package (and all other sizes) equal to $p_1$. The initial supply curve for housing services in Z-sized packages is labeled $S_1$. $S_1$ is fairly steep, indicating that in the short run only small changes in the quantity supplied can be brought about. The implementation of the rent voucher plan would shift the demand curve to $D'$. In the short run the price would rise to $p_2$, and there would be only a small increase in quantity supplied. (A decline in the average vacancy rate brought about because prospective tenants show up more frequently or because owners are induced by the higher price to spend less time sampling prospective tenants could account for this initial increase in quantity.) At $p_2$, economic profits are made by those who offer packages of Z units of housing services. This will induce owners of different sizes of packages to filter their units to size Z. This increase in supply is shown as a righward shift of the short-run supply curve, and it continues until the price per unit of housing services in the Z-sized package (as well as all other sizes) again becomes equal to the long-run average cost of housing services. If the long-run average cost increases during

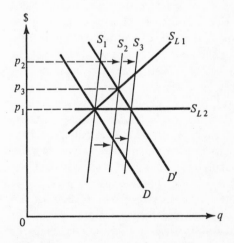

**Figure 7-12.**
Supply and demand of Z-sized packages.

this process the final price will be above the initial price. Earlier we saw that upward shifts of the long-run average cost curve result in a positively sloped long-run market supply curve. Suppose the long-run market supply curve is $S_{L1}$. This would mean that filtering would continue until the short-run supply curve had shifted to $S_2$, and the new equilibrium price would be $p_3$. If long-run average cost did not increase, the long-run market supply curve would be $S_{L2}$, and the short-run supply curve would stop shifting when it reached $S_3$. In this case the new equilibrium price per unit of housing services would be $p_1$—just what it used to be. Clearly the claim that a rent voucher plan would merely result in higher rents and no appreciable increase in the quantity of desirable dwelling units is incorrect. It fails to recognize the long-run market adjustments to shifts of demand.

## Gifts of Specific Resources versus Cash Gifts [11]

A gift is made whenever someone receives something from another person and pays for it an amount (possibly zero) less than its market value. A gift can be in the form of specific goods or it can be in cash. A rent voucher, since it can be used only to purchase housing services, is an example of the former type. The dollar value of the gift is the difference between the voucher's face value and the amount the recipient pays for the voucher. If the recipient places a value on the gift that is less than its cost to the giver, it would be more efficient (at least from the recipient's point of view) for an equivalent gift in cash to be given. This is easily seen by breaking a gift of specific resources down into its component parts, which are:

A. The market value of the specific goods received. In our example this is the face value of the rent voucher.

[11]This discussion is based on Alchian and Allen, *Exchange and Production, op. cit.* pp. 166-172.

B. The maximum amount of money the recipient would have been willing, on his own, to pay for the specific goods that are received in the gift. In our example this is the price of $Z$-sized packages which, if it existed, would have induced the recipient of the voucher to buy a $Z$ package of housing services on his own. (He doesn't buy a $Z$ package, without the voucher, because the actual price exceeds this hypothetical price.)

C. The amount of money the recipient, on his own, in fact does spend on the type of good given in the gift. In our example this is the amount of money the recipient actually spends on housing services before he receives a voucher.

D. The amount of money the recipient pays for the specific goods received in the gift. In our example this is the amount that the recipient pays for the voucher. In what is commonly called "outright gifts" this amount is zero.

The difference between $A$ and $D$ ($A - D$) is the cost that the giver of the gift incurs. He could conceivably give a cash gift of the same amount. Since $B$ is the value that the recipient places on the specific goods, $B - D$ is the value that the recipient places on the gift, and the difference between $A$ and $B$ is pure waste from the recipient's point of view. He receives something that costs the giver $A - D$, but he thinks what he receives is worth only $B - D$. The recipient would much prefer to receive cash equal to $A - D$ because $B - D$ of cash would make up for the gift of specific resources, and $A - B$ would be left over to acquire other things.

If $B$ exceeds $A$, the recipient would already be purchasing $Z$-sized packages, since the value he places on them exceeds their market price. In this case a voucher used to pay a portion of the rent would simply free an equivalent amount of cash to use to acquire other things. In general $C - D$ is cash that is freed for purchasing other things, but if $B$ exceeds $A$, $B$ will equal $C$.

The difference between $B$ and $C$ is the value the recipient places on the additional specific resources made available to him because of the gift. In our example it is the difference between the value he places on a $Z$-sized package of housing services and the value he places on the housing services he consumes before receiving the voucher. (Remember, to an economist the "value" placed on something is merely the amount of money that a person chooses to spend on that thing, given its unit price and his real income.)

We have noted that if $A$ exceeds $B$ there is waste from the recipient's point of view. This may not be waste from the giver's point of view. The giver may not consider the cash gift to be the equivalent of the gift of specific resources. In our example the giver could want to give only housing services and nothing else. He could think that the recipient simply has a false sense of values. If the recipient were sufficiently informed, or sufficiently intelligent, he would realize that the "true value" of a $Z$-sized package of housing services was $A$ and not just $B$. If the giver gave a cash gift the recipient would purchase a somewhat smaller sized package of housing services than the $Z$ package. He would purchase a larger package than he previously did because his budget constraint has changed, but he would not purchase enough housing services to please the giver. The giver would think that the recipient was "wasting" a part of the gift, perhaps on alcohol, tobacco, or rock records. It is for this reason that we see many gifts given in the form of specific resources rather than in cash. In the public sphere, politicians simply don't trust the poor to use cash gifts intelligently.

## Looking Ahead

The purpose of this chapter was to explain the working of open markets that are characterized by sellers who are too small, relative to the demand for what they sell, to have any appreciable effect on market price. Hopefully the example of the housing market has reinforced your understanding of such markets. In the next two chapters we consider another type of market—the "price searcher" market. The first of these chapters will develop the price searcher model and the second will use that model to discuss cartels and mergers.

## Questions for Discussion

1. Evaluate this statement:

    There is no role for advertising in price taker markets. Neither is there any role for inventories in price taker markets.

2. Explain the following:

    Disregarding governmentally controlled prices, no firm must take any price except an equilibrium price.

3. Evaluate the quality of the economics lesson taught by the following problem from an elementary arithmetic text.

    If a grocer purchases bread at 20 cents per loaf, what price must be charged if he is to earn a 50% profit?

4. Why is it correct to say that although not all firms have equally capable decision makers, all firms will experience the same unit cost in long run equilibrium?

5. Construct an analysis of the market for restaurant services on the model of the market for housing services presented in this text.

6. Make a list of ten items whose relative price has fallen since 1968.

7. Make a list of five price taker markets that have been closed (entry and other forms of rivalry eliminated) by government action.

8. Congress often complains that private firms do not label their products honestly. Can you think of an honest label for a bill to reduce prices below market-determined levels? What label would Congress put on such a bill?

9. Apply Alchian's gift analysis to a program that rations gasoline with ration coupons which the original recipient:

    (a) cannot sell to another person and
    (b) can sell to another person at any mutually agreeable price.

# 8
## Price Searchers

A seller is a price searcher if he has some discretion over the price he can charge. At a higher price he will sell less than at a lower price (the first fundamental law of demand again), but if the seller is sufficiently large relative to the total demand for the product he sells that he will not lose all (or most) of his customers to rivals when he raises his price, there is a range of prices that he can pick from to charge. Since the market does not dictate what price to charge (as it does for price takers) the seller must search for the price that is optimal from his point of view—that is, the price at which his profits will be maximum.

### Price and Marginal Revenue

Marginal revenue, you will recall from the last chapter, is the change in total revenue collected by a seller when his selling price changes sufficiently to cause a one-unit change in the quantity sold. A decrease in price sufficient to cause a one-unit increase in the quantity sold causes a change in total revenue equal to the new price (the amount that all units are now sold for) less the decrease in revenue collected from the original amount sold. The original amount sold brings in less revenue because each of these units now

sells for a lower price (the new price) than it did before. For any given market demand curve the decrease in price that is necessary to cause only a one-unit increase in the quantity demanded is very small. Since a single price taker sells only a small quantity relative to the total demand, there is practically no resulting decrease in total revenue when this small price decrease is applied to the small quantity originally sold. Thus for a price taker there is no significant difference between price and marginal revenue. Such is not the case for a price searcher.

Consider a given market demand curve. In order to increase the quantity sold on the market by one unit, price must be decreased by some small, specific amount. Whether the market is made up of numerous sellers or only one seller, the necessary change in price is the same. This small decrease must be applied to the number of units originally sold. An individual price searcher is larger relative to the market demand than is an individual price taker. The number of units to which the price drop is applied is sufficiently large that the difference between price and marginal revenue cannot be ignored. Marginal revenue is significantly less than price for price searchers. In the last chapter we saw that the formula for marginal revenue is

$$MR = p - \frac{\Delta p}{\Delta q} q \qquad (8\text{-}1)$$

where $p$ is the new selling price, $\Delta p/\Delta q$ is the (absolute value of the) slope of the demand curve, and $q$ is the original amount sold (the amount sold before the price was changed enough to cause the one-unit change in quantity). Equation 8-1 can be rewritten as

$$MR = p\left(1 - \frac{\Delta p}{\Delta q}\frac{q}{p}\right) \qquad (8\text{-}2)$$

Since

$$\frac{\Delta p}{\Delta q}\frac{q}{p}$$

is the reciprocal of the formula for the price elasticity of demand, another form of the marginal revenue formula is

$$MR = p\left(1 - \frac{1}{\epsilon}\right) \qquad (8\text{-}3)$$

where $\epsilon$ is the (absolute value of) price elasticity of demand.

Consider Figure 8-1. Since a price searcher can raise his price without losing most of his customers, and lower his price without being inundated with customers, he does not perceive a horizontal demand curve as a price taker does. Rather, he perceives a negatively sloped demand curve such as that labeled $D$ in the diagram. (For the moment we will assume that the demand curve is a straight line.) From the horizontal axis formula for price elasticity of demand in Chapter 3 we know that the price elasticity of demand equals 1 at one-half the quantity demanded at a zero price. The quantity demanded at a zero price (where the demand curve cuts the horizontal axis) is $0T$; half of that quantity is $0B$; thus (the absolute value of) the price elasticity of demand at point $E$ on the demand curve is 1. The demand curve depicts the price that corresponds to each quantity; price is average revenue; thus the demand curve could be called the average revenue curve. Our formula for marginal revenue tells us to compute marginal rev-

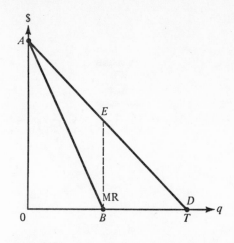

**Figure 8-1.**
Price searcher's demand and marginal revenue.

enue at any given quantity by subtracting the reciprocal of the price elasticity of demand from 1 and multiplying the result by the price that corresponds to the specified quantity. Thus the marginal revenue at quantity $0B$ is price times $1 - 1/1$, or zero.

The vertical axis formula for the price elasticity of demand in Chapter 3 tells us that the price elasticity of demand at the point where the demand curve cuts the vertical axis is infinite. Thus the marginal revenue at that point is $p(1 - 1/\infty)$, which equals price.

We conclude that the curve that represents marginal revenue can be derived from the demand curve. In the case where the demand curve is a straight line the marginal revenue curve cuts the horizontal axis halfway between origin and the point where the demand curve cuts the horizontal axis. The marginal revenue curve cuts the vertical axis at the same point where the demand curve cuts the vertical axis. A straight-line demand curve generates a straight-line marginal revenue curve.

If the demand curve is not a straight line it will not be sufficient to find two points on the marginal revenue curve and connect them in order to generate the entire marginal revenue curve. Marginal revenue must be calculated for each quantity, but fortunately that is easy to do. Consider Figure 8-2, where the demand curve is labeled $D$. The formula for marginal revenue (Equation 8-3) can be written as

$$MR = p - p/\epsilon \qquad (8\text{-}4)$$

We can apply the vertical axis formula for the price elasticity at any given point by constructing a tangent line to the demand curve at the point in question. The vertical axis formula was derived in Chapter 3 by multiplying the reciprocal of the slope of the demand curve by the ratio of the price to the quantity at the point being examined. Since the slope of a tangent line to a particular point on a curve equals the slope of the curve at that point, we can use the tangent line just the way we used the straight-line demand curve. Label the point where the tangent line cuts the vertical axis $R$. Label the price that corresponds to the point in question $P$. The vertical axis formula for $\epsilon$ is then $OP/PR$ (see Chapter 3). Equation 8-4 is then

$$MR = OP - \frac{OP}{OP/PR} = OP - PR \qquad (8\text{-}5)$$

For example, in Figure 8-2 the point that depicts marginal revenue at quantity $OC$ is point $M$. It is derived by starting at point $A$ ($AC = OP$) and coming down an amount equal to $PR$ ($AM = PR$). To trace out the entire marginal revenue curve it would be necessary to construct a tangent line to

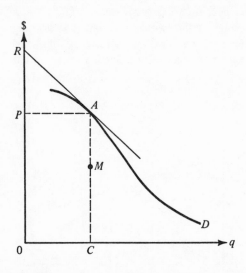

**Figure 8-2.**
Marginal revenue with nonstraight-line demand curve.

each point on the demand curve and follow this procedure in each case.

## Individual and Market Demand Curves[1]

If there were only one seller of a product which in the minds of buyers had no close substitutes, the market demand curve would be the demand curve faced by that seller. This is a special case of price searchers commonly called "monopoly." With two or more sellers of what is in the minds of buyers the same or nearly the same product, the market demand curve would no longer be the demand curve faced by an individual seller. In fact, with two or more rival sellers it is difficult to say for sure just what sort of demand curve an individual price searcher will perceive. Two types of curves could logically be perceived by an individual price searcher who is not a monopolist.

One of these curves depicts what would happen to the quantity the individual seller would sell if, when he changed his price, each of his rivals also made the same change in price. This curve is sometimes called the "market share" curve. It depicts the share of the total quantity sold that will be sold by the individual seller if all sellers of the product charge the same price. In Figure 8-3 curve $D$ is the market demand curve. If only one seller of the product exists, he will confront the market demand curve. If there were two sellers of equal size the market share curve for each would be represented by the line labeled $MS_2$. If the price were $p_1$ each seller would sell $OC$ units and the total quantity sold would be twice $OC$, or $OF$. If both sellers reduced their price to $p_2$ there would be an increase of $FG$ in the total quantity demanded. Each seller would increase the quantity he sells by $CE$. (Twice $CE$ equals $FG$.)

[1] The following discussion is based on Edward Chamberlin, *The Theory of Monopolistic Competition* (Cambridge, Massachusetts: Harvard University Press, 1933).

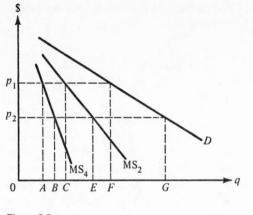

**Figure 8-3.**
Market share curves.

If there were four sellers of equal size each would face the market share curve labeled $MS_4$. At each price each seller would service a quarter of the total quantity demanded. At $p_1$ each would sell $0A$, and four times $0A$ equals $0F$, which is the total quantity demanded at price $p_1$. If each seller reduced his price to $p_2$ the quantity demanded would again increase by $FG$, and each seller would service one-fourth of this increase. Each would experience an increase of $AB$ in the quantity he sells.

The market share curve for any seller depicts what happens to the quantity purchased from that seller when all sellers act in concert with respect to changes in price.

The second type of demand curve faced by each seller depicts what happens to the quantity purchased from the seller when he changes his price and none of his rivals follow suit. In Figure 8-4, the initial price is $p_1$, and the depicted firm's share of the market at that price is $0A$. Its market share curve is labeled MS. If this firm lowered price to $p_2$, and all of its rivals did the same, the quantity sold by the depicted firm would increase to $0B$. However, if its rivals did not lower their prices, the increase in the quantity sold by the firm that did would be larger than $AB$. Perhaps this firm's entrepreneur would expect the quantity sold to increase to $0D$. In that case the demand curve he perceives would be the one labeled $d$. The amount of the increase of the quantity sold depends on the extent

to which buyers regard the product of the depicted firm to be a good substitute for the products of that firm's rivals. The demand curve labeled $d'$ indicates less substitutability in the minds of buyers than is indicated by the demand curve labeled $d$, because the price reduction brings about an increase in quantity sold of only $AC$ instead of $AD$. The greater the substitutability in the minds of buyers the flatter will be this second type of demand curve.

With only two rivals selling a given type of product it is highly unlikely that either of them would base his pricing decisions on the assumption that the other's price will remain unchanged. In other words, under these circumstances it is unlikely that the rivals will perceive demand curves such as those labeled with the lower case $d$'s. With only a few sellers the pricing decisions of any one of them affect the others substantially. Rivals are unlikely to ignore each other's pricing decisions when the effects of those decisions are large. Thus when there is a small number of rivals it is generally assumed that each seller considers its market share curve to represent the demand information relevant to its decision making.

With numerous sellers the effects of the pricing decisions of one of them would be spread out over all of them, so that their effect on any single rival would be small. Under these circumstances it is likely that a single seller would feel safe in assuming that his rivals will not necessarily follow his price changes. The individual seller would

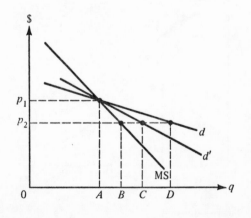

**Figure 8-4.**
Possible demand curves facing price searcher.

consider one of the flatter demand curves — the ones we have labeled with a lower case $d$ — to represent the demand information relevant to its decision making. For future reference let's call this curve the *ceteris paribus* demand curve, to emphasize that the seller assumes that all prices but his own will be held fixed. Of course it is frequently the case that individual sellers who make decisions based on the assumption that their rivals will not follow suit are unpleasantly surprised when their rivals in fact *do* follow suit. When this happens each seller is forced to move along his market share curve rather than his *ceteris paribus* demand curve. For example, suppose a seller's market share curve and *ceteris paribus* demand curve are those labeled MS and $d_1$, respectively, in Figure 8-5. Each seller charges price $p_1$. If the depicted seller perceives his demand curve to be $d_1$, he may decide that the profit-maximizing price for him to charge is $p_2$. (In the next section we will see how the profit-maximizing price is determined.) If when he changes his price to $p_2$ all of his rivals do likewise, he will increase the quantity he sells by only $AB$ (a movement along his market share curve) rather than $AC$. The demand curve that he then perceives if he again assumes that his rivals will not follow his price changes becomes that labeled $d_2$.

## The Price Searcher's Optimum Price

The main distinction between a price taker and a price searcher is that the former perceives an almost horizontal demand curve, while the latter perceives a substantially negatively sloped demand curve. Thus for a price taker there is no difference between price and marginal revenue, while for a price searcher marginal revenue is significantly less than price. The profit-maximizing rule is the same for both price takers and price searchers: produce the quantity at which marginal cost equals marginal revenue. Marginal cost is the addition to cost when one more unit is produced, and marginal revenue is the addition to revenue when that additional unit is sold. As long

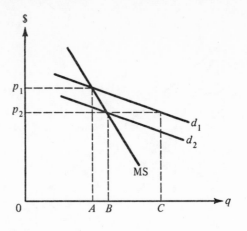

**Figure 8-5.**
Surprise movement along market share curve.

as the addition to cost is less than the addition to revenue when one more is produced and sold, profit will increase.

The curve labeled $D$ in Figure 8-6 is the demand curve perceived by the individual price searcher we are examining. If the price searcher is a monopolist, that demand curve is the market demand curve for the product he sells. If the price searcher has rivals, the demand curve he perceives may be his market share curve or it may be what we have called a *ceteris paribus* demand curve. In all cases, however, the perceived demand curve will be negatively sloped. From the negatively sloped demand curve we can derive the corresponding marginal revenue curve. It is labeled MR in the diagram.

The quantity at which profit is maximum is $q^*$, for only at $q^*$ does marginal cost (MC) equal marginal revenue. Since the decision maker perceives $D$ to be the curve that tells him what quantity he will sell at each price, he sees that he should charge $p^*$. Only if price is $p^*$ will he sell quantity $q^*$. If he charged a price equal to $AE$, he could sell only $0A$ units per period. At this quantity, marginal revenue is $AH$ and marginal cost is $AG$; thus if an additional unit were produced and sold, profit would increase by $GH$ dollars. If $Aq^*$ additional units were produced and sold, profit would increase by the number of dollars represented by area $GHI$. Hence it is profitable to lower the price from $AE$ to $p^*$. If the price searcher charged a price equal to

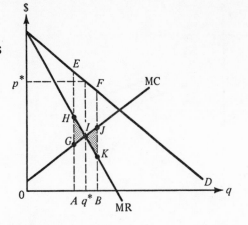

**Figure 8-6.**
Price searcher's optimum price.

*BF* he would sell quantity *OB*. At this quantity marginal cost is *BJ* and marginal revenue is *BK*. If one unit less were produced, cost would decrease by *BJ* and revenue would decrease by *BK*, so profit would increase by *KJ* dollars. If *Bq\** fewer units were produced, profit would increase by the number of dollars represented by area *KIJ*. Hence it is profitable to raise the price from *BF* to *p\**. If the price searcher were charging a price that made his quantity sold *any* amount other than *q\** he could increase his profit by changing his price so that *q\** will be sold.

## Price Searcher Equilibrium— Closed Market

If we add an average cost curve to Figure 8-6, we can determine whether the price searcher earns an economic profit. In Figure 8-7 we depict an economic profit of *TW* per unit. The price searcher chooses to produce at the rate *q\**, and average cost at that output rate is *q\*T*, while average revenue (price) is *q\*W*. The average cost curve includes normal profit as a cost; hence *TW* is the per-unit economic profit. Generally, economic profit attracts rival sellers, and the competition of these interlopers eliminates the economic profit. But if entry into the market is blocked the price searcher will enjoy the economic profit for as long as the demand and cost conditions remain as we have depicted them.

The most commonly observed block to entry is legal restrictions. In fact, historically the word "monopoly" meant sellers who were protected from rivals by government decrees that granted the monopolist exclusive access to the market. Yellow Cab has an exclusive franchise to service downtown Los Angeles and the Los Angeles International Airport. Other cities also grant monopoly rights to cab companies. No one may open a liquor store in most cities without first acquiring permission from some government agency. If an economic profit is made by existing liquor store owners they need not fear the arrival of new rivals, because they can count on the government to protect them. Government agencies enforce official prices on all kinds of liquor. Competition by price is illegal. Professional licensure laws pertaining to such sellers as doctors, dentists, barbers, and morticians are another example of legal impediments to entry. In these cases the government in effect grants those who are already in the market the power to decide who shall be allowed to enter.

The cost curves in Figure 8-7 are long-run cost curves. Our theory pretends that the price searcher (in open as well as closed markets) estimates (makes guesses about?) the demand conditions that confront him. From this he estimates marginal revenue. He also estimates the position of his cost curves; i.e., he tries to determine

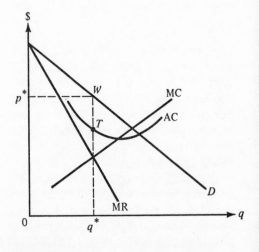

**Figure 8-7.**
Closed market price searcher equilibrium.

the least-cost way to produce each output rate. He selects the output rate that equates his perceived marginal revenue with his perceived marginal cost and proceeds to construct the scale of plant that minimizes average cost for the selected output rate. He will frequently guess incorrectly about the relationship between demand and cost. Ford guessed incorrectly with respect to the Edsel, and Kaiser guessed incorrectly with respect to the Henry J. The more accurate the guesses the more profitable the enterprise will be, and profitable enterprises are imitated by other entrepreneurs. Our theory identifies what appears to be the profit-maximizing price to charge, given the decision maker's perception of demand and cost conditions. We know that the more successful firms will be those that (1) have the more correct perceptions of market conditions and (2) come closest to the actual profit-maximizing decisions. These firms will endure and be imitated while others disappear from the scene. No actual decision maker need ever directly use our marginal cost equals marginal revenue criterion. Whatever the decision rules actually employed, the ones that will in fact lead to success are those which yield the same decisions as those indicated by our criterion. By a process of natural selection existing firms come to behave as if they acted according to our model.[2]

## Price Searcher Equilibrium— Open Market

In the absence of legal impediments to entry, the existence of economic profit will (with exceptions to be discussed later in this chapter) attract rival sellers who will try to sell the same or nearly the same product. If a price searcher is in the situation depicted in Figure 8-7 in an open market, rivals will be attracted onto the scene. As additional sellers enter the market the demand curve perceived by the original sel-

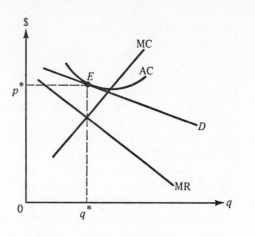

**Figure 8-8.**

Open market price searcher equilibrium.

ler will shift to the left (at each price he will sell less because there are more sellers sharing the market) and become flatter (any unmatched increase in price will result in a larger decrease in the quantity sold because buyers have additional alternative sellers from whom they may buy). Also, the cost curves may shift up. As entry proceeds the interlopers will likely bid up resource prices. This shifting of the demand and cost curves will continue until there is no longer any economic profit. Such a situation is depicted in Figure 8-8. Marginal cost equals marginal revenue at $q^*$. The price that must be charged if $q^*$ is sold is $p^*$. Point $E$ represents this optimal combination of quantity and price. If there is to be zero economic profit, price must equal average cost. This means that the average cost curve must either just touch the demand curve at point $E$ or cut the demand curve at that point. But if point $E$ represents maximum profit the average cost curve cannot cut the demand curve, for if it did, profit could be increased by reducing $q$ below $q^*$. If profit can be increased it obviously cannot already be maximum. The zero economic profit condition can only be represented by a tangency between the average cost curve and the demand curve.

It is not necessary that there be numerous rival sellers in order to have zero economic profit. In fact, with only one seller of a product there may be zero economic profit because that one seller must consider

[2]Armen Alchian, "Uncertainty, Evolution, and Economic Theory," *Journal of Political Economy* (June 1950).

potential rivals as well as actual rivals. A seller may adopt a price that generates only a normal profit, even though he could make some economic profit in the short run, because he recognizes that the economic profit will attract rivals. The interlopers will dissipate the economic profit, and once they are established as sellers in the market they may be more effective innovators than the original seller and so may make it impossible for him to earn even a normal profit. The single seller could well be better off not to attract attention to himself and to his market.

It is the openness of the market and the resulting actual or potential competition that exerts discipline on sellers. This openness means that resources will be allocated to higher valued uses in price searcher markets as well as price taker markets. In the last chapter we saw that an increase in the demand for a product created economic profit for its producers. This economic profit attracted additional resources into its production. A decrease in demand for a product would generate economic losses and lead to fewer resources being used for its production. Changes in demand have the same effects in open price searcher markets. If buyers want smaller cars more than they used to, it will be profitable for General Motors, Ford, Chrysler, and American Motors to produce additional small cars. If they continue to produce larger cars, alternative suppliers (foreign manufacturers) will service the buyers and the American firms will incur losses. If the U.S. market were closed to foreign manufacturers this threat would not exist, and there would be less incentive to respond to the demand change.

## Comparison of Price Takers and Price Searchers

If markets are open, zero economic profit will be earned by both price searchers and price takers when the entry and exit processes are completed. The important difference between price takers and price searchers derives from the fact that for price searchers marginal revenue is significantly less than price, while for price takers it is not. Both sorts of firms seek to maximize profits by producing the quantity that sets marginal cost equal to marginal revenue. Thus for the price taker marginal cost is set equal to selling price, while for the price searcher the selling price will be greater than marginal cost.

Consider Figure 8-9. The market demand curve is labeled $D$. If the market were a price taker market there would be numerous firms, and the market supply curve ($S$) would be the horizontal addition of the individual firms' marginal cost curves. The market price, the one that each price taker would take, would be $p_T$, and the total quantity supplied and demanded would be $q_T$. If there were only one seller in the market, he would face the same market demand curve. To facilitate the comparison let us suppose that the monopolist's marginal cost curve would be the same as the price takers' summed marginal cost curve. The single seller of the product could not ignore the difference between price and marginal revenue. His marginal revenue would be the same as the marginal revenue of the price-taking group *as a whole*. In the last chapter we saw that when price is lowered enough to sell an additional unit, the marginal revenue to the one price taker who sells the additional unit is practically the same as the new price, while the marginal revenue to the group as a whole is much less than the new price because the lower price means lower

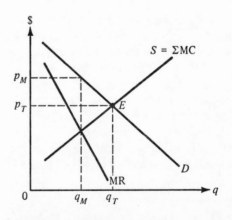

**Figure 8-9.**
Comparison of price taker and price searcher.

revenue collected on the large amount previously sold in the market. The monopolist in this exercise can be thought of as the group as a whole. The monopolist would wish to produce quantity $q_M$, for that quantity sets his marginal cost equal to his marginal revenue. The monopolist would charge $p_M$, which is definitely greater than marginal cost.

Marginal cost is the value in alternative uses of the resources required to produce an additional unit of the specific good in question. Price measures the value that buyers place on an additional unit of the good. Since for a price searcher price is greater than marginal cost, the value placed on an additional unit is greater than the value of the alternative things that could be produced with the resources that are necessary to produce an additional unit. For this reason it is often said that resources are not efficiently allocated in price searcher markets. In a price taker market there is no difference between marginal cost and price; hence the value of an additional unit of a given good is equal to the value placed on alternative goods that could be produced with the same resources. Resources are efficiently allocated by price taker markets. Price searcher markets will always produce less than the ideal amount of any good. In our diagram the ideal amount is $q_T$, but a monopolist would produce $q_M$.

Some theorists, noting this misallocation of resources, claim that price searcher markets can be made to produce the efficient amount—the amount produced by a group of price takers—by setting a ceiling on the price that can be charged. In Figure 8-9, if a ceiling price of $p_T$ is imposed on the monopolist his marginal revenue curve is $p_T E$ for any quantity up to $q_T$. The usual marginal revenue curve over that output range becomes irrelevant because it only pertains to prices higher than $p_T$. The monopolist would then equate marginal cost with his new marginal revenue and produce $q_T$. In effect, the monopolist becomes a price taker—he must take the price that the government sets.

If this sounds like a good idea you should pause for a moment to consider one question: how does the government know where the curves are? Private firms constantly strive to attain least possible cost because it is profitable for them to do so. If a price ceiling is imposed the incentive is diminished and the government agency in charge will have to base its decisions on experienced marginal cost, not least marginal cost. Only least marginal cost reflects value in alternative uses. Furthermore, even if the government agency once had an accurate picture of the relevant curves, how would it know when the picture changes? Demand and cost are not static. Our curves constantly shift. Private owners of firms find it difficult to keep up with the shifts, and all each has to worry about is his own firm. How could a government agency keep accurate track of many separate firms? Don't let the simplicity of our geometry trick you into thinking that it is easy to identify optimal points in the real world.

## Barriers to Entry[3]

We have seen that the openness of a market affects how responsive the market will be to changes in demand. A decentralized, private property, voluntary exchange economy allocates resources toward higher valued uses if markets are open to new rivals. It cannot do this as well if markets are closed. It is of some importance, therefore, to consider some forces that are generally thought to close many markets.

1. **Legal Barriers** We have already considered the legal barrier, and we have noted that it is very frequently observed. We have mentioned occupational licensure, taxicab franchises, and government agency controls in liquor and milk as examples. To this list we can add many others. The Civil Aeronautics Board restricts entry and other forms of competition among airlines. (The CAB will be discussed in the next chapter.) The Interstate Commerce Commission restricts entry and prohibits price competi-

[3]This discussion follows George J. Stigler, *The Theory of Price*, 3rd. ed. (New York: Macmillan, 1966), pp. 220–227.

tion among truckers and railroads. And government regulation prevents entry and price competition among banks. In all of these cases there is alleged to be some "public interest" at stake, although it is difficult to imagine any results other than lower prices if these regulations were removed.

Patents are another example of a legal impediment to competition and some case can be made that patents serve a useful purpose. Patents are issued to inventors to protect them from having their inventions copied for a period of 17 years. Without patents it would be very difficult to enforce private property rights in ideas. Innovation and discovery are very costly processes, but imitation is not. Without patents innovators would have less incentive to incur the costs of innovation.

**2. Economies of Scale** If the long-run average cost curve of a *single firm* declines over most of the output represented on the *market* demand curve, only one or a few firms may be able to actually produce and sell the product. Figure 8-10 depicts this situation. The market demand curve is labeled *D*, while the long-run average cost curve of a single firm is labeled LAC. The single firm could produce (for example) quantity $0A$, charge $0P$, and earn an economic profit of $BE$ per unit. However, if a second firm of equal size entered the market each firm would have the market share curve labeled MS. There is no output where this market share curve lies above the LAC curve. In other words there is no quantity for which the unit cost is not greater than the price that could be received by each of the two firms. At $0P$ each firm would sell only $0C$, and at $0C$ unit cost exceeds $0P$ by $RS$. There is only room for one firm in this market.

Usually the relationship between the market demand curve and a single firm's long-run average cost curve is as depicted in Figure 8-11. The firm experiences decreasing returns to scale (rising long-run average cost) at an output far smaller than the total quantity demanded on the market at most prices. The relevant comparison is between the long-run average cost curve for a single

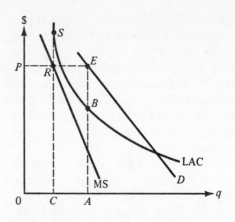

**Figure 8-10.**
Natural monopoly.

firm and the market demand curve. We can see in Figure 8-11 that even if there were eight firms of equal size there would still be portions of each firm's market share curve that lie above the long-run average cost curve. The curve labeled $MS_2$ represents two firms, each selling half the total quantity demanded at each price. $MS_4$ represents four firms, and $MS_8$ is the market share curve for eight firms of equal size.

The case in which there is room for only one producer in a market is called a "natural monopoly." A public utility company (one that sells natural gas, electricity, water, or telephone services) is the classic example. It is simply not economic to have more than one company service each of these markets in a given geographical area. Public utility commissions have been set up in every state to regulate these companies.

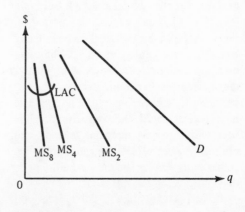

**Figure 8-11.**
Absence of economies of scale.

Since economies of scale preclude entry into the market by rivals it is generally thought to be necessary to control the prices and other terms of trade offered by natural monopolists. If it is rivalrous behavior that disciplines sellers, where rivalrous behavior would not be observed it is necessary to substitute an alternative form of discipline.

However, it has been shown that such regulatory agencies are not necessary in public utilities.[4] An alternative way to cope with a natural monopoly situation is to have public ownership of the plant and equipment used to provide the service and have open market bidding (every two years, for example) for the right to use that plant and equipment. That is, there could be competition for the right to service a market for a specified period of time whenever there could not be competition in the actual sale of services, due to economies of scale. In other words, there could be competition *for* the market, rather than competition *in* the market. Many rival entrepreneurs could be in on the bidding for the right to service a given area. Each bidder would have to guarantee a fixed return to the public owner of the plant and equipment to cover depreciation and interest costs. The winning bid would be the one that offered the lowest prices to consumers over the life of the contract. This simple procedure would go a long way toward getting politics out of rate setting by public utility commissions.

Because of regulation by public utility commissions, telephone rates have been constant over long periods of time. At these fixed money rates it is not possible to make private service available in sparsely populated rural areas unless the telephone company incurs substantial losses. As a result, private service in such areas is often hard to get. Ever since 1965 we have had an accelerating inflation in the United States. With service rates fixed by public utility commissions that vote according to political expediency rather than sound economics, the real prices collected by the phone companies and other utilities decrease. The result is that the companies try to avoid losses by lowering their costs. Quite often the only way they can do this is to allow the quality of the services to deteriorate. Under the Demsetz plan these undesirable effects of regulation would be avoided.

**3. Ownership of Vital or Superior Resources** If existing firms own all the known supply of a raw material necessary to make a given product, new rivals cannot effectively enter the market. This barrier to entry is only a short-run barrier because, over time, alternative sources of the raw material will be found and a changing technology will make possible the use of alternative raw materials. At the beginning of World War II the U.S. was cut off from its supply of rubber, yet substitutes were found which turned out to be superior to natural rubber.

Sometimes the superior resource in question is the entrepreneur himself. Ford Motor Company dominated the automobile market for so long precisely because of the extraordinary ability of Henry Ford. No other entrepreneur was nearly as successful. If the human ability to run an enterprise in a given market is very scarce—is possessed by only one or two people—these people will make above-normal profits. They will collect a *rent* on their superior ability. The above-normal profits will not be competed away, because no one has the ability to be an effective rival. Superior entrepreneurial ability is also only a "short-run" barrier to entry since it is often true that superior entrepreneurs do not necessarily breed children who become superior entrepreneurs.

**4. "Imperfect" Capital Market** It is sometimes said that if it takes a lot of (financial) capital to set up shop in an industry, the existing sellers in that industry are effectively protected from new rivals. Even if an above-normal profit is made in the automobile industry, for example, new automobile manufacturers will not emerge because they need too much money to get

---

[4]Harold Demsetz, "Why Regulate Utilities?", *Journal of Law and Economics* (April 1968).

started. It is extremely difficult to raise the start-up capital.

One of the functions of the financial capital market (the market in stocks, bonds, and other financial assets) is to enable an entrepreneur to obtain start-up funds. If the entrepreneur can convince others that he is capable of successfully entering a market he can obtain the funds by borrowing them (issuing bonds) or by offering part ownership rights to others (issuing stock). Since information is not free, not every potentially successful entrepreneur will be able to convince others of his ability. Those who are frustrated by their inability to convince others will complain of an "imperfect" capital market. It is true that if information were free a "perfect" capital market would provide funds to all who could earn a rate of return in excess of the market rate of interest. But information is not free. Lenders and investors must use real resources to gather information about the entrepreneurs who are competing for their funds. Mistakes will be made, in the sense that some projects that eventually fail will be funded while others that would have been successful do not get funded. This indicates an "imperfect" capital market only in the sense that the market would do a better job of allocating investment funds if information were free. That amounts to the same thing as saying we all would be better off if we had never been evicted from the Garden.

Because of information costs, entry into industries that involve huge amounts of plant and equipment may be impeded. Empirically, however, there is no evidence that this is an important impediment to competition. For nonregulated industries there does not seem to be any correlation between rates of return and the market share of giant firms.[5]

### Price Discrimination and Multipart Pricing

Up until now we have implicitly assumed that a seller charges the same price to all who purchase from him. This uniform price is announced and buyers are told they may purchase all they want at that price. But alternative pricing techniques are commonly observed in the business world. One technique is to charge one price to one set of buyers and another price to another set. The buyers in each group are still told that they may purchase all they want at the announced price. This tactic is called price discrimination if there are no cost differences which account for the price differences. Another technique is to tie the per-unit price charged to the amount purchased. Each buyer is told the amount that much be purchased in order to obtain a given price. There is a sliding scale of prices based on quantity purchased. This technique is called multipart pricing.[6]

In order to engage in either of these tactics the seller must be a price searcher. Clearly, if the seller has no discretion over the price he charges, he cannot charge different prices to different groups or tie the price to the quantity bought.

**Price Discrimination** If a seller sells to two or more distinct submarkets, and if the elasticity of demand at a given price is different in the submarkets, the seller can increase his profits by charging a different price in each submarket, even if there is no difference in the marginal cost of servicing each submarket. (Stores that charge a higher price in some neighborhoods than in others may not be price discriminators because the difference in price may be accounted for by differences in cost. Insurance rates are higher in areas with high incidences of theft, burglary, vandalism, etc.) Suppose there are two submarkets, $A$ and $B$, and that marginal cost is the same in each. Let the price elasticity of demand in $A$ be $\epsilon_A$ and that in $B$ be $\epsilon_B$, and let $\epsilon_A > \epsilon_B$. Recall that the formula for marginal revenue is $p(1 - 1/\epsilon)$. If the seller

---

[5]George J. Stigler, *The Theory of Price, op. cit.*, p. 224n.

[6]Sometimes it is called first or second degree price discrimination, while what we have called price discrimination is sometimes called third degree price discrimination.

charged the same price in each submarket, the marginal revenue in each would have to be different. Marginal revenue in $A$ equals $p_A(1 - 1/\epsilon_A)$ while the marginal revenue in $B$ equals $p_B(1 - 1/\epsilon_B)$. If $p_A = p_B$ the marginal revenue in $A$ would be bigger than the marginal revenue in $B$, because $(1 - 1/\epsilon_A)$ is larger than $(1 - 1/\epsilon_B)$. Given the total amount produced, more should be delivered to submarket $A$ and less to submarket $B$. The addition to revenue in $A$ ($MR_A$) would be bigger than the reduction in revenue in $B$ ($MR_B$). More could be sold in $A$ only if the price in $A$ fell. Less made available to $B$ would make the price in $B$ go up. Units of the goods should be transferred from $B$ to $A$ until the gain in revenue in $A$ is not larger than the loss of revenue in $B$. At this point total revenue will be maximum. If

$$MR_A = MR_B$$

then

$$p_A(1 - 1/\epsilon_A) = p_B(1 - 1/\epsilon_B).$$

Since $\epsilon_A$ is bigger than $\epsilon_B$, $p_A$ must be smaller than $p_B$. The higher price will be charged in the submarket that has the smaller elasticity.

We can show this situation graphically. Consider Figure 8-12. We know that whatever total quantity is produced, it will be divided between the two submarkets so that the marginal revenue in $A$ ($MR_A$) equals the marginal revenue in $B$ ($MR_B$). If $MR_A > MR_B$, additional revenue can be obtained by taking units away from B and selling them in $A$. Since marginal revenue will be equal in the two submarkets our profit-maximizing rule tells us to equate the common marginal revenue with marginal cost. The curve labeled $D_A$ is the demand curve in $A$, and that labeled $D_B$ is the demand curve in $B$. The individual marginal revenue curves are labeled $MR_A$ and $MR_B$ respectively. If marginal revenue is to equal $0R$ in each submarket the quantity supplied to $A$ must be $q_A$ and the quantity supplied to B must be $q_B$. The total quantity that must be supplied if the common marginal revenue is to be $0R$ is $q_T$. We

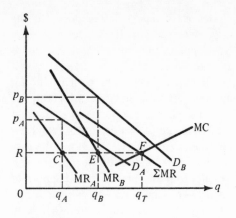

**Figure 8-12.**
Price discrimination.

could consider any other value for the common marginal revenue and see what the total quantity supplied must be if that is to be the actual common marginal revenue. The line that keeps track of these total quantities for the various common marginal revenues is merely the horizontal sum of the individual marginal revenue curves. It is labeled $\Sigma MR$ in the diagram. The profit-maximizing total quantity is the one which equates the common marginal revenue with marginal cost. We see that that is $q_T$. The total is divided by sending $q_A$ to market $A$ and $q_B$ to market $B$. The price in $A$ will be $p_A$, and the price in $B$ will be $p_B$.

Clearly the seller must be able to prevent those who buy in the low-price market from reselling to those who buy in the high-price market if his price discrimination is to succeed. Services, unlike physical commodities, are consumed immediately upon purchase, and hence are impossible to retrade. For this reason price discrimination is more likely to be observed with those kinds of goods. Consider medical services. Rich people are charged higher doctors' fees than are poor people. The rich exhibit less price elasticity of demand than do the poor because the fees are likely to be a smaller portion of the real income of the rich. The poor show more sensitivity to changes in doctors' fees because their budgets are so limited. The poor have a higher propensity to turn to such substitutes for physicians as patent medicine, self-care, and faith healers than do the rich. Most people consider it a fine act of charity for physicians to charge lower prices to the poor, and perhaps it is. However, you should note that it is profitable for physicians to lower their prices to the poor if the alternative is that the poor would not buy any physician services. A higher price leads to higher total revenue when demand is inelastic, and it leads to lower total revenue when demand is elastic. It is quite easy for physicians to identify the separate markets and to prevent resale from the poor to the rich—it is impossible for a poor recipient of an appendectomy to resell it to another at a higher price.

The medical services example of price discrimination illustrates that such practices can have what many would consider to be desirable consequences. With price discrimination the poor get to consume more medical services than they would without price discrimination. As another example, the airlines used to be able to offer discount fares to youth. The Civil Aeronautics Board outlawed that practice in early 1974 on the grounds that the low youth fares were discriminatory. Well, in fact, they were discriminatory. Young people have a more elastic demand for air travel than, for example, businessmen. An airline company would naturally respond to this fact by charging businessmen higher fares than young people. The effect of this price discrimination was to attract many young people to air travel, and thereby to make airplanes more full than they otherwise would be. Did the Civil Aeronautics Board act in the "public interest?" You decide.

Another widespread example of price discrimination is the use of trading stamps that give "free" merchandise to the savers of the stamps. While it may be possible for a gasoline dealer to identify which of his customers are rich and therefore have a relatively inelastic demand for gasoline and which are poor and so are more sensitive to price changes, it is not possible to post two prices, one for the rich and one for the poor. Even if a dealer could force his customers to different pumps according to their real income, it is impossible to prevent one group from reselling to the other. Trading stamps can solve this problem.

Time is more valuable to a rich person than to a poor person. Rich people are likely to take whatever stamps they receive and throw them away. They simply cannot be bothered with putting the stamps in books, storing the books, and visiting the redemption centers. A gasoline dealer can raise his price to all his customers to the optimum level for the group with low price elasticity of demand, and he will not lose his other customers because they are given a partial rebate when they cash in their stamps. The "free" merchandise lowers the true price of gasoline for anyone who actually redeems them. The poor are more likely to redeem them so the poor generally end up paying a lower price for gasoline than do the rich. Of course the gasoline dealer does not get to use this device for a zero price. He must pay for the stamps he gets from the stamp company. The price he pays for the stamps reflects the expected redemption rate. The more people who throw away the stamps the lower the price the stamp company will charge.

Sometimes price discrimination is necessary if a product is to be produced and sold at all. Consider Figure 8-13. There are two submarkets. Demand in the first is represented by $D_1$ and demand in the second by $D_2$. The total demand for the product is the horizontal sum of these two demand curves, and it is labeled $D_T$ in the diagram. The long-run average cost curve for a single firm (LAC) is everywhere above the total demand curve. This means that if the same

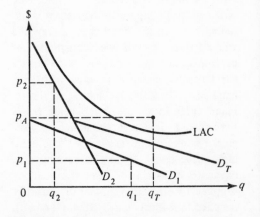

**Figure 8-13.**
Price discrimination to survive.

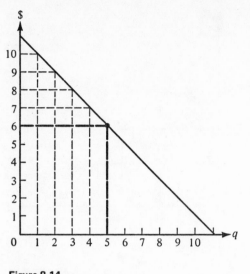

**Figure 8-14.**
Consumer surplus.

worth at least $9 to him.[7] The third unit must be worth at least $8, the fourth unit must be worth at least $7, and the fifth unit must be worth at least $6. If the seller charged the uniform price of $6 the buyer would receive a *consumer surplus* on the first four units. Consumer surplus is the difference between the amount paid for a unit of a good and the value the buyer places on the unit. The buyer values the first unit at $10 and pays only $6 for it. On that unit he obtains a consumer surplus of $4. The consumer surplus on the second unit is $3, on the third unit it is $2, and on the fourth unit it is $1. There is no consumer surplus on the last unit bought since it is valued at $6, and $6 is the price that is paid. The last unit bought is called the *marginal unit* and the first four units bought are referred to as the *inframarginal units.* If a uniform price of $6 is charged the consumer will receive a total of $10 of consumer surplus on the inframarginal units.

Now why should our seller limit himself to charging a uniform price? If he can get the buyer to pay the full value the buyer places on each unit, the seller will capture the consumer surplus for himself. He will collect $10 more revenue. There are a number of ways in which the seller could do

price were charged in both submarkets there is no quantity for which the price would not be less than unit cost. This product would not be produced unless the seller could employ price discrimination. If he charged $p_2$ in Market Two and $p_1$ in Market One he would sell a total quantity of $q_1 + q_2 = q_T$. The average price—computed by dividing the total revenue collected by the total quantity supplied—would be $p_A$. This average price is bigger than unit cost, hence the product could be sold profitably.

**Multipart Pricing** Under price discrimination buyers in each submarket are told they can purchase as much as they want at the stated price. A different price is charged in each submarket, but within a submarket there is a uniform price. The amount the buyer pays per unit is independent of the number of units he buys. Multipart pricing permits the seller to obtain still more total revenue from the units he sells. Figure 8-14 depicts the demand curve of an individual buyer for the product sold by a monopolist. If the seller charges $6 per unit this buyer will purchase 5 units per time period. Since the buyer would purchase one unit if the price were $10, that one unit must be worth at least $10 to him. Since he would buy two units if the price were $9, the second unit must be

---

[7]Contrast two situations: The buyer buys two units at $9 each, or he buys two units paying $10 for the first and $9 for the second. In the first case the buyer exchanges $18 for two units, and in the latter case he exchanges $19 for the same two units. Clearly the buyer is less well off in the second case. He has $1 less real income. Having paid $10 rather than $9 for the first unit, he may value the second unit at less than $9. The demand curve indicates that he places a $9 value on the second unit, but in Chapter 3 we saw that the demand curve is derived by confronting the individual with a series of relative prices, each of which applies to *all* units the individual chooses to buy while his real income is held constant. Only under these circumstances does the demand curve accurately indicate the value placed on each unit. However, this lost real income effect from multipart pricing is likely to be tiny, especially if the good in question does not represent a large part of the individual's total expenditure. This is because the effect of the lost real income is spread out over all things the individual buys. For simplicity we shall ignore this real income effect in what follows.

this. If the consumer paid the full value for each unit he buys, the average price he would pay would be $10 + 9 + 8 + 7 + 6$ divided by 5. This equals $40/5 = 8$. The seller could tell the buyer he could buy one unit at $10, but if he bought 5 units he could have them for $8 each. This quantity discount could induce the buyer to buy the five units. Alternatively the seller could announce a "special sale" —one unit for $10, two for $19, three for $27, four for $34, and five for $40. The purpose of this sliding scale of prices is to extract consumer surplus. It may seem that the buyer is getting a break, but with a uniform price of $6 the consumer would also purchase only five units. The total amount he would spend would be $30. Under the sliding scale of prices he pays $40. Two for $19 is a cheaper unit price ($19/2 = $9.50) than $10, but if $10 were the uniform price only one unit would be bought, not two.

Again with reference to Figure 8-14, we can see another way in which sellers can extract consumer surplus from buyers. At a simple, uniform price of $6 per unit the buyer would buy five units and enjoy a consumer surplus of $10. One way for the seller to capture that surplus is to charge the buyer $10 as an admission fee to the store and then tell him there is a simple, uniform price of $6 for each unit. Inspection of the demand curve indicates that the buyer would still choose to purchase five units. The admission fee device is the way in which consumer surplus is captured at Disneyland.

Public utilities engage in multipart pricing. You pay a higher price per kilowatt of electricity on the first 100 kilowatts than you do on the second 100 kilowatts. The same is true for natural gas and water. While the utilities do not attempt to extract all of your consumer surplus by charging the maximum price for each unit, they extract some of the consumer surplus that you would have if they charged a uniform price that made you consume the same amount you consume under the sliding scale. In Figure 8-15 we see that if a uniform price of $p_3$ were charged, the quantity demanded would be $q_3$. Consumer surplus would be represented by the

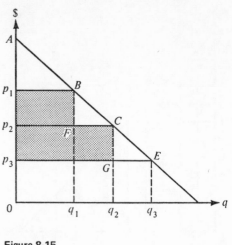

**Figure 8-15.**
Public utility pricing.

area $Ap_3E$. The utility does not charge $p_3$ for all units. It sets an initial price of $p_1$ and recognizes that the quantity demanded will be $q_1$. (We are assuming the utility knows the position and shape of the typical buyer's demand curve.) Hence for consumption rates in excess of $q_1$ it charges a lower rate. A uniform price of $p_2$ would induce consumption of $q_2$, so the utility knows that it will sell $q_2 - q_1$ additional units if it lowers its price to $p_2$ on units above $q_1$. Additional consumption can be induced by lowering the price still more on units consumed in excess of $q_2$. Specifically, if the price for such units is lowered to $p_3$, $q_3 - q_2$ additional units will be sold. The buyer receives some consumer surplus on the first $q_1$ units (equal to the area $Ap_1B$), some on the next $q_2 - q_1$ units (area $BFC$), and some on the last $q_3 - q_2$ units (area $CGE$), but he does not receive the same amount of consumer surplus that he would if the uniform price were $p_3$. The shaded area in the diagram represents the consumer surplus that the utility has captured by its multipart pricing.

Multipart pricing offers one solution to the pricing dilemma that theorists have always considered when marginal cost is less than average cost. In Figure 8-16 we depict a utility with its customary economies of scale (falling long-run average cost). When average cost declines, marginal cost is less than average cost. Suppose you are charged by the Public Utilities Commission with the responsibility of setting the price a utility can charge. Earlier in this chapter we saw that efficient allocation of resources requires that price equal marginal cost. If you set price at $p_2$ customers will demand $q_2$, and at $q_2$ marginal cost equals $p_2$. However, since marginal cost is less than average cost, the utility will incur losses equal to $RS$ per unit. The efficient price carries with it the necessity of subsidizing the utility out of general tax money. If you set the price at $p_1$ the quantity demanded will be $q_1$, and at $q_1$ average cost equals $p_1$. Since price and average cost are equal the firm earns only a normal rate of return. There is no need to subsidize the utility with general tax money. If you had to pick between these two uniform prices, which would you choose? You must either subsidize the utility or tolerate an inefficient allocation of resources.

Multipart pricing offers a way out of this dilemma. The efficient allocation of resources requires only that the value that buyers place on an *additional* unit be equal to the addition to total cost when the additional unit is produced. If the utility is permitted to charge a price higher than $p_2$ for some inframarginal units it can raise enough revenue to cover the loss from a uniform price of $p_2$. The last units purchased could be sold for $p_2$, thus meeting the efficiency criterion.

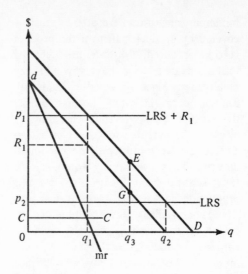

**Figure 8-17.**
Price taker licensees.

## Patents and Royalties[8]

Earlier in this chapter we noted that patents are an anticompetitive device in the sense that they make entry into some markets more difficult than it otherwise would be. We also saw that patents perform the useful function of defining and enforcing private property rights in ideas. In this section we use our price searcher model to determine the optimal royalty rate for the holder of a patent on a new product to charge when he licenses others to sell the product. This analysis will explain why, when only one firm is licensed to sell the product, the contract between the patentee and the seller stipulates a minimum quantity that must be sold or a maximum price that can be charged. In addition, this exercise illustrates how our abstract model can be employed to understand real-world events.

In Figure 8-17 the market demand curve for the product is labeled $D$. It shows for each output rate the maximum price that can be charged per unit of the product. The horizontal line labeled LRS shows the

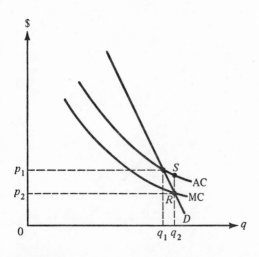

**Figure 8-16.**
Public utility pricing.

[8]This section is based on John S. McGee, "Patent Exploitation: Some Economic and Legal Problems," *Journal of Law and Economics* (October 1966).

minimum long-run unit cost that must be covered by producing firms if the product is to be produced. If $q_2$ were produced the maximum unit price buyers would pay would be $p_2$. Since this equals the unit production cost (including normal profit) there would be no revenue per unit left over for the patentee to collect as a royalty. If $q_3$ were produced the maximum unit price buyers would pay would be $q_3E$. If we subtract from this price the per-unit production cost we see that $q_3G$ per unit would be available for the patentee to claim. If for each $q$ we subtract the per-unit production cost from the maximum price buyers would pay, we will trace out the line labeled $d$ in the diagram. This line depicts the maximum per-unit royalty that the patentee could charge for each rate of output. It is the demand curve faced by our price searching monopolist holder of the patent, and the marginal revenue curve derived from it is labeled mr. The line labeled $CC$ shows the patentee's unit licensing and policing costs. The optimum royalty rate from the patentee's point of view is $R_1$. If he licenses many sellers of the product—i.e., if the product is sold competitively—the market price for the product will be $p_1$, for $p_1$ equals the sum of the royalty rate and the per-unit production cost. At price $p_1$ the quantity demanded will be $q_1$.

It is in the patentee's interest to see that the product is produced at the least cost possible, since his royalty cannot be larger than the difference between the maximum price buyers will pay and the unit production cost. If the long-run average cost curve for the typical producer turns up at relatively small output rates, it will be in the patentee's interest to license many producers so that each will operate at the minimum point of his long-run average cost curve. In the previous diagram this minimum point was assumed to be at a unit cost equal to $p_2$. In the absence of such diseconomies of scale, since the patentee's policing costs are lower the fewer the number of producers he must police, he may wish to license only one producer. In Figure 8-18 the curves labeled $D$, $d$, and mr have the same interpretation they did in

the previous diagram. The line labeled PC represents the patentee's marginal policing cost. MC is the marginal cost (and average cost) curve for the single producer. The optimal royalty rate from the patentee's point of view is $R$. The optimal quantity to be produced and sold, again from the patentee's point of view, is $q_p$. The sum of $R$ and MC equals $p_p$ — the optimum price for the product from the patentee's point of view. MC + $R$ is now the producer's total marginal cost. This single producer will try to equate *his* total marginal cost with *his* marginal revenue. His marginal revenue curve is labeled MR. Thus from the producer's point of view the optimal price and quantity are $p_M$ and $q_M$. The patentee must force the producer to charge a lower price—namely $p_p$. For this reason the license contract may specify a maximum price that the producer may charge, or it may specify that he sells a minimum quantity, namely $q_p$.

## An Exercise

Arab oil-producing countries have recently drastically increased the tax (royalty) they charge the oil companies that sell their crude oil. We can see that there is an optimum tax per barrel of crude oil by applying the same techniques that

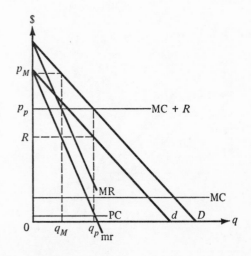

**Figure 8-18.**
Price searcher licensee.

we used for patents. See if you can construct the analysis.

In the next chapter we shall use the tools developed in the last two chapters to analyze the economics of cartels and mergers.

## Questions for Discussion

1. Evaluate the following:

   A price taker is a quantity searcher, and a price searcher is a quantity taker.

2. Evaluate this statement:

   If there is excess demand (or excess supply) in a price taker market, the sellers in that market are actually price searchers.

3. Explain what is wrong with the following:

   A price taker's marginal revenue is practically the same as his selling price, while a price searcher's marginal revenue is substantially less than his selling price. The reason for the difference is that price does not have to be lowered to sell an additional unit in a price taker market, but price does have to be lowered to sell an additional unit in a price searcher market.

4. Under what circumstances is a price searcher likely to perceive his market share curve as the demand curve he faces? When is he likely to perceive a *ceteris paribus* curve as the demand curve he faces? List at least two price searchers in each category.

5. Evaluate the following:

   Advertising is an anticompetitive device used to create or extend monopoly power.

What is an operational meaning of "monopoly power?"

6. Explain the following:

   Our models of the behavior of decision makers in profit-maximizing firms do not assert that real-world decision makers in such firms make decisions on marginal principles.

7. Evaluate the following:

   Most sellers are price searchers. They can thus be induced to increase the quantity they offer for sale if they are forced to take governmentally controlled prices that are below their optimum prices. Hence, laws setting ceiling prices below what prices would otherwise be will not result in shortages.

8. Why is it not necessary under the Demsetz proposal for the plant and equipment used by a public utility to be publicly owned?

9. Evaluate the following:

   Exclusive ownership of vital or superior resources is not a barrier to entry, since interlopers could bid either for the ownership or the use of the resources. Existing owners don't have to be the users of the resource.

10. Is the United States' progressive income tax a form of price discrimination? What is the good being sold? What is the basis of the discrimination? Is there any meaning to the price elasticity of demand for that good?

11. Construct a diagrammatic analysis modelled after the text's discussion of patents and royalties to show that it is not possible for an oil refiner to increase his profits by acquiring ownership of the competitive retail gasoline stations that sell his gasoline unless this concentration of ownership reduces retailing costs.

# 9
# Cartels and Mergers

A cartel is an agreement among independent sellers to act together with regard to their marketing decisions. Although these sellers maintain their independence as separate business entities, they make decisions with the welfare of the group as a whole in mind rather than engaging in rivalrous behavior with each other. A merger is a formal joining together of two or more separate business entities into a new single business entity. A horizontal merger involves two or more firms that sell the same product in the same market, while a vertical merger involves two or more firms that operate at different stages of the creation and sale of a product. A merger of a firm that produces shoes with another firm that retails the shoes is a vertical merger, while the merger of two firms each of which manufactures shoes is a horizontal merger.

## The Instability of Cartels[1]

Unless a cartel is protected by some government agency (e.g., the Civil Aeronautics Board protects airlines and the Interstate Commerce Commission protects truckers)

it is likely that the parties to the collusion will soon begin to engage in rivalrous behavior which will destroy the cartel. Cartels generally refer to such behavior as "cutthroat competition," but it is generally the members of the cartel whose throats are cut, not those of consumers.

In Figure 9-1 we depict one reason why cartels are inherently unstable. In panel **B** the market demand curve and the market supply curve are labeled $D$ and $S$ respectively. The market supply curve is the horizontal sum of the marginal cost curves of the numerous independent sellers in the market. In the absence of collusion the market price would be $p_1$, and any single seller, one of which is depicted in panel **A**, would produce the quantity that made marginal cost equal $p_1$. The horizontal axis of panel **A** is a stretched-out version of the horizontal axis in panel **B**. If each inch represents $Q$ units of output in panel **B**, each inch represents $1/n$ times $Q$ units of output in panel **A**, where $n$ is the number of individual sellers in the market. Without collusion the single seller would produce $q_1$, and the total quantity supplied (and demanded) in the market would be $Q_1$.

If any single seller were to sell an additional unit his marginal revenue would be insignificantly different from $p_1$. For the group as a whole, however, marginal reve-

[1]This section is based on George Stigler, *The Theory of Price, op. cit.*, pp. 231–236.

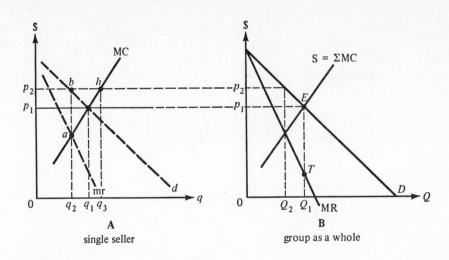

**Figure 9-1.**
Cartel pricing.

nue would be significantly below market price. The curve that represents marginal revenue for the group as a whole is labeled MR in panel **B**. We can think of the group as a whole as a monopolist that faces the market demand curve *D*. The marginal revenue curve derived from this market demand curve is the group's marginal revenue curve.

Suppose that all the independent sellers meet in a smoke-filled room and agree to cut back the quantity that each supplies until the total quantity supplied is $Q_2$. This would raise the market price to $p_2$, the optimum price for the group to settle on, because it is the price that gets buyers to purchase $Q_2$, and at $Q_2$ the group's marginal revenue equals the group's marginal cost. (The group's marginal cost curve is merely the sum of the individual marginal cost curves.)

We can show that the optimum price is $p_2$ from the individual colluder's point of view as well as the group's point of view as long as all firms have identical marginal cost curves. We shall consider the more realistic case of diverse marginal cost curves in a later section. Since all the sellers act in concert, when one seller reduces the quantity he supplies there *will* be a perceptible effect on price. If a single seller acted alone his demand curve would be almost horizontal at $p_1$, but since what one does they all do, each individual will perceive his *mar-*

*ket share* curve to be the relevant demand curve.

In the last chapter we saw that an individual's market share curve is steeper than the market demand curve. The individual's market share curve is labeled *d* in panel **A** of Figure 9-1. It appears to be parallel to the market demand curve in panel **B**, but it really isn't, since the horizontal scale of panel **A** is stretched out relative to the horizontal scale of panel **B**. A movement of a given distance on the horizontal scale of panel **A** results in a movement of the same distance on the horizontal scale of panel **B** because any move by the individual in panel **A** is duplicated by all the other individual sellers. The difference between $Q_1$ and $Q_2$ in panel **B** is *n* times the difference between $q_1$ and $q_2$ in panel **A**. The individual's marginal revenue curve is labeled mr in panel **A**, and we can see that the optimum quantity to supply is $q_2$, while the optimum price is $p_2$.

The group as a whole makes more profit with the collusion than without it. We know this because with the collusion the group's marginal revenue equals the group's marginal cost. Without the collusion the group as a whole supplies $Q_1$. At $Q_1$ the group's marginal revenue is $Q_1 T$ and its marginal cost is $Q_1 E$. Since the latter is bigger than the former, profits are increased by reducing the quantity supplied. The extra profit from the collusion will be divided up among the colluders.

If this makes you wonder why firms ever act rivalrously, consider the following difficulties involved in establishing and maintaining a cartel.

**1. The Free Rider** Each colluder is expected to supply only $q_2$ in panel **A** of Figure 9-1. $q_2$ is each firm's quota, but the cartel must enforce the quota. Each colluder realizes that if he alone supplies more than $q_2$ the effect on price will be nil. Each colluder sees $p_2$ as the price that he must take. If he acts alone $p_2$ is his marginal revenue. The quantity that maximizes his profit (as long as the others continue to charge $p_2$) is $q_3$. By increasing his quantity to $q_3$ the individual seller sees a gain of profit represented by area *abh*. Since this opportunity is available to any of the colluders the probability is very high that one or a few will seize it. When that happens the others will follow suit and the market price will decline. The group's interest will be subordinated to individual interest as sellers return to their rivalry. A cartel is sometimes called a gentlemen's agreement, but as Stigler has quipped, "The participants seldom are, or long do."[2]

Not only is there a temptation for each existing seller to get a "free ride" on the anticompetitive behavior of his fellows, but the same temptation presents itself to new sellers. If the collusion creates economic profits new firms will be established. These new firms will produce the quantity that sets their marginal costs equal to the collusion price. Their additional supply will reduce the market price.

The cartel that was most in the news in early 1974 was the Organization of Petroleum Exporting Countries (OPEC), an organization dominated by its Arab members. These sellers of crude oil colluded to cut back the availability of crude to a level that would support a world price that OPEC considered optimal from its point of view. Non-Arab members of the cartel (Iran and Venezuela, for instance) increased their production in response to the chance to free-ride on the new higher price. Toward the middle of 1974 there were signs that the most important member of the cartel, Saudi Arabia, was growing impatient with the cartel price as it became clear that people in Europe and the United States were capable of doing without a lot more oil than they thought they could. If the OPEC cartel goes the way of most cartels, individual members will increasingly cheat on their production quotas, and the world crude oil price will fall.

Rivalry from interlopers or sellers outside of a cartel is frequently avoided by enlisting the aid of some government agency to keep the outsiders out. The Civil Aeronautics Board offers a fine example in the United States. A carrier must get permission from the CAB if it is to fly any particular route across state lines. If a particular route, such as New York to Los Angeles, is heavily traveled and the carriers on that route are making large profits, no additional carriers could service the route. The CAB won't let them. Prior to 1938 commercial airline companies made up an ordinary competitive industry. Airline companies could service any route they wanted to. The only regulations imposed on them were concerned with safety (the responsibility of the Federal Aviation Administration), not economics.[3] Now, however, the airline industry is not an ordinary competitive industry. The CAB sets routes and sets fares—*minimum* fares which are also maximum fares. But it does not control frequency of flights or size of aircraft. In section 3 below we shall see the implications of this omission.

**2. Different Marginal Cost Curves** In section 1 we assumed that each seller's marginal cost curve was in the same position so that equal quotas resulted in equal marginal costs. Suppose, however, that the marginal cost curve for one seller is in a

---

[2]*Ibid.,* p. 230.

[3]George W. Hilton, "Why We Have Full Airports and Empty Airplanes: The Case for Scrapping the CAB," *Airliners International* (Winter 1974).

different position from that of another seller. Figure 9-2 depicts the resulting difficulty. Assume that there are only two sellers and that the collusive agreement is that each will supply half of the quantity demanded at each price. The market demand curve is labeled $D$. The line marked $MS_2$ is both the demand curve perceived by each seller under the collusive agreement and the marginal revenue curve for the group as a whole. Each seller perceives the line labeled mr as his marginal revenue curve. The lines labeled $MC_A$ and $MC_B$ are the marginal cost curves for firm $A$ and firm $B$ respectively. The optimum price for $A$ is $p_A$ while that for $B$ is $p_B$. $A$ and $B$ will fight over the price that should be set.

Moreover, neither $p_A$ nor $p_B$ is the optimal price to charge from the point of view of the group as a whole. Cartel profits are maximized when the cartel's marginal revenue equals its marginal cost. The group's cost is minimized for any total quantity produced when each firm has the same marginal cost. If the marginal cost for $A$ is $5 (when four units are produced by $A$) and that for $B$ is $7 (when 8 are produced by $B$) the same total quantity (12 units) could be more cheaply produced if less were produced by $B$ and more by $A$. One less produced by $B$ reduces total cost by $7, and one more produced by $A$ increases total cost by $5. Such a reallocation of production would reduce total cost by $2.

The cartel's marginal cost curve depicts the total quantity produced when each firm is producing the quantity that makes its marginal cost equal the other's marginal cost. It is formed, therefore, by simply adding the individual marginal cost curves horizontally. In Figure 9-2 we see that the cartel's optimum price is $p_C$, the optimum total quantity is $0E$, and that total is ideally made up of $0a$ from $A$ and $0b$ from $B$. The common marginal cost is $0C$, and this is equal to the cartel's marginal revenue.

The cartel faces a serious problem in trying to get its members to agree to this optimum quota and optimum price. Of course if a governmental agency makes the quotas and price a matter of law the cartel need not worry about its members engaging in "cutthroat competition."

**3. Nonprice Rivalry** Sometimes cartel members avoid price competition but compete in different ways. For example, airline companies cannot compete in price because the CAB enforces the cartel's pricing scheme. Airlines then compete by offering zero-priced champagne, more leg room, better in-flight meals, more cabin attendants, etc. One picture used in an advertisement showed an airplane with only one passenger in the cabin, being attended by three stewardesses. This lucky passenger was offered delicious food and copious drink. This picture more than any thousand words depicts the results of CAB regulation. One cannot help but think that the passenger who was the center of all this attention would prefer the lower prices that would result from price competition even though that would mean a fuller plane and less individual attention.

Earlier we saw that the CAB does not control the frequency of flights made by any airline on a specific route, nor does it control the size of the aircraft used on the flights. As a result the airlines compete by offering more frequent flights in order to create in the minds of their clientele the notion that they "are ready when you are." It is easier to offer emoluments in wide-bodied planes than in standard jets. As a result we have frequent flights using 747's, DC-10's, and L-1011's, which are

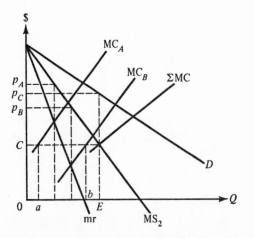

**Figure 9-2.**
Different marginal costs.

most often over half empty.[4]

The most persuasive evidence that, in the absence of regulation, airline fares will fall can be found in California. The CAB does not control fares of airlines that operate only within one state. Pacific Southwest Airlines (PSA) is such a carrier. It flies only within California. PSA offers almost no emoluments on its flights. The only thing available at a zero price is soft drinks. The fare from San Francisco or Oakland to Los Angeles is $16.50. This is 46% of CAB-regulated fares for trips of the same distance.[5] According to one expert cited by Hilton, airline fares could be reduced by as much as one third by deregulation, for a reduction of some $2 billion in the nation's annual air transport bill.[6]

On September 9, 1974, *The Wall Street Journal* reported that the CAB had denied permission to Laker Airlines to service the London to New York route. Laker Airlines is a small British company that has three DC-10s. It wanted to offer a no-frills flight across the Atlantic for $125 one way. This is one-third of the standard economy class fare. If the passengers wanted food or drink they would have had to pay extra for it. There was absolutely no question about Laker's ability to meet standard safety requirements. The CAB simply was afraid of allowing any direct price competition to disturb the idyllic extortion practiced by the cartel that it supervises. Ironically, the CAB's denial came at the same time that President Ford was expressing concern about high prices in general.

Rivalrous behavior is the natural response of one seller to another. If one type of rivalry is suppressed another type will take its place. This rivalrous behavior will increase costs so that cartel profit will be eliminated just as it would be with price rivalry. With price competition the cartel profit is eliminated by decreases of price, and with other forms of rivalry it is eliminated by increases in cost.

## The Market Concentration Doctrine[7]

Collusion among few is easier to carry off than collusion among many. If there are only two firms that must agree, negotiation is less difficult than if there are twenty. For this reason it is often assumed that in highly concentrated industries—ones where the largest four firms have an aggregate market share of over 50%—firms are likely to collude so that together they can exert "monopoly power" over the market. Monopoly power is the power to avoid rivalrous behavior from others. The market concentration doctrine states that a reliable index of monopoly power is the extent to which the output of an industry is produced by a few firms. According to this doctrine markets that are concentrated are markets in which monopolistic or anticompetitive behavior is practiced. On March 12, 1973, Senator Philip Hart introduced a bill that would establish an industrial reorganization commission whose job it would be to force the breakup of large firms whenever it was observed that the largest four firms in any market had an aggregate market share of over 50%.

Since the Sherman Antitrust Act was passed in 1890 it has usually been necessary for the prosecution to demonstrate that firms have actually engaged in anticompetitive practices in order for the courts to in any way penalize the defendant firms. The Hart bill would reverse this tradition. It would make the existence of concentration sufficient cause for a divestiture order. It would not require that the prosecution prove that any actual anticompetitive practices have been used. Bigness would be declared bad in and of itself. The Hart bill is an expression of faith in the market concentration doctrine.

In the study referred to in the last footnote, Demsetz presented evidence that the market concentration doctrine is false—that the extent to which a market is

---

[4]*Ibid.*, p. 51.

[5]*Ibid.*, p. 53.

[6]*Ibid.*, p. 53.

---

[7]This section is based on Harold Demsetz, *The Market Concentration Doctrine* (American Enterprise Institute, Hoover Policy Study 7, August 1973).

### Table 9–1   Rates of Return

| Aggregate Market Share of Largest Four Firms | Size of Firm's Total Assets | | | |
|---|---|---|---|---|
| | Under $500,000 | $500,000 to $5,000,000 | $5,000,000 to $50,000,000 | Over $50,000,000 |
| 10-20% | 6.9% | 9.7% | 10.9% | 10.2% |
| 20-30 | 5.3 | 8.9 | 9.6 | 9.7 |
| 30-40 | 5.1 | 8.7 | 9.9 | 10.4 |
| 40-50 | 4.6 | 9.1 | 10.0 | 8.8 |
| 50-60 | 4.8 | 10.3 | 10.2 | 13.2 |
| Over 60 | −1.3 | 10.0 | 10.9 | 20.3 |

concentrated in no way indicates the extent of monopoly power. We have already seen that potential competition can be just as effective a curb on monopoly power as actual competition. Even if there is only one seller of a product his pricing strategy is designed with the threat of interlopers in mind. But that is not all. Demsetz reasoned that if collusive behavior is present in concentrated industries the smaller firms in the industry should benefit from the collusion as well as the large firms. Even if the small firms are not a party to the collusion they would benefit from it since they could act as free riders on the anticompetitive price. Demsetz examined the figures for the average of 1963 and 1969 rates of return (before tax profit as a percent of total assets) of firms in various industries. The firms were classified by size of firm and also by the extent of industry concentration. The above table[8] contains the relevant data.

First of all, if we examine each column we see that there is no strong indication of a positive correlation between rates of return and industry concentration for *any* size firm. The only possible exception is firms that have over $50 million in assets where the four-firm market share is above 50%. For small firms (the first column) there seems to be a negative correlation between the four-firm market share (or industry concentration) and rates of return. It appears that only the very large firms get increasing rates of return as industrial concentration increases. This only makes sense if the largest firms in concentrated indus-

tries are more efficient (i.e., have lower costs) than smaller firms, for if the high rates of return were due to collusion the small firms would benefit as well as the large firms. Since small firms in concentrated industries are worse off than the small firms in nonconcentrated industries we must conclude that collusion does not exist in industries that are concentrated. In other words we must reject the market concentration doctrine. Bigness is not bad in and of itself. In fact, Demsetz' findings indicate that if the large firms in concentrated industries are broken up the result will be higher prices for the products that are produced by those firms.

Demsetz also examined the correlation coefficients between rates of return and market concentration by firm size for 1969 and 1970 data.[9] The correlation coefficients for the various size firms are:

| Size ($ thousands) | Correlation Coefficient |
|---|---|
| Under 10 | −.09 |
| 10-25 | −.10 |
| 25-50 | −.40 |
| 50-100 | .00 |
| 100-250 | −.14 |
| 250-500 | −.23 |
| 500-1000 | −.09 |
| 1,000-2,500 | −.07 |
| 2,500-5,000 | −.27 |
| 5,000-10,000 | .00 |
| 10,000-25,000 | −.06 |
| 25,000-35,000 | −.05 |
| 35,000-50,000 | +.20 |
| 50,000-100,000 | +.05 |
| Over 100,000 | +.24 |

[8]*Ibid.*, p. 21.

[9]*Ibid.*, p. 25.

Again the only positive correlation (and it is weak) between profit rates and concentration is for larger firms; the correlation is negative, if it is anything, for smaller firms. The data clearly reject the market concentration doctrine. If the Hart bill were to become law the result would be a reduction of industrial efficiency, not a diminishing of monopoly power.

## Horizontal Mergers

If we contrast two situations, one where there are numerous price taker sellers and the other where there is a single seller—a monopolist—we generally expect to see a higher price and a smaller quantity in the latter case than in the former. This will always be true as long as the marginal cost curve for the monopolist is the same as the horizontal sum of the marginal cost curves of the individual price takers. If such sellers merged together to form a single monopolistic firm the net result would be a deadweight "welfare" loss. That is, there would be a reduction in consumer surplus that would not be offset by a corresponding gain to producers, and a portion of what was previously "producer surplus" would be lost to both producers and consumers (although total producer surplus would increase). Producer surplus is defined in a manner exactly analogous to the definition of consumer surplus. A marginal cost curve depicts the lowest per-unit price that a producer must get if he is to supply each of the indicated quantities. In Figure 9-3, if $q_2$ is to be supplied sellers must receive at least $q_2B$ per unit, while if $q_1$ is to be supplied sellers must receive at least $q_1E$ per unit. If this were a price taker market the quantity that would be supplied would be $q_1$ and the price would be $p_1$. Producer surplus would be the sum of the differences between $p_1$ and each of the minimum prices indicated on the supply curve for quantities between zero and $q_1$. Producer surplus would be area $Cp_1E$. Consumer surplus would be area $Rp_1E$. If a merger took place, and if the monopolist's marginal cost curve were the same as the original supply curve, the quantity supplied

would become $q_2$ and the price would be $p_2$. Consumer surplus would be area $Rp_2A$, and producer surplus would be area $p_2ABC$. Area $p_1p_2AE$ would be lost consumer surplus, but part of it, area $p_1p_2AF$, is captured by the producer. That area becomes part of producer surplus. Area $AFE$ is the part of lost consumer surplus that is not converted into producer surplus. In addition, area $FEB$ used to be a part of producer surplus and now it is captured by neither consumers nor the producer. Area $ABE$ is, therefore, a deadweight loss—one group has lost and the other group has not gained. It is a net "social" or "welfare" loss.

If you think this analysis suggests that horizontal mergers should be prevented, consider the importance of our assumption that the merged firm's marginal cost curve is the same as the horizontal sum of the price takers' marginal cost curves. Usually a horizontal merger is carried out because the merged firm can operate with lower costs than the composite costs of many firms acting individually. When we wish to consider whether there is a net social loss or gain from a merger we must take these cost reductions into account.

In Figure 9-4 we assume that originally the long-run market supply curve that exists with many individual firms is LRS. (The horizontal supply curve means that there is no producer surplus to start with;

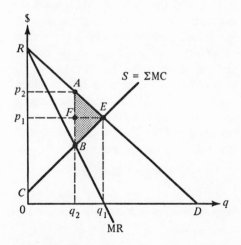

**Figure 9-3.**
Deadweight loss.

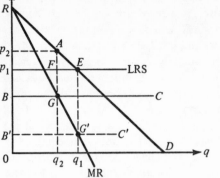

**Figure 9-4.**
Merger with decreased costs.

hence the analysis is greatly simplified without any loss of generality.) The initial price is $p_1$ and the initial quantity is $q_1$. Consumer surplus is area $Rp_1E$, and there is no producer surplus. If when the merger is carried out unit cost declines to $0B$, and is constant, the monopolist's marginal cost curve becomes $BC$. Price will be $p_2$ and quantity will be $q_2$. Consumer surplus is reduced by $p_1p_2AE$, but $p_1p_2AF$ of that becomes producer surplus. Only area $AFE$ is deadweight loss. Against this loss of consumer surplus that is not acquired by the producer we must set area $p_1FGB$, which now is producer surplus and before was neither producer nor consumer surplus. This area of new producer surplus was brought into existence by the reduction in costs occasioned by the merger. If area $p_1FGB$ is larger than area $AFE$ there is a net social gain from the merger. If the merger reduced unit cost to $0B'$, the merged firm's marginal cost curve would be $B'C'$ and the price would be the same as the price before the merger. In this case there would be no lost consumer surplus, but there would be new producer surplus equal to area $B'p_1EG'$. There is clearly a net social gain from the merger.[10]

## Vertical Mergers

In Figure 9-5 we depict two independent firms. Panel **A** depicts a price taker

---

[10]This analysis follows John S. McGee, *In Defense of Industrial Concentration* (New York: Praeger, 1971), Chap. 5 and 6.

seller of an intermediate good ($I$), and panel **B** depicts a price searcher seller of the final product ($F$) which uses $I$ in its production. Both horizontal axes measure quantity of $I$. The price searcher seller of $F$ is a price taker buyer of $I$. That is, he is one of many buyers of good $I$. He buys such a small portion of the total purchases of $I$ that he cannot appreciably affect the price of $I$ by his decision to buy more or less of it. He can buy all he wants at the going price, but he cannot buy any if he offers any price below the going price. The going price for $I$ is $0P$ in panel **A**. This equals the marginal cost of $I$ ($MC_I$) from the point of view of the manufacturer of product $F$. The curve that represents the marginal cost of the *production* of $I$ is labeled $MC_P$ in panel **A**.

$MC_I$ depicts the increase in cost that the manufacturer of $F$ experiences when he purchases an additional unit of $I$. In order to discern what quantity of $I$ he will want to purchase, we must consider the increment to profit that the manufacturer of $F$ experiences when he purchases enough additional $I$ to produce (and sell) an additional unit of $F$. When an additional unit of $F$ is sold the manufacturer of $F$ gets additional revenue—this is merely his normal marginal revenue. Not all of this marginal revenue is a gain from the use of product $I$, for in addition to purchases of the intermediate product the manufacturer of $F$ incurs other incremental costs (such as those for labor). If we subtract these other incremental costs from the marginal revenue from selling $F$ we have the increment to profit that can be attributed to the purchase and use of the additional $I$. This "marginal net revenue" from the use of $I$ ($MNR_I$) must be compared with the marginal cost of the use of $I$ (its purchase price) in order to determine how much $I$ to use. To illustrate, suppose the marginal revenue from the sale of $F$ is \$8 and the incremental cost involved in producing an additional unit of $F$ exclusive of the costs of the additional intermediate product needed is \$5. When one more $F$ is produced and sold there is \$3 (\$8 − \$5) net revenue coming in. One more $F$ will be produced and sold if, and only if, the cost of

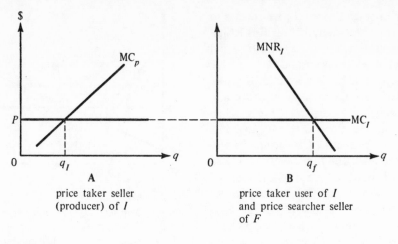

**Figure 9-5.**

Separate firms.

purchasing the additional $I$ is not greater than this $3.

The line that represents the marginal net revenue from the use of $I$ is labeled $MNR_I$ in panel **B** of Figure 9-5. The price taker seller of $I$ maximizes his profit by producing $q_I$ of $I$, while the price searcher seller of $F$ maximizes his profit by purchasing $q_f$ units of $I$ to use in the manufacture of $F$.

Suppose the two firms merge so that they are now two divisions of one firm. Division I produces the intermediate product, and division F produces the final product. Figure 9-6 combines the two panels of Figure 9-5. If division I were independent it would produce $q_I$ at the going price $OP$. If division F were independent it would purchase $q_f$ of $I$ at that same going price (which is division F's marginal cost of $I$). In order for the merged firm to maximize its total profit each of the divisions should do precisely the same as they would do if they were independent.

If division I produced $q_I$ and sold it on the open market its profit would be area $HPA$.[11] If division F used $q_f$ of $I$ and purchased all of it on the open market, its profit would be area $GPC$. The merged

firm's total profit would be the sum of these two areas. It would get the same total profit if division I transferred $q_I$ to division F and division F brought only $q_f - q_I$ on the open market. Division I's profit would decrease by area $HPA$, but division F's profit would increase by exactly the same amount. The effective marginal cost curve for division $F$ would be $HAC$, because the firm must incur the marginal production cost of the first $q_I$ units. In practice, when division I transfers $q_I$ to division F, division I is credited with an amount of receipts equal to what it would get if it sold $q_I$ on the open market. Division F is charged with an identical amount of expense. In effect division I sells to division F at the going market price. This accounting prac-

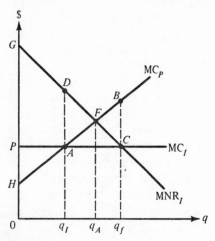

**Figure 9-6.**

Vertically-merged firm with open market purchases.

[11] Since all of the curves in the diagram represent *marginal* variables, totals are represented by the areas beneath the respective marginal curves. Thus total cost for division I is area $0HAq_I$, while total revenue is area $0PAq_I$ and profit is area $HPA$.

tice enables each division's performance to be evaluated accurately. Of the firm's total profit, division I contributes area $HPA$ and division $F$ contributes area $PGC$.

If the two divisions were told to ignore the external market and to produce and use the amount of $I$ that made the marginal production cost of $I$ equal to the marginal net revenue from using $I$, $q_A$ would be produced and used. The firm's profit would be area $HGF$, which is area $AFC$ short of the profit from allowing the divisions to respond to the market price independently. If division I were instructed to supply division F with $q_f$, profits would be reduced by area $ABC$. If division F were instructed to use only $q_I$, profits would be reduced by area $ADC$.

In Figure 9-7 we depict the case where the profit maximizing quantity for division I $(q_I)$ is larger than the profit maximizing quantity for division F $(q_f)$. If the divisions act independently, division I would transfer $q_f$ to division F and sell $q_I - q_f$ on the open market. Division I would be credited with receipts from division F equal to the receipts it would receive if it sold $q_f$ on the open market, and division F would be charged with the same amount as an expense. Division I's profit would be area $HPA$, and division F's profit would be area $PGC$. If the firm produced and used the amount that equates $MNR_I$ with $MC_P$ $(q_A)$, its total profit would be area $HGF$, which is area $CFA$ short of the profit from allowing the divisions to act independently. If division I produced only $q_f$, profit would be reduced by area $BCA$. If division F were instructed to use $q_I$, profit would be reduced by area $CAD$.[12]

Since the profit maximizing rule for the merged firm is to allow each division to do what it would do if it were independent, what is the purpose of vertical mergers? Usually it is thought that when one firm acquires one of its suppliers or one of its customers it is for the purpose of acquiring additional monopoly power. However, the final product manufacturer in our example

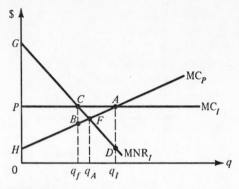

**Figure 9-7.**
Vertically-merged firm with open market sales.

did not acquire any additional monopoly power when it acquired a price taker producer of the intermediate product. If a manufacturer of shoes acquires a retail seller of shoes he does not acquire any additional monopoly power. Even if he doesn't allow the retail store to buy from any other supplier, these other suppliers have other retail stores to which they may sell.

There are three reasons for vertical mergers.[13] First, vertical mergers facilitate the implementation of price discrimination. If an intermediate product manufacturer (such as a manufacturer of steel or aluminum) perceives different price elasticities of demand for his product as it is fabricated into different final products, he will benefit from becoming a fabricator. Since the different elasticities are exhibited for the intermediate product as it is embodied in the final product, the manufacturer can more easily exploit these differences if he is also the manufacturer of the final product. Second, vertical integration can be used to offset monopoly power of suppliers. If there is a cartel of suppliers of some intermediate product, a manufacturer of a final product could assure himself of cheaper supplies by entering the intermediate product market himself. It is for this reason that many industrial users of oil are acquiring oil companies and exploring for new sources for oil on their own. Third, vertical integration may effectively raise entry costs to new rivals. If all the suppliers

---

[12]This analysis is based on Jack Hirshleifer, "On the Economics of Transfer Pricing," *Journal of Business* (July 1956).

[13]George Stigler, *The Theory of Price, op. cit.*, pp. 237–238.

of an intermediate product are controlled by a cartel of manufacturers of the final product, any new manufacturer who wishes to enter the market must not only raise enough capital to set up to manufacture the final good, he must also acquire the capital to set up as a supplier of the intermediate good. We have already seen that because of information costs it is sometimes difficult for an interloper entrepreneur who would carry out a successful operation to raise the money necessary to get going.

Up to this point in the text we have discussed markets for produced goods and services, but we have not explicitly examined the supply and demand for inputs. The next chapter is, in part, devoted to that examination.

## Questions for Discussion

1. Evaluate the following:

    Pan American Airways hasn't generated an accounting profit since 1968. Other airlines also show little or no profit for some years. This evidence clearly demonstrates that the CAB does not operate a cartel for the benefit of the airlines. Without the CAB's fare regulation, airlines would become profitable because they could raise their fees.

2. In the 1870's and 1880's, numerous railroads were formed to take advantage of the economic profit created by then existing privately operated railroad cartels. These interlopers set off a rate war that reduced railroad revenue to the level of operating costs. In 1887, in response to demands from the railroads, Congress created the Interstate Commerce Commission (ICC). The ICC immediately set out to try to establish an orderly cartel. It wasn't until 1920 that Congress gave the ICC sufficient powers to achieve that goal and by then railroads were clearly a declining industry. Since then the ICC has attempted to rescue the railroads from their fate as a declining industry by restricting competition among railroads, barges, and trucks. Outline what would have happened if, in 1887, Congress had followed a policy of "masterful inaction" —i.e., did nothing. (According to George Hilton this would have been the best policy.)

3. Evaluate:

    All workers in a unionized plant must be forced to join the union because nonmembers would be free riders.

4. It is often asserted that firms or cartels with monopoly power set "administered prices" without regard for market constraints. What do you think an "administered price" is? Is it anything different from a price searcher's optimum price? Do price searchers operate without regard for market conditions?

5. On October 20, 1974, the *San Francisco Examiner* reported that Republican gubernatorial candidate Houston Flournoy was against the repeal of California's fair trade law for alcoholic beverages. Flournoy's reasoning was that without the fair trade law, which sets minimum prices on each kind of alcoholic beverage, the mom-and-pop liquor stores would be driven out of business by the bigger retail sellers who would then raise prices higher than they are under the fair trade law. What do you think of Flournoy's grasp of economics? In the same article, Democratic gubernatorial candidate Jerry Brown was reported to have said that the economics of the milk industry made the removal of minimum retail prices for milk unwise. His solution was to appoint consumer representatives to the board that sets the minimum prices. What do you think of Brown's grasp of economics?

6. Construct a diagram to show gains and losses from a horizontal merger where a merged firm's marginal cost curve is positively sloped below the positively sloped supply curve that exists without the merger.

7. Construct the diagrammatic analysis of a vertical merger of a price searcher seller of an intermediate good with a price taker seller of a final good that embodies the intermediate good.

# 10
# Distribution Theory

The amount of real income a person receives is determined by the amount of resources he owns, the price the services of those resources sell for, and the individual's willingness to sell such services. Resources include land (natural resources) and capital (human and nonhuman). A person's human capital is his stock of mental and physical abilities acquired biologically or through education, training, and experience. Labor is the service yielded by human capital. Nonhuman capital includes such things as machines, buildings, and dams that are themselves produced by human effort and used to produce other things. If we are to understand why some people have less real income than others we must inquire into what determines the amount of resources individuals own, what determines the prices of the services of those resources, and how individuals choose between work and leisure.

## Quantity of Resources Owned

Although people are equal before the law, they are clearly not equal in ability, intelligence, training, education, and experience. Two people who are born with the same mental and physical capabilities (i.e., who inherit the same amount of

human capital) may well become owners of unequal amounts of human capital. Some of the difference may be due to voluntary decisions of the two individuals. Person A elects to strive to acquire training and/or education while Person B, having a stronger taste for leisure, does not.

Some of the difference may be due to unequal access to training and education. It is often difficult to borrow money to finance an education because the lender cannot claim the resulting human capital as collateral. This difficulty could prevent some individuals whose families are poor from acquiring educational services. Public schools at all levels which charge zero, or nearly zero, tuition are intended to alleviate this problem. Another way to alleviate the problem, at least at the college level, would be to rely exclusively on private institutions that charge full cost tuition, but to provide low interest loans, which would be paid back with interest after graduation, to any academically qualified student who wanted them. If the only problem we wish to address is the accessibility of educational services to academically qualified students from poor families, such a program would be sufficient, and it would have the advantage that those who benefit from the educational services are the ones who would pay for them. While there probably is some general public benefit from the provision of general education for citizenship, that kind of education is not what is provided at the college level. College level education is generally career-related, so that while what the degree holder does may benefit others, he gets paid for it. The benefit to others is captured as a benefit to the degree holder, hence there are no "spillover" benefits for the public at large.

Some mistakenly think that a person who borrows money to acquire an education does not get the same financial benefit from the education as one who does not have to borrow. The borrower, they argue, starts off after school with a debt over his head and the nonborrower does not. Suppose the cost of an education is $6,000. A person who has $6,000 can pay the price, but one who does not must borrow. If the person with the $6,000 elects to spend it on an education he cannot use it to purchase, say, bonds. If bonds pay 8% interest this person is in effect borrowing $6,000 from himself at 8%. After he graduates he must earn $6,000 plus the interest he could have earned on the bonds before he receives any *net* return from his investment in human capital. The borrower must earn $6,000 plus whatever interest the loan contract specifies before he receives any *net* return from his investment in education. The borrower must pay an outsider back, while the other person must pay himself back. If the borrower borrows the $6,000 for any interest rate less than 8% the net gain from the education will be larger for the borrower than it is for the nonborrower. To be sure, you are better off if you have to pay yourself back rather than someone else. But this is just another way of saying it is better to be rich than to be poor. The proposition that the net gain from investing in education is independent of initial wealth stands quite apart from the fact most individuals prefer wealth to poverty. A system of full tuition at all colleges and universities coupled with a program that made low interest loans available to students would not, therefore, discriminate against the poor.

An alternative sometimes considered is to charge full tuition but to permit the tui-tion plus interest to be paid over (say) a ten-year period after graduation. Such a "deferred tuition" plan was recently suggested by the Governor of California as a solution to funding problems in the University of California and California State University and Colleges. Of course, students at these institutions are opposed to such a system because they currently receive their education essentially as a gift from California taxpayers. Anyone who receives something at less than cost will oppose any plan that makes him pay the full cost. In fact if loans are made at interest rates below the market rate the student borrowers will still be receiving their education at less than full cost. The money that is loaned to them could yield a higher rate of return for the lenders (the taxpayers).

Volition plays some part in the determination of the ownership of nonhuman as well as human resources. Two individuals with equal incomes from their human capital may choose to save at different rates. The one who saves more will gradually acquire more nonhuman capital and/or land than the other. Two individuals with the same stock of human capital may earn different incomes because one has a stronger taste for leisure than the other. The one with the lower income will accumulate smaller claims on nonhuman capital and land even though he saves the same percentage of his income as does the person to whom leisure is less valuable.

Some human capital, nonhuman capital, and land may be acquired through inheritance. Many are concerned that inheritance of nonhuman capital and land gives an "unfair" advantage to those who are so blessed. These same people do not display the same concern for the "unfair" advantage that comes from inherited human capital. Some consider it all right for a father to use up his wealth purchasing human capital for his children (providing them with an education and enriching experiences), but if the same father uses his wealth to purchase nonhuman capital (e.g., a business enterprise) which he then turns over to his children, they consider it unfair. Those who assert that accumulations of nonhuman capital and land should be confiscated by government at the death of those who accumulate it do not also claim that the government should reduce the height of Bill Walton because this inherited human characteristic is not evenly distributed.

The question of what is "fair" or "unfair" is beyond economic analysis. Many feel that one of the human rights each person has is to use his property in any way that he wishes, subject only to the constraint that he does not engage anyone else in involuntary exchange. One thing that a person may wish to do with his property is give it away. While some people may approve if a wealthy man gives his property away to a search for a cancer cure and disapprove if he gives it away to his son, some others may have the opposite attitude. It is purely a matter of individual value judgments. For our purposes we merely note that inheritance is one of the determinants of the amount of human and nonhuman resources a person owns. In the United States less than 10% of all income payments received arise from the ownership of inherited nonhuman wealth.[1]

Simple luck is another determinant of the amount of resources owned. Human capital is affected by sickness and accident, and nonhuman capital and land are affected by natural disasters such as floods, fires, storms, and earthquakes.

In sum, there are four determinants of the amount of human and nonhuman resources owned by a given individual in a voluntary exchange economy:

1. *choices* made concerning work and leisure and rates of saving and investment (in both human and nonhuman capital)

2. *access* to sources of human and nonhuman capital

3. *inheritance,* which determines the individual's initial endowment of physical and mental ability as well as his initial endowment of other forms of wealth such as land, stocks, and bonds

4. *chance* or luck

## The Prices of Services of Resources

Whenever we discuss any price we use the tools of supply and demand. Earlier in this book we discussed the prices of goods and services produced by business firms and sold to households. We shall now use similar tools to discuss the prices of productive services sold by household owners of resources to business firms. We shall see that what determines the price any resource owner can collect for the productive services of that resource is the demand for the service relative to the number of other resource owners who can make that service available. If it takes you a long time to learn how to tear paper into precisely even strips, that does not mean that you will earn a high income performing this service. Because there is no demand for such a service, its performer will not successfully sell the service. Truck drivers earn more income than high school music teachers because there is more demand for truck drivers (relative to the supply) than there is for music teachers. The supply of truck drivers is severely restricted by the Teamsters Union. High school music teachers do not have a union that is strong enough to eliminate competition for music teaching jobs. Clearly, if we want to understand the different earnings from different occupations we must analyze the demand for and supply of productive services.

**A. Short-Run Demand Curve for Productive Services** Labor is the productive service that is derived from the resource we call human capital We shall focus on the demand for labor services, but we could just as easily concentrate on any other productive service. The theory would be the same.

In Chapter 4 we adopted the convention that in the short run labor is the only input

[1]George J. Stigler, "The Intellectual and the Market Place," reprinted in Leonard S. Silk, *Readings in Contemporary Economics* (New York: McGraw Hill, 1970), pp. 59–65.

that can be varied. There is a fixed amount of plant and equipment and the operator of the firm must decide how much labor to hire. As always we assume that the decision maker's only concern is to maximize profit. It is profitable to hire an additional unit of labor only if the resulting addition to revenue exceeds the resulting addition to cost. The change in revenue per unit change in labor used is $\Delta R/\Delta L$. It equals the change in output that results per unit change of labor, $\Delta q/\Delta L$, times the change in revenue per unit change in quantity of output sold, $\Delta R/\Delta q$; that is;

$$\frac{\Delta q}{\Delta L} \cdot \frac{\Delta R}{\Delta q} = \frac{\Delta R}{\Delta L}$$

The change in output per unit change in labor is called the marginal product of labor ($MP_L$). The change in revenue per unit change in quantity of output sold is called marginal revenue (MR). If the firm that hires the labor is a price taker seller of the product, marginal revenue equals price; hence

$$\frac{\Delta R}{\Delta L} = MP_L \cdot p_x$$

where $p_x$ is the product price. In this case $\Delta R/\Delta L$ is called the *value of the marginal product of labor* ($VMP_L$). If the firm that hires the labor is a price searcher seller of the product, marginal revenue is less than price, and $\Delta R/\Delta L = MP_L \cdot MR$. This is called the *marginal revenue product of labor* ($MRP_L$). In all cases $\Delta R/\Delta L$ is the additional revenue collected by the firm when it hires an additional unit of labor, and it is also the reduction in revenue that results when one unit less of labor is used. Since our discussion is carried out within the context of a two-input model with one input—capital—held fixed, the additional revenue of concern is merely the gross revenue collected from selling the additional output. If there were more than one variable input to be considered the additional revenue of concern would be the gross revenue collected from selling the additional output less payments that had to be

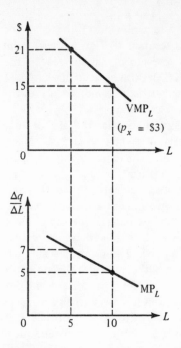

**Figure 10-1.**

Deriving the value of marginal product of labor curve.

made to the owners of the other variable inputs.

We know from Chapter 4 that a profit-maximizing firm will always use an amount of labor that is in the range where $MP_L$ is declining and below the average product of labor ($AP_L$). The curve that depicts the value of marginal product must also be downward sloping, for the marginal product is merely multiplied by market price. In Figure 10-1 the relevant portion of an $MP_L$ curve is drawn in the bottom panel. When the amount of labor used is 5, the use of an additional unit will result in 7 additional units of output. When the amount of labor used is 10, the use of an additional unit will result in 5 additional units of output. If the firm is a price taker, and if the product price is $3, the value of the marginal product curve will appear as it is in the top panel. When the amount of labor used is 5, the use of an additional unit will result in an increase of $21 ($3 times 7) in revenue. When the amount of labor used is 10, the use of an additional unit will result in an increase of revenue of $15 ($3 times 5). The marginal product of labor is monetized by multiplying by the product price.

In Figure 10-2 we again depict the relevant portion of an $MP_L$ curve, but this time we suppose that the firm is a price searcher. Since marginal revenue declines as additional units of output are sold, the $MRP_L$ curve must be steeper than the $VMP_L$ curve. For example, when $MP_L$ is 7 (at 5 units of $L$) marginal revenue would be (say) $2; thus $MRP_L$ would be $14 ($2 times 7). When 10 units of labor are used, more total output is produced than when 5 units of labor are used, so the marginal revenue that we use to multiply $MP_L$ by will be less than $2. It could be, for example, $0.50. In that case $MRP_L$ would be $2.50 ($0.50 times the $MP_L$ of 5).

The $VMP_L$ curve and the $MRP_L$ curve are the short-run demand for labor curves for price takers and price searchers, respectively. (The analysis is "short run" because the amount of plant and equipment used is held fixed.) Both $VMP_L$ and $MRP_L$ are the addition to revenue that the firm collects when an additional unit of labor is used. This addition to revenue is the benefit of using an additional unit of labor. If the firm is a price taker buyer of labor services it can purchase all it wants at the pre-

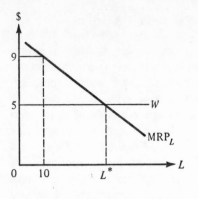

**Figure 10-3.**
Optimum quantity of labor.

vailing market wage, but it cannot purchase any at a lower wage rate. The wage rate is then the cost of using an additional unit of labor. Suppose the prevailing wage for a given type of labor is $5 per hour. A standard workday is eight hours, so this wage could also be expressed as $40 per day. The horizontal axis of Figure 10-3 measures the number of people working a standard workday. The vertical axis is in units of dollars per hour. For example, when 10 people work a standard workday the marginal revenue product is $9 per hour. This means that if an eleventh person were hired to work a standard workday the resulting additional output per day would bring in an additional $72 per day, or $9 per hour. It is clearly profitable to hire the eleventh person. Additional people will be hired until $MRP_L$ does not exceed the $5 wage rate ($W$). The profit-maximizing quantity of labor to hire is $L^*$. The firm in Figure 10-3 is a price searcher seller of output (because the $MRP_L$ curve and not the $VMP_L$ curve is used), but it is a price taker buyer of labor. The horizontal line at $5 indicates that the firm can purchase all the labor it wants at $5 per hour, but it cannot purchase any if it offers a lower wage.

At this juncture it is essential to recall that the marginal product of labor is *not* the amount of output produced by an additional unit of labor. In Chapter 4 we saw that the marginal product of labor is the additional output produced when an additional unit of labor is used. The amount that the additional worker produces is the

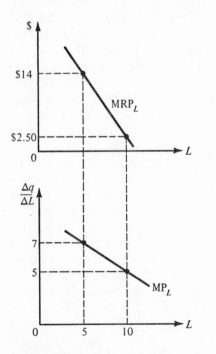

**Figure 10-2.**
Deriving the marginal revenue product of labor curve.

average product of labor $(AP_L)$.[2] All work-ers produce the average product. When an additional worker is hired, that worker pro-duces some output, *but he also changes the amount that all other workers produce.* Since the relevant range is the region of declining average product, when an addi-tional worker is hired he *reduces* the amount produced by each of the workers who were already hired. Suppose that when 10 workers are working each pro-duces 20 units of output (i.e., the *average* product is 20 units), and that when an eleventh is hired each of the 11 workers produces 19 units (i.e., the *new* average product is 19 units). The marginal prod-uct—the addition to output when the eleventh is hired—is then 9 units. The amount that the eleventh person produces is 19. This is the same amount that all others produce when he is there, but be-cause he causes each of the first 10 workers to produce one unit less, the net increase in output—the marginal product—is 9 units. We have seen that a firm that is a price taker buyer of labor will hire the amount of labor that makes $MRP_L$ (or $VMP_L$ for price taker sellers of output) equal the wage rate. This means that each worker is paid an amount of dollars equal to the de-crease in revenue that the firm would ex-perience if any single worker were to stop working. *It does not mean that a worker is paid an amount of dollars equal to the revenue the firm collects from what that worker produces.*

Each worker produces the average prod-uct of labor; hence the revenue that the firm collects from what a worker (together with capital) produces equals the price each unit sells for multiplied by the *aver-age product* of labor. Product price times average product of labor is always larger than either $VMP_L$ or $MRP_L$. This is so be-

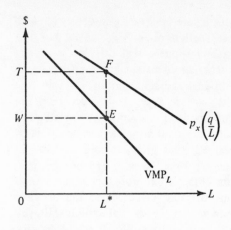

**Figure 10-4.**
Division of total revenue.

cause in the relevant range $MP_L$ is less than $AP_L$, and MR either equals (price taker) or is less than (price searcher) product price.

Figure 10-4 illustrates the relevant magnitudes. In the short run, profit equals the difference between total revenue $(p_x q)$ and the sum of variable cost $(WL)$ and fixed cost. If the firm is a price taker seller of output the relevant demand curve for labor is the $VMP_L$ curve. If the wage rate is $W$ the quantity of labor demanded will be $L^*$. Variable cost will be area $0WEL^*$. If we multiply the average product of labor $(q/L)$ by the product price we get the curve labeled $p_x(q/L)$. If we multiply $p_x(q/L)$ by $L^*$ we get the total revenue collected by the firm when it hires $L^*$ units of labor. Area $0TFL^*$ equals this total revenue. Total revenue minus variable cost is then area $WTFE$. This amount is what is availa-ble for fixed cost and profit.

Note that when $L^*$ units of labor are hired the $VMP_L$—the amount of revenue the firm would lose if one unit less of labor were used—is $L^*E$. Each worker is paid this amount. The amount of revenue the firm collects on the amount produced by any single unit of labor is $L^*F$. A worker is not paid the value of what "*he* produces"—this is the product price times the *average* prod-uct. Instead each worker is paid an amount equal to the decrease in revenue the firm would experience if any one worker quit—this is the value of the marginal prod-uct and it is the full value of each worker to the firm. If each worker were paid the value of what "*he* produces" there could never be any revenue left over for fixed cost and profits.

When we compared price takers and price searchers in Chapter 8 we observed that with a given market demand for a product the total quantity supplied by a group of price takers is greater than the total quantity supplied by a single price searcher. Each price taker equates marginal cost and product price, but a price searcher equates marginal cost and marginal revenue. Since marginal revenue is less than price, price will be larger than marginal cost for a price searcher. We said in Chapter 5 that this is an indication that insufficient resources are devoted to the product produced by the price searcher. Now we have seen that a price taker seller of output equates his $VMP_L$ with the wage rate. Note that if $p_x(MP_L) = W$, $p_x = W/MP_L$. In Chapter 5 we saw that $W/MP_L$ equals marginal cost. Saying that a price taker equates $VMP_L$ with the wage is just another way of saying that for a price taker price equals marginal cost. If $MR(MP_L) = W$, $MR = W/MP_L = MC$. Saying that a price searcher sets $MRP_L$ equal to the wage rage is just another way of saying that he equates marginal cost and marginal revenue.

Since MR is less than $p_x$, $MRP_L$ is less than $VMP_L$. In Figure 10-5 the $VMP_L$ curve depicts the demand for labor by a firm that is a price taker, while the $MRP_L$ curve depicts the demand of the same firm if it were a price searcher. The underlying

marginal product of labor curve is the same for both $VMP_L$ and $MRP_L$. If the firm were a price searcher and the wage rate were $W$, $L_1$ units of labor would be hired. At the same wage $L_2$ units would be hired if the firm were a price taker. At $L_1$ we see that the value that consumers place on the additional output produced when one more worker is used is $L_1 T$ (the product price times the number of additional units produced when one more unit of labor is used). The cost of using an additional unit is merely $W$. This is just another way of seeing that too few resources (in this case labor) are used by price searchers.

Throughout this discussion we have assumed that each employer is a price taker buyer of labor services. This is a fairly realistic assumption, since even if a firm is a monopolistic seller of some product it is only one of many firms that hire a given kind of labor. In the early part of the Twentieth Century and before, there were numerous instances in which labor in a given city or town had only one or two potential employers. A New England mill town, for instance, was usually characterized by one dominant employer. Such an employer did not have to accept the prevailing wage rate as being beyond his control. We will discuss employers in this situation later in this chapter. Right now the main point to be recognized is that because of the automobile and other transportation and communication devices, the extent to which labor is restricted to only a few employers has been greatly diminished. Labor markets are now at least regional, if not national and international. The passage of time has greatly increased the amount of rivalry among employers for employees.

**B. Long-Run Demand Curve for Productive Services** In the long run a firm can alter the amount of capital it uses as well as the amount of labor. In Chapter 5 we saw that when the ratio of the wage rate to the user cost of capital changes, the optimum (least-cost) input combination for each output rate also changes. This suggests that when there is a change of the wage rate and a constant user cost of capital the firm will want to alter the amount of capital it uses

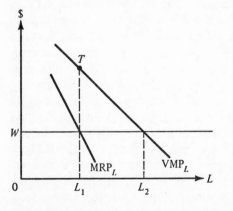

**Figure 10-5.**
Comparison of price taker and price searcher.

along with the amount of labor it uses. When it does so the marginal product of labor curve (and therefore the $VMP_L$ and the $MRP_L$ curves) shifts. In Chapter 4 we saw that, in the relevant range, when additional (less) capital is used with a constant amount of labor the marginal product of labor increases (decreases). Similarly, when additional (less) labor is used with a constant amount of capital the marginal product of capital increases (decreases).[3] A given $VMP_L$ or $MRP_L$ curve is the demand curve for labor only so long as there is a constant amount of capital.

The top panel of Figure 10-6 is an isoquant-expansion path diagram such as that used in Chapters 4 and 5. The bottom panel depicts the demand curves for labor. We begin at point $A$ in both diagrams. The wage rate is $W_1$ and the quantity of labor demanded is $L_1$. The ratio of the wage rate to the user cost of capital, together with the isoquants, generates the expansion path labeled $0E_1$ in the top panel. Quantity $q_1$ is produced with the optimal input combination $K_1$ and $L_1$. The initial demand curve for labor ($VMP_L$ or $MRP_L$) is labeled $D_s$ in the bottom panel. Let us suppose that the wage rate declines to $W_2$. In the bottom panel we can see that the quantity of labor demanded at first becomes $L_2$. The lower wage rate, together with an unchanged user cost of capital, generates another expansion path, labeled $0E_2$ in the top panel. With unchanged capital, and labor increased to $L_2$, we move to point $B$ in both diagrams. The amount of output produced becomes $q_2$. (With changed costs the optimal output rate changes.) The increased labor use increases the marginal product of capital. With an unchanged user cost of capital this means that the firm will want to use additional capital. When full equilibrium is restored, in other words, the firm will use more capital than it initially

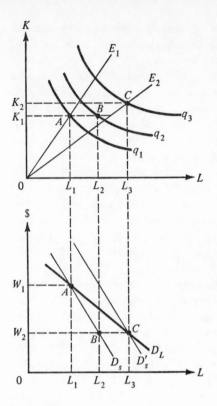

**Figure 10-6.**
Long-run demand curve for labor.

did. Additional capital shifts the short-run demand for labor curve to the right. We assume that the new equilibrium amount of capital is $K_2$ in the top panel. This assumption, together with the new expansion path, determines the new equilibrium output rate, $q_3$, in the top panel. The fact that the output rate must change when the use rates of inputs change is obvious enough, but it has at least one implication that must be emphasized: changes in the amount of capital used are not the only thing that will shift the short-run demand curve for labor. If the depicted firm is a price taker seller of its output, presumably all other sellers of the product will also increase output in response to the decreased wage rate. When they do so the price of the product will fall; hence for a given marginal product of labor the value of the marginal product will decline. If the depicted firm is a price searcher seller, the additional output will mean that marginal revenue will decrease; hence for a given marginal product of labor the marginal revenue product will decline. In the bottom panel we have

---

[3]These relationships must hold for the case of constant returns to scale. With other kinds of production functions it is possible to demonstrate mathematically some situations where they do not hold. Nevertheless they hold most of the time, and they are empirically and pedagogically useful generalizations.

depicted the net result of the increase in capital and decrease of product price or marginal revenue as a shift of the short-run demand curve for labor from $D_s$ to $D'_s$. The new optimal input combination is $K_2$ and $L_3$. As the short-run demand curve for labor shifts the firm moves from point $B$ to point $C$ in both diagrams. The firm's long-run demand curve for labor is formed in the bottom panel by connecting the initial point of full equilibrium (point $A$) with the new point of full equilibrium (point $C$). It is labeled $D_L$. You can test your understanding of this exposition by going through the analysis for the case of an increase of the wage rate.

The market demand curve for a given type of labor is the horizontal sum of the demand curves of individual firms for that type of labor. Some buyers of a given type of labor will be price taker sellers of output, while others will be price searcher sellers of output. At each wage rate we add together the quantity demanded by each user of the type of labor in question.

**C. Determinants of the Price Elasticity of Demand for Inputs** The price elasticity of demand for an input will be higher the more easily that other inputs can be substituted for it; that is, the *technical feasibility* of substitution affects the price elasticity of demand. The extent to which machinery can substitute for the services of a nurse is extremely limited. A hospital administrator will only slightly decrease the quantity he demands of nursing services when the price of such services rises. Machines can much more easily substitute for laboratory technicians. When laboratory technician wages increase, therefore, there is a greater reduction in the quantity of technician services demanded.

A commonly used measure of the technical feasibility of substitution is the *elasticity of technical substitution*. The lower case Greek letter "sigma" ($\sigma$) is the symbol most often used to represent this elasticity. $\sigma$ is defined as the percentage change in the ratio of capital to labor that is caused by a 1% change of the ratio of the wage rate ($W$) to the user cost of capital ($\phi$) when there is no change in the quantity of output pro-

duced. Suppose, for example, that the ratio of the wage rate to the user cost of capital falls by 10% and this induces a substitution of labor for capital such that if the same output rate were produced the ratio of $K$ to $L$ would fall by 20%. Then $\sigma$ would be 2. There would be a 2% drop in the $K/L$ ratio per 1% drop in the $W/\phi$ ratio. A change of the ratio of $K$ to $L$ with a constant output rate is a movement along an isoquant. The more sharply convex the isoquant the lower the elasticity of technical substitution. The higher the elasticity of technical substitution the higher will be the price elasticity of demand for a given input.

The price elasticity of demand for a given input is also affected by the price elasticity of the supply of substitutes. The more elastic the supply of a substitute the less the increase in price that must be paid to acquire additional units of it. Thus if the price of a given input increases its users can turn to the substitute and have to pay only a small price increase. On the other hand, if the elasticity of supply of the substitute is low, large increases in price must be paid when additional units of it are used. The users of the given input will be less likely to turn to a substitute if they must pay greatly higher prices when they do so. We conclude that the greater the price elasticity of supply of a substitute the greater will be the price elasticity of demand for a given input.

Third, the price elasticity of demand for an input will be greater the greater the price elasticity of demand for the products that are produced with the input. The more elastic the demand for the product the more the quantity sold will fall when the price of the product rises. A given increase in the price of an input will result in some increase in the price of the product. If the quantity demanded of the product falls by a large amount there will also be a large decrease in the quantity of input demanded to produce the output. If buyers buy less of the product, firms will employ less inputs to produce the product. If the given increase in product price that results from the increase in input price causes only a small reduction in the quantity demanded of the product, there will be a correspondingly small reduction in the quantity of input demanded.

Finally, the amount of time that firms have to adjust to a change of the wage rate will affect the size of the resulting change in the quantity of labor demanded. Our derivation of the long-run and short-run demand curves for labor revealed that the second fundamental law of demand stated in Chapter 3—that the price elasticity of demand is greater in the long run than it is in the short run—holds for input demand as well as product demand. This implies, for example, that whereas in the short run there may be only a small reduction in the amount of farm labor used in response to a large increase in farm wage rates, in the longer run, when growers have had time to adapt to a new optimal output rate and to attain the new least-cost combination of capital and labor, there will be substantial reductions in the quantity of farm labor used.

**D. The Supply Curve of Labor** Our theory of what determines the quantity of a product available in a market in Chapters 7 and 8 is also applicable to the supply of non-human inputs. Nonhuman inputs are, after all, produced by firms and sold to other firms; hence the suppliers of nonhuman inputs are either price taker or price searcher sellers of their products. We need no special theory for them. However, we do need to construct a separate theory for the supply of the services of human capital. Owners of human capital can choose whether to sell labor services or to consume labor services in the form of leisure. The tools that we use to analyze this choice process are the same as those we used to analyze the choice processes of individual buyers of more than one good—indifference curves and budget constraints.

Figure 10-7 shows an indifference curve that depicts the trade-off between income (a good) and work (a bad). Recall from Chapter 2 that a "good" is something the individual prefers more of to less of; we can also say that a "bad" is something the individual prefers less of to more of. In this analysis we assume that work is something people don't like to do. They will only do

it if they are sufficiently remunerated for it. In Chapter 3 we listed three basic assumptions of indifference curve analysis. The third assumption was that the more an individual has of any good the less he will pay (in real terms, not money terms) to get an additional unit of the good. In Figure 10-7 we begin at point $A$. An increment of income (the good) equal to $AC$ is given to the individual. The maximum amount the individual is willing to pay (the amount that keeps him on the initial indifference curve) to get this increment of income is $CD$ units of work (the bad). The first thing we notice is that an indifference curve between a bad and a good must be positively sloped. More of the good must be compensated for by *more* of the bad if the individual is to stay on the same indifference curve. The third assumption of Chapter 3 tells us that the indifference curve must be convex toward the work axis. If instead of starting at point $A$ we start at point $B$, and give the individual the same increment of income ($BE$ equals $AC$), the maximum amount he is willing to pay for it is less than before. It is $EF$, whereas before, when the individual had less income, it was $CD$. An indifference map depicting the individual's attitude toward all possible combinations of work and income consists of many such positively sloped lines that are convex to the work axis. The combinations that are preferred to the combinations represented by the one indifference curve in Figure 10-7 would lie on indifference

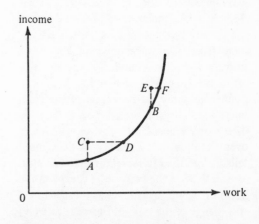

**Figure 10-7.**
Indifference curve for bad and good.

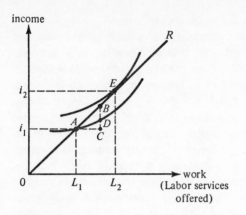

**Figure 10-8.**
Optimum combination of income and work.

curves that are generally northwest of the one in the figure. Less preferred combinations would lie on indifference curves that are generally southeast of the one in the figure.

Figure 10-8 depicts the relevant budget constraint and the individual's optimum combination of income and work. The budget constraint starts at the origin, for if zero hours are worked income will be zero.[4] If $L_1$ units of labor service are offered and the wage is $W$, income will be $WL_1$, which equals $i_1$. If $L_2$ units of labor service are offered and the wage continues to be $W$, income will be $WL_2$, which equals $i_2$. The line $OR$ gives us the income that will be earned for each possible amount of labor service offered. Its slope equals the wage rate, $W$. If the wage rate were to fall the budget line would still begin at the origin, but it would be flatter. If the wage rate increased the budget line would be steeper. The budget line is a straight line because for each increment of work the resulting increase in income is constant. Each additional unit of work raises income by the wage rate. Suppose the individual is at point $A$ on his budget constraint. He would be willing to offer $AC$ additional units of labor service if he got paid any amount over $CD$ in income. The budget constraint tells us that he can obtain $CB$ additional

units of income for $AC$ additional units of labor service. He thus moves from point $A$ to point $B$ on the budget constraint line. He will continue to make such moves until the extra income he can get for extra work (the slope of the budget line) no longer exceeds the minimum amount he will accept for extra work (the slope of the indifference curve). Point $E$ represents the optimum combination of income and work, $i_2$ and $L_2$ respectively. Its optimality is indicated, as is usual in indifference curve analysis, by the tangency between an indifference curve and the budget constraint.

Let us now examine the individual's response to an increase of the wage rate. In Figure 10-9 the individual is in initial equilibrium at point $A$. Income is $i_1$ and work offered is $L_1$. The wage rate increases so that the budget line shifts from $OR_1$ to $OR_2$. This change in the wage rate has two effects: it increases the price of leisure and it gives the individual additional income from an unchanged amount of work. The price of leisure is merely the income that could be earned if the time were spent working instead of in leisure. From the first fundamental law of demand we know that the worker will decrease his consumption of leisure, which is the same thing as saying that additional work will be offered. However, since the individual can earn $i' - i_1$ extra income by continuing to offer only $L_1$ units of work, he is richer now that he was before. If leisure is a normal

---

[4]If the individual has some nonlabor sources of income, the budget constraint would begin above the origin on the vertical axis.

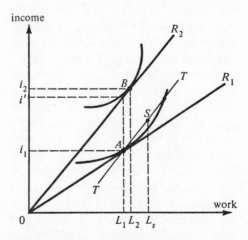

**Figure 10-9.**
Income and Substitution Effects.

good the increased income will induce the individual to consume additional leisure. By constructing budget line $TT$ we can see how the individual would respond to the increased price of leisure if he didn't have the $i' - i_1$ extra income. That budget line has the same slope as $OR_2$ so it depicts the higher wage rate, but it passes through point $A$. In effect we have subtracted $i' - i_1$ income from the amount the individual earns by offering $L_1$ units of work. He makes the same income at $L_1$ as he used to, so there is no extra income to make him consume more leisure. Under these circumstances of a pure rise in the real price of leisure the individual will unambiguously consume less leisure (work more) than before. He would, for example, move to point $S$ on $TT$, offering $L_s$ units of work. Only points northeast of $A$ on $TT$ are on higher indifference curves. The increase from $L_1$ to $L_s$ is called the *substitution effect* of the higher wage rate. Now we can add back the $i' - i_1$ income, making the budget line $OR_2$. This added income will, if leisure is a normal good, induce the individual to consume more leisure (work less). The work offer declines from $L_s$ to $L_2$. This decline is called the *income effect* of the higher wage rate. The net result, adding the substitution effect and the income effect together, is to increase the work offer from $L_1$ to $L_2$.

This analysis suggests that an individual's labor supply curve is positively sloped with respect to the wage rate. But the substitution effect need not always dominate the income effect, so we can imagine a backward-bending individual labor supply curve, especially at high wage rates. At low wage rates the substitution effect of a wage increase is likely to dominate the income effect because the individual is not yet rich enough to seriously contemplate cutting hours worked. At higher wage rates income earned will be larger, so that an increase in the wage rate may indeed be accompanied by a reduction in hours worked. In any case we can clearly say that an individual's labor supply curve gets steeper as the wage rate increases. The market supply curve for a particular kind of labor is merely the horizontal sum of the individual supply curves.

Although our choice theory does not rule out backward-bending individual, and therefore market, supply curves of labor in the short run, we can rule out backward-bending long-run market supply curves. In the long run individuals who are in one occupation can switch occupations by acquiring the necessary training. If the wage rate paid to one type of labor increases enough to induce workers already in the occupation to decrease the quantity of labor they offer, this is likely to attract outsiders into the occupation. If the cost of the retraining is no greater than the present value of the income difference between the two occupations, such interoccupational transfers will take place.[5] Of course if access to the more profitable occupation is blocked by legal obstacles such as licensing requirements or by a requirement of membership in a union, the extent of interoccupational transfers will be diminished.

**E. Determination of the Wage for a Particular Type of Labor** We have noted that a price taker seller of a product who is a price taker buyer of labor services equates his $VMP_L$ with the prevailing wage for the type of labor he uses; a price searcher seller of a product who is a price taker buyer of labor services equates his $MRP_L$ with the going wage for the type of labor he uses. The wage a particular type of labor receives is determined by the interaction of the total supply of that labor type and the total demand for that labor type. Essentially the relationship between the market supply and demand for labor of a given type and the individual user of the labor is depicted in Figure 10-10. The curve labeled $d$ in the left panel is the demand curve of one user for a given type of labor. The price the individual price taker buyer of the labor services must take is determined by the intersection of the total market demand and supply curves which are depicted in the right panel. The market clearing

---

[5]We shall discuss discounting and present value calculations in the next chapter.

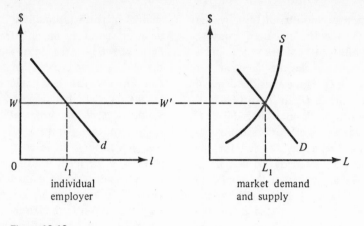

**Figure 10-10.**
Price taker buyer of input.

wage is $0W$ and the profit-maximizing quantity of this labor for the depicted individual employer to use is $l_1$. The total quantity supplied and demanded is $L_1$.

However, we frequently observe long-run interindustry differences in the wages paid to labor of a given type. In order to analyze this fact we must disaggregate the total demand and supply curves for labor of a given type into demand and supply curves for labor of that type in different industries. Although all price taker users of a given type of labor face horizontal individual supply curves such as that labeled $WW'$ in Figure 10-10, the price taker buyers of the services of that labor type in Industry $A$ could well have to take a wage that is different from that taken by

employers of the same kind of labor in Industry $B$.

Ordinarily we would expect that if the going wage paid to a given type of labor in Industry $A$ were higher than that paid to the same kind of labor in Industry $B$, workers would transfer from $B$ to $A$ until the differential disappeared. Figure 10-11 depicts this process. The demand curves of all the employers in Industry $A$ are summed to yield $D_a$ in the left panel. The same sum over the employers in Industry $B$ yields $D_b$ in the right panel. The short-run labor supply curve in Industry $A$ is labeled $S_a$, and that for Industry $B$ is labeled $S_b$. Movements along these two supply curves indicate changes in the quantity of labor services offered by workers already employed

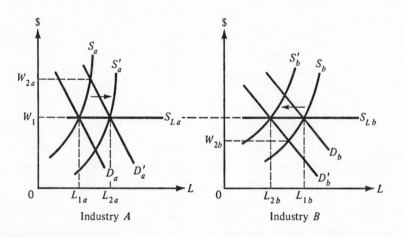

**Figure 10-11.**
Responses to demand shifts.

in the respective industries. Initially the wage is $W_1$ in both industries. Suppose now that product $A$ becomes very popular with consumers while the demand for product $B$ declines. This causes the demand for labor to shift to $D_a'$ in Industry $A$ and to $D_b'$ in Industry $B$. Workers in Industry $B$ are told to accept layoffs or wage cuts because of the decline in demand for the product. The wage decreases to $W_{2b}$ in Industry $B$ and there is some reduction in the quantity of labor used. The expanding demand for labor in Industry $A$ drives the wage rate up to $W_{2a}$, and there is some increase in the amount of labor used there. Since the labor employed in Industry $B$ has the same abilities and skills as the labor employed in Industry $A$, the higher wage rate in $A$ will attract employees from $B$ as soon as the differential becomes known. As labor leaves Industry $B$ and seeks employment in Industry $A$ the short-run supply curve shifts toward $S_b'$ in $B$ and toward $S_a'$ in $A$. If there are no barriers to labor mobility such as union rules, and if workers consider the nonpecuniary aspects of employment to be the same in both industries, the reallocation of labor in response to the demand shifts will continue until the wage rate is again made equal in the two industries. This occurs when wage rate $W_1$ is restored in both industries, with $L_{2a}$ employed in $A$ and $L_{2b}$ employed in $B$. The long-run supply curves in Industry $A$ and Industry $B$ are, under these circumstances, horizontal lines. They are labeled $S_{La}$ and $S_{Lb}$, respectively. With such mobility of workers between industries any wage differences between the industries must be only temporary. Any shift of demand between industries must ultimately result in the wage rate returning to its previous level in all industries, providing that the total demand and supply of labor of the type in question do not change.

Labor in fact is not as mobile as this analysis requires. One major reason is that workers do not consider employment in one industry a perfect substitute for employment in another, even when the type of work involved is the same. For example, some workers have strong geographical preferences. For some it would take a sub-

stantial increase in pecuniary income to get them to consider moving from the San Francisco Bay Area to the Midwest. If these people were paid the same wage in San Francisco as they could make in the Midwest (in purchasing power terms) they would be receiving a *geographic rent*. Some decrease of their San Francisco wage would not induce them to leave. Since they are receiving a payment in excess of the minimum necessary to keep them in San Francisco, they are receiving a rent. A person may not be enticed to move by a higher wage rate, because of family ties and friendships in his present location. The steadiness of employment within a given industry might be another factor accounting for immobility of some workers. Some workers have a strong aversion to risk. They will discount any wage differences to take into account the probability of unemployment.

Under these circumstances there will be "equalizing differences" in wage rates between industries that use the same kind of labor. Differences in pecuniary income make up for differences in the nonpecuniary aspects of employment. Even if initially the supply and demand conditions in two industries happened to bring about equal wage rates, if anything should happen to make the wage rates unequal—such as a demand shift—the equality would not be restored. We depict such a situation in Figure 10-12. The initial demand curves in Industry $A$ and Industry $B$ are $D_a$ and $D_b$, respectively. Suppose that, given the different tastes and preferences of workers regarding the nonpecuniary aspects of employment in the two industries, the initial supply curves in Industry $A$ and Industry $B$ are $S_a$ and $S_b$, respectively. The wage rate would equal $W_1$ in both industries. If buyers of products $A$ and $B$ change their buying patterns so that the demand for product $A$ increases while the demand for product $B$ decreases, the demand for labor in Industry $A$ would shift to $D_a'$, and in Industry $B$ it would shift to $D_b'$. Again workers in Industry $B$ would be faced with layoffs and wage cuts. The wage would fall to $W_{2b}$. The increase in demand in Industry $A$ will increase the wage there to

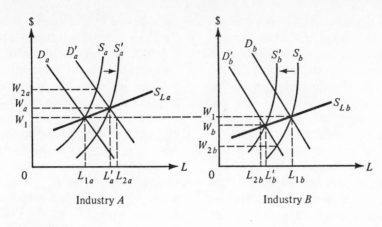

**Figure 10-12.**
Equalizing wage differences.

$W_{2a}$. The higher wage in $A$ than in $B$ will, as soon as it becomes known, induce workers to move from employment in $B$ to employment in $A$. The supply of labor in $A$ will shift to the right, while that in $B$ will shift to the left. The increase of supply in $A$ will diminish the wage there, while the decrease of supply in $B$ will increase the wage there. If some workers in Industry $B$ are willing to work in $B$ even if the wage there is less than in $A$, the supply shifts will stop before $W_1$ is reestablished in both industries. The equilibrium wage in Industry $A$ would be (for example) $W_a$, while that in Industry $B$ would be $W_b$. The quantity of labor employed in $A$ would be $L'_a$ rather than $L_{2a}$ as before. In Industry $B$ the amount employed would be $L'_b$ rather than $L_{2b}$. Labor will have been reallocated in response to the changes in the desires of the buyers of the products, but the reallocation will not be as extensive in this case as it was in the previous case. The higher wage in Industry $A$ will mean that the marginal cost of each firm will be higher than it was in the previous case, hence the optimal total output of Industry $A$ will be reduced. Similarly, in Industry $B$ marginal cost will be lower and the optimal total output higher than in the previous case of more extensive reallocation.

Both industries face positively sloped long-run labor supply curves—$S_{La}$ in $A$, and $S_{Lb}$ in $B$. This indicates that the workers in the two industries do not consider employment in one a perfect substitute for employment in the other. When the total demand for a given type of labor does not change relative to its total supply, but one industry demands more while another demands less, the industry that demands more will have to pay a higher wage than it did before, while the industry that demands less will be able to pay a lower wage than it did before.

Of course, the tastes and preferences of workers for the various nonpecuniary aspects of employment are not the only barriers to perfect labor mobility. Minimum wage laws and restrictive union practices can have similar effects. This is illustrated in Figure 10-13. Initial demand and supply curves in Industry $A$ and Industry $B$ are $D_a$ and $S_a$, and $D_b$ and $S_b$, respectively. The initial wage is $W_1$ in both industries. Suppose now that $W_1$ is set as the legal minimum wage. Since the wage would be $W_1$ anyway, there are no ill effects from the legislation, and some politician makes points with voters who do not understand economics. However, as Hayek never tires of pointing out, we do encounter problems as soon as market conditions change. Suppose that the demand for labor in Industry $A$ shifts to $D'_a$ while the demand for labor in Industry $B$ shifts to $D'_b$. The wage rate will rise in Industry $A$ to $W_u$, but the wage rate in Industry $B$ cannot fall. If it could it would fall to $W'$ and eliminate the excess supply of labor that was induced by the demand shift. Since the wage continues to be $W_1$ in Industry $B$, there will be an excess supply of labor in that industry of $L_{3b} - L_{1b}$. Ordinarily these unemployed workers would transfer to Industry $A$, shifting the supply of labor there to $S_a'$ and returning the wage rate to $W_1$. As long as the total demand for this type of labor has not decreased relative to the total supply (and if we ignore the problem of equalizing differences), the equilibrium wage will be $W_1$ in both industries. Since the minimum wage is $W_1$, the legislation will have no lasting effect. However, if the total demand for this type of labor decreased relative to its total supply the new equilibrium wage would be less than $W_1$. Since the wage could not fall there would be a continuous excess supply of labor (unemployment) in the market for this type of labor.

Assume that the equilibrium wage is $W_1$, but that the workers in Industry $A$ are unionized. When the demand shifts to $D_a'$ in that industry the union negotiates a wage increase to $W_u$. The wage would have become $W_u$ anyway, but now the union officers get to make points with the rank and file. More important, the union officers can keep the wage at $W_u$. The workers displaced from Industry $B$ can be effectively kept out of Industry $A$ by the union contract that specifies $W_u$ as the wage. The effective labor supply curve is a horizontal line at $W_u$ out to the quantity of labor that is ordinarily supplied at $W_u$. That quantity will be $L_{3a}$ because it includes workers from $B$ who are attracted by the high wage in $A$. To get more workers than $L_{3a}$, higher wages than $W_u$

are indicated by the normal supply curve $S_a'$. The effective labor supply curve is the line $W_u R S_a'$. The dashed portion of $S_a'$ is irrelevant because the union contract specifies that the wage cannot be below $W_u$. Employers are told they may have all the workers they want up to $L_{3a}$ if they pay $W_u$, but they cannot have any if they pay less. Given that the demand for labor in Industry $A$ is $D_a'$, the quantity of labor that will be hired will be $L_{2a}$. Workers represented by the difference between $L_{3a}$ and $L_{2a}$ will be prohibited from offering to work for any less than $W_u$ in Industry $A$. If they did so they would be branded as "scabs." These same workers are excluded from reemployment in Industry $B$ by the legislation that specifies $W_1$ as the minimum wage. Perhaps they end up on welfare rolls.

## Monopsony

Up to now we have treated employers as price taker buyers of labor services. Each employer was considered to be one of many employers of a given type of labor. The wage rate paid to any type of labor was determined by the interaction of the many buyers and sellers of the labor service. Suppose, however, there is only one employer of a given type of labor. In Chapter 8 we saw that when there is only one seller of a given product, that seller faces the market demand curve for the product. When

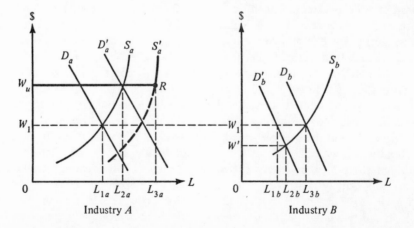

**Figure 10-13.**
Effects of union and minimum wage.

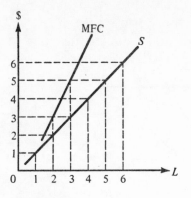

**Figure 10-14.**
Marginal factor cost and supply.

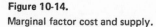

there is only one *buyer* (that is what the word "monopsony" means) of a given type of labor services, that buyer faces the market supply curve for that type of labor. The single buyer makes up the whole of the buying side of the market, hence he can affect the wage rate paid by his decision to hire more or less labor. Since the market supply curve is positively sloped, the more labor he wants to hire the higher the wage he must pay. Think of the market supply curve of labor as a *supply price* curve. Each worker has a minimum price that he will insist on receiving if he is to perform the task the employer wants done. This minimum price—or supply price—is different for each worker. One may be willing to work the standard work week at a pay rate of $1 per hour, while another will not do so unless he receives $2.50 per hour. Presumably the first worker has less attractive alternative employment opportunities or places a lower value on leisure than the second worker does. Figure 10-14 depicts a positively sloped market supply price curve labeled *S*. There is one worker who will work the standard workweek for an hourly wage rate of $1. There is another who will do the job for an hourly wage rate of $2, a third who will do it if the hourly wage rate is $3, and so on. If the employer hires one person it will be the one who will work for $1 per hour. If a second person is hired that person will have to be paid $2 per hour, and if the employer pays a uniform wage—equal pay for equal work—the first person will also be paid $2. In that case the hourly wage bill increases by $3

when the second person is hired. This increase is made up of the $2 paid to the second worker plus the added $1 paid to the first worker. We call this increase the *marginal factor cost* (MFC). Suppose now that the employer hires a third person. That person must be paid at the rate of $3 per hour, and if a uniform wage is paid to all workers the hourly marginal factor cost will be the $3 paid to the third worker plus the $1 increase paid to each of the first two workers. Thus, MFC equals $5. The line labeled MFC in Figure 10-14 keeps track of the additional cost when one more worker is hired. It is the curve that is marginal to the supply curve. The supply curve gives the wage paid per unit of *L*—it is the *average factor cost*. When a third person is hired the addition to the hourly wage bill is $5, and each worker is paid at the hourly rate of $3.

Figure 10-15 depicts the optimal amount of labor for a monopsonist to hire. The curve that keeps track of the addition to revenue when one more unit of *L* is hired is the marginal revenue product curve ($MRP_L$). The curve that keeps track of the addition to cost when one more unit of *L* is hired is the curve labeled MFC. A profit-maximizing monopsonist will hire additional workers until the resulting addition to revenue no longer exceeds the resulting addition to cost. $MRP_L$ no longer exceeds MFC at point *E*. The optimum quantity of *L* to hire is *L**, and each worker is paid *W** as the hourly wage.

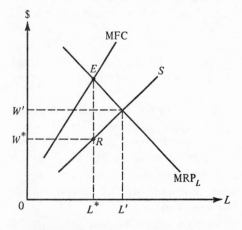

**Figure 10-15.**
Nondiscriminating monopsonist.

Note that whereas an employer who is a price taker buyer of labor services pays a wage equal to the addition to revenue that results when the last person is hired, the monopsonist does not. In Figure 10-15 the addition to revenue when one more unit of labor is hired is $L^*E$. The wage paid is $L^*R$. The difference arises because the wage rate is the marginal factor cost for a price taker buyer, while for the monopsonist the marginal factor cost exceeds the wage.

The marginal factor cost exceeds the wage because when one more person is hired the workers who are already employed receive the same wage as the new person. Actually, if there were such a thing as a monopsonist—the only employer of a given type of labor—he would probably not pay all workers the same wage. He would pay each worker whatever that worker's supply price is. The first worker would get $1 per hour, the second would get $2 per hour, etc. When an additional worker is hired the hourly wage bill will go up only by the amount paid the additional worker. The other workers continue to get paid their supply prices. Such an employer is sometimes called a "perfectly discriminating" monopsonist. He is actually engaging in multipart pricing of the input. A seller of a product who gets each buyer to pay his demand price for the product, and a buyer of an input who pays each seller only his supply price for the service, are both engaging in multipart pricing. If the employer depicted in Figure 10-15 were such a "perfectly discriminating" monopsonist he would hire $L'$ units of $L$. The last worker hired would be paid an hourly wage equal to $W'$. All the other workers would be paid whatever their respective supply prices were.

Suppose that a monopsonist does not engage in multipart pricing. He pays a uniform wage to all workers of a given type. In Figure 10-16 we see that the amount of $L$ hired would be $L^*$, and the uniform wage paid would be $W^*$. Suppose now that the employees of the firm form a union and get a contract that specifies $W_u$ as the uniform wage. The supply curve the employer now faces is $W_uRS$. The employer

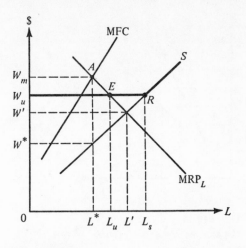

**Figure 10-16.**
Effect of higher wage.

can hire as many workers as he likes up to $L_s$, but he must pay each worker $W_u$. If he wants more workers than $L_s$ he will have to pay a higher uniform wage (indicated by the $RS$ segment of the supply curve). The monopsonist's marginal factor cost is $W_u$ for all units of $L$ up to $L_s$. He cannot hire any workers at less than $W_u$. He is in effect a price taker buyer up to $L_s$ units. The price he must take is that specified in the union contract. Under these circumstances the quantity of labor hired will be $L_u$, for at point $E$ marginal factor cost equals marginal revenue product. An increase of the wage has, in this case, been accompanied by an *increase* in the quantity of labor hired (from $L^*$ to $L_u$). In fact, if the union contract specified any wage less than $W_m$ the result would be to increase the amount hired to some amount greater than $L^*$. This is because, although the wage rate has increased, the marginal factor cost has actually decreased. Without the union contract the marginal factor cost was $L^*A$. With a contract that specifies a wage less than $W_m$ the marginal factor cost is less than $L^*A$.

Note that this result does not hold in the case of a perfectly discriminating monopsonist. Such a monopsonist would hire $L'$ in the absence of a union contract. The last worker would be paid $W'$. If a union were formed that set a uniform wage in excess of $W'$, less than $L'$ would be hired. However, all workers whose supply prices were less than $W'$ and who continued to work would be paid the contract wage, where before they were paid only their supply prices. These workers would clearly benefit from the union contract even though the amount of employment would be reduced.

## The Role of Unions

It is widely believed that labor unions, representing workers, went through a "long and bitter struggle" to attain "decent" wages and "decent" working conditions. It is also widely believed that if unions were to disappear the old "sweatshop" days would return. In a very significant book W. H. Hutt points out many reasons to doubt this conventional idea.[6] We have already seen that a firm hires an additional worker if, and only if, the resulting extra revenue is at least as large as the resulting extra cost. No firm can for long get away with paying a worker less than his value in alternative employments. Suppose a worker could produce some thing or perform some service that generates an extra $8 per hour for his present employer, but that he is paid only $2 per hour. In addition, suppose that if he worked for another employer he would generate an extra $6 per hour. It would be profitable for this second employer and this worker to seek each other out. At any wage less than $6 per hour but greater than $2 per hour both could be made better off. This means that it is *profitable* for the first employer to pay at least $6 per hour. The notion that it is always profitable for an employer to pay low wages rather than higher wages is simply incorrect. It is *profitable* for the first employer to pay $6 per hour rather than $2 per hour in our example. The key is the value of the worker's services in alternative employments. Without unions a worker will be paid at least his value in alternative employments. (In a moment we shall discuss the problem of the worker *knowing*

[6]W. H. Hutt, *The Strike-Threat System: The Economic Consequences of Collective Bargaining* (New Rochelle, N.Y.: Arlington House, 1973).

about his alternatives and alternative employers *knowing* about the worker.)

Why, then, were wages so low and working conditions so bad before the advent of significant unionization? First we must note that wages and working conditions *together* constitute a worker's "pay." A given "pay" could consist of high wages and poor working conditions or low wages and good working conditions. From the mid-Eighteenth Century to the first third of the Twentieth Century workers' pay was low, but improving, in both dimensions, because their productivity was low but improving. The value of a given worker in all employments was low because of the state of technological progress. Workers were paid their value in alternative employments, but that value was low. It was so low, in fact, that it was necessary for urban families to put their children to work in factories, exactly as rural families put their children to work on farms, in order to support themselves as a unit. Technological progress that enabled more to be produced with the same amount of labor or the same amount to be produced with less labor (i.e., that increased the productivity of labor) emancipated children from the factories. It would have been impossible to generate sufficient political support for child labor legislation unless people came to believe that the family could survive without the children's help. That same technological progress *made necessary* the gradual improvement of a worker's pay. It was made necessary because of the rivalry among employers to hire anyone whose marginal revenue product exceeded the wage that the worker would accept. Since workers' productivity increased, their pay had to increase. This increase could have been either in the form of higher wages or better working conditions. As it happened it occurred in both forms.

According to Hutt (and he cites a lot of evidence to support himself), unions as a whole have obtained for workers what the workers would have received anyway due to the normal market rivalry among employers. Where unions obtained more than this they did so by strike or threat of strike, and they did so at the expense of consumers and workers who were priced out of employment by the higher-than-market wage rates. They did *not* obtain their goals at the expense of investors.

Hutt believes that the right to strike (the right of a group of workers collectively to refuse to work, without facing the prospect that others will be hired in their place) should be abolished. It is not necessary for the protection of workers in general, it creates a warfare mentality among managers and workers, it interferes with the freedom of nonstrikers to offer themselves to work at whatever terms of trade suit them, and it forces the monetary authorities to create inflation in order to overcome the unemployment effects of wages above market clearing levels.

Unions would have valuable services to perform for their members even if they were denied the right to strike. Since it is a worker's value in alternative employments that protects him against "exploitation" by his current employer, anything which makes it easier for workers to discover what their alternatives are and makes it easier for alternative employers to know the terms of trade at which they can obtain workers would be beneficial to union members. One of the useful roles of a union would be to serve as a clearinghouse for this kind of information. The job of the union would be constantly to look for the best terms of trade for each of its members. Another useful function for the union would be to finance its members' moving and relocation expenses when they opt to change employers. A third useful function would be to institute legal proceedings against any collusion among employers to keep wage offers below what they would otherwise be (i.e., to protect its members from monopsony by application of the antitrust laws).

## Bilateral Monopoly

Since antitrust legislation in the United States does not pertain to unions there can be such a thing as a steelworkers' union and an automobile workers' union. While it

is illegal for the producers of steel to collude in the determination of prices and quantities supplied of steel, it is not illegal for the employees of the different steel firms to collude on setting the prices and quantities supplied of what they sell—labor services. Since there is one union that represents all steel workers, the manufacturers of steel are permitted to act together in their negotiations with the steelworkers' union. Thus we frequently see industry-wide negotiations in the steel and automobile industries as well as in other industries. The union officers meet and negotiate with a group that represents all the employers in the industry. The union is the monopolist seller of labor services, and the employers' group is the monopsonist buyer of labor services.

In Figure 10-17 the demand curve for labor services is labeled $D$. Since the union is a monopoly seller of the labor services it will be interested in the marginal revenue from selling additional labor services. The marginal revenue curve is labeled MR. The labor supply curve is the union's marginal cost curve in the sense that it depicts the minimum payment each worker will insist on getting to keep for himself—his supply price. When the union sells one more unit of $L$ that unit must be paid at least the amount that is indicated on the supply curve. The maximum amount the union officers can collect for themselves in dues is the difference between the supply price and the price actually paid for labor services. Assuming that the union officers want to maximize their "profit"—the sum of the differences between the contract wage and each member's supply price—they will want to sell $L_u$ units of labor services and charge a wage equal to $W_u$. (They equate their marginal cost and their marginal revenue.) The area that represents the possible dues collected is area $TW_uAB$. The employers' group is the monopsonist buyer of labor services. It will want to equate its marginal factor cost with its marginal revenue product. It will want to hire $L_e$ units of $L$ and pay $W_e$ per hour as the uniform wage. The union wants a wage equal to $W_u$ and the employers' group wants a wage equal to $W_e$. The dif-

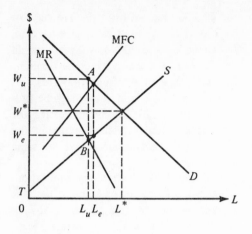

**Figure 10-17.**
Bilateral monopoly.

ferences are settled in "collective bargaining" sessions. If there were no union and numerous independent employers of this type of labor, the wage that each employer would pay would be $W^*$, and the total amount of labor hired would be $L^*$.

## The Negative Income Tax

As long as people own different amounts of human and nonhuman resources, and as long as there are different prices for the services of those resources, there will be an unequal distribution of income. This is true in all societies. In those societies where government plays a large role in the economy, the rich will be those who are skilled at political manipulation. Although there are few money millionaires in the Soviet Union, there is a well defined group of political millionaires who have absolute control of public policy. In an economy where government plays a lesser role there will be fewer political millionaires and more money millionaires. If government has no power the possession of political influence will not yield high returns. High incomes will come mainly from market transactions.

Nevertheless, many people are concerned about the extreme ends of the income scale. The problem of the very rich and the very poor is at the heart of the continuous controversy about the relative merits of free enterprise and socialist

systems. Some who favor free enterprise attempt to ameliorate the plight of the very poor by direct intervention and control of some markets. Minimum wage legislation is a very good example of this strategy. Unfortunately, as we have seen, the poor are not helped by minimum wage legislation, for if the real value of an individual's marginal revenue product is less than the minimum wage corrected for inflation, that individual will not be hired. The poor are poor because they are the least productive. Lack of education, training, and experience is the reason why they don't command a high wage in the first place. A minimum wage means that no firm will be willing to hire the poor to give them the training and experience that will eventually permit them to escape from poverty. Minimum wage legislation also makes it difficult for labor markets to adjust to changes of demand and supply conditions. If the demand for a given type of labor service decreases relative to its supply, those who are thus displaced from their jobs may well have to accept a lower wage in order to find alternative employment. There is no guarantee that the buying patterns of consumers will always set a market value on a given type of labor service that is not lower than the minimum wage. The main result of minimum wage legislation is to increase the number of people who are permanently unemployed. Just as we cannot cure the common cold by passing a law against it, we cannot cure the problem of individuals having only a low marginal revenue product to sell to employers by passing a law that specifies a minimum wage.

The most effective way to raise the real value of an individual's marginal revenue product is to permit that person to acquire training—especially on-the-job training. If wage rates were determined by voluntary exchange, employers could be induced to hire the poor and give them on-the-job training. If a worker loses his job because consumers' valuation of the product that he produces decreases, he could then acquire alternative abilities by offering to work for a low wage. When he acquires training and experience in the provision of goods and services on which buyers place a high value, his wage will go up. If the real wage he receives is less than the real value of his marginal revenue product another employer could increase his profits by offering to pay a somewhat larger wage that is still below the real value of the worker's marginal revenue product. Rivalrous bidding among employers will ultimately result in a wage not substantially different from the worker's marginal revenue product.

A scheme to aid those whose marginal revenue product is low—one that would permit those who are able to acquire a higher marginal revenue product to receive on-the-job training and that would also take care of those who cannot increase the value of their marginal revenue product (disabled people)—is the negative income tax. In fact, the negative income tax could replace every single welfare and assistance plan that we now have to help unfortunate people.

Current tax law in the United States defines taxable income as earnings minus a per-person exemption of $750, and minus automatic or itemized deductions. Suppose deductions were $2,000. This would mean that a family of four would have a taxable income ($I_T$) equal to $E - \$5,000$, where $E$ is earnings. However, if $E$ is less than $5,000, taxable income is *zero*. Negative values for taxable income are not permitted. Whether the family earns $5,000 or $2,500, taxable income (and therefore tax) is the same—zero. Milton Friedman has suggested that taxable income should be defined as $I_T = E - \$5,000$, and that negative values for $I_T$ should be permitted.[7] If a family earns $2,400, taxable income would be $-\$2,600$. Friedman suggests that the tax rate applied to negative values of $I_T$ be 50%. When $I_T$ equals $-\$2,600$, the tax would be $-\$1,300$. This means that the Treasury would send a check to the taxpayer for $1,300. The taxpayer's total income would be the earnings of $2,400 plus

the $1,300 received from the Treasury, or $3,700. If the family's earnings were zero, $I_T$ would be $-\$5,000$, and the tax would be $-\$2,500$. The family's income would be the $2,500 received from the Treasury. The real value of the plan would be protected against inflation by increasing the amount subtracted from earnings in the definition of taxable income at the same rate as the rate of inflation.

To more fully illustrate the implications of such a scheme let us suppose that the tax rate applied to negative values of $I_T$ is 60%. Zero earnings would generate a negative tax of $3,000. This $3,000 would be a minimum guaranteed income. If earnings were $1,000, the negative tax would be $2,400, and total income would be $3,400. The family would, in effect, keep $400 of the $1,000 it earned, since the check it receives from the Treasury would decrease by $600 (from $3,000 to $2,400).

Under present welfare schemes, if an additional dollar is earned the welfare check decreases by a dollar. Individuals on welfare are not given any incentive to find work, since the tax rate on their earnings is 100%. With a negative income tax scheme, where the tax rate on negative values of $I_T$ is 60%, the tax rate on earnings is only 60%. Individuals are thus always better off working than not working. Moreover, the only bureaucracy needed for this scheme is the Internal Revenue Service. The checks from the Treasury would be a matter of legal right, just as the Treasury has a legal right to receive taxes from those who have a positive taxable income. There would be no necessity for the multitude of welfare agencies and welfare employees at the local, state, and federal levels. No recipient of a negative tax would have to tolerate having social workers checking up on him to ensure that welfare regulations are not being violated—there simply would be no welfare regulations. The money saved from this substantial reduction of the costs of administration, together with the money that is now in fact distributed to welfare recipients (rather than welfare employees), would probably be enough to pay for the scheme. Friedman indicates that the administration costs of existing programs

---

[7] Milton Friedman, *Capitalism and Freedom* (Chicago: University of Chicago Press, 1962), Chap. 12.

amount to approximately \$2,000 per poor person per year.

With a negative income tax plan there would be no reason to restrict the movements of wage rates in response to changes in labor market conditions. Some have mistakenly said that a negative tax scheme would depress wage rates because employees would know that if wages are low the Treasury will make it up, so they would not have the usual incentive to get the highest wage they can. This reasoning is false because, as we have seen, the Treasury does *not* make up for lower wages on a dollar-for-dollar basis. If the tax rate on negative values of taxable income is 60% the Treasury makes up only 60 cents on each dollar of lost income. The individual gets to keep 40 cents of each additional dollar earned, so he can still improve his situation by getting the highest wage possible. Because of rivalry among employers, each of whom wants to hire anyone whose wage is less than his marginal revenue product, the highest wage that any worker can get will in fact not be substantially less than his marginal revenue product.

It must be emphasized that the attractiveness of the negative income tax plan rests on its ability to replace all of our existing welfare, social security, and minimum wage programs. If a negative income tax plan were implemented on top of all existing programs, the costs to taxpayers who earn positive taxable incomes would be unbearable. In 1970 President Nixon proposed a negative income tax plan to the Congress. He called it a Family Assistance Plan (FAP). Milton Friedman did not support FAP precisely because it would merely have been added to the multitude of other welfare-type plans already in existence.

A particularly horrendous example of the side effects of coping with the poverty problem by direct interference in a market is afforded by the "gasoline crisis" of early 1974. At that time Americans all across the country had to wait in long lines to purchase gasoline. The Federal Energy Office (FEO) controlled how much gasoline was allocated to each area, and its allocation decisions forced gas stations to close their pumps most of the day. If dealers were to make the gas the government permitted them to have last over the period between deliveries, they could not pump gas all of the working day. Therefore, at any given time as many as 50% of the gasoline stations in an area closed their pumps, forcing buyers to line up at the other 50% of the pumps.

All of this was unnecessary. As we saw in Chapter 7, an earlier large reduction of the supply of oil from the Mideast (after the Six-Day War of 1967) did not result in such a mess. The fact that there was a reduction in the supply of oil relative to its demand did not have to mean long lines at gasoline stations, nor did it have to mean that the government had to take over the job of allocating oil and oil products. By now you understand how the market would respond to a decrease of supply relative to demand for oil. The relative price of oil would rise, causing people to *choose* to cut back on their consumption of oil products, and causing suppliers to *choose* to search for ways of obtaining additional supplies of oil. The high price means additional profit, and additional profit calls forth additional supplies. Prices were permitted to rise somewhat, but the FEO did not permit the price to rise to the market clearing level. The excuse used was that the poor would be discriminated against by a free market price. The price had to be kept down to help those who could not afford higher prices. The FEO tried to attack the problem of poverty by controlling the price of one of the products that the poor buy. As a result everyone stood in line for two or three hours to purchase gasoline. I conjecture that most of those whom the FEO claimed to help would have preferred to pay a higher pump price rather than to pay the price of having to waste so much time standing in line. This conjecture could have been tested by permitting dealers to have two pump prices: one high price and one low price. The higher price could have been set at whatever level was necessary to keep the line at that pump down to four or five cars. The lower price could have been set at whatever level made the bureaucrats happy. Each person could then have chosen whether he wanted to pay a low money price and a high time price or a high money price and a low time price. (Incidentally, the consensus among economists at the time was that the free market price for regular gasoline would have been approximately 60 cents per gallon.[8])

Controlling the prices of individual commodities is not a very efficient way to assist the poor. If we had a negative income tax plan which ensured that everyone had some minimally acceptable purchasing power, we could at the same time benefit from the efficiency with which the market allocates resources and makes the amount wanted of anything equal to the amount that is available.

In the next chapter we develop the tools that are necessary to analyze the decision to alter the amount of human and non-human capital one owns or uses. This involves time more explicitly than anything we have thus far done, and thus it also involves interest rates.

## Questions for Discussion

1. Evaluate the following:

   An egalitarian distribution of income is less natural than unequal distribution of income.

2. Make a list of the "externalities" of elementary and secondary education. An externality in this context is a benefit that an educated person confers on others for which the educated person cannot charge a fee. If there are such externalities, individuals would not have sufficient incentive to acquire on his own the optimum amount of education (that amount where the benefit of additional education is no longer greater than its cost).
   Make a list of such externalities for college education.

3. Evaluate the following:

   The laws of supply and demand cannot apply to labor because labor is not a commodity to be bought and sold like machines.

4. Evaluate the following:

   Capital itself clearly is productive—more is produced with it than without it—but the ownership of capital is not productive. The owner contributes nothing, hence capital would continue to be just as productive if its ownership were collectivized.

5. Draw one isoquant that exhibits a high elasticity of technical substitution and another that exhibits a low elasticity of technical substitution.
   Draw one isoquant that exhibits a zero elasticity of technical substitution and another that exhibits an infinite elasticity of technical substitution.

6. Evaluate the following:

   Since labor unions have as much monopoly power as any corporation or group of corporations, the antitrust laws ought to apply to unions as well as to corporations. One way to do this would be to make it illegal for any single union to have members other than the workers of a single firm. For example, there would be one union for General Motors' employees and a separate union for Ford's employees.

7. Make a list of four colluding groups of employers that could be called monopsonists.

8. Evaluate the following:

   The social security tax is paid by both employers and employees. The employers pay half and the employees pay half. (First assume that the aggregate supply of labor has zero price elasticity and then assume some positive price elasticity of supply.)

---

[8]The *Wall Street Journal* (February 27, 1974).

# 11
# Capital Values and Investment Decisions

In Chapter 4 we developed our production theory using two inputs—the services of labor and the services of nonhuman capital. In the last chapter we noted that the services of labor come from a durable stock called human capital. Nonhuman capital services also derive from a stock, and in this chapter we shall consider how decision makers within firms decide whether to purchase additional stocks of nonhuman capital. People, each one the owner of his own stock of human capital, also make similar decisions when they consider acquiring education and training, and we shall consider the decision process from this vantage point as well. The nonhuman capital purchases that we usually think of in regard to a firm are purchases of a plant, equipment, and land, but advertising is an expenditure on another kind of nonhuman capital, namely *brand name capital*. A capital expenditure is one that results in the acquisition of an asset that can be used over an extended period of time. Acquiring additional durable assets is called *investing*. Since the firm's investment decisions involve time they also involve uncertainty, because no one knows for sure what the future holds. Our first task, therefore, is to discuss how time and uncertainty are handled.

## Why There Is a Positive Rate of Interest

Money is effective purchasing power over all other goods. Ask yourself how much, in the absence of inflation, of this ability to buy other goods you would be willing to give up today in exchange for one dollar of purchasing power next month. Your immediate response is likely to be that since, without inflation, a dollar today has the same generalized purchasing power as a dollar next month you would be willing to exchange a dollar today for a dollar next month. But immediate responses are sometimes not the wisest, and this is one of those times. By giving up a dollar today in exchange for a dollar next month you are giving up the ability to purchase goods during *this* month, and next month's dollar cannot restore that ability. You are postponing the enjoyment of what you could buy with a dollar, and you are receiving nothing for that sacrifice. Most people would insist on some reward for giving up the *current use* of their purchasing power. In other words, they would be willing to give up less than a dollar today in exchange for a dollar next month. This payment for the sacrifice of *current use* is called interest.

Consider a person who receives a large real income this month but faces zero income receipts next month. He would not have to be paid to not use part of his income this month and instead save some of it for use next month. If it were impossible for him to receive any interest, he would still postpone the use of part of the purchasing power available to him this month. He could, for instance, leave part of his income untouched in his checking account, in a safe deposit box, or in a cookie jar. But he wouldn't lend the money to anyone else unless he received a positive interest rate (even with no risk of default), because when someone else has it he loses the option to use it in the current month. He couldn't, in other words, change his mind halfway through the month and use the money then. That option has a positive value.

We have seen why lenders insist on *receiving* a positive interest rate; now let's consider why borrowers are willing to *pay* a positive rate of interest. There are two reasons. First, a borrower gets *earlier availability* of what he buys with the money than he would if he waited to accumulate sufficient purchasing power directly out of his own income receipts. Borrowers, just like lenders, generally prefer current availability to later availability. Second, there are always many investment projects (e.g., construction of a plant and acquisition of equipment, or acquisition of training and education) which yield a positive rate of return—i.e., which generate a flow of receipts in excess of the outlay originally made to undertake the investment. Clearly it makes sense to borrow money, and pay interest on that money, if you can use the money to acquire durable assets that yield a rate of return in excess of the interest rate paid on the loan. (Later in this chapter we shall see how to compute the rate of return on an investment.)

In sum, interest rates are greater than zero because if the rate were zero the amount of money people would want to borrow would greatly exceed the amount that other people would want to lend. There would, in other words, be an excess demand for loan funds. Interest is the price

that establishes a zero excess demand for loan funds. It is the price that coordinates the plans of borrowers and lenders. It is positive because people place a positive value on earlier availability (the jargon is that individuals exhibit positive *time preference*) and because of the ability of real capital to yield a positive rate of return.

## Present Values

Suppose you want to buy a guitar that has a price tag of $100. You have $100, but there are other things you want to spend it on, so you ask your father for the price of the guitar. Your father agrees to give you the $100 providing that you agree to pay it back in one year, together with an additional $5 in interest. If you accept your father's offer, how much will the guitar cost you? Most people would say that the guitar will cost $105, but they would be wrong. You could take the $100 that you wanted to use for some other purpose and put it in a savings account that pays 5%. At the end of one year, when the payment to your father is due, you could withdraw your deposit plus the interest it had earned and pay him off. From today's point of view all that it costs you to pay off an obligation of $105 one year from now is the amount of money you need right now to put into the bank so that in one year you will have accumulated $105. In our example that is merely $100. We say the *present value* of $105 to be paid (or received) one year from now, when the rate of interest that can be earned is 5%, is $100. The real cost of the guitar is merely the other things you can buy with the $100 that you need to put into the bank in order to accumulate the $105 in one year.

Even if you do not have the $100 to put into the bank, the cost of the guitar is still only $100. If you take the $100 you borrow from your father and put it in the bank you will be able to pay him off at the end of the year. The net cost to you of the series of transactions will be zero. If you use the $100 to purchase the guitar you are giving up the bank account that pays your father off. The cost of the guitar is the

$100 needed to open the savings account.

Actually the cost of the guitar can be less than $100, for you can do much better than a mere 5% savings account. Triple A corporate bonds pay over 8% interest. At 8% interest, how much money do you need right now so that at the end of one year $105 will be accumulated? In other words, what is the present value of $105 to be paid one year from now when the rate of interest you can earn is 8%? All we need do is find $V_0$ (present value) in the following equation:

$$(1 + .08)V_0 = \$105$$

$$V_0 = \frac{\$105}{1.08} = \$97.22$$

Ninety-seven dollars and twenty-two cents will accumulate to one hundred and five dollars in one year if the annual rate of interest is 8%. Your father is giving you a gift after all. You get a $100 guitar for only $97.22. He is giving up an opportunity to earn 8% so that he can lend to you at 5%. You could take the $100 that he lends to you, invest it at 8% for a year, pay him $105, and keep the $3 difference.

The present value $(V_0)$ of a sum of money paid (or received) in one year $(S_1)$ when the annual rate of interest is $r$ times 100% is found by the formula:

$$V_0 = \frac{S_1}{1 + r}$$

Suppose you had to pay someone $120 two years from now and the annual rate of interest you can earn is 8%. How much money would you need right now to invest so that it would accumulate to $120 at the end of two years? In other words, what is the present value of that $120 obligation that comes due in two years? Let $V_0$ stand for the necessary starting money. At the end of one year the accumulated amount would be $V_0 (1 + .08)$. This is the amount that you begin the second year with, so at the end of the second year the amount accumulated would be

$$(1 + .08) [V_0 (1 + .08)],$$

or

$$(1 + .08)^2 V_0$$

which must equal $120. Therefore the present value of $120 paid two years from now is:

$$V_0 = \frac{\$120}{(1 + .08)^2} = \$102.84$$

In general the present value $(V_0)$ of a sum of money received (or paid) $i$ years in the future $(S_i)$ with an annual rate of interest of $r$ times 100% is:

$$V_0 = \frac{S_i}{(1 + r)^i} \qquad (11\text{-}1)$$

A dollar to be paid or received in the future is worth less than a dollar in the present, *and this has nothing to do with inflation.* The fact that one can take less than a dollar now and invest it so that it will build up to a dollar in the future is the underlying important fact. The present value of any specified future amount of money is merely the amount you need right now to invest so that at the end of the specified period of time you will have accumulated the specified amount of money.

Equation 11-1 can be rewritten as

$$V_0 = S_i [1/(1 + r)^i]$$

The term in the square brackets is merely the present value of one dollar $i$ years in the future when the interest rate is $r$ times 100%. Table 11-1 gives the present value of one dollar paid or received at the end of various numbers of years with various rates of interest. The table permits us to check on our calculation of the present value of $120 paid two years in the future at 8% interest. We see that the present value of one dollar two years in the future at 8% interest is $.857. Since we want the present value of $120, we merely multiply .857 times $120 and that gives us $102.84. From the table we can see that if we start today with 25 cents it will accumulate to

## Table 11-1 Present Value of One Future Dollar
### (What a Dollar at End of Specified Future Year Is Equivalent to Today)

| Year | 3% | 4% | 5% | 6% | 7% | 8% | 10% | 12% | 15% | 20% | Year |
|---|---|---|---|---|---|---|---|---|---|---|---|
| 1 | .971 | .962 | .952 | .943 | .935 | .926 | .909 | .893 | .870 | .833 | 1 |
| 2 | .943 | .925 | .907 | .890 | .873 | .857 | .826 | .797 | .756 | .694 | 2 |
| 3 | .915 | .890 | .864 | .839 | .816 | .794 | .751 | .711 | .658 | .578 | 3 |
| 4 | .889 | .855 | .823 | .792 | .763 | .735 | .683 | .636 | .572 | .482 | 4 |
| 5 | .863 | .823 | .784 | .747 | .713 | .681 | .620 | .567 | .497 | .402 | 5 |
| 6 | .838 | .790 | .746 | .705 | .666 | .630 | .564 | .507 | .432 | .335 | 6 |
| 7 | .813 | .760 | .711 | .665 | .623 | .583 | .513 | .452 | .376 | .279 | 7 |
| 8 | .789 | .731 | .677 | .627 | .582 | .540 | .466 | .404 | .326 | .233 | 8 |
| 9 | .766 | .703 | .645 | .591 | .544 | .500 | .424 | .360 | .284 | .194 | 9 |
| 10 | .744 | .676 | .614 | .558 | .508 | .463 | .385 | .322 | .247 | .162 | 10 |
| 11 | .722 | .650 | .585 | .526 | .475 | .429 | .350 | .287 | .215 | .134 | 11 |
| 12 | .701 | .625 | .557 | .497 | .444 | .397 | .318 | .257 | .187 | .112 | 12 |
| 13 | .681 | .601 | .530 | .468 | .415 | .368 | .289 | .229 | .162 | .0935 | 13 |
| 14 | .661 | .577 | .505 | .442 | .388 | .340 | .263 | .204 | .141 | .0779 | 14 |
| 15 | .642 | .555 | .481 | .417 | .362 | .315 | .239 | .183 | .122 | .0649 | 15 |
| 16 | .623 | .534 | .458 | .393 | .339 | .292 | .217 | .163 | .107 | .0541 | 16 |
| 17 | .605 | .513 | .436 | .371 | .317 | .270 | .197 | .146 | .093 | .0451 | 17 |
| 18 | .587 | .494 | .416 | .350 | .296 | .250 | .179 | .130 | .0808 | .0376 | 18 |
| 19 | .570 | .475 | .396 | .330 | .277 | .232 | .163 | .116 | .0703 | .0313 | 19 |
| 20 | .554 | .456 | .377 | .311 | .258 | .215 | .148 | .104 | .0611 | .0261 | 20 |
| 25 | .478 | .375 | .295 | .232 | .184 | .146 | .0923 | .0588 | .0304 | .0105 | 25 |
| 30 | .412 | .308 | .231 | .174 | .131 | .0994 | .0573 | .0334 | .0151 | .00421 | 30 |
| 40 | .307 | .208. | .142 | .0972 | .067 | .0460 | .0221 | .0107 | .00373 | .000680 | 40 |
| 50 | .228 | .141 | .087 | .0543 | .034 | .0213 | .00852 | .00346 | .000922 | .000109 | 50 |

$1 in 18 years if the rate at which we invest it is 8%. Thus $1 invested at 8% for 18 years will accumulate to $4, and the present value of $4 paid 18 years in the future is $1.

## The Firm's Investment Decision

Suppose you are the manager of a firm and you are trying to decide whether to purchase a new machine. The price tag on the machine is $25,000. You estimate that the machine will last for five years, after which you can sell it for scrap for $S$. How should you make your decision? You must *estimate* the amount of additional profit for each of the five years; i.e., you must estimate the difference between your profit with the machine and your profit without the machine for each year of the life of the machine. Let $\pi_i$ be the amount by which your estimate of profit with the machine exceeds your estimate of profit without the machine in the $i$th year. You will have five numbers, $\pi_1, \pi_2, \pi_3, \pi_4,$ and $\pi_5$. This set of estimates is called the *expected incremental profit stream.* In order to obtain these expected additions to profit (plus the scrap value of the machine) you must today pay $25,000 to purchase the machine. Suppose that triple A corporate bonds yield an 8% annual rate of return. If you calculate the present value of the expected incremental profit stream plus the estimated scrap value, using 8% as the interest rate, you will get the amount of money that is needed to buy bonds with today so that you can get from the bonds the same return stream expected from the machine. (You can use bonds to duplicate the expected incremental profit stream by selling various amounts of the bonds in each of the five years. The proceeds from the sale plus the interest on the bonds would make up your return in any given year.) The present value of the machine is:

$$V_0 = \frac{\pi_1}{(1 + .08)} + \frac{\pi_2}{(1 + .08)^2} +$$

$$\frac{\pi_3}{(1 + .08)^3} + \frac{\pi_4}{(1 + .08)^4} +$$

$$\frac{\pi_5}{(1 + .08)^5} + \frac{S}{(1 + .08)^5}$$

Suppose, for example, that the expected incremental profit in each of the first three years is $8,000, for each of the last two years it is $2,000, and the estimated scrap value is $100. We can use Table 11-1 to compute the present value of the machine. It is

8,000(.926) + 8,000(.857) + 8,000(.794) +

2,000(.735) + 2,000(.681) +

100(.681) = $23,516.10

This present value figure is the amount of money that you need today to buy bonds with which you can duplicate the expected return stream from the machine. You need $25,000 to get this return stream through the purchase of the machine, and only $23,516.10 to get it through bonds. You should decide not to purchase the machine.

The expected incremental profit stream is only an estimate. It is as good as your sales and costs forecasts and no better. It is not a guaranteed return. On the other hand, the returns from bonds are more certain. If you hold bonds to maturity the return is virtually certain, but if you sell them before maturity there is some risk that the selling price may be low on the day you choose to sell. Since the returns from bonds are more certain than the return on the machine you may want to add a *risk premium* onto the 8% bond rate when you make your present value calculation. Suppose the expected incremental profit stream is such that your present value calculation—using 8%—comes out to $26,000. That would mean you could get the return stream by buying $26,000 worth of bonds or by buying $25,000 worth of machine. The machine appears to

be a good investment. However, the return stream is more doubtful with the machine than with bonds, so perhaps the machine is not a good investment after all. If you had used 9% instead of 8% in your present value calculations the present value of the machine would be lower. Using the bond rate of return as the discount rate biases the result of the calculations in favor of buying the machine because it ignores the greater uncertainty of the machine's return stream. Using a higher rate of interest to compute the present value of the machine's return stream offsets the bias of the calculations.

The wealth-maximizing decision rule to use in deciding whether to undertake any investment project (buy a machine, construct a building, undertake an advertising campaign, or purchase some land) is to compare the present value of the project's return stream with the cost of the project. Each project will have its own appropriate rate of interest to use in the present value calculations (called that project's *discount rate*), depending on the amount of uncertainty the manager attaches to the expected return stream. Let the present value of the expected return stream be $V_0$ and the price tag on the project be $C_0$; the profit-maximizing decision rule is to undertake any project for which it is the case that $V_0$ exceeds $C_0$ and not to undertake any others. $V_0 - C_0$ is called the project's *net present value*. If there are insufficient funds to undertake all projects with positive net present values, the project with the highest net present value should be undertaken first, the project with the next highest net present value should be undertaken next, and so on.

### The Internal Rate of Return

For any given expected return stream there is a rate of interest that will make the present value of the expected return stream equal the cost of the project. That interest rate is called the *internal rate of return*. It is $\rho$ in:

$$\frac{\pi_1}{(1 + \rho)} + \frac{\pi_2}{(1 + \rho)^2} + \cdots +$$

$$\frac{\pi_n}{(1 + \rho)^n} = C_0$$

where $\pi_i$ is the return expected in the $i$th year, $n$ is the number of years of life of the capital good, and $C_0$ is the cost of the capital good. The internal rate of return is the interest rate which if applied to $C_0$ would generate the expected return stream. With a known expected return stream and a known cost of the project we merely compute the rate of return that is implicit in the relationship between the two. Let $r$ be the discount rate that is used to compute the present value of a project. This is the bond rate of interest adjusted for risk. Let $\rho$ be the internal rate of return. For any given expected return stream, if $r$ is bigger than $\rho$, $V_0$ will be less than $C_0$. This is so because $\rho$ is defined as the discount rate that makes $V_0$ equal $C_0$. If the actual discount rate used is bigger than $\rho$, the expected return stream will be discounted to a number smaller than $C_0$. Similarly, if $r$ is smaller than $\rho$, $V_0$ will be bigger than $C_0$. If we interpret $r$ to be the cost of tying up the money in the investment project (after all the manager could buy bonds with the money, so the rate of interest he could make on the bonds is sacrificed when the money is used for the investment project), we can restate our investment decision rule in terms of $\rho$ and $r$: undertake any project for which the internal rate of return exceeds the bond rate of interest (adjusted for risk). As long as all such projects can be undertaken this internal rate of return rule will lead to the same decisions as the net present value rule.

However, if because of insufficient funds not all projects which pass the internal rate of return test can be adopted, it would not always be correct to adopt the projects in order of the magnitude of their respective internal rates. Consider Figure 11-1. The vertical axis of the figure measures net present value, while the horizontal axis measures alternative discount rates. The higher the discount rate that is used to make present value calculations,

the lower will be the net present value. The relationship between the discount rate and net present value is shown for two projects, $A$ and $B$. The higher the discount rate that is used, the more important early returns are relative to later returns. This is because the discount rate that is applied to later periods is raised to higher and higher powers. We divide an expected return due in two years by $(1 + r)^2$, while we divide the return expected in ten years by $(1 + r)^{10}$. At high discount rates, therefore, early returns will dominate the calculations, while at lower discount rates later returns are more of an influence. Look back at Table 11-1. The table clearly shows that for high rates of interest the number used to multiply the expected returns by in order to compute present values gets very small fairly soon. For example, for $r = 20\%$ any returns expected past the seventh year are greatly reduced in the present value calculation. For $r = 15\%$ returns expected beyond the ninth year are heavily discounted. Suppose project $A$ gave small returns in the early years but very large returns later on, and project $B$ gave a more uniform flow of expected returns over its life. At high discount rates project $A$ would have a lower net present value than project $B$, because the early returns would dominate both calculations. At lower discount rates, later returns have more influence on the net present value calculation than at high discount rates,

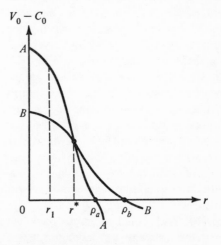

Figure 11-1.
Alternative investment projects.

hence project $A$ will have a higher present value than project $B$. Project $A$ is said to be a "later" project than project $B$ because its expected returns are concentrated at later dates.

Since the internal rate of return for any project is defined as the rate of interest that makes its net present value zero, we see in Figure 11-1 that the internal rates for $A$ and $B$ are $\rho_a$ and $\rho_b$ respectively. Since $A$ is "later" than $B$, $\rho_a$ will be smaller than $\rho_b$. Suppose that either project $A$ or project $B$ could be undertaken, but not both. Which one should the manager undertake? If the internal rate of return rule is used project $B$ will be chosen; but if the appropriate discount rate is less than $r^*$, for instance $r_1$, the appropriate project to adopt is $A$, since its net present value is the larger one. The current market value of a firm (or that firm's common stock) is the present value of its expected net earnings over time. An investment project with a large net present value adds more to a firm's worth than a project with a smaller net present value.

The internal rate of return approach to the investment decision may be expressed in terms of marginal revenue and marginal cost. If we array all potential investment projects according to their internal rates of return we will trace out a downward sloping step function which we can treat as a marginal revenue schedule. In Figure 11-2, there are six potential investment projects— $A$ through $F$. Project $A$ requires an outlay of $2 million and has an internal rate of return equal to 14%. Project $B$ requires an outlay of $1 million and has an internal rate of return of 12%. Project $F$ has the lowest internal rate of return—2%—and it requires a $2 million outlay. The thick step lines trace out a marginal revenue schedule in that they tell us the additional return (net revenue), in percentage terms, that will be forthcoming as each additional project is undertaken. How many of these investment projects should be undertaken? To answer that question we must have some indication of the marginal cost of investing. If the firm uses internally generated funds for investment, the marginal cost of investment is the per-

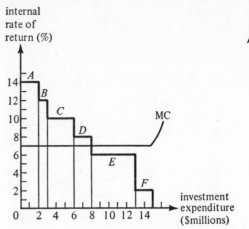

**Figure 11-2.**
Marginal revenue and marginal cost of investment.

centage interest rate that the firm could earn if it put its money into bonds. If the firm borrows money with which to make the investment, the marginal cost investment is the interest rate it pays to its creditors. Corporations borrow money by issuing bonds, so in both cases we can say that the marginal cost of investment (in percentage terms) is merely the interest rate on corporate bonds. Suppose that rate is 7%, and the depicted firm can obtain up to $14 million at that rate but must pay higher rates of interest if it wants additional funds. The marginal cost curve is labeled MC in the diagram. Only projects $A$ through $D$ should be undertaken, for only those projects have internal rates of return in excess of the marginal cost of investment funds.

Figure 11-3 shows a smooth curve for marginal revenue of investment. This idealized curve would exist if the firm could make arbitrarily small investment expenditures. It is downward sloping because each of the arbitrarily small projects is arrayed in descending order of internal rates of return. With such a marginal revenue schedule the firm would spend $I^*$ on investment, because for any investment expenditure less than $I^*$ the return from additional investment expenditure exceeds the cost of the additional investment expenditure.

It must be emphasized that this approach to the firm's investment decision is

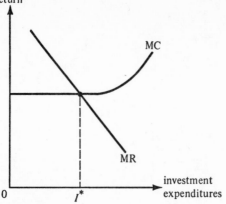

**Figure 11-3.**
Idealized marginal revenue and marginal cost of
investment.

$$\sum_{i=1}^{5} \frac{100}{(1 + r)^i} = 100 \sum_{i=1}^{5} \frac{1}{(1 + r)^i}$$

where $r$ is the discount rate (most frequently the rate of return on triple A corporate bonds) and the Greek capital "sigma" means "the sum of." The last term in the equation says that in order to find the present value of a $100 annuity for five years we merely find the present value of a $1 annuity for five years and then multiply by 100. Table 11-2 gives the present value of $1 annuities for various periods of time at various rates of interest. To illustrate its use, suppose that when you retire you have savings of $25,000. You plan to buy triple A corporate bonds with it, and you plan at the end of each year to spend the interest you receive plus some money that you get by selling some of the bonds. What constant amount of money will you have to spend each year if you want the bonds to last for 15 years and if the rate of interest on the bonds is 7%? From the table we see that you get a one-dollar 15-year annuity for each $9.11 you have. Since you have $25,000 you can get 25,000/9.11 such one-dollar annuities. In other words, your 15-year annuity would be $2,744.24.

Another example of the use of this important table involves the value of the educational services you purchase. Suppose you will receive your college degree when you reach age 21 and that average life expectancy for people like you is 71. In addition, suppose you estimate that on the average your annual income with the college degree will be $4,000 higher than it would have been with only a high school diploma. What is the pecuniary value of your college degree at age 21? It is merely the present value of a 50-year annuity of $4,000. Using an 8% discount rate we see that this is $4,000 (12.2) = $48,800.

valid only so long as all projects for which the internal rate of return exceeds the cost of the investment funds can actually be undertaken. If this is not true the projects that should be adopted are those with the highest net present values, regardless of internal rate of return. For example, with reference to Figure 11-2, if only $5 million is available for investment we may want to undertake project $C$ before project $B$. Although project $B$ has a higher internal rate of return than project $C$, project $B$ is a small project and may add less to the net worth of the firm than project $C$.

## Annuities

An *annuity* is a level series of annual payments for a specified number of years. If I purchase a five-year $100 annuity, this means that at the end of each of five years I will receive $100. The maximum price (demand price) I will pay for such an annuity is its present value. Its present value is

$$V_0 = \frac{100}{(1 + r)} + \frac{100}{(1 + r)^2} + \frac{100}{(1 + r)^3} +$$

$$\frac{100}{(1 + r)^4} + \frac{100}{(1 + r)^5} =$$

## Occupational Choice

Let us consider the question of occupational choice.[1] Suppose it is graduation

---

[1]This example follows George J. Stigler, *The Theory of Price, op. cit.*, pp. 258–259.

**Table 11-2  Present Value of Annuity of One Dollar, Received at End of Each Year**

| Year | 3% | 4% | 5% | 6% | 7% | 8% | 10% | 12% | 15% | 20% | Year |
|------|------|------|------|------|------|------|------|------|------|------|------|
| 1 | 0.971 | 0.960 | 0.952 | 0.943 | 0.935 | 0.926 | 0.909 | 0.890 | 0.870 | 0.833 | 1 |
| 2 | 1.91 | 1.89 | 1.86 | 1.83 | 1.81 | 1.78 | 1.73 | 1.69 | 1.63 | 1.53 | 2 |
| 3 | 2.83 | 2.78 | 2.72 | 2.67 | 2.62 | 2.58 | 2.48 | 2.40 | 2.28 | 2.11 | 3 |
| 4 | 3.72 | 3.63 | 3.55 | 3.46 | 3.39 | 3.31 | 3.16 | 3.04 | 2.86 | 2.59 | 4 |
| 5 | 4.58 | 4.45 | 4.33 | 4.21 | 4.10 | 3.99 | 3.79 | 3.60 | 3.35 | 2.99 | 5 |
| 6 | 5.42 | 5.24 | 5.08 | 4.91 | 4.77 | 4.62 | 4.35 | 4.11 | 3.78 | 3.33 | 6 |
| 7 | 6.23 | 6.00 | 5.79 | 5.58 | 5.39 | 5.21 | 4.86 | 4.56 | 4.16 | 3.60 | 7 |
| 8 | 7.02 | 6.73 | 6.46 | 6.20 | 5.97 | 5.75 | 5.33 | 4.97 | 4.49 | 3.84 | 8 |
| 9 | 7.79 | 7.44 | 7.11 | 6.80 | 6.52 | 6.25 | 5.75 | 5.33 | 4.78 | 4.03 | 9 |
| 10 | 8.53 | 8.11 | 7.72 | 7.36 | 7.02 | 6.71 | 6.14 | 5.65 | 5.02 | 4.19 | 10 |
| 11 | 9.25 | 8.76 | 8.31 | 7.88 | 7.50 | 7.14 | 6.49 | 5.94 | 5.23 | 4.33 | 11 |
| 12 | 9.95 | 9.39 | 8.86 | 8.38 | 7.94 | 7.54 | 6.81 | 6.19 | 5.41 | 4.44 | 12 |
| 13 | 10.6 | 9.99 | 9.39 | 8.85 | 8.36 | 7.90 | 7.10 | 6.42 | 5.65 | 4.53 | 13 |
| 14 | 11.3 | 10.6 | 9.90 | 9.29 | 8.75 | 8.24 | 7.36 | 6.63 | 5.76 | 4.61 | 14 |
| 15 | 11.9 | 11.1 | 10.4 | 9.71 | 9.11 | 8.56 | 7.60 | 6.81 | 5.87 | 4.68 | 15 |
| 16 | 12.6 | 11.6 | 10.8 | 10.1 | 9.45 | 8.85 | 7.82 | 6.97 | 5.96 | 4.73 | 16 |
| 17 | 13.2 | 12.2 | 11.3 | 10.4 | 9.76 | 9.12 | 8.02 | 7.12 | 6.03 | 4.77 | 17 |
| 18 | 13.8 | 12.7 | 11.7 | 10.8 | 10.1 | 9.37 | 8.20 | 7.25 | 6.10 | 4.81 | 18 |
| 19 | 14.3 | 13.1 | 12.1 | 11.1 | 10.3 | 9.60 | 8.36 | 7.37 | 6.17 | 4.84 | 19 |
| 20 | 14.9 | 13.6 | 12.5 | 11.4 | 10.6 | 9.82 | 8.51 | 7.47 | 6.23 | 4.87 | 20 |
| 25 | 17.4 | 15.6 | 14.1 | 12.8 | 11.7 | 10.7 | 9.08 | 7.84 | 6.46 | 4.95 | 25 |
| 30 | 19.6 | 17.3 | 15.4 | 13.8 | 12.4 | 11.3 | 9.43 | 8.06 | 6.57 | 4.98 | 30 |
| 40 | 23.1 | 19.8 | 17.2 | 15.0 | 13.3 | 11.9 | 9.78 | 8.24 | 6.64 | 5.00 | 40 |
| 50 | 25.7 | 21.5 | 18.3 | 15.8 | 13.8 | 12.2 | 9.91 | 8.25 | 6.66 | 5.00 | 50 |

day from high school and you are 17 years old. You must choose between two occupations, $A$ and $B$. You can begin occupation $A$ immediately after a brief period of on-the-job training, and the average annual income (in dollars corrected for inflation) you expect from occupation $A$ over a 50-year period is $8,000. Using Table 11-2 we see that the present value of an $8,000 annuity for 50 years (at 8%) equals $8,000 times 12.2, which is $97,600.

Occupation $B$ requires a college degree which takes four years to obtain. The costs of acquiring the college degree are of two sorts—direct schooling costs, which include tuition, fees, and books, and the four-year delay before earnings begin in occupation $B$. Let's assume that the direct schooling cost are $3,000 per year. The present value of a four-year $3,000 annuity (from Table 11-2, again using 8% as the discount rate) is $3,000 times 3.31, which equals $9,930. Let $X$ be the average annual income from occupation $B$. The present value of an an-

nuity of $X$ for 46 years is (again at 8%) 12.1 $X$. But earnings do not begin for four years, so we must compute the present value of this lump sum. From Table 11-1 we see that the present value of $1 received four years in the future is $.735; hence the present value of the earnings from occupation $B$ is .735 times 12.1$X$.

What value must $X$ have if the present value of net earnings in occupation $B$ equals the present value of earnings in occupation $A$? In other words, what must $X$ be if occupation $B$ pays just enough to cover its costs? (The present value of earnings in occupation $A$ is the opportunity cost of the present value of the net earning in occupation $B$.)

We must solve for $X$ in:

$$.735(12.1)X - \$9,930 = \$97,600$$

$$8.89X = \$107,530$$

$$X = \$12,095.61$$

An average annual income of $12,095.61 (in dollars corrected for inflation) from occupation B would mean that you will just break even if you pick occupation B. Anything in excess of that is economic profit. With open markets the existence of economic profit would attract others into occupation B until the economic profit was eliminated. If entry were blocked by, for example, occupational licensure laws, those in occupation B would continue to earn the economic profit.

You should note that by using Table 11-2 we can convert any nonconstant series of annual payments into an equivalent annuity. For example, a person's *permanent income* is the annuity that can be bought with the lump sum of money that equals the present value of the unequal annual incomes that he expects to earn.[2] Although our incomes may vary substantially from year to year, we all have some idea about what our average or normal annual income is. Permanent income is merely a particular kind of average. Assume for simplicity that you receive only three annual income payments. In the first year your income equals $2,000, in the second it equals $23,000, and in the third it equals $1,000. The present value of these income payments is (at 8%): $2,000(.926) + $23,000(.857) + $1,000(.794), which comes to $22,357. We can convert this amount into a three-year annuity (or an annuity of *any* length) by finding the present value of a $1 annuity for three (or any number of) years at 8%. Table 11-2 shows that we can purchase one $1 three-year annuity for every $2.58 we have. Thus the three-year annuity that is equivalent to the three very unequal annual payments is $22,357/2.58, which equals $8,665.50. If he were concerned with only three years, an economist would say your *permanent income* was $8,665.50. If the three unequal annual payments were the only income you received, and you had 20 years left to live, the three payments would

[2]See Milton Friedman, *Price Theory: A Provisional Text* (Chicago: Aldine, 1962), pp. 244–245.

equal a permanent income of $22,357/9.82, which is $2,276.68. The three unequal payments occurring in the first three years would be equivalent to twenty equal payments of $2,276.68 each.

## Perpetuities

A *perpetuity* is an annuity that lasts forever. (Although you don't live forever, you can pass the ownership rights to the perpetuity on to your heirs.) The British government issues bonds they call consols. These are merely bonds that never mature. They are a claim to a perpetual annual payment equal to the face value of the bond times the rate of interest printed on the face of the bond. If the face value of the bond is £1,000 and the stated rate of interest is 4%, the owner of the bond will receive £40 per year until he decides to sell it. The new owner of the bond will then receive £40 per year until *he* decides to sell it. How much would you be willing to pay for such a perpetuity? The maximum price I would pay for it is the present value of the annual payments, where the interest rate that is used in the present value calculations is the current market rate of interest (the current yield on triple A corporate bonds). The present value of the £40 perpetuity is:

$$V_0 = 40 \left[ \frac{1}{(1 + r)} + \frac{1}{(1 + r)^2} + \frac{1}{(1 + r)^3} + \cdots \right] \quad (11\text{-}2)$$

There is no last term because the payments never end. This does not mean that the sum will be indefinitely large. Note that

$$\frac{1}{(1 + r)^i}$$

can also be written as

$$\left( \frac{1}{1 + r} \right)^i$$

and that for all values of $i$ this expression is positive and less than one. For simplicity let's substitute $Z^i$ for

$$\left( \frac{1}{1+r} \right)^i$$

Equation 11-2 can then be rewritten as:

$$V_0 = 40(Z + Z^2 + Z^3 + \cdots) \quad (11\text{-}3)$$

Equation 11-3 can be rewritten as:

$$V_0 = 40Z(1 + Z + Z^2 + \cdots) \quad (11\text{-}4)$$

The term in the parentheses of Equation 11-4 is the sum of an infinite geometric series with a base ($Z$) that is positive but less than one. From elementary algebra we know that the sum of such an infinite series is $1/(1 - Z)$. We see, therefore, that:

$$V_0 = 40Z \, \frac{1}{1-Z} \quad (11\text{-}5)$$

If we now substitute $1/(1 + r)$ for $Z$, Equation 11-5 becomes

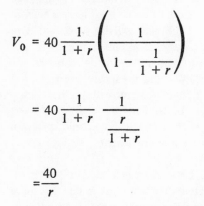

$$V_0 = 40 \frac{1}{1+r} \left( \frac{1}{1 - \frac{1}{1+r}} \right)$$

$$= 40 \frac{1}{1+r} \, \frac{1}{\frac{r}{1+r}}$$

$$= \frac{40}{r}$$

The present value of a perpetuity of $\$y$ is merely $y/r$, where $r$ is the current market rate of interest.

Suppose the interest rate printed on the bonds is 4%. This merely means that the annual payment received per bond will be 4% of the face value of the bond. If the current market rate of interest is 10% a perpetuity of $40 will have a present value of 40/.1, which equals $400. If you pay any more than $400 for one bond the rate

of return you will make will be less than 10%. If you pay $800, for example, the actual rate of return you would make would be 40/800, which is 5%. Why earn only 5% when the going market rate of return is 10%? When the market rate of interest is 10% people will abstain from buying any $40 perpetuity until its price falls to $400—no matter *what* the face value of the claim to the perpetuity (e.g., a bond), or the printed rate of interest. The rate of interest that is printed on a bond is called that bond's *coupon rate*. The amount of money the holder of a bond receives at the end of each year that he holds it is always the coupon rate times the face value of the bond. The actual rate of return earned on the bond would equal the coupon rate only if the puchase price of the bond equaled its face value.

The simplest way to purchase a perpetuity is to "deposit" some money in a savings account that specifies some passbook interest rate. The amount you deposit is the purchase price of the perpetuity. You and your heirs could withdraw each year's interest on the deposit forever. Of course, if the market rate of interest on bonds is greater than the passbook rate, the present value of your perpetuity would be less than the amount of the deposit. This merely means that bonds are a better buy than savings passbooks.

## Some Further Applications of Present Value Calculations

Now that you are familiar with these concepts we can address some issues that were beyond our reach before.

**Conservation** You need not search too long to find someone who is convinced that when resources are privately owned they will be used up much more rapidly than if they are publicly owned. In Chapter 4, with the fishing example, we saw that this widely held view is incorrect because when a resource is privately owned the users of the resource will be charged for its use. Moreover, the charge is not merely some randomly selected amount, it is the precise amount that forces each user of the resource to recognize his impact on the total supply of the resource.

Consider a thousand-acre forest that is privately owned. There are many uses for the forest. One possible use is as a source of lumber and lumber products. The owner of the land has every incentive to see to it that the lumber is not harvested at excessively rapid rates. After all, the market worth of the thousand acres is the present value of the expected earnings from its use. This includes not merely earnings this year or this decade, it includes earnings over the lifetime of the owner and of the owner's heirs. The private owner is forced to take the future into consideration because the current value of the land depends to an important extent on its future earning capacity. A private owner will, therefore, implement that cycle of harvesting trees and planting new ones that best serves the desires of the public (it is the public that buys lumber and lumber products) over the long run.

Contrast that situation with one where the thousand-acre forest is publicly owned, and the government gives permits to lumber companies to cut the timber. No individual decision maker in the government has his own private wealth at stake when the permits are given. The permits will be given on the basis of short-run political gain rather than the long-run future use of the land. The lumber company that gets the permit this year could well lose it next year, so the company will want to cut as much timber as possible without any regard for the future.

You may think that no timber should be cut because the best use of the forest is as a natural wilderness area for present and future generations to enjoy. But present and future generations also benefit from lumber and lumber products. Which benefit outweighs the other? Many assert that the benefits from the wilderness area far exceed the benefits from lumber and lumber products, and many others assert the reverse. The only objective test we have of the extent to which an individual benefits from anything is the price that he is willing to pay to obtain it.

It is misleading to depict the bidding process as "the people versus the lumber companies." The lumber companies' bids are limited by what their customers are willing to pay for lumber and lumber products. "The people" want wilderness areas, and they also want lumber and lumber products. A private owner of a forest can discover the value that "the people" place on its use as a wilderness area by charging admission to those who wish to so use it. Because the private owner wants to maximize his wealth he will apportion the use of the forest according to the relative demands for its use. The owner will try to devote the land to the use from which he gets the highest marginal revenue. If the demand for its use as a wilderness area is strong it may turn out that the marginal revenue from this use exceeds the marginal revenue from the alternative use even when all one thousand acres are devoted to the wilderness use. In this case the whole area will be used as a wilderness area. The reverse could also be true. Or, it could well happen that after the first (say) five hundred acres are used as a wilderness area, the marginal revenue from using the land as a source of lumber will exceed the marginal revenue from its use as a wilderness area. In that case the land will be apportioned so that the marginal revenues from both uses are equal. The important point is that the private owner has the incentive to seek out the highest valued use. With political determination of land use there is no such test of the relative values "the people" place on alternative uses of the land.

**The Used Textbook Market**[3] It is often stated that textbook publishers have their authors produce new editions frequently, in order to cope with the used book market. As students you are aware that your campus bookstore will buy back any text that is to be used again in the near

---

[3]The discussion in this section is based on what may be called an "oral tradition" at UCLA. It was first suggested by Aaron Director (University of Chicago) to Armen Alchian, and Professor Alchian has made it standard fare in the theory classes at UCLA.

future. (The bookstore generally pays somewhat less than half of the original price you paid for a new book, and it resells the book to another student for around two-thirds to three-fourths of the new book price.) This means that new book purchases from the publisher will be less than they would be without the used book market, so the publisher tries to eliminate this competition by putting out a new edition every two or three years. Students are reluctant to buy a used copy of the first edition if other students are purchasing new copies of the second edition. They fear they will miss some important discussion that was not contained in the first edition.

Now it is certainly true that at any price set by the publisher he would prefer to sell more books than less books. However, the price the publisher can charge for a new book is affected by whether or not the initial buyer can resell the book. A student's demand price (the maximum price he is willing to pay) for the book is the sum of the value of the direct educational services he receives from the book while he owns it and the present value of the amount that he can sell it for in the future. You are less reluctant to pay $11 for a book when you think you can resell it than you would be if you knew you could not resell it. By making the book more durable, and hence resalable, the publisher is able to collect a higher price from the initial purchaser than he could if the book fell apart after only one use. The publisher collects revenue from the initial owner and from all subsequent owners of a durable book all at one time—at the time of the initial purchase. Morever, the difference between the unit cost of producing a durable book and the unit cost of producing a nondurable book is relatively small. If the publisher produced a book that fell apart after one use he could sell a new book to each student in each time period, but he would also have to incur that book's production costs in each time period. If the publisher produced a more durable book that the first buyers could resell, he could in effect still collect revenue from future students because the present students would have higher demand prices due to the possibility of resale. He would incur higher production costs in the first period, but his production costs would be lower in subsequent periods. The publisher will select the strategy that maximizes his profits.

We can illustrate these points more completely by the use of a diagram or two. Assume that the publisher is deciding whether to publish a book that will last only one time period and therefore cannot be resold, or a book that will last two periods and therefore can be resold by the initial buyers. Assume also that all initial buyers in fact do resell the book, and that no new books are sold by the publisher in the second period. In Figure 11-4 the line labeled $D_1$ is the market demand price curve perceived by the publisher for the one-period book. (The demand prices that the publisher perceives are always the buyers' demand prices less an amount per copy to cover the bookstores' operating costs, which include a normal profit.) The maximum price per unit that the publisher could charge if he wanted to sell quantity $0A$ per period is $0B$. Any individual student's demand price is merely the money value that the student places on the educational benefit of reading the book during the single time period. If the two-period book could be resold by the initial buyers for the initial purchase price, you might be

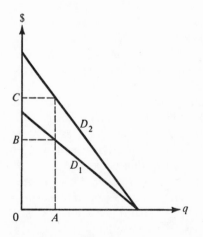

**Figure 11-4.**
Demand price curves for one- and two-period books.

tempted to say that the demand price at each quantity would be twice the demand price indicated on $D_1$. But this would be incorrect. The demand price would be the sum of the money value of the direct educational benefits of the book and the *present value* of the resale price. After all, the resale doesn't take place until the second period. Futhermore, the resale price will be less than the initial purchase price because the second group of students has lower demand prices for underlined and otherwise marked-up books. (Remember that we are discussing demand prices net of the bookstores' operating costs. The first group of students does not collect the full amount of the second group's demand prices.) The market demand price schedule perceived by the publisher for the two-period book is labeled $D_2$ in Figure 11-4. At each quantity the demand price for the two-period book is the sum of the money value of the direct educational benefits of the book (the demand price indicated on $D_1$) and the present value of the buy-back price. If the publisher wants to sell $0A$ copies of the two-period book the maximum price he can charge is $0C$ per copy. $BC$ is the present value of the resale price that would exist if $0A$ copies were placed on the used book market at the end of the first period.

In Figure 11-5, the curves labeled $D_2$ and $D_1$ are the market demand price curves perceived by the publisher for the two-period and the one-period books, respectively. The curves labeled $MR_2$ and $MR_1$ are the marginal revenue curves that are derived from the respective demand price curves. Line $AC_1$ is the marginal and average cost curve for producing the one-period book. Line $BC_2$ is the marginal and average cost curve for producing the two-period book. $BC_2$ is higher than $AC_1$, but not twice as high. It does not cost twice as much to produce a two-period book as it does to produce a one-period book. If the publisher produces the one-period book the optimum quantity to sell is $q_1$ and the price that sells that amount is $p_1$. Profit in each of the two periods would be area $p_1FHA$. Viewed from the present, the total profit over the two periods would be area $p_1FHA$ plus a smaller area which would represent

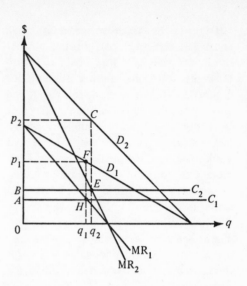

**Figure 11-5.**
Impact of used book market on publisher's profits.

the present value of the profit received in the second period. If the publisher produces the two-period book the optimum quantity to produce would be $q_2$, and the price that sells that quantity is $p_2$. Profit in the first period would be area $p_2CEB$, and there would be no profit in the second period. If area $p_2CEB$ exceeds area $p_1FHA$ plus an area equal to the present value of $p_1FHA$, the publisher would be better off producing the two-period book even though his second-period sales would be zero. Such is the case in Figure 11-5; thus we must conclude that the used book market does not necessarily act against the interest of publishers.

To be sure, the publisher would be better off if he could sell $q_2$ per period at $p_2$ per copy, but buyers will not pay $p_2$ per copy in the absence of the used book market. Perhaps a shortsighted publisher will try to trick buyers into thinking that resale is possible and then put out a new edition at the end of the first period to kill off the resale market. A publisher who did that could get away with it only once. Buyers would catch on to this practice, and their demand prices for his book would soon decline.

You probably have heard the charge that many manufacturers of consumer durable goods practice something called "planned obsolescence." Can you now see why manufacturers may not be interested in such a practice?

**Predatory Pricing**[4]  In 1911 John D. Rockefeller's Standard Oil (N.J.) Co. was prosecuted for violations of the Sherman Antitrust Act. One of the allegations brought against Rockefeller was that in markets where he faced substantial competition he forced his rivals out of business by cutting his oil prices far below his own costs, thus attracting his rival's customers. His rivals, who were smaller than he, could not afford to sell below costs for any length of time and so were forced to sell out to Rockefeller. In 1958 John S. McGee presented a theoretical argument that such "predatory pricing" was a higher cost way of getting rid of rivals than a simple direct purchase of the rivals' assets without an intervening predatory price war. In the same article McGee examined the historical evidence and demonstrated that Rockefeller in fact did *not* use predatory price wars to eliminate his rivals. The widely held belief to the contrary is nothing more than a myth. Rockefeller bought out his rivals at attractive prices, and in many cases the previous owners remained on the job as Rockefeller's managers at equally attractive salaries. In this section we shall see why it is generally unprofitable for a potential monopolist to use predatory pricing against his rivals.

To begin with you should take special note of the fact that the term "predatory pricing" refers to a seller's practice of cutting his prices below *his own cost* in order to drive rivals out of the market. If a large seller has lower costs than smaller sellers there are economies of scale, and the large seller could lower his price and attract and service additional customers while still making at least a normal profit. If the other firms cannot earn a normal profit at the lower price it is inefficient to have more than one large firm. The relationship

of the market demand curve and a single firm's long-run average cost curve indicates a natural monopoly. Such was not in 1911 (and still is not) the case with oil.

Suppose there is one large seller ($R$) and a small seller ($S$) who is $R$'s rival. If $S$ were not on the scene $R$ could earn a return stream that includes economic profit, but with $S$ on the scene $R$'s return stream (and $S$'s) consists of only competitive returns (normal profit). The minimum price that $S$ would sell his assets for is the present value of the competitive return stream $S$ expects to earn. Let's call that amount $V_S$. The present value of the economic profit that $R$ would make if $S$ were not on the scene ($V_R$) is the maximum price $R$ can afford to pay to get rid of $S$. No matter how rich $R$ is, the value of the monopoly power he is seeking is only $V_R$, and it would be irrational for him to pay more than $V_R$ for it. You can be sure that $R$ didn't get rich by paying a price for *anything* that exceeded the value of that thing to him.

If $V_R$ is bigger than $V_S$ there is some price that $R$ could pay and $S$ would accept to go out of business. For just a little more than $V_S$, $R$ could acquire control of $S$'s assets and immediately enjoy monopoly returns. He would not have to worry about anyone else acquiring the assets at a later date. If $R$ opts to engage in predatory pricing, his return stream during the period of the predation not only will not contain any economic profit, it will consist of economic losses. The return stream after the price war can at most be what it would have been if he bought $S$'s assets immediately. Therefore, the present value of $R$'s return stream with predation, even if the price war is successful, is necessarily less than $V_R$. In addition, $R$ still must acquire control of $S$'s assets. The price war may have driven $S$ out of business, but $S$'s plant and equipment do not vanish. There are many other entrepreneurs who see the importance of these assets to $R$, and hence they will be bidding to acquire the assets, planning to keep them out of operation until $R$ is forced to stop taking losses. Thus even after a successful price war $R$ will have to pay a price not too much lower than $V_S$ to acquire control of the assets so

---

[4]The discussion in this section is based on John S. McGee, "Predatory Price Cutting: The Standard Oil (N.J.) Case", *Journal of Law and Economics* (October 1958).

that he can either retire them or integrate them into his own operation.

Since predatory pricing is an inefficient way of getting rid of existing rivals, if $R$ wants to acquire monopoly power he should do it by direct purchase of $S$'s assets without an intervening price war. Of course $R$ wants to pay as small a price as possible (that will be close to $V_S$) not only because a low price means a low cost of getting rid of existing rivals, but also because he wants to discourage new rivals from coming on the scene. If $R$ acquired the reputation of paying prices in excess of $V_S$, entrepreneurs not already in business might set up the assets necessary to enter without ever planning to operate them. It would appear that $R$ was willing to guarantee an above-normal return on the interloper's investment. If it is known that $R$ pays only the competitive value of the assets, new entrepreneurs would have no reason to prefer to enter $R$'s industry over any other industry.

If the present value of $S$'s expected return stream, $V_S$, is bigger than the present value of $R$'s monopoly return stream, $V_R$, $R$ could not afford to buy $S$ out immediately. As we have seen, even after a price war $R$ would have to pay a price not much below $V_S$ to acquire control of $S$'s assets, hence predatory pricing is even more foolish under these circumstances than when $V_R$ exceeds $V_S$.

As McGee has shown, John D. Rockefeller was far too shrewd to try to drive out rival firms by predatory pricing. He acquired his monopoly power by the more profitable route of direct purchase of his rival's assets without an intervening period of predation.

## Questions for Discussion

1. You are a lawyer for the defendant in a civil lawsuit arising from the death of a family head in a car accident. The lawyer for the plaintiff asserts that the deceased's earning power must be replaced by granting the plaintiff judgment for the sum of all the earnings the deceased could reasonably have expected to make from the time of his death to the time of his expected retirement. How do you respond?

2. (a) Evaluate this argument of St. Thomas Aquinas concerning interest:

   For some goods, such as wine, there cannot be use without consumption. These goods are fungible goods. There are other goods, such as a house, for which use does not imply consumption. In the former case it is impossible to charge for use as distinct from charging for the good itself. In the latter case it is possible to charge for use without surrendering ownership. Money is a fungible good, hence interest is unnatural.

   (b) What is natural about a positive rate of interest?

3. Why do market rates of interest rise whenever people expect increasing inflation in the future?

4. When you purchase a triple A corporate bond you get a claim to a fixed annual interest payment equal to the coupon rate of interest times the face value of the bond. This interest payment continues until the bond matures (assuming you don't sell the bond before then), at which time you receive the face value of the bond. How do you calculate the actual percentage yield you make on the bond? Can you think of an easy-to-use formula that would give you a good approximation of the actual percentage yield?

5. If a law were passed that applied a 100% tax to all nonhuman wealth owned at time of death, would people care more or care less about conservation? Why?

6. Evaluate the following:

   The way to get people to keep future generations in mind as they make current decisions concerning scarce natural resources is allow them to hold private property rights over these resources, which they can transfer at death to their heirs.

7. Evaluate the following:

   In order to preserve our natural wilderness and beach areas for future generations, we must place such areas under public control.

8. Construct a diagrammatic analysis of planned obsolescence based on the text discussion of the used textbook market.

9. Evaluate the following:

   If the present value of an interloper's expected competitive return stream exceeds the present value of an extablished monopolist's expected monopoly return stream, predatory pricing by the monopolist could be a wise idea if there were no effective (financial) capital market.

# 12
## Futures Trading

This book is about markets, and one of the more important but least understood markets is that in standardized contracts for future delivery of commodities such as soybeans, pork bellies (bacon), wheat, frozen orange juice, coffee, and eggs. It is widely believed that such trading benefits speculators at the expense of producers, distributors, and consumers, and that it makes prices for these commodities more volatile than they would otherwise be. At the outbreak of the Korean War President Truman declared that such trading should be banned because it would interfere with the flow of the supply of food both at home and for the fighting troops. In the summer of 1973 Senator Alan Cranston of California asserted that futures trading was responsible for the high and increasing prices of agricultural commodities that existed at that time. The purpose of this chapter is to show why President Truman and Senator Cranston were wrong. Futures trading *reduces* the volatility of the prices of agricultural products, and ensures a more even flow of supply of those commodities than would otherwise exist. It is indispensable to those who are actually engaged in the production, processing, and distribution of agricultural commodities, for it permits them to diminish the riskiness of their enterprises. It permits those who have a taste or preference for risk bearing to take over the risk from those who do not.

### The Mechanics of Futures Trading

In many instances contracts are made which specify future delivery. The purchaser of a house makes a contract with a builder of a house today which requires the builder of the house to provide a house to the buyer at some date in the future. The buyer of a new car frequently gets nothing immediately except a piece of paper that obligates the car dealer to deliver a car outfitted with specified accessories at some future date. A farmer makes a contract to deliver some specified amount of wheat to a grain elevator operator at a specific date in the future at a price that is agreed on today. All of these cases are examples of *forward contracts*. A forward contract is a contract that is entered into on one date that requires the delivery of some service or commodity at a future date. Such contracts can be made by any two transactors, at any place, at any time, for any quantity of the service or commodity.

A *futures contract* resembles a forward contract in that it calls for final execution in the future but it differs from a forward contract in that it can be made only for commodities that are listed on a formal commodities exchange market (such as the Chicago Mercantile Exchange, the Chicago Board of Trade, and the New York Coffee and Sugar Exchange), it must be for standard quantities of the commodity (e.g., 5,000 bushels in the case of soybeans, 40,000 board feet in the case of lumber, and 15,000 pounds in the case of frozen orange juice concentrate), it calls for delivery at standard times (e.g., delivery dates for frozen pork bellies are February, March, May, July, and August), and it can be entered into only via the intermediation of a broker.

Any person, after he signs the necessary papers and puts down an initial deposit at the office of a broker, can buy or sell futures contracts. When he "buys" a futures contract today he merely enters into an agreement to accept delivery of a specified amount of a commodity at a specified date in the future and to pay the price specified in the futures contract. Delivery is made to standard delivery points (specified public warehouses), not to the buyer's home. The buyer merely gets a warehouse receipt that gives him title to the actual commodity that physically exists and is stored at the specified delivery point. The price that is specified in the futures contract is called the *futures price*. For example, at the Chicago Board of Trade the closing futures price on October 17, 1973, for December wheat was $4.17. The wheat futures contract is for 5,000 bushels, and the quoted price is in dollars per bushel. Therefore if one were to buy one contract (and one cannot buy less) for December wheat he would enter into an agreement to accept delivery of 5,000 bushels of wheat at a time in December chosen by the seller and to pay (in December) $4.17 times 5,000 = $20,850. On the other hand, if one were to "sell" a December wheat futures contract on October 17, 1973, he would thereby agree to deliver 5,000 bushels of wheat any day he chooses in December to the specified delivery point and to accept $20,850 (in December) in payment.

Whether one is a buyer or a seller he must pay his broker some fraction (usually 10%) of the dollar value of the contract at the time the contract is bought or sold. This is called the *margin payment*, and it is the only money that changes hands at the time of the initial purchase or sale of the futures contract. The broker's commission is paid only after the customer is no longer bound by the futures contract in question. The margin payment is not a fee paid to the broker, it is a down payment that the customer makes on the futures transaction.

How does a transactor become "no longer bound" by a futures contract that he buys (or sells)? The most obvious way is to wait until the delivery date and to accept (or make) delivery at the agreed-on price. Only about 1% of futures contracts are settled in this way. The other 99% become no longer binding because the transactor "closes his position." A person who holds futures contracts to accept delivery in the future (i.e., one who has *bought* futures contracts) is said to have a "long position." A person who holds futures contracts to deliver in the future (i.e., one who has *sold* futures contracts) is said to have a "short position." A person who is "long" has some commodity coming to him. One who is "short" must deliver commodities. A long (short) with respect to a given delivery date can close his position by selling (buying) an equal number of contracts for the same delivery date. In other words, a person who is long can rid himself of the obligation to accept delivery by incurring an obligation to deliver an equal amount of the commodity on the same delivery date. The second obligation cancels out the first, leaving the transactor free of both obligations.

Let us take a more careful look at how this works. Suppose that on Day 1 Mr. A buys one contract for May soybeans at $5.10 per bushel (the standard soybean contract is for 5,000 bushels). Someone had to sell the contract to him. For every long there has to be a short. Let's call the one who is short Mr. B. On Day 5 the price for May soybeans is $4.80. Mr. B is delighted. He has agreed to deliver May soybeans at $5.10 and now he can buy a May futures contract which will guarantee him that he can acquire soyeans in May at $4.80. That is why he went short in the first place—he expected the May soybean price to fall relative to its price on Day 1. *Shorts expect prices to fall.* If he thinks that $4.80 is as low as the price is going, Mr. B will buy a May futures on Day 5 from Mr. C. Now why should Mr. B have to wait until May to get his profit? He has two contracts that determine for certain what will happen in May. Since his profit is guaranteed why can't he get it now? *He can.* In fact the rules of every commodity exchange prohibit him from keeping his two contracts until May. As soon as he buys the futures contract that offsets his original short position, his position is *automatically* closed. The exchange's clearinghouse immediately will pay him the profit he would make if he waited until May and executed both contracts. (Of course this profit is reduced by the amount of the broker's commission.) Since Mr. B has made a profit he may if he wishes also tell his broker to return the margin payment that he originally made.

Let's suppose the price goes the other way. If the price by Day 5 rises to $5.30 Mr. B will be very unhappy. He originally went short because he expected the price to fall, but it has risen. If this price rise convinces him that the price will not eventually fall, he will want to limit his losses to those that he has already suffered, so he again closes his position by buying a May soybean futures. This time he must pay into the exchange's clearinghouse an amount exactly equal to the loss that he would realize if he waited until May to execute his two contracts. The margin payment that he originally gave to his broker would be used for this purpose. Brokers always see to it that the amount of money the customer has put down is enough to cover the losses the customer suffers from his position. If the customer holds on, and the value of his position deteriorates so much that the margin payment is not enough to cover his losses, the broker will issue a *margin call.* This means that the customer must pay in an additional amount of money—at least enough to cover his losses. (Actually brokers insist that the amount paid in be more than enough to cover the losses.)

Mr. B has closed his position, but what about Mr. A and Mr. C? They too can close their positions any time they wish. Mr. A, who is long (he purchased a contract on Day 1), could close his position by selling a contract for the same delivery date, i.e., he would have to go short to close his long position. Mr. C, who is short (he sold a contract on Day 5 for, let's say, $4.80), could close his position by making an offsetting long transaction. Mr. A took a long position because he expected the price for May soybeans to rise. If the May futures price falls and he does not think it will rise again he may close his position by selling a May futures and paying the loss into the clearinghouse. On the other hand if the May futures price rises and he does not think it will rise any more, he may close his position again by selling a May futures. Under these circumstances he will make a profit and receive payment from the clearinghouse. Of course he always has the option of maintaining his long position until the delivery date and actually accepting delivery of the soybeans. Mr. C took his short position because he expected the price to fall. If it does he can close his position and take his profit. If the May futures price rises he may want to close his position to limit his losses. Again Mr. C has the option of maintaining his short position until delivery time. If he does that he will have to actually acquire 5,000 bushels of soybeans, deliver them to the designated public warehouse, and deliver the warehouse receipt to someone with an open long position. There must be such a person because even if A has closed his position someone had to buy A's contract from him.

Let's suppose that Mr. A and Mr. C do not close their positions, and they hold the contracts until May. Now Mr. A is obliged to accept delivery of 5,000 bushels of soybeans at $5.10 per bushel. Mr. C is obliged to deliver 5,000 bushels of soybeans and to accept $4.80 per bushel in full payment thereof. Mr. C delivers the warehouse receipt to the exchange's clearinghouse and receives his payment from the clearinghouse, which then passes the warehouse receipt on to Mr. A, who then must pay the clearinghouse at $5.10 per bushel. The clearinghouse makes a profit on this operation, but that profit is exactly offset by the loss it suffered back on Day 5 when it paid Mr. B the profit he made when his position was closed. The clearinghouse never nets any profit from its operation. It is merely the conduit of funds. Its operating expenses are paid by fees levied on brokers.

Of course there is one way that Mr. A and Mr. C could close their positions before the delivery date and still not involve any additional transactors. A is long one contract and could close his position by selling a contract. If it coincidentally happens that Mr. C is the buyer of that contract he would also have closed his position. Of course Mr. A and Mr. C would not deal directly with each other. All buying and selling is done through brokers and is executed through the clearinghouse. Nevertheless it is *possible* that such a coincidence could occur. If Messrs. A, B, and C were the only individuals who traded in this particular contract there would be no open positions on trading day. As we said before, only about 1% of futures contracts are still binding on delivery day. The number of open positions that exist on any day for a given futures contract is reported in the financial section of many daily newspapers under the name *open interest*.

Every commodities exchange sets a limit on the amount that the price of a given futures contract can change in either direction on one day. For example, the Chicago Board of Trade sets a limit of 25 cents per bushel (increase or decrease) on wheat futures contracts. This limit is ostensibly for the purpose of limiting the losses that traders can suffer on any one day. However, these limits do not serve that purpose. On some days no trade occurs in some commodity because there is either no buyer or no seller. For example, when the Russian wheat purchase in 1972 became known, there were a number of open short positions held by people who had previously anticipated that the price of wheat futures would fall. However, as soon as the news of the agreement with the Russians was out everybody anticipated increased prices. Thus, for several days, the opening bid prices for all the wheat futures contracts

were at the allowed maximums, with no one willing to sell. Consequently, no trading took place in wheat for those days and as a result those who had previously sold wheat short lost $1,250 per day for each contract they held (5,000 bushels times 25 cents per bushel = $1,250). This is not an insignificant point, for it often happens that news of unanticipated crop failures, bumper crops, or some government action, anywhere in the world, will greatly affect peoples' expectations about future prices.

## The Transactors:
## Speculators and Hedgers

By now you are probably wondering why such an elaborate system of betting on the course of prices in the future ever emerged. The first step toward understanding the role of the futures market is to note that for those commodities that are traded on this market there are actually two markets: the *spot* or *cash* market, and the *futures* market. The cash market involves the actual production, processing, and distribution of the commodities. The buyers and sellers in this market are those whom we normally think of when we envisage the economic chain that gets commodities from the producer to the consumer. Contracts in the cash market call for various amounts of various qualities of the various commodities to be delivered at various times and places, depending on the desires of those who enter into the contracts. Prices in the cash market are called *spot prices*. The spot price of soybeans on any specific day is the number of dollars that must be paid on that day in order to actually acquire a bushel of soybeans "on the spot." Spot prices are the prices we usually think of when we discuss the price of the actual commodity.

The futures market is not really a market for the actual commodities. It is a market in *contracts* for future delivery of standardized quantities and qualities of commodities to standardized delivery points on standardized dates. Today's prices of such contracts are called futures prices, and as we have seen the overwhelming majority of such futures contracts are closed out before the delivery of any actual commodity is made. All kinds of people trade in the futures market. On November 30, 1959, there were 8,075 open positions in the soybean futures market. These positions were held by 252 grain merchandisers and exporters, 99 livestock feeders and dealers, 1,617 farmers, 103 professional speculators, 235 physicians, 117 lawyers, 252 salesmen, 46 housemaids and private detectives, 56 brokers, 408 housewives, 34 students, 648 retired people, and 22 unemployed people.[1]

Some people who trade in the futures market—such as farmers, grain merchandisers, and livestock feeders—also trade in the cash market as their main source of income. Others—such as physicians, students, and housewives—are not involved in the cash market except as consumers of the final products. Producers, processors, and distributors in the cash market trade in the futures market to *hedge*. Hedging is simply a way of reducing the risk of losses from unforeseen changes in the prices of the actual commodities. The operator of a grain elevator buys wheat from farmers at harvest time and stores it, gradually selling it off to processors over the period between harvests. He stands the chance of suffering large losses if the spot price of wheat unexpectedly falls while he holds it in inventory. Of course he is delighted whenever the spot price unexpectedly rises. The price he paid the farmer was based on his (and the farmer's) expectation of low prices between harvests, so if the spot price actually rises he will make a windfall profit.

The grain elevator operator can greatly reduce the risk from unforeseen price changes by agreeing with another person (such as a lawyer or a housewife or a professional speculator) that he will give that person whatever gains he makes from unforeseen price increases in exchange for that person's agreement to pay the elevator operator any losses that he suffers from unforeseen price decreases. The elevator oper-

ator can do this simply by selling futures contracts in wheat for approximately the same amount of wheat that he has in his inventory. As he sells his inventory he will close out his position on the same amount of futures.

Let's take a more careful look at how this reduces the elevator operator's risk. Suppose that on December 1 an elevator operator purchases 5,000 bushels of wheat from a farmer. He pays the farmer a price based on the then spot price for wheat that he can expect to receive when he sells to the processor (the spot price at the Chicago terminal elevator). Let's say that that spot price is $4.80 per bushel. He then bears the risk that the spot price will decline while he is holding the wheat in inventory. With the difference between the spot price that he receives and the price he paid the farmer he must cover his operating costs and in addition make at least a normal profit. If the spot price declines the resulting loss could wipe out the profit from his operation. To reduce this risk, at the same time that he purchases the wheat from the farmer he sells a March futures contract (one futures contract in wheat is always for 5,000 bushels) for $5.00 per bushel. The futures price will ordinarily be higher than the spot price by the costs of storage, insurance, and interest for the period of time from the present to the delivery day. If the futures price were higher than this, many speculators would sell futures contracts while planning to actually make delivery with commodities purchased on the spot market. This would lower the futures price. If the futures price were lower than this, many speculators would buy futures contracts planning to accept delivery and resell on the spot market. This would raise the futures price. Competition between speculators will ordinarily ensure that all such profitable transactions are made. If you think that any given futures price is out of line you should act on your belief. If you think a given futures price is too high relative to the spot price and carrying costs you should sell futures contracts. If you think the futures price is too low you should buy futures contracts. If you are correct in your belief, i.e., if you have out-

[1]Thomas A Hieronymus, *Economics of Futures Trading* (New York: Commodity Research Bureau Inc., 1971), p. 58.

guessed the market, you will be wealthier. If you are wrong you will be poorer.

In any case let's get back to our elevator operator. Suppose he decides to sell his 5,000 bushels of wheat on the spot market in February, but that spot prices have fallen. The best he can get, let's say, is $4.60 per bushel. He loses 20 cents per bushel on his transactions in the spot market. Since he no longer holds the wheat in inventory he will buy a March futures contract to close his position on the futures market. If the futures price fell by the same amount as the spot price he would gain 20 cents per bushel on futures transactions. The gain in the futures transactions reimburses him for the loss in the spot transactions. In this case the speculator reimburses him for the losses he suffered from unfavorable changes of the spot price.

Suppose that the spot and futures prices of wheat both increased by the same amount. Under these circumstances the elevator operator would sell his wheat in February at a higher price than he paid for it in December. He would have that gain to add to the profit he gets from charging for his normal service. However, when he closes his position on the futures market he will lose by the same amount. He originally sold a contract for $5.00 per bushel and now he must (in effect) buy it back at a higher price. The loss in the futures transactions offsets the gain from the spot transactions. In this case he gives the speculator the gain he made from favorable changes of the spot price.

The hedging that we have just described is called the *selling hedge*. Some transactor is long on the actual commodity (has bought some of the actual commodity to hold in inventory), and to protect himself against losses in the spot value of his commodity he has gone short in the futures market (has sold futures contracts for, as nearly as possible, the same amount of the commodity). Of course the reverse situation is also possible, and it would call for a *buying hedge*. Consider the case of a livestock feeder whose role is to buy (say) cattle from ranchers and to feed them to make them ready for slaughter. He may today enter into a forward contract with a

meat packer to sell a certain number of cattle after the feeding period. The price that the feeder and the packer would agree on would reflect, among other things, the expected cost of the feed over the feeding period. Once the forward contract is made, the feeder bears the risk that the price of feed would unexpectedly rise. He can reduce the risk by using the futures market. The essence of his hedge would be an agreement to give the speculator any windfall profit from a decline in the price of feed in return for the speculator's promise to reimburse the feeder if the price of feed increased.

Suppose that when the feeder makes his agreement with the packinghouse the spot price of soybean meal is $155 per ton. He bases his agreement with the packer on this price. If during the feeding period the spot price unexpectedly rises, the feeder will incur larger costs but will not be able to receive a higher price for his cattle. He can reduce this risk by buying a futures contract for soybean meal at the same time that he enters into his forward contract with the packer. Assuming that the spot price and the futures price move together, such a move would eliminate any risk of loss and any hope of gain from unexpected spot price changes. If the spot price unexpectedly rises, the feeder is worse off as regards his cattle operation, but he is better off from his futures transaction. With rising prices, when he closes his long position in the futures market he will receive a check from the clearinghouse that will reimburse him for the loss from his forward contract. With falling spot and futures prices he will gain from his forward contract, but he will lose a commensurate amount when he closes his long futures position and makes his payment to the clearinghouse.

Thus we see that hedgers both buy and sell futures contracts when they open their hedge. Those who wish to open a selling hedge are those who hold inventories of the actual commodity. They will sell futures contracts. Those who wish to open a buying hedge are those who have sold an actual commodity forward. They will buy futures contracts. When it comes time to close the hedges, the selling hedgers will buy futures contracts and the buying hedgers will sell futures contracts.

If the spot and futures prices for a given commodity move by exactly the same amount and in the same direction, the hedge will be perfect. The hedger stands neither to lose nor to gain from unforeseen spot price changes. The difference between the spot price and the futures price of a commodity is called the *basis*. If the spot price and the futures price move by the same amount the difference between them—the basis—is constant. However, the basis is not always constant. This fact provides the mechanism whereby futures prices affect the rate at which the actual commodity will be consumed between harvest periods. In the next section we consider this mechanism.

## The Time Allocation of Consumption

When a crop is harvested all of it could be made available for current consumption. This would mean that the price of the commodity would be very low at harvest time because of the large supply relative to the demand. Later in the interharvest period, however, the price of the commodity would be very high because most of the crop would already be used and the available supply would be small relative to demand. One way to cope with this problem is to have a central authority ration out the crop over the interharvest period so that a more even flow of supply will be assured. A more even flow of supply will mean less volatile prices. Another way to accomplish the same objectives is to have a system of futures trading.

As we have seen, there is a great deal of profit to be made by outguessing the market. Thousands of people examine crop reports and other market conditions in the hope that they can forecast what prices will be in the future. Current futures prices are a result of the interplay of all of these individuals. Futures prices are therefore good indicators of what actual spot prices will be in the future. If a given futures price is high relative to the estimated future spot price, individual speculators will

sell futures contracts; if the futures price is low relative to the estimated future spot price, individual speculators will buy futures contracts. Futures prices represent a consensus forecast of future spot prices.

When futures prices increase relative to current spot prices (taking carrying charges into account), holders of unhedged inventories of the commodities will decrease the rate at which they are selling for current use and thus increase the amount that will be available later in the interharvest period. They hold back on their inventories in the expectation of selling at a higher price in the future. The decrease in the supply of commodities for current use will raise today's spot price, but the increase in the supply of commodities for later use will make the future spot price lower than it otherwise would be. The higher spot price today induces consumers to consume less today and permits a lower price in the future. If the futures price decreases relative to the spot price, holders of unhedged inventories will interpret this to mean that in the future they will be able to sell for less favorable terms than in the present, hence they will be induced to sell more now, leaving less for later. This will mean that today's spot price will be lower than it otherwise would be and the future spot price will be higher than it otherwise would be.

Holders of hedged inventories can also be induced to hold back for future use. Think in terms of the speculator bidding against the current consumer. If the speculator outbids the current consumer the futures price will increase relative to the spot price. In other words *the basis will change*. The hedger is indifferent to movements in spot and futures prices *only if they move together by the same amount*. Consider the grain elevator operator we discussed in the last section. If the spot price of wheat goes up he is better off from his spot transactions, but this is offset by the fact that he loses when he closes his futures position. Suppose the futures price goes up by more than the increase in the spot price. The loss from his futures transaction would be greater than the gain from his spot transaction. He will not wish to close his futures position under these circumstances, hence he will not "close" his spot position (i.e., he will not sell wheat in the spot market for immediate use). The speculator's bidding has raised the futures price by more than the current consumers' bidding has raised the spot price. Speculators are the representatives of consumers in the future. This change in the basis will mean that present consumption will be decreased, but future consumption will be increased.

If spot prices increased by more than futures prices—i.e., if current consumers outbid the speculators who represent future consumers—the gain the elevator operator makes from his spot transactions would be greater than the loss he would suffer when he closed his futures position. This would induce the elevator operator to close his futures position, thereby freeing him to release grain for current consumption. This will mean that current spot prices will be lower than they otherwise would be, and future spot prices will be higher than they otherwise would be.

In a falling market—i.e., with both spot and futures prices falling—the elevator operator would be induced to hold back on grain if the spot price fell by more than the futures price. Here again the loss he would suffer if he sold wheat for current use would be greater than the gain he would make when he closed his futures position. He would thus be induced not to close his futures position so that he could continue to hold grain in storage. If the futures price fell by more than the spot price the reverse would be true. Here the loss he would suffer from selling in a declining spot market would be less than the gain that he made from closing his futures position. He would thus be induced to close his futures position and sell grain on the spot market. Current consumers would have outbid future consumers in the latter case, and the reverse would hold in the former case.

## The Volatility of Prices

Do speculation and futures trading in general make prices fluctuate more widely than they otherwise would? You do not have to search very far to find a politician or a news commentor who will say so. But our analysis reveals that this is wrong. Suppose that, because of weather conditions, half of the new, growing soybean crop is destroyed during the interharvest period. This will mean that when the existing harvested crop is used up the price of soybeans will rise drastically because of the greatly reduced supply relative to the demand. The currently available harvested crop is sufficient for the quantity demanded at the current price, but the excess demand in the coming period will mean that there will be a big difference between the current spot price and next period's spot price. The effect of futures trading is to diminish this jump in prices. The news of the crop damage will almost immediately result in higher futures prices relative to spot prices. This will induce holders of both hedged and unhedged inventories to decrease their rate of sales for current use, making more available for future use. The current spot price will rise, but there will be less excess demand in the future period, so the future spot price will be lower than it otherwise would be. The difference between the current spot price and the future spot price will be greatly diminished. There will be less price volatility.

The speculators did not cause the destruction of the crop. They converted knowledge of its destruction into market signals that induced others to increase the amount available in the future period, thus partially compensating for the crop damage. Of course this means that less is available for current use, but blame Mother Nature, not the speculator. The speculator's behavior means that instead of feast now and famine next period, we can enjoy moderate consumption in both periods.

If speculation is profitable for the speculator it must result in more price stability, not less. Consider the speculator who has an open long position. He maintains that position because he thinks that the current futures price is unrealistically low relative to the spot price and the carrying charges. He thinks he knows something that the consensus of the market does not know. Perhaps his cousin, a soybean farmer, has told him that the coming harvest will be lean. If he is right this information will eventually become generally known and the futures price will rise, so our speculator will make a profit. His initial purchase of the futures contract put some bit of upward pressure on the futures price. It was a signal to others to take a look at the existing price to see if it is realistic. If our speculator is right the rest will follow, and current holders of inventories will be induced to hold larger amounts for deferred consumption. This will mean that the spot price will be less volatile. If he is right the futures price would have gone up anyway, so his action does not increase the volatility of the futures price.

Suppose he is wrong. If his action causes others to do the same, so that the futures price increases, holders of inventories will hold larger amounts for deferred consumption. When it becomes generally known that the coming harvest will be abundant rather than lean, the futures price will fall by a large amount, and our speculator as well as any others who guessed wrong will suffer losses. The current spot price will have risen in response to the initial increase in the futures price, and the abundant harvest will mean that next period's spot price will be very much lower. Price volatility has increased, but this is because the speculators guessed wrong. They suffer losses when they guess wrong, so it is not true that futures trading provides the incentive to speculators to make prices less stable.

At the beginning of this chapter we noted that President Truman and Senator Cranston did not understand that futures trading assures less price volatility and more even supply flows than would be observed in the absence of futures trading. Can you now explain these facts to Senator Cranston?

## Questions for Discussion

1. Why would you expect that the usual difference between any two futures prices for a given commodity would equal the carrying costs (interest, storage, and insurance) for the amount of time between the two dates for which the futures prices are quoted?

2. A futures price is an estimate. An estimate of what?

3. Explain how a speculator agrees to reimburse a hedger for any losses the hedger makes due to unexpected price changes in exchange for the hedger's agreement to give the speculator any gains made from unexpected price changes.

4. Evaluate the following:

   If the basis increases, holders of hedged inventories are induced to decrease the amount they make available for current consumption, while hedgers are induced to increase the amount they make available for current consumption when the basis decreases.

5. Explain the following:

   Speculators make profits only when they reduce price volatility.
   Speculators gain nothing from increased price volatility.

6. Who gains when futures trading for a given commodity is prohibited (as it has been for onions)? Who loses?

7. Sketch out how hedging in foreign exchange could be used by companies and individuals in one country who trade with companies and individuals in another country. Is hedging more useful in a system of floating (market determined) exchange rates than in a system of fixed (controlled) exchange rates? Why?

8. Futures trading is most beneficial whenever there is uncertainty about future market conditions. Could futures trading in crude oil be helpful during the "energy crisis"? How?

# 13
# General Equilibrium, Property Rights, and the Coase Theorem

Up to this point in the text each market (product or input) has been examined in isolation. For example, when we discussed the housing market in Chapter 7 we did not discuss how the supply and demand for automobiles may affect that market. Our discussion of the housing market used the technique known as partial equilibrium analysis. In partial equilibrium analysis we treat each market as if it were independent of all other markets, so that we can concentrate on the many effects of changes of a good's own relative price on the amount available and the amount wanted of that good. A more complete analysis requires that we recognize that the relative price of gasoline, for example, can have significant effects on the supply of and demand for housing. Moreover, changes in the relative price of goods that we may think have nothing to do with the housing market must also exert some effect (perhaps very tiny) on the housing market. This follows from the general structure of a voluntary exchange economic system. In the first part of this chapter we will examine this interrelatedness of markets by introducing general equilibrium analysis.

It is customary in intermediate level textbooks such as this to include a section of a chapter, or an entire chapter, on "welfare economics." Welfare economics has

nothing to do with welfare schemes such as Aid to Dependent Children or the negative income tax. Rather, it is concerned with describing the technical conditions that exist when an economy is in a perfectly competitive general equilibrium state. Welfare economics was developed by mathematical economists who were interested in rigorously demonstrating the optimality of a decentralized voluntary exchange economy in competitive equilibrium. As an adjunct to this intellectual exercise it is possible to demonstrate that since the conditions for perfect competition do not exist, and since there are such things as "externalities" in the real world, we cannot expect an actual decentralized voluntary exchange economy to generate an economic optimum.

In my view, little of value comes from a discussion of the properties of a state of perfectly competitive general equilibrium. Perfect competition does not exist, so whatever its features it is irrelevant to any discussion involving the merits of decentralized voluntary exchange economic systems. As Hayek constantly reminds us, the chief advantage of a decentralized voluntary exchange economy lies in the fact that the world's best expert on any good does not know as much individually as the market does collectively. No amount of central planning, with or without a computer, is capable of responding to changes of economic conditions as efficiently as a decentralized market. This chapter does not, therefore, discuss welfare economics.

Recent work on externalities demonstrates that they are a problem only where there are high costs of defining, enforcing, and exchanging private property rights. It makes more sense to concentrate on the etiology of externality problems so that we can find ways around them, rather than to try to demonstrate how the existence of externalities affects general equilibrium equations and thus makes impossible what we already knew was impossible anyway—the attainment of perfectly competitive general equilibrium. The last sections of this chapter will, therefore, discuss the problem of externalities using the modern property rights approach.

## Say's Principle and General Equilibrium[1]

Assume that each transactor (a decision making unit such as a person, a household, or a firm) is neither a thief nor a philanthropist. That is, no transactor *plans* to acquire any amount of any good without *planning* to offer some thing(s) of equal value in exchange, and no transactor *plans* to give any amount of any good to another transactor without *planning* to receive something(s) of equal value in exchange. Suppose that a given transactor has some amount of money, $m_0$, with which to purchase two goods, $X$ and $Y$. From Chapter 3 we know that the transactor's budget constraint, if all the $m_0$ must be spent, is

$$p_x q_x + p_y q_y = m_0 \qquad (13\text{-}1)$$

where $q_x$ and $q_y$ are the quantities of $X$ and $Y$ bought, and $p_x$ and $p_y$ are the money prices of $X$ and $Y$ respectively. Equation 13-1 describes the set of pairs of $q_x$ and $q_y$ that can be purchased. Out of

this attainable set the transactor chooses the one pair that he considers better than the others. Let the chosen purchase plan be $q_x^*$ and $q_y^*$. From Equation 13-1 we know that

$$p_x q_x^* + p_y q_y^* - m_0 = 0 \qquad (13\text{-}2)$$

If the transactor plans to hold on to some money rather than spend it all, Equation 13-2 becomes

$$p_x q_x^* + p_y q_y^* + m^* - m_0 = 0 \qquad (13\text{-}3)$$

where $m^*$ is the amount of money that the transactor plans not to spend. Equation 13-3 can be generalized by noting that the transactor could begin with some amount of $X$ and some amount of $Y$ as well as some money. Let $q_{x0}$ and $q_{y0}$ be the transactor's initial endowment (starting amount) of good $X$ and good $Y$ respectively. Not only can he plan to use money to purchase $X$ and Y, he can also plan to use his initial endowment of $X$ and $Y$ to purchase more $X$ or more $Y$ or more money. The transactor's budget constraint is then

$$p_x(q_x^* - q_{x0}) + p_y(q_y^* - q_{y0}) +$$
$$(m^* - m_0) = 0 \qquad (13\text{-}4)$$

The term $p_x(q_x^* - q_{x0})$ is the money value of the transactor's planned *excess demand* for good $X$. If it is positive the transactor plans to acquire more $X$ than he started with, while if it is negative he plans to get rid of some $X$ in order to get some more $Y$, or some more money, or both. The planned excess demands for $Y$ and for money have similar interpretations. Notice that the money value of the excess demand for money is written as $(m^* - m_0)$. There is no need to multiply this quantity by a price because the money price of money is one. In other words, we could write the excess demand for money as

$$p_m(m^* - m_0),$$

where $p_m = 1$.

We can rewrite Equation 13-4 as

[1]This exposition of Say's Principle follows Axel Leijonhufvud, "Classnotes on Say's Principle," mimeo.

$$p_x \Delta q_x + p_y \Delta q_y + \Delta m = 0 \qquad (13\text{-}5)$$

where $\Delta q_x$, $\Delta q_y$, and $\Delta m$ are planned changes in the amount of $X$, $Y$, and money respectively. The "planned change" is the difference between the amount the transactor starts with and the amount he plans to end up with after exchange with other transactors—i.e., it is the physical amount of the planned excess demand.

Equation 13-5 can be further generalized to the case of $n - 1$ nonmoney goods plus money. Nonmoney goods are such things as labor services and bonds, as well as such things as records and shirts. Instead of calling the goods $X$, $Y$, and $m$, let's label them by numbers. Equation 13-5 becomes

$$p_1 \Delta q_1 + p_2 \Delta q_2 + p_3 \Delta q_3 + \cdots +$$

$$p_{n-1} \Delta q_{n-1} + \Delta q_n = 0 \quad (13\text{-}6)$$

where $\Delta q_n$ is the planned excess demand for money. Equation 13-6 is Say's Principle for any individual transactor.[2] It says that the net value of an individual transactor's trading plan is zero. If, for example, $p_1 \Delta q_1$ is positive the transactor is planning to increase his holdings of good one. He has a planned excess demand for good one. Since the transactor is not a thief, he must at the same time plan to reduce his holdings of some other good(s), possibly money, in order to pay for his planned increase in his holdings of good one. Thus if $p_1 \Delta q_1$ is positive there must be either some other good, good $t$, for which $p_t \Delta q_t$ is negative (the transactor has a planned excess supply of that good) to the same extent that $p_1 \Delta q_1$ is positive, or there is a set of goods for which the transactor has a planned excess supply such that the total money value of the planned excess supply equals the money value of the planned excess demand for good one. In general, the money value of the sum of the planned excess demands

_____

[2]Named for Jean Baptiste Say (1767–1832), the French classical economist who is, along with James Mill, given credit for first enunciating the principle.

must necessarily be equal to the money value of the sum of the planned excess supplies.

The same point can be made in an alternative fashion. Suppose that the transactor has a planned excess supply of some particular good. For that good, call it good $t$, $p_t \Delta q_t$ is negative. This simply means that the transactor wants to end up with less of good $t$ than he starts with. Because the transactor is not a philanthropist he does not plan to give any of good $t$ away. His planned reduction of his holdings of good $t$ must be matched by a planned increase in his holdings of some other good(s). Again we see that the money value of the total of the planned excess supplies must equal the money value of the total of the planned excess demands. At the level of the individual transactor, Say's Principle merely states that the transactor is neither a thief nor a philanthropist.

From Equation 13-6 which states Say's Principle for an individual transactor we can derive the aggregate version of Say's Principle. Suppose there are $k$ transactors in the economy, and that all transactors face the same money prices for $n$ goods, including money. In the following tabulation each row represents the trading plans of a single transactor, and in each column we represent the planned excess demand for a single good. (A negative excess demand is an excess supply.)

In this array $p_i \Delta q_{ij}$ represents the money value of the $j$th transactor's planned excess demand (excess supply if negative) for good $i$. Each row is merely Equation 13-6 for an individual transactor. The first row is the first transactor's trading plan, the second row is the second transactor's trading plan, and so on. Of course, the net trading plan of each transactor must equal zero, so the sum in each row is zero, and the sum of all rows together must be zero. In the row labeled "Market Excess Demands" $p_i X_i$ is the total excess demand, adding the excess demands of all transactors together, for good $i$. The total (or market) excess demand for any of the $n$ goods could be either positive or negative, but since each of the transactors must have a net trading plan equal to zero, the sum of

|  | Good 1 | Good 2 | $\cdots$ | Good $n-1$ | Good $n$ (money) | Sum |
|---|---|---|---|---|---|---|
| Transactor 1 | $p_1 \Delta q_{11}$ + | $p_2 \Delta q_{21}$ + | $\cdots$ + | $p_{n-1}\Delta q_{n-1,1}$ + | $\Delta q_{n1}$ | = 0 |
| Transactor 2 | $p_1 \Delta q_{12}$ + | $p_2 \Delta q_{22}$ + | $\cdots$ + | $p_{n-1}\Delta q_{n-1,2}$ + | $\Delta q_{n2}$ | = 0 |
| $\vdots$ | $\vdots$ | $\vdots$ | | $\vdots$ | $\vdots$ | $\vdots$ |
| Transactor $k$ | $p_1 \Delta q_{1k}$ + | $p_2 \Delta q_{2k}$ + | $\cdots$ + | $p_{n-1}\Delta q_{n-1,k}$ + | $\Delta q_{nk}$ | = 0 |
| Market excess demands | $p_1 X_1$ + | $p_2 X_2$ + | $\cdots$ + | $p_{n-1} X_{n-1}$ + | $X_n$ | = 0 |

the market excess demands over all goods must be zero. Thus if $p_1 X_1$ is positive (if there is more of good one wanted than is available in the market) there must be some other good(s) for which there is an offsetting negative planned excess demand (excess supply).

The aggregate version of Say's Principle states that the sum of the planned market excess demands must be zero. It will be zero no matter what the value of the $n-1$ money prices of the nonmoney goods. If the price of good one is such that there is a market excess demand for the good, the price of good one is below its equilibrium value. There must be at least one other price that is above its equilibrium value, because a market excess demand must be matched elsewhere by a market excess supply, since the total money value of the planned market excess demands must be zero. *Say's Principle holds for any arbitrary list of prices.*

General equilibrium is defined as a state in which each planned market excess demand is zero. That is, general equilibrium (*GE*) exists when *each* $X$ in the row marked "Market Excess Demands" is zero. Clearly if each $X$ is zero, the sum of the planned excess market demands is also zero; thus we see that *GE* is a special case of the general constraint known as Say's Principle. While Say's Principle holds for any arbitrary list of prices, general equilibrium does not. For *GE* to hold, each price must have that one value that makes the quantity of its good demanded and the quantity supplied equal. The list of prices that accomplishes this task is called the general equilibrium price vector. The gen-

eral equilibrium price vector brings about full coordination between the plans of the buyers and the sellers of each of the $n$ goods. Each transactor can carry out all of his planned purchases and sales without finding that the sellers he faces have run short or the buyers he faces have already purchased all they want to purchase. The individual plans of the $k$ transactors "mesh" when the price list that exists is the general equilibrium price vector.

## Effective Demand, Tatonnement, and Walras' Law

Throughout our discussion of Say's Principle we emphasized that the transactions involved were only *planned* transactions, not *actual* transactions. The aggregate version of Say's Principle could be succinctly stated as "the sum of the planned market excess demands must be zero." Say's Principle holds for any arbitrary list of prices, but only when the price list is the general equilibrium price vector will all transactors be able to carry out their plans. Suppose, for example, that the prices of two goods were not equilibrium prices. (Why did I not say the price of only one good?) One price is above its equilibrium value, and the other price is below its equilibrium value. (Why could not both prices be above their equilibrium values?) This means that the amount that some transactors are planning to purchase of one good is less than the amount that other transactors intend to sell of that good. The existing price of this good is higher than its equilibrium value. Not all of those transactors who have a planned excess supply of the good can carry out their plans at the existing price. Only a portion of those with planned excess supplies will be successful in finding transactors with planned excess demands for the same good. For the good whose price is too low the reverse is true. Not all of the transactors with plans to purchase the good can execute their plans because transactors with plans to decrease their holdings of the good in the aggregate plan to release less than the other transactors in the aggregate want.

Suppose there are two sets of transactors—households and firms—and two nonmoney goods—labor services and widgets. Households demand widgets and supply labor services, while firms demand labor services and supply widgets. Additionally, suppose that the price of labor services is above its general equilibrium value and the price of widgets is below its general equilibrium value, so that there is a market planned excess supply of labor services and a market planned excess demand for widgets. Households plan to sell more labor services than firms plan to buy, and firms plan to supply fewer widgets than households plan to buy. Say's Principle assures us that the money value of the planned excess supply of labor services is equal to the money value of the planned excess demand for widgets, but because of the disequilibrium prices the plans of the separate transactors are not mutually consistent and not all plans can be carried out. Households that are unsuccessful in selling all the labor services they plan to sell will have a *planned* (and actual) excess supply of labor services which will correspond to a *planned* excess demand for widgets. But in an economy that uses money as a medium of exchange this planned excess demand for widgets cannot be *effective* unless the households' plans to sell labor services (for money) are successfully carried out.[3] (We

assume the households have no assets they could sell for cash except at "distress prices.") Labor is not bartered for widgets in a money economy. To quote Clower, in such an economy "Money buys goods, and goods buy money; but goods do not buy goods."

We have an *effective demand failure.* Buyers of widgets would buy more widgets (execute their planned excess demands) only if they could first sell additional labor services (execute their planned excess supplies) for *money*. It is necessary to have *money* to purchase widgets; hence the transactors fail to make their planned excess demands effective. Money is more than just one of the $n$ goods. The distinguishing characteristic of money is that it is the only source of effective purchasing power over other goods. In an economy where any good represents effective purchasing power over any other good there is no need for the good called money to exist at all. (More about this later.)

One of the early pioneers in mathematical economics was Leon Walras. He was concerned with whether there is such a thing as a general equilibrium price vector. That is, starting each transactor out with some amount (possibly zero) of each of $n$ goods including money, is there necessarily a list of prices of the $n - 1$ nonmoney goods that will establish zero planned excess demand in each market—i.e., establish general equilibrium? We have just seen that unless there is zero planned excess demand in each market, not all transactors will be able to execute their plans. If some transactors are successful in executing their plans and others are not, there will be a redistribution of the $n$ goods away from the pattern of the initial endowment before general equilibrium is established. If a general equilibrium is eventually established, it will be with a starting distribution of the goods different from the initial one, so the general equilibrium price vector that is eventually established will not be uniquely related to the initial endowment pattern. Walras wanted to discover if for each initial endowment pattern there was a general equilibrium price vector. That is, he wanted to see if for each starting distribu-

[3]R. W. Clower, "A Reconsideration of the Microfoundations of Monetary Theory," *Western Economic Journal* (1967); and "The Keynesian Counterrevolution: A Theoretical Appraisal," in F. H. Hahn and F. Brechling, eds. *The Theory of Interest Rates* (New York: Macmillan, 1965).

tion of the $n$ goods there was at least one price list that could induce each transactor to make buying and selling plans that would immediately result in zero planned market excess demand in each of the $n$ markets. Mathematically this involves solving a system of simultaneous equations where the prices of the $n - 1$ nonmoney goods are the unknowns, and the initial endowments are parameters. There are $n$ different excess demand equations. Each equation contains the $n - 1$ nonmoney prices as unknowns. Each equation is set equal to zero, and the values of the $n - 1$ nonmoney prices that make the equations zero are then computed. (Although there are $n$ equations, there are only $n - 1$ independent equations, since from Say's Principle we know that if $n - 1$ excess demands are zero the other one must also be zero.)

We can depict the search for the general equilibrium price vector in nonmathematical terms by adopting a fictional exchange scenario that Walras called *tatonnement*. Each transactor has initial amounts (perhaps zero) of each of the $n$ goods. All transactors bring their endowments to a central location called a marketplace. There is an auctioneer at the marketplace whose job it is to try out various price lists until he finds the general equilibrium price vector. The auctioneer calls out a list of prices at random. Each transactor is told to decide how much of each good he wants to purchase or sell at the prices called out by the auctioneer. Each transactor makes his plans known to the auctioneer, and the auctioneer then totals up the amount of desired purchases and desired sales for each good. If the desired purchases and the desired sales of each good are equal, the price list that the auctioneer called out is the general equilibrium price vector, and all transactors are instructed to actually carry out their purchase and sale plans. If, however, the auctioneer discovers that there are some goods for which planned purchases are not equal to planned sales, *no actual exchange is allowed*, not even for goods with zero planned excess demands. The auctioneer must then call out a different price list.

The new price list will be different from the first one in that the price for any good for which there was a planned excess demand will now be higher than before, and the price for any good for which there was a planned excess supply will now be lower than before. When the auctioneer calls out the new price list the transactors again make known (to the auctioneer) their desired purchases and sales at the new prices. The auctioneer again totals up the desired purchases and sales of each good. If there is zero planned excess demand for each good with this new price list, the new price list is the general equilibrium price vector, and the transactors are instructed to actually execute their planned purchases and sales. If the auctioneer discovers any nonzero planned excess demands the transactors are told that no actual exchange may occur and that the auctioneer will try yet another price list. The auctioneer keeps "groping" (the literal meaning of *tatonnement*) his way to the general equilibrium price vector in this manner. No actual exchange is carried out by anyone until the auctioneer determines that the last price list he called out is actually the general equilibrium price vector. Since no actual exchange takes place until the general equilibrium price vector is determined, the general equilibrium price vector that emerges is related to the specified initial endowments (the parameters of the general equilibrium equations).

The *tatonnement* process is, as we observed before, a fictional scenario. It has no real-world counterpart. Walras offered it merely so that his readers could have some sort of economic framework within which to understand the meaning of the simultaneous solution of the excess demand equations. The turning of the mathematical crank to find the values of the prices in the general equilibrium price vector in no way duplicates actual market processes. This kind of mathematical economics can be very misleading. It has led some to think that we do not need markets and market processes to establish coordination among all transactors. (These people generally call themselves "market socialists.") They think that to replace normal market processes a central planning board must only construct the system of simultaneous equations and then put the equations into a computer (a substitute for the auctioneer) for a solution. The resulting prices, when announced, will induce transactors to behave in mutually consistent ways. All Walras did was to show that for each initial endowment pattern there was a price list that could establish general equilibrium. It is a huge leap in logic from that to the conclusion that the act of solving the simultaneous equations can in any way substitute for real-world market processes. To begin with it is inconceivable that any central planning agency could collect the information that is needed to even construct the relevant excess demand equations. Remember, market excess demands are the result of the millions of individual decisions made by individual transactors. No computer in the world has the capacity to handle that much information.

Furthermore, even if the planning board could construct the excess demand equations, and even if there was a computer that could handle the problem, the market process would not be matched. Market conditions are not static. Tastes and preferences change, costs change, existing supplies of materials and resources get depleted, new sources of materials and resources are discovered, etc. It is impossible for a central planning board to keep abreast of all these changes; that is, it is impossible for a central planning board to keep its equations up to date. Decentralized markets can handle these changes much more speedily because the information does not have to be collected in any central place. Each transactor is made aware of changed market conditions by changes in the real prices of the things he buys and sells. He need not worry about other information.[4]

Forgetting that the *tatonnement* process is nothing but a fictional scenario constructed to correspond to the simultaneous solution of excess demand equations led many economists to forget that Say's Principle refers only to *planned* excess demands, not to *effective* excess demands. In the *tatonnement* process there is no difference between planned and effective excess demand. Plans are not executed (do not become effective) until the general equilibrium price vector is called out. With the general equilibrium price vector, all planned excess demands are effective excess demands. For this reason it became customary for mathematical economists to ignore the difference between planned and effective excess demands. Say's Principle came to be known as Walras' Law, and Walras' Law was generally thought to state that the sum of the money values of the market excess demands (both planned *and* effective) must equal zero. As we have seen, it is only necessary that the sum of the money values of the *planned* excess demands be zero. This is what we mean by Say's Principle. As Clower demonstrated in the second paper cited in footnote 3, the sum of the money values of the *effective* excess demands is *at most* zero. It could well be *negative*, as was the case in our example of labor services and widgets. In that example there was a planned and effective excess supply of labor services. In other words, there was some unemployment. Corresponding to that excess supply of labor was a planned (Clower called it "notional") excess demand for widgets that could not be made effective because in a money economy the transactors with an excess supply of labor must first sell it for money before the widgets can be bought.[5]

In the Walrasian *tatonnement* process money has no unique attributes. An excess supply of *any* good is effective in transmitting upward pressure on the price of the good for which there is the corresponding excess demand. The instructions given to the auctioneer require that he adjust the

[4]It is F. A. Hayek who speaks most eloquently on these matters. Throughout his *Individualism and Economic Order* (Chicago: University of Chicago Press, 1948), he repeatedly demonstrates the impossibility of replacing markets with computers.

[5]See also Axel Leijonhufvud, *On Keynesian Economics and the Economics of Keynes* (Oxford: Oxford University Press, 1968), pp. 81–102.

price of the good in excess demand upward and that of the good in excess supply downward. In real-world markets there is upward pressure on the price of a good only if money expenditures on the good exceed the money value of planned sales. In the absence of the auctioneer only an excess supply of money puts upward pressure on prices. If any good can be used to effectively purchase any other good there can be no effective demand failure, and there is no reason for the good called money to exist.

This discussion of Say's Principle and the difference between planned and effective excess demands is crucial for the understanding of the model that John Maynard Keynes constructed in his *General Theory*. According to Axel Leijonhufvud (see footnote 5), Keynes' model is not the traditional income-expenditure model that Keynesian economists have for so long used to interpret the *General Theory*.[6]

## The Geometry of Walrasian General Equilibrium

The easiest way to depict Walrasian general equilibrium is with the Edgeworth exchange box that we discussed in Chapter 2. You should review that section of Chapter 2 to make certain you remember how the exchange box is constructed and how to read it.

Suppose there are two transactors, $A$ and $B$, and two goods, $X$ and $Y$. $A$'s initial endowment of $X$ and $Y$ ($E_A$) is $X_{0A}$ and $Y_{0A}$ respectively, while $B$'s endowment ($E_B$) is $X_{0B}$ and $Y_{0B}$. Suppose the price of $X$, $p_x$, and the price of $Y$, $p_y$, are such that the budget constraints faced by $A$ and $B$ are as they are drawn in panels **A** and **B** respectively of Figure 13-1. The two budget lines are parallel since both transactors face the same prices. (Since our geometry

limits us to only two goods there is no actual money that serves as a medium of exchange. The prices are in units of some arbitrary standard, say unicorns. Thus if the unicorn price of $X$ is 2 and the unicorn price of $Y$ is 1, one $X$ will exchange for two $Y$'s. Prices such as these are called *accounting prices*.) At their respective endowment points $A$ and $B$ are on the dashed indifference curves in the two panels. If the auctioneer called out prices such that the budget constraints are as drawn in the figure, Transactor $A$ would have a planned excess demand for $Y$ of $Y_A^* - Y_{0A}$ and a planned excess supply (negative excess demand) of $X$ equal to $X_A^* - X_{0A}$. Transactor $B$'s planned excess demands (positive and negative) would be $X_B^* - X_{0B}$ for $X$, and $Y_B^* - Y_{0B}$ for $Y$. $A$ and $B$ plan to move to indifference curves $A^*$ and $B^*$ respectively. The accounting value of $A$'s excess demand for $Y$ equals the accounting value of his excess supply of $X$, and the accounting value of $B$'s excess demand for $X$ equals the accounting value of his excess supply of $Y$. (Both transactors are merely planning to move along their budget constraints.) Moreover, since both transactors face the same prices, the extent to which $A$'s excess demand for $Y$ exceeds $B$'s excess supply of $Y$ is matched by the extent to which $A$'s excess supply of $X$ exceeds $B$'s excess demand for $X$. There is a market excess demand for $Y$ ($ED_y$) and a market excess supply of $X$ ($ES_x$). The existing prices are not equilibrium prices, but, by Say's Principle, $ED_y = ES_x$.

Figure 13-2 depicts this same situation in an Edgeworth exchange box. To construct the box we rotate $B$'s diagram 180 degrees and superimpose $B$'s endowment point on $A$'s endowment point. Since the budget lines have the same slope they will coincide and pass through the common endowment point, point $E$ in the figure. At the indicated prices $A$ plans to attain indifference curve $A^*$ by moving from point $E$ to point $F$. $B$ plans to attain indifference curve $B^*$ by moving from point $E$ to point $G$. These plans are inconsistent, since the transactors cannot move to two different points at the same time. If $A$ is to attain point $F$, $B$ must be willing to give $Y_A^* -$

[6]For a brief statement of Leijonhufvud's analysis see his *Keynes and the Classics* (Institute of Economic Affairs, Occasional Paper 30, 1969). The complete title of John Maynard Keynes' 1936 magnum opus is *The General Theory of Employment, Interest, and Money*.

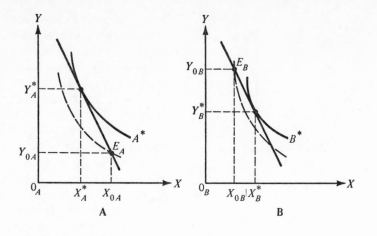

**Figure 13-1.**
Planned excess demands.

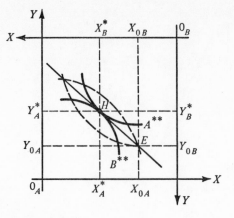

**Figure 13-3.**
Equilibrium prices.

the original endowment point, $E$. Thus general equilibrium exists at the point where the budget line that reflects the general equilibrium price vector (and passes through the original endowment point) cuts the contract curve.

Consider Figure 13-4. The initial endowment point is point $E$. Transactor $A$ is originally on indifference curve $A_1$, and Transactor $B$ is on indifference curve $B_1$. The contract curve is line $CC'$. Point $S$ on the contract curve is a point of tangency between one of $A$'s indifference curves and one of $B$'s indifference curves. However, the dashed straight line through point $S$ that has the same slope as the two indifference curves at point $S$ does not pass through point $E$. For that reason $S$ is not a point of general equilibrium. The transactors could not travel along this line and get from $E$ to $S$. Can we say that there must be at least one point on the contract curve between point $R$ and point $T$ that is a general equilibrium point? In other words, can we say that there is at least one straight line that has the same slope as the common slope of the tangent indifference curves along the contract curve that also passes through point $E$?

Because point $R$ is on the contract curve, one of $B$'s indifference curves is tangent to $A_1$ at point $R$. The common slope of those indifference curves is the same as the slope of the dashed tangent line to $A_1$ at point $R$. Because of the convexity of $A_1$, that dashed tangent line must pass to the

*left* of point $E$. Since point $T$ is on the contract curve, one of $A$'s indifference curves is tangent to $B_1$ at point $T$. The common slope of those indifference curves is the same as the slope of the dashed tangent line to $B_1$ at point $T$. Because of the convexity of $B_1$ (with respect to $B$'s origin) that dashed tangent line must pass to the *right* of point $E$. As we move from point $R$ to point $T$ we go from a tangent line that passes to the left of $E$ to a tangent line that passes to the right of $E$. One of the intervening tangent lines must pass through $E$ unless there are breaks or discontinuities in $A$'s and $B$'s preference orderings. If we assume that no such discontinuities exist we can say that for each initial endowment there is at least one price list that will establish general equilibrium.

Our discussion of general equilibrium has been conducted within the framework of a pure exchange economy. Production has not been considered at all. Transactors were simply endowed with specified quantities of all $n$ goods. A more complete discussion of general equilibrium in the Walrasian tradition would include production as well as exchange. For our purposes, however, it is not necessary to expand our discussion. We have seen the approach and some of the problems of general equilibrium analysis. A more complete discussion would require a more explicitly mathematical exposition.

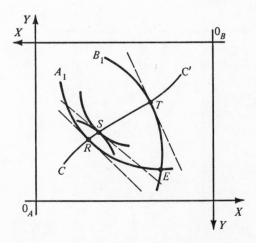

**Figure 13-4.**
Existence of general equilibrium price vector.

## Externalities and Property Rights

An "externality" is said to exist when the action of Transactor $A$ affects others—adversely or positively—and Transactor $A$ is not forced to pay for the adverse effects of his action or does not receive payment for the positive effects of his action. Since $A$ does not have to reimburse those he harms, the harm is "external" to him. In other words he is not forced to take it into consideration when he decides what actions to take—he does not "internalize" the harm. Likewise, since $A$ does not receive payment for the beneficial effects of his action these beneficial effects are "external" to him. He ignores the beneficial effect of his actions because he gets nothing out of it. Again, it is said that $A$ does not "internalize" the benefit. Since $A$ does not internalize the harmful effects of some of his actions he will carry out more of these actions than is "socially optimal." The "socially optimal" amount of any action to undertake is that amount which equates the marginal cost of the action to its marginal benefit. Since $A$ does not perceive all of the marginal cost (to others as well as himself) he will undertake too much of the action. Similarly, if $A$ does not perceive all (to others as well as himself) of the marginal benefit of some action he will not undertake enough of that action. He will choose to undertake less than the "socially optimal" amount of the action.

In Chapter 4 we discussed the example of the number of fisherman who would choose to fish on a lake under alternative types of rights to the lake. In the region where the average catch (catch per fisherman) declines, when one more person comes on the lake each fisherman catches less than before. The total catch increases by less than the amount that the new person catches, because each of the other fishermen now catches less fish. We saw that with communal rights to the lake the new fisherman was not in any way forced to take into consideration the effect he has on other fishermen. This effect is, therefore, an example of an externality. We also saw that with private property rights to the

lake the new fisherman was forced to internalize the effect he had on the catch of others. This is because the private owner of the lake charged a fee which induced fishermen to come onto the lake until the marginal catch ($MP_F$) was equal to the opportunity cost ($0C$) of fishing. The marginal catch (the amount the total catch increases when one more fisherman comes to the lake) equals the catch of the new fisherman (the average catch) minus the decrease in the amount of fish caught by the people already on the lake, which equals the change in the average catch ($\Delta AP_F$) times the number of fishermen already on the lake ($F$). In symbols, therefore,

$$AP_F - \Delta AP_F F = 0C.$$

This can be rewritten as

$$AP_F = 0C + \Delta AP_F F.$$

The opportunity cost of fishing is the only cost that the fisherman would consider under communal rights, but with private property rights he is forced also to consider his effect on the catch of others. This effect is $\Delta AP_F F$, and this is the amount of the fee collected by the profit-maximizing owner of the lake.

Private property rights are a way of forcing transactors to internalize their effects on others. In fact there is some evidence that private property rights naturally emerged in history whenever it became beneficial to cope with the problem of externalities. Harold Demsetz discusses the case of the American Indians known as the Montagnes who inhabited large regions around Quebec.[7] Before the advent of the fur trade the Montagnes hunted primarily for food and the few furs that they used themselves. There were no private property rights to hunting land. Anyone could hunt as intensively as he pleased in any area. The hunting land was, in other words, community property. Like the fishermen in the

---

[7] Harold Demsetz, "Toward a Theory of Property Rights," *American Economic Review* (May 1967).

example we just discussed, individual hunters had no reason to consider that the intensity with which they hunted affected the success of others' hunting. The externality existed, but it simply was not important enough to do anything about. The advent of the fur trade changed the importance of the externality. The value of furs to the Indians greatly increased because they could now exchange them for goods they had never seen before. Since the value of furs became so high, the intensity of hunting increased. The greater the intensity of hunting the more severe the externality problem and the more important it became to conserve and husband the game. The Montagnes began to assign exclusive hunting rights in defined areas to individual families. The Indians saw that if game were to be husbanded—that is, if care were to be taken that an appropriate mix of reproduction and killing was instituted—the simplest way to accomplish the task was to give each individual a personal stake in husbanding. Thus private property rights emerged as the natural solution.

The Indians from the southwestern plains of what is now the United States did not develop a similar property rights system, but the Indians of the American Northwest did. Our theory of the evolution of property rights explains the difference. There were no animals in the southwestern plains that were of comparable commercial importance to the fur-bearing animals of the forested areas around Quebec. Moreover, the animals that did inhabit the southwestern plains roamed over great distances. It is very difficult to prevent such animals from crossing over the boundaries of private hunting areas; therefore the husbanding activity of one private property owner would become someone else's gain. The high cost of internalizing the effects of one person's actions on others and the relatively low commercial value of establishing the necessary rights meant that it was not economic for private property rights to emerge at that time. On the other hand, forest animals similar to those around Quebec inhabited the American Northwest, and this region was frequently visited by sailing schooners which served the fur trade; thus private property rights naturally emerged there.

## The Coase Theorem

In certainly one of the most important articles ever written about the problem of externalities, Ronald H. Coase demonstrated that with private property rights the only time that externalities can result in "market failure" (the inability of voluntary exchange to result in an optimum allocation of resources) is when exchange costs are high.[8] Exchange costs are the costs involved in getting individuals together to bargain, the costs involved in the negotiations or bargaining itself, and the costs involved in carrying out the bargain. Most of the salient points of the Coase theorem are best made with an example.

Suppose a cattle ranch exists beside a farm, and there is a strip of land between the ranch and the farm to which private property rights have not been assigned. Since the rights to this strip of land are unassigned, the farmer decides to plant crops on it. However, since the rights are unassigned the rancher feels no compunction in allowing his cattle to feed on the crops. The farmer sues the rancher for crop damage. If the judge decides in favor of the farmer he is in effect assigning the rights to use the land to the farmer. If he decides in favor of the rancher he is assigning the rights to the rancher. You may think that if the judge decides in favor of the farmer the strip of land will be used only to grow crops, and if the judge decides in favor of the rancher the farmer will cease to grow crops there and the land will be used only for grazing cattle. Coase demonstrated that that is incorrect. Let the additional profit per year that the farmer would earn if he got to use the land be $V_F$ and the additional annual profit that the rancher would earn if he got to use the land be $V_R$. If $V_F$ is bigger than $V_R$ the land will be used by

---

[8]Ronald H. Coase, "The Problem of Social Cost," *Journal of Law and Economics* (October 1960).

the farmer even if the judge decides in favor of the rancher. If $V_F$ is smaller than $V_R$ the land will be used by the rancher even if the judge decides in favor of the farmer. This will be true as long as the exchange costs involved in the farmer and the rancher getting together to bargain are not too high. (We will see how high is "too high" shortly.)

Suppose that $V_F$ = $1,000, $V_R$ = $600, and the judge decides in favor of the rancher. The rancher would be willing to let the farmer use the land if the farmer paid an annual user fee of any amount in excess of $600. All the land brings in to the rancher if he uses it himself is $600, so he could be induced to rent the land by a payment of (say) $601. If the farmer doesn't get to use the land he loses $1,000, so he will be willing to pay up to that amount to use the land. If the exchange costs involved in setting up and executing the rental agreement do not exceed $400 (the difference between $V_F$ and $V_R$), the two transactors can come to a mutually beneficial rental agreement, and the farmer will get to use the land. If the judge decides in favor of the farmer, with $V_F$ = $1,000 and $V_R$ = $600, there is no price the rancher could pay which the farmer would accept for permission to use the land. The farmer would use it himself. If $V_F$ exceeds $V_R$ the farmer will use that land no matter what the judge decides. *As soon as the rights are assigned to some transactor they can be exchanged. If exchange costs are not too high the rights will ultimately reside with the transactor who places the highest value on them.*

Suppose that the reverse ordering of the relative values of the land to the farmer and the rancher existed. With $V_F$ = $600 and $V_R$ = $1,000, if the judge decides in favor of the farmer, the rancher will use the land because he can afford to pay up to $1,000 for the use of the land while the farmer would be happy to receive anything over $600 as a rental payment. If the judge decides in favor of the rancher, the rancher will use the land rather than rent it to the farmer because the minimum the rancher would accept as a rental payment is $1,000, and the maximum the farmer would be willing to pay is $600.

Although the way the land is used is independent of the initial assignment of the rights to the land, the wealth of the farmer and the wealth of the rancher are affected by the initial assignment of rights. If the farmer gets the rights when $V_F$ is less than $V_R$, the rancher will use the land, but the farmer will receive payment for its use. If the rancher were given the rights he would use the land without having to make payment to the farmer. Clearly the person to whom the rights are assigned is wealthier than he would be if the other person received the rights.

Conflict over the use of the land existed only when the rights to its use were unassigned. As soon as the rights are assigned the conflict is resolved through voluntary exchange.

Coase points out that all externalities are reciprocal in nature, hence all externalities can be internalized as long as exchange costs are sufficiently low. The classic example of externalities that is used in most textbooks is the factory that emits smoke which dirties the surrounding neighborhood. There are two possible assignments of the rights to use the air. If the rights are assigned to those in the neighborhood surrounding the factory, the factory owner can bring the value of the air as a waste disposal system to the attention of his neighbors by offering to pay them for their permission to dirty the air. If the rights are assigned to the factory owner, his neighbors can bring the value they place on clean air to his attention by offering to pay him to forego emitting smoke or to install smoke abatement equipment. If exchange costs are not greater than the difference between the value of the air as a waste disposal system and the value of clean air, the outcome will be the same no matter how the rights are assigned. There is merely another example of the situation that we illustrated with the farmer and the rancher.

If the rights to use the air are unassigned there is an externality. We can think of the factory owner as a perpetrator of a harm who does not have to pay for the harm he perpetrates; thus he emits too much smoke. If we do so we are implicitly making the value judgment that the rights to use the air ought to be assigned to the factory owner's neighbors. On the other hand, with the rights unassigned, the factory owner could be thought of as conferring a benefit on his neighbors that he wouldn't be paid for if he incurred the expense of installing smoke abatement equipment; thus he will not install sufficient smoke abatement equipment (he will emit too much smoke). If we view the externality in this way we are implicitly making the value judgment that the rights to the use of the air ought to belong to the factory owner. There is only one externality, but it can be thought of in these two different ways. This is what Coase means by the reciprocal nature of all externalities. If we prevent one group from harming a second group we are in fact harming the first group for the benefit of the second. The question of which group *should* be assigned rights is beyond the competence of economists. It is purely a philosophical or ethical question.

The example of the factory's smoke differs from the farmer-rancher example only in that exchange costs are likely to be higher in the smoke case than in the other. The farmer and the rancher must negotiate only with each other. The factory owner must negotiate with numerous separate neighbors. The neighbors could conceivably form a coalition for purposes of bargaining with the factory owner, but there is still the problem of the members of the coalition negotiating with each other as to what common front to present to the factory owner. The effects of the rancher's actions on the farmer (and vice versa) are always internalized because of the low exchange costs involved. In fact we never think of the relationship between the farmer and the rancher as an externality problem, although in the absence of the assignment of the rights to the land there clearly is an externality problem in every sense of the term. Dirty air is an externality problem precisely because of the difficulty of assigning private property rights to clean air, and because, even if the rights could be assigned, the costs involved in exchanging those rights would be very high.

In sum, the Coase theorem states the following: if the property rights to any resource are assigned rather than unassigned, and if exchange costs are sufficiently low, the ultimate *use* of the resource is independent of the initial assignment of the rights to the resource (although the initial assignment of rights does affect the wealth of the transactors involved).

## The NFL Player Draft

Let us consider the National Football League's annual player draft in light of the Coase theorem. The NFL owners assert that the reason for the draft is to equalize the talent among the 26 member teams and so to heighten the competition of the game. As long as the NFL owners are wealth maximizers—i.e., as long as they regard their teams as business investments—the Coase theorem indicates that the distribution of talent among the teams is independent of which team gets the draft rights to any player. The value of any player to a wealth-maximizing team owner is the present value of the expected additional net revenue the player could generate for the owner over his playing life. The owner estimates the effect of the player on the team's success (both immediately and in the future) and thus the gate receipts and television revenues that the team can generate. A team that gets into the playoffs generates more net revenue for its owner than a team that does not, and a team that gets into the Super Bowl generates even more net revenue than that. The value of a star college player to the owner of a team that already makes a habit of getting into the playoffs (such as the Oakland Raiders) is likely to be less than the value of that player to the owner of a losing team. If the draft rights to the star player were given to a winning team rather than to a losing team, the player would still most likely end up with the losing team. The owner of the losing team would be willing to pay a price for the rights to the player that would exceed the minimum price the owner of the winning team would be willing to accept. No matter what the initial assignment of rights, they come to reside with the transactor who places the highest value on them, as long as exchange costs are not too high. Exchange costs among NFL owners are actually fairly low. They are always in close touch, and they have a formal mechanism for exchanging rights to players.

The NFL owners make up a monopsonistic cartel, and the draft assures the owners that the prices paid to the players will not be much higher than the players' supply prices. The owners capture the gain from the bidding for the rights to a player. Without the draft players could hold out for the highest bid. The highest bid for a given player would come from the team that placed the highest value on his services, but the player would capture the difference between his supply price and that team's demand price. With the draft the player would end up with the same team as without the draft, but the gains from the competitive bidding for a player's services would accrue to the owner of the rights to the player's services rather than to the player himself.

The reason the draft rights are assigned in inverse relationship to a team's success is that the owners realize that a player will ultimately end up with the team to which he can contribute the most. By assigning the initial draft rights to a given player to the team that is likely to place the highest value on the player, the owners save all of the exchange costs involved in realigning the rights to the player.

## Pollution

We have already discussed the problem of the factory that emits smoke that dirties the surrounding neighborhood, in the context of the Coase theorem. The Coase theorem does more than help us understand why smoke emission and other forms of pollution continue to be a problem (because of the high costs of defining and exchanging rights in air and water); it also points the way to possible solutions of the problem.

Pollution is always the by-product of the production of some good or goods (things that people want to have produced). Smog is the by-product of transportation by vehicles powered with internal combustion engines. We could eliminate smog overnight simply by making all internal combustion engines illegal. But that would not eliminate the smog *problem*. The smog *problem* is that in order to get something we want we must also tolerate something we don't want (i.e., bear a cost). Outlawing internal combustion engines would allow us to escape from what we don't want by giving up what we do want. The optimum amount of smog is not zero. The optimum amount of smog is the amount that exists when the marginal benefit from smog abatement is no longer bigger than the marginal cost of smog abatement.

The Coase theorem tells us that if private property rights could be defined in clean air, and if exchange costs were zero, we would have the optimum amount of smog. If each person had an enforceable right to the air surrounding him he could exclude nonpayers from the use of the air. He would sell the rights to the air (permit pollution of the air) only if the polluters were willing to pay him a price higher than the value of clean air to him. The maximum price that polluters could bid would be limited by the value buyers place on the good the polluter produces. (Remember, pollution is always the by-product of the production of goods.) Thus pollution would occur only to the extent that its marginal benefit (to the buyers of the polluters' goods) exceeded its marginal cost (the value of the clean air to the owners of the clean air).

Of course exchange costs are not zero, so not all of the instances where the marginal benefit exceeds the marginal cost will result in an optimum exchange. More importantly, it is physically impossible to assign enforceable property rights in air to each individual. Person A's air cannot be kept separate from Person B's air. Since no one has enforceable rights to air it can be used by polluters at a zero price, and since polluters pay only a zero price they will pollute to an extent that far exceeds the optimum amount of pollution.

One possible way to cope with this problem is for the population to come to some sort of consensus (via the political process) on what the desired amount of pollution is. The government could then print pollution permits which it would auction off to the highest bidders. The total number of permits would be held to the number that would result in the desired amount of pollution. The winning bids would come from those polluters who produced the goods that consumers value most highly. The cost of the pollution permits would be a production cost just like the cost of raw materials. This would mean consumers would pay higher prices for their goods, but when pollution rights are available at a zero price these consumers are imposing a cost on others that they are not forced to take into consideration (i.e., there is an externality). If pollution rights had to be paid for, each consumer would be forced to decide if the benefit he derived from the good was worth the full cost of making the good available. Goods would be produced and sold only to the extent that they were worth their full cost. We would have a more nearly optimal amount of pollution.

## Conclusion

Throughout this text I have tried to demonstrate that microeconomics is more than just the bending of curves and the manipulation of equations. The basic notions in microeconomics are few and simple. When they are properly understood they can shed light on a wide variety of actual events in the real world. Prices and markets are just as relevant today as they ever were. The mechanics of the manipulation of elaborate economic models is just as sterile today as it has always been. My hope is that the teaching of microeconomics will move away from rigid formalism and toward the exposition of markets as efficient devices for communicating information and attaining coordination of independently made plans without central direction. If that should happen, future editions of this text will contain even less curve-bending than this one does. If that should fail to happen, students cannot help but come to the conclusion that microeconomics exists merely to give employment to teachers of its mysteries.

## Questions for Discussion

1. Evaluate the following:

   (a). Say's Principle (SP) says the economy is always in overall equilibrium.

   (b). Since economists before Keynes believed in SP, they were unable to understand depressions.

   (c). SP indicates that if all markets are left alone they will be self-regulating.

   (d). SP is a libel on the human race.

2. What is the difference between Walras' Law and Say's Principle?

3. Sometimes the expression "Say's Law" is used to refer to Walras' Law for a barter economy—an economy that does not use a meduim of exchange. Can there be an effective demand failure in a barter economy?

4. Evaluate the following:

   In Walrasian tatonnement money has no unique attributes. There is no reason for money to exist in such a system. Indeed any Walrasian tatonnement model that contains money as one of the goods is internally inconsistent.

5. Suppose all prices in a money-using economy were quoted in terms of an imaginary unit of account such as unicorns. How would money prices be calculated? Would an equiproportionate change in the unicorn price of each good affect any market? Would an equiproportionate change in the money price of each good affect any market?

6. Suppose alternatively that:

   (a). producers of new products are assigned the right to sell new products without compensating competitors who are thereby injured, and

   (b). producers of new products must obtain permission from the sellers of related old products before they can sell their new products.

   In which situation would new products be introduced more frequently? Why? What are you assuming?

7. Suppose that government is considering whether to undertake some activity that will benefit some citizens and harm others. Evaluate the decision rule that instructs the government bureaucrat to:

   (a). attempt to buy the benefited group's permission to not undertake the activity and

   (b). attempt to buy the permission of the harmed group to undertake the activity.

   Whichever permission can be obtained at the lowest price will be acted on.

8. Can you see how a military draft involves an externality? Why is this an externality caused by forbidding negotiation rather than an externality caused by the intrinsically high cost of negotiation?

# Index

**A**

accounting prices, 216
advertising, 13, 101–102, 103
   as investment, 181
   in price taker markets, 106–107, 111
Alchian, Armen A., 16n, 39n, 40n, 51n, 96n, 98, 123n, 131n, 192n
Allen, William R., 16n, 39n, 40n, 51n, 123n
American Medical Association, 22
annuities, 188
Arrow, Kenneth J., 107n
average–marginal relationship, 62–63, 77
atomistic, defined, 106

**B**

Bailey, Martin J., 38n
Baird, Charles W., 22n
barriers to entry, 21–23, 100, 115, 116, 130, 133–136, 168, 190
barriers to labor mobility, 168, 170, 171
basis
   defined, 205
   trading, 205–206
Baumol, William J., 99n
Becker, Gary, 4n, 27n, 36n, 38n, 119n
bilateral monopoly, 176–177
budget constraint, 27–31
   and labor supply, 167

**C**

capacity, 90–91
cartel
   analysis of, 145–149

defined, 106n, 145
*ceteris paribus* demand curve, 128–129
Chamberlin, Edward, 127n
child labor legislation, 175
Civil Aeronautics Board, 23, 133, 138, 145, 147, 148–149
Clower, Robert W., 213, 213n, 215
Coase, Ronald H., 96n, 220, 220n
Coase theorem, 220–222
   and the NFL player draft, 222–223
   and pollution, 223–224
collusion, 106, 106n, 145–149
competition
   as rivalrous behavior, 13, 102, 106
   assumptions of perfect, 100
   perfect and equilibrium price, 107
   perfect and information, 13, 99–103
   perfect and welfare economics, 209–210
   perfect as benchmark, 13, 102
   process vs. equilibrium state, 13, 101–102
conglomerates, 99, 106
conservation, 191–192
consumer price index, 2–4
consumers as employers, 98
consumer surplus, 139
   and mergers, 151–152
   and multi-part pricing, 139–141
contract curve, 24, 217–218
costs, definitions (see also opportunity costs)
   average variable, 76
   continued possession (fixed) 74–75
   long run average, 85–87
   long run marginal, 91–92
   marginal, 76, 78–79
   operating (variable), 75
   total, 77
coupon rate of interest, 191

**D**

demand
  alleged exceptions to first law of, 39–41
  first fundamental law of, 37–41
  income elasticity of, 34–36
  price elasticity of, 41–42
  real vs. money income constant, 45–46
  second fundamental law of, 42–43
  and Slutsky equation, 43–45
demand price, defined, 9
Demsetz, Harold, 96n, 98, 135, 135n, 149, 149n, 150, 219, 219n
diminishing returns, 68–69
Director, Aaron, 192n
discount rate, 185

**E**

economic profit, defined, 21
  function of, 21, 100, 113–118, 120–123, 130–132
economies of scale, 69–70, 87–90
  and natural monopoly, 134–135
Edgeworth box, 23–25, 216–218
Edgeworth, Francis Y., 23n
education loans, 157–158
effective demand failure, 213, 215–216
efficiency
  economic (achieving least cost), 83–84
  technical, 54–56
elasticity of demand
  cross price, 46
  income, 34–36
  price, 41–42
  for labor, 165–166
  and market demand curves, 47–48
  and marginal revenue, 126
  and Slutsky equation, 44–45
  and total revenue, 48
elasticity of technical substitution, 165
employer–employee distinction, 97–98
Engel curve, 33–34
  defined, 27
  aggregate, 36–37
  and income elasticity, 34–35
Engel, Ernst, 27n
equalizing differences, 170
excess demand
  defined, 9, 210
  planned vs. effective, 215–216
excess supply, defined, 9, 211
exchange
  costs of, 20, 24, 220–222
  and middlemen, 20–21
  mutual gains from, 19–20
expansion path, 84–85
  and long run demand for labor, 163–165
expected incremental profit stream, 184
externalities
  and congestion, 81
  defined, 63, 219, 224
  and education, 157–158
  and pollution, 221–222, 223–224
  and property rights, 63, 210, 219–224
  reciprocal nature of, 221–222
  and welfare economics, 209

**F**

Federal Energy Office, 179–180
financial capital market, 135–136
firm
  contractual claims in, 97–98
  definition, 96
  monitoring in, 96–97
  residual claims in, 97–98
forward contract, defined, 199
"free" vs. "zero price", 16
Friedman, Milton, 16n, 38n, 39, 39n, 178, 178n, 179, 190n
futures contract, defined, 199–200
futures prices
  and carrying costs, 203–204
  defined, 200, 202
  as predictors of future prices, 205

**G**

gasoline lines, 113, 179–180
general equilibrium
  defined, 212
  existence of, 213–214, 218
  price vector, defined, 212
  and Say's Principle, 212
Giffen good, 45n
gifts, cash vs. in-kind, 123–124
goods
  defined, 1
  free, 16
  inferior, and indifference curves, 33n
  superior and inferior, 33–34
    and Slutsky equation, 45
  substitutes and complements, 46–47
  zero price, 16

**H**

Hart, Senator Philip, 150
Hayek, F. A., 101n, 101–102, 105, 105n, 171, 209, 215n
hedge
  buying, 204–205
  selling, 204–205
hedging, 203–205
Hieronymus, Thomas, 203n
Hilton, George W., 147, 149
Hirshleifer, Jack, 154n
horizontal mergers
  analysis of, 151–152
  defined, 145
housing market, 120–123

human capital, defined, 157
Hutt, W. H., 98, 175–176, 175n

**I**

illegal campaign contributions, 119
implicit rental rate, 52–53
imputation of costs, 115–116
income effect, 44
    and labor supply, 168
    and multipart pricing, 139n
    and Slutsky equation, 45
indifference curves, definition
    and construction, 16–19
inflation
    cause, 7
    definition, 7
    and relative prices, 6–7, 118
inheritance, 158–159
interest rates, existence of, 181–182
internal rate of return, defined, 185–186
Interstate Commerce Commission, 133–134, 145,
    155
investment decision rules, 184–188
isocosts, 82–83
isoquants
    convexity of, 57–58
    defined, 55
    and number of processes, 58
    and technical efficiency, 57

**K**

Kessel, Reuben A., 22n
Keynes, John M., 216, 216n
Klein, Lawrence R., 46n
Knight, Frank H., 79n, 80
Kuhn, Thomas S., 15, 15n

**L**

labor demand curves
    long run, 163–165
    short run, 159–163
labor supply curves, 166–167
labor unions, 171–172, 174–176
Laker Airlines, 149
Lancaster, Kelvin, 53n
Leijonhufvud, Axel, 8n, 210n, 215n, 216, 216n
long position, defined, 200
long run, defined, 69, 77, 81, 92

**M**

margin call, 201
margin payment, defined, 200
marginal evaluation, defined, 17
marginal product
    and average product, 61–63

of capital, defined, 59
    of labor, defined, 59
marginal rate of substitution, defined, 17
marginal rate of technical substitution, 59–60
marginal revenue
    defined, 108–109
    and price searcher, 125–127
    and price taker, 108–109
market basket, defined, 3
market concentration doctrine, 149–151
"market failure", defined, 220
market share curve
    in cartels, 146
    defined, 127–128
market structure, 99–103
Marshall, Alfred, 8n
Marshallian homeostat, 8–13
McGee, John S., 141n, 152n, 195, 195n
middleman's functions, 20–21
Miller, Roger Leroy, 113n
minimum wages, 5–6, 171–172, 177–178
monopolistic competition, 100, 101
monopoly
    ambiguity of, 101
    defined, 100
monopsonist, perfectly discriminating, 174
monoposony, 172–175
    and the NFL, 223
multipart pricing, 139–141

**N**

natural monopoly, 134–135
"needs" vs. "wants", 17–18
negative income tax, 6, 177–180
net present value, defined, 185
NFL player draft, 222–223

**O**

Oakland Raiders, 222
occupational choice, 188–190
occupational licensure, 22, 115, 130, 168, 190
oil shortage, 113, 179–180
oligopoly, 100, 101
Olsen, Edgar O., 106n, 120n
on-the-job training, 177–178
open interest, defined, 202
open vs. closed markets, 21–23, 101, 102
    equilibrium in, 130–132
    and occupational choice, 190
opportunity cost, 64, 73
optimum consumption basket, defined, 32
Organization of Petroleum Exporting Countries,
    147

**P**

Pacific Southwest Airlines, 149
partial vs. general equilibrium, 209

patents, 134, 141–142
permanent income, 190
perpetuities, 190–191
Pigou, A. C., 70
planned obsolescence, 192–195
planning curve, 89
politicians, 7, 112, 113, 119, 120, 124, 199, 206
pollution, 221–222, 223–224
    (see also "property rights" and "externalities".)
predatory pricing, 195–196
present values, 168, 182–184
price discrimination, 136–139, 136n
    in monopsony, 174
price taker–price searcher distinction, 100, 102
    examples of, 102–103
price–wage controls, 5, 7, 40, 113, 118–120,
    179–180
    and price searchers, 133
process rays
    defined, 53
    combinations of, 55
producer surplus
    in mergers, 151–152
    in unions, 176–177
product differentiation as competition, 101
production function
    defined, 51–52
    and returns to scale, 70n, 86n, 164n
profit, 21, 98, 98n
    as a goal in corporations, 99
    economic, defined, 114
    normal, defined, 100, 114
property rights
    and buffalo extinction, 63
    and congestion, 79–81
    and conservation, 192
    evolution of, 219–220
    and externalities, 63, 219–224
    and manager behavior, 39, 69
    and patents, 134
    and pollution, 221–222, 223–224
    and resource use, 63–66, 219–220
public utility commissions, 134–135

**Q**

quality
    and competition, 101–102
    and price, 40–41

**R**

real income
    changes of with fixed relative prices, 29
    constant with changes of relative prices, 29–31
    and consumer price index, 4
    defined, 4
relative prices
    as conveyors of information, 4–6, 215
    and consumer price index, 2
    as coordination devices, 6, 111–113, 119,
        214–216
    defined, 2
    and inflation, 6–7, 118
rent, 74, 115–116, 135, 170
resource allocation, price taker vs. price searcher,
    132–133, 163
returns to scale, 69–70, 87–90
risk premium, 185
Rockefeller, John D., 195–196

**S**

Say, Jean Baptiste, 211n
Say's Principle, 210–212
    and general equilibrium, 212
    vs. Walras' Law, 215
scabs, 172
scale of plant adjustments, 113–116
scarcity
    and competition, 6
    defined, 1
    and tradeoffs, 16
Sherman Antitrust Act, 149
short position, defined, 200
short run, defined, 60, 69, 74, 92
shut down decision, 77, 110, 113
slums
    demand for, 120–121
    and rent vouchers, 120–123
Slutsky, E. E., 44n
Slutsky equation, 44–45
socialists, market, 214–215
speculators
    and price volatility, 206–207
    as representatives of future consumers,
        205–206
spot (cash) market, 202
spot (cash) price, 202
stages of production, 66–69
Stigler, George, 102, 102n, 133n, 136n, 145n,
    146, 154n, 159n, 188n
strike, right to, 176
substitution effect, 43–44
    and labor supply, 168
    and Slutsky equation, 45
sunk costs, 74
supply price, defined, 9

**T**

*tatonnement*, 9n, 214–215
time preference, 182
total product curve, 60–63
    critical points, 62, 68
trading stamps and price discrimination, 138
transactor, defined, 4, 210

**U**

used textbook market, 192–195